ARTIFICIAL INTELLIGENCE AND SECURITY IN COMPUTING SYSTEMS

**THE KLUWER INTERNATIONAL SERIES
IN ENGINEERING AND COMPUTER SCIENCE**

Jerzy Sołdek, Leszek Drobiazgiewicz (Eds)

ARTIFICIAL INTELLIGENCE AND SECURITY IN COMPUTING SYSTEMS

9th International Conference, ACS '2002
Międzyzdroje, Poland
October 23-25, 2002
Proceedings

KLUWER ACADEMIC PUBLISHERS
BOSTON/DORDRECHT/LONDON

Distributors for North, Central and South America:
Kluwer Academic Publishers
101 Philip Drive
Assinippi Park
Norwell, Massachusetts 02061 USA
Telephone (781) 871-6600 /Fax (781) 681-9045
E-Mail: kluwer@wkap.com

Distributors for all other countries:
Kluwer Academic Publishers Group
Post Office Box 322
3300 AH Dordrecht, THE NETHERLANDS
Telephone 31 786 576 000 / Fax 31 786 576 474
E-Mail: services@wkap.nl

 Electronic Services <http://www.wkap.nl>

Library of Congress Cataloging-in-Publication Data

9th International Conference, ACS 2002 (Międzyzdroje, Poland)
Artificial Intelligence and Security in Computing Systems /
Edited by Jerzy Sołdek, Leszek Drobiazgiewicz.
p.cm. (The Kluwer international series in engineering and computer science).
Expansions of selected papers that were presented at the Advanced Computer Systems conference, held October 23-25 2002 Międzyzdroje (Poland) organized by Technical University of Szczecin.
Includes bibliographical references.
ISBN: 1-4020-7396-8 (alk. paper)
1. Artificial Intelligence. 2. Computer Security. 3. Agents. I. Sołdek, Jerzy
II. Drobiazgiewicz, Leszek. III. Title. IV. Series.

Copyright © 2003 by Kluwer Academic Publishers

All rights reserved. No part of this work may be reproduced, stored in a retrieval system, or transmitted in any form or by any means, electronic, mechanical, photocopying, microfilming, recording, or otherwise, without the written permission from the Publisher, with the exception of any material supplied specifically for the purpose of being entered and executed on a computer system, for exclusive use by the purchaser of the work.

Permission for books published in Europe: permissions@wkap.nl
Permissions for books published in the United States of America: permissions@wkap.com

Printed on acid-free paper.

Printed in the United States of America.

Table of Contents

Preface .... *vii*

Chapter 1
Artificial Intelligence Methods and Intelligent Agents

FACCHINETTI GISELLA, FRANCI FRANCESCO,
MASTROLEO GIOVANNI, PAGLIARO VITTORIO, RICCI GIANNI
    From a logic map to a fuzzy expert system for the description
    of the Middle East destabilization 3

FRANCESCO FORTE, MICHELA MANTOVANI,
GISELLA FACCHINETTI, GIOVANNI MASTROLEO
    A Fuzzy Expert System for Auction Reserve Prices 13

WALDEMAR UCHACZ, ZBIGNIEW PIETRZYKOWSKI
    Vessel traffic optimization using a linear model with fuzzy coefficients 23

ALICJA MIESZKOWICZ-ROLKA, LESZEK ROLKA
    Variable Precision Rough Sets 33

JACEK CZERNIAK, HUBERT ZARZYCKI
    Application of rough sets in the presumptive diagnosis
    of urinary system diseases 41

JANUSZ MORAJDA
    Neural Networks and Their Economic Applications 53

MARCIN PLUCIŃSKI
    Application of data with missing attributes in the probability RBF
    neural network learning and classification 63

IZABELA REJER, ANDRZEJ PIEGAT
    A method of investigating a significance of input variables
    in non-linear high-dimensional systems 73

ROMAN ŚMIERZCHALSKI
    Evolutionary Algorithm in Problem of Avoidance Collision at Sea 81

YUGO ITO, SHIN-ICHI MIYAZAKI,
YOSHINOBU HIGAMI, SHIN-YA KOBAYASHI
    Improvement and Evaluation of Autonomous Load Distribution Method 91

PRZEMYSŁAW RÓŻEWSKI, ANTONI WILIŃSKI,
OLEG ZAIKINE, KRZYSZTOF GIŻYCKI
    Idea of the National System of Education and Verification Traffic's
    Knowledge as a Tool of Traffic Safety Increasing 101

EDWARD NAWARECKI, GRZEGORZ DOBROWOLSKI,
MAREK KISIEL-DOROHINICKI
    Distribution of Resources by Means of Multi-Agent Simulation Based on
    Incomplete Information 111

PABLO GRUER, VINCENT HILAIRE,
JAROSLAW KOZLAK, ABDER KOUKAM
    A multi-agent approach to modeling and simulation
    of transport on demand problem 119

OREST POPOV, ANNA BARCZ, PIOTR PIELA, TOMASZ SOBCZAK
    Practical realization of modelling an airplane
    for an intelligent tutoring system 127

PIOTR PECHMANN, JERZY SOŁDEK
    Model of Natural Language Communication System
    for Virtual Market of Services 137

BOŻENA ŚMIAŁKOWSKA
    Models of Integration in Decision Support Systems 153

KHALID SAEED
    Object Classification and Recognition using Toeplitz Matrices 163

Chapter 2
Computer Security and Safety

MIROSŁAW KURKOWSKI, JERZY PEJAŚ
    A Propositional Logic for Access Control Policy in Distributed Systems 175

JERZY PEJAŚ
    Certificate-Based Access Control Policies Description Language 191

MARIAN SREBRNY, PIOTR SUCH
    Encryption using two-dimensional cellular automata with applications 203

MARCIN GOGOLEWSKI, MIROSŁAW KUTYŁOWSKI
    Secure data storing in a pool of vulnerable servers 217

KAMIL KULESZA, ZBIGNIEW KOTULSKI
    On automatic secret generation and sharing
    for Karin-Greene-Hellman scheme 227

TADEUSZ GAJEWSKI, IZABELA JANICKA-LIPSKA, JANUSZ STOKŁOSA
    The FSR-255 family of hash functions with a variable length of hash result 239

MIROSŁAW KURKOWSKI, WITOLD MAĆKÓW
    Using Backward Strategy to the Needham-Schroeder
    Public Key Protocol Verification 249

TADEUSZ CICHOCKI, JANUSZ GÓRSKI
    OF-FMEA: an approach to safety analysis
    of object-oriented software intensive systems 261

JANUSZ GÓRSKI, JAKUB MILER
    Providing for continuous risk management in distributed software projects 271

IMED EL FRAY
    About Some Application of Risk Analysis and Evaluation 283

KRZYSZTOF CHMIEL
    Linear Approximation of Arithmetic Sum Function 293

Preface

The book contains the selected papers from Conference of Advanced Computer Systems (ACS)'2002 in the fields of Artificial Intelligence and Computer Security &Safety.

The Conference, organized for the ninth time, acts as international forum for researches and practicioners from academia and industry with a forum to report on the latest developments in advanced computer systems and their application within methods of artificial intelligence, intelligent agents, computer security & safety, image processing & biometric systems, computer graphics & visualization and software engineering. The main directions of the conference were problems of artificial intelligence and computer security. There were chosen 27 the best papers between all 85 articles of conference. These 27 papers are organized in two chapters.

Chapter I "Artificial Intelligence Methods and Intelligent Agents" contains 17 papers, including 10 dedicated for the applications of artificial intelligence methods and 7 concerned intelligent agent applications.

G. Facchinetti et al. in the paper "From a logic map to a fuzzy expert system for the description of the Middle East destabilization" describe the actual political situation of Middle East by using the fuzzy expert system.

In another paper F. Forty, G. Facchinetti et al. use "A fuzzy expert system for auction reserve prices" focusing on the issue of a rieliable reserve price: important both for the sellers as for the purchasers. The paper is a preliminary effort to apply the fuzzy sets theory to the multiattributes valuation of art goods.

W. Uchacz and Z. Pietrzykowski present the use of fuzzy linear programming for vessel traffic optimisation on the Świnoujście – Szczecin fairway. The L-R representation of fuzzy number was used for the model description.

A. Mieszkowicz – Rolka and Leszek Rolka in their paper consider the evaluation of human decision model basing on measures of the variable precision rough sets theory. Decision tables were generated and investigated in case of control of dynamic plant (aircraft).

J. Czerniak and H. Zarzycki describe the model of the expert systems which will perform the presumptive diagnosis of two diseases of urinary system. This is an example of the rough sets theory application to generate the set of decision rules in order to solve a medical problem.

J. Morajda in the article "Neural networks and their economic applications" outlines basic types of neural networks and presents their selected application in marketing, finance and other areas of business and economy.

M. Pluciński in his paper presents an application of the probability RBF neural network to classification of samples with missing attributes and tuning of the network with incomplete data.

I. Rejer and A. Piegat in their article introduce a new method of investigating a significance of input variables in non-linear multi-dimensional systems. The method was used to build a ranking of significance for 19-dimentional system of an unemployment rate in Poland in years 1992 – 1999.

R. Śmierzchalski in his paper presents the evolutionary algorithm for computing the near optimum trajectory of a ship in given sea environment. By taking into account certain boundaries of the manoeuvring region, along with navigation obstacles and other moving ship, the problem of avoiding collisions at sea was reduced to a dynamic optimisation task with static and dynamic constrains. Result of algorithm parameter, having the form obtained using the program for navigation situation, are given.

In the article "Improvement and evaluation of autonomous load distribution method" authors proposed a new load distribution algorithm for multi-computer systems and applied it on a workstation cluster to compare it with some methods proposed in the past.

In the paper "Idea of the national system of education and verification traffic knowledge as a tool of traffic safety increasing" authors present the education system based on knowledge management. The system is developed for the sake of the European drivers' education standards.

B. Smialkowska in her paper presents an overall charakteristics of methods aiming at integration of enterprise's management information systems and decision support systems. The method is based on virtual data warehouse concept with a database of decision modelling methods and database of models.

In the paper "Object classification and recognition using Toeplitz Matrices" the derived Toeplitz forms are applied to verify the projected view of the given images for recognition. The results of experiments good and encouraging for algorithm extension to apply on other applications like handwritten script, spoken-letter image and varieties of geometrical patterns including views of three dimensional objects for the sake of classification and recognition.

The last set of four papers concern the problems of multi-agent systems applications.

E. Nawarecki et al. consider a problem in which distribution and transportation of resources depend on incomplete and uncertain information about availability or demand. Agent-based simulation is proposed as a convenient and efficient tool. The chosen experiments with the model are reported together with interpretation and some general remarks.

In the paper "A multi-agent approach to modelling and simulation of transport on demand problem" authors focus on a model of multi-agent system for simulation of transport on demand. The system performs efficient allocation of vehicles to dynamically incoming transport orders.

O. Popov et al. in their paper describe the general design and an example of practical realisation of the simulation system for a light airplane, created as a part of an intelligent multi-agent tutoring system for civil aviation. Structure of the simulation system is based on two modules: the simulation kernel and the user interface. Both modules communicate with each other as well as with the other parts of an intelligent tutoring system through the network, which makes the simulation system a suitable tool for use in distance learning.

P. Pechman and J.Sołdek present a model of communication system with computers by using natural language. Model was built based on results of their research of semantic analysis and sentence generation in Polish language used in human – computer dialogue. Multi-agent system structures and specified agent functions related to communication based on natural language, are described. Achievability of the proposed system of the virtual market of services and functions intended for agents are also discussed.

Chapter II "Computer Security and Safety" contains 10 papers related to the problems of security, cryptography, safety and risk management.

M. Kurkowski and J. Pejaś in their article propose the logic-based model for interpreting the basic events and properties of the distributed access control systems. They provide a convenient formal language, an axiomatic inference system, a model of computation, and semantics. They prove some important properties of this logic and show how our logical language can express some access control policies proposed so far.

J. Pejaś in the paper "Certificate – based access control policies description language" describes the language to support security and management of distributed systems. This policy language is based on a declarative, object-oriented Ponder language presented in Damianou. The language is flexible, expressive and extensible to cover the wide range of requirements implied by the current distributed systems paradigms.

M. Srebrny and P. Such in their papers present a new symmetric cryptosystem, based on two dimensional cellular automata. Enciphering uses both left- and right-toggle rules. Enhanced cryptographic power is obtained by designing some simple geometric transformations on squares of bits of information. As an application, a software system "IPI Protect" is presented which integrates with MS Word for protecting the documents against unauthorized modifications while allowing free viewing and printing.

M. Gogolewski and M. Kutyłowski consider the problem of secure data storing in a pool of vulnerable servers. In order to elude the threat described one may store multiple copies of data in a pool of data servers. However, in order to limit the costs, the number of copies must be limited. Again, this provides a chance for an adversary to attack only the few servers actually storing the copies of data relevant for him.

In this paper they design a simple and elegant method for secure storing of encrypted data based on Rackoff-Simon onion protocol used previously against traffic analysis.

M. Kulesza and Z. Kotulski examine the problem of automatic secret generation and sharing for Karin-Greene-Hellman scheme. They show how to simultaneously generate and share random secret. Next, they propose a method of automatic sharing of a known secret. They discuss how to use extended capabilities in the proposed method.

In the paper "The FSR-255 family of hash functions with a variable length of hash result" a family of cryptographic hash functions with a variable length of hash result, is presented. The hash functions are defined by some processing structures based on seventeen 15-stage stage non-linear feedback shift registers. The feedback functions can be modified by the user to customize the hash function. Hardware is designed for implementing as a full custom ASIC, and is optimized to increase the processing rate.

M. Kurkowski and W. Maćków present in the paper the application of new fast method of verification of cryptographic authentication protocols to verification of the Needham-Schroeder Public Key Authentication Protocol. They present a verification algorithm, its implementation and some experimental results. For the verification of correctness property they apply a backward induction method.

T. Cichocki and J. Górski present in their paper an extension to the common FMEA method in such a way that it can be applied to safety analysis of systems that are developed using a recently popular object oriented approach. The method makes use of the object and collaboration models of UML. The method supports systematic way of failure mode identification and validation. The verification process provides hints for possible redesign of components. Experiences of using the method for a railway signalling case study are also reported.

J. Górski and J. Miler present a concept of continuous risk management in distributed software development projects. The concept is particularly relevant for critical software applications where risk management is among main project management activities. The approach recognises that effective and open communication is the prerequisite for successful risk management. Therefore, it concentrates on providing to the project stakeholders a broad and highly available communication channel through which they can communicate risk-related information The description of a tool that embodies those concepts and reports from some validation experiments are also included.

I. El Fray in his paper consider some application problems of risk analysis and evaluation. At present every company which want to exist on the market should introduce consistent security policy and risk management mechanisms within the company to guarantee information accessibility, confidentiality and integrity. The paper is focused on risk evaluation based on some model enterprise and in accordance with known and accepted risk management methods.

Szczecin, March 2003   Professor Jerzy Sołdek

                                              Chairman of International
                                              Program Comittee Committee

INTERNATIONAL PROGRAM COMMITTEE

J. Sołdek	Poland
S. Ablameyko	Belarus
R. Drechsler	Germany
M. Adamski	Poland
A. Bartkowiak	Poland
W. Bielecki	Poland
Ch. Chu	France
Z. Czech	Poland
A. Dolgui	France
N. Enlund	Sweden
V. Evdokimov	Ukraine
G. Facchinetti	Italy
R. French	USA
J. Górski	Poland
A. Javor	Hungary
S. Kabayashi	Japan
G. Kuchariew	Poland
W. Kulba	Russia
E. Kuriata	Poland
C. Moraga	Germany
K. Myszkowski	Germany
A. Naeve	Sweden
W. Pedrycz	Canada
J. Pejaś	Poland
A. Piegat	Poland
J. Pieprzyk	Australia
O. Popov	Poland
D. Puzankov	Russia
W. Rucinski	Poland
R. Sadykhov	Belarus
B. Sovetov	Russia
M. Srebrny	Poland
R. Stankovic	Yugoslavia
J. Stoklosa	Poland
W. Swinarski	USA
A. Verlan	Ukraine
J. Weglarz	Poland
O. Zaikin	Poland

Advanced Computer Systems '2002 was organized by: Technical University of Szczecin (Poland), Albert-Ludwigs-University (Germany), University of Technology of Troyes (France) and was held in cooperation with:Belarussian Academy of Sciences (Belarus), Electrotechnical University of Sankt Petersburg (Russia), Polish Academy of Sciences (Poland), University of Goettingen (Germany), Ukrainian Academy of Sciences (Ukraine), Warsaw University of Technology (Poland).

Chapter 1

Artificial Intelligence Methods and Intelligent Agents

From a logic map to a fuzzy expert system for the description of the Middle East destabilization

FACCHINETTI GISELLA[1], FRANCI FRANCESCO[2],
MASTROLEO GIOVANNI[1], PAGLIARO VITTORIO[2], RICCI GIANNI[1]
[1] *University of Modena and Reggio Emilia Italy,*
[2] *Interproduction / Ce.A.S.-Rome Italy, facchinetii@unimo.it, franci@ips.it, mastroleo@unimo.it, vittorio.pagliaro@tin.it, ricci@unimo.it*

Abstract: In this paper we present a first attempt to describe the present situation of the Middle East area by a fuzzy logic map. By it we design a fuzzy expert system that evaluate the level of destabilization in the same area. In this map are present the political and geographical "actors" that influence the level of destabilization. The connections between the "actors" are expressed in a linguistic framework, like "if the United States influence increases than the Israeli radicalism is fortified" and so on. Using this map, built by experts in International Policy and Terrorism, we have tried to translate it in a fuzzy expert system, with the idea to obtain a numerical level of destabilization of the area we have considered. Making a continuous monitoring of the situation, the system makes possible to understand the behaviour of this complex situation, and shows what are the actions that increase or decrease the destabilization. It suggests what are the actions useful to reduce this level.

Key words: Fuzzy cognitive map, fuzzy expert systems, Middle East area destabilization level, sensibility analysis

1. INTRODUCTION

In this paper we present a first attempt to understand and to evaluate the Israeli-Palestinian situation. The problem complexity has carried us to decide to approach this problem using not-classical logics so that the fuzziness of the concepts involved in the description may be captured. The way, we have selected, is to describe the different realities involved in this situation and their implication by a Fuzzy Cognitive Map and then to translate it by a fuzzy expert system that let us a way to produce a numerical value. This value gives the destabilization level of the Middle East area.

We have decided to use a fuzzy expert system for two motivations. The designed map is the translation of what the experts think about the involved variables and the connection between them. The implications (arrows and their strength) are a way to design the rules that connect the variables.

The logic map presents a dynamic design of the Middle East situation. So, the experts have decided with us to simplify the map, cutting all the arrows, which produce loops, leaving those that correctly describe the situation.

This is first try to produce a model, which is able to evaluate, in a numerical way, the destabilization level of that area. The interest for this numerical level is high, as it is possible to utilize this value in a monitoring phase. This paper has been presented in the conference "the Glocal Strategies" organized by Ce.A.S. "Centre of the high studies for the fight against politic violence and terrorism (Priverno, Italy, 15/18 May 2002), where mathematicians and experts of geopolitics, politics, anti-terrorism, intelligence and of security were present.

2. FUZZY LOGIC FOR THE SOCIAL COMPLEXITY

The complexity of the social system requires dynamic "laboratories" of analysis, if we want to deal with it. We have not to operate against the complexity, but in favour of it, thinking about the complexity as a value. For example, one of chances that the complexity offers is to plan and to act for local and no-local strategies. The complexity of the social system shows this paradox exactly as a chance, an opportunity, and not as a difficulty or an obstacle. A clear antinomy appears: local and no-local, a thing and its opposite. Antinomy and paradox offer the incentive which induces us to find or, at least, to look for other logic approaches, other ways to analyse in order to not to be paralysed or obliged to be local *or/aut* global.

The "system of the social- political relations" is a part and a representation of a complex social system at the same time. Some features of a complex social system need an analysis in which we must accept:
- The contradictions and the difficulty of contextualization in the social situations, which are interconnected among them.
- Some situations are oppressed by the critical state of a certain social dynamism.
- "Hidden" and unclear aspects, which are beyond the observed social phenomena.

At this point we can consider different reasoning that let us the possibility:
- To think about the vague, the ambiguities, the ideas and doubtful qualitative sentences.
- To stress the limits of the assertions, which feel the effects of the uncertainty and the subjectivity of the representation,
- To relate them. Nets, maps, logical connections.

Fuzzy logic provides an innovative instrument in order to include and then to manage these one and other problems. It can be useful to deal with the fuzziness, which is in the social system or in the geopolitics. The instruments offered by fuzzy logic can be used not only for the problems of engineering, but also in the social, political problems in which the parties are persons, facts and interactions. They are not definable, they are never true or false in an unequivocal way.

If we want to deal with them with classic reasoning, we would realize that "everything is vague in a measure of which we do not realize until we try to make it precise" (Bertrand Russell).

3. THE ARABIAN PALESTINIAN SITUATION

We analyse the Arabian Palestinian situation. Is it local or global?

| It is global | 1 | If we think that this situation is the reason of the destabilization of the whole scenery of the Middle East, and also the reason of the participation of the great part of the globe |

| It is local | 0 | It is a problem that concerns only the life and the death in the Israeli and Palestinian streets. |
| It is enough ... a few... too much... local and global | Between 0 and 1 | It is not so clear if it concerns only global questions or only local questions. |

According to us, it is both the things and it means that we have to "sail" in that area between 0 and 1. If we want to describe this area we need of linguistic variables, which help us to outline the situation. Fuzzy logic, instrument borne to manage the linguistic variables, will allow us to set up analysis, to obtain interesting results, to describe the situation of "glocal strategy" related to the Arabian Palestinian situation where we find an "armed peace" or the suicide as "vital élan", and so on.

This situation cannot be resolved in accordance with the classical meaning of this word. Only an "abstract" hope can exist and this is the hope that each conflict of decision can find a logical solution, but it is a false expectation. This fact is confirmed by the K. Arrows "theorem of impossibility". This theorem says that: in a decisional process, the problem to find a series of method to perform, which have to satisfy the preference of the single individual, has no solution.

Probably it is not absolutely necessary a "theory of the whole", but it is necessary to make the most of give the uncertainty, the complexity, the "vagueness" and to the scientific systems, which are able to manage all these things. These scientific systems operate with new approaches, which "learn" from the continuous changing of the events and of the dates, which do not define areas with crisp borders but areas of "survival" and cohabitation of different realities.

4. A LOGIC MAP FOR THE MIDDLE EAST AREA

In order to understand, we propose to use the instrument of Fuzzy Cognitive Maps (FCM), complex "nets" of complex events; thus we have at our disposal a model upon which we can trace "relations", "interactions", and quantify reciprocal "weight" and relational dynamism.

In substance, we introduce the "actors" in the scenery, the "rules" which define a link or casual connection (if...then...). For example $C_X \rightarrow_+ C_Y$ means that the event C_X causes an increase and a worsening of the event C_Y. (The contrary is when there is the sign –). In the same place of the signs + and –, we can put the numbers between 0 and 1 (just like before) which are corresponding to some linguistic variables (much, a few, in a certain amount..). Each arrow of the figure 1, defines a fuzzy rule IF-THEN

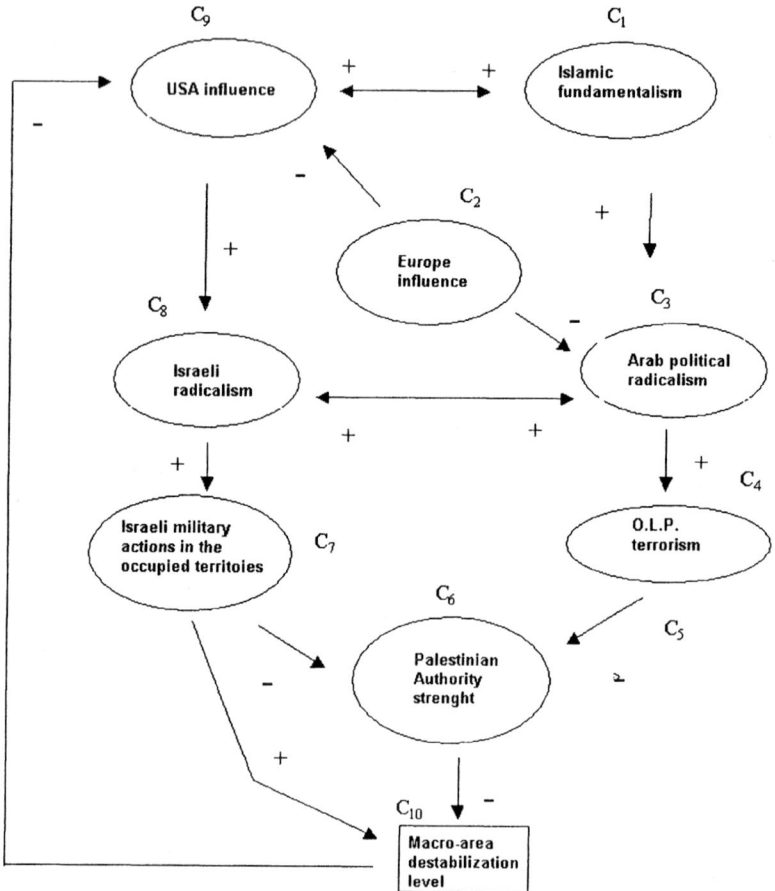

Fig. 1. The logic map of the Israeli an-Palestinian situation

The fuzzy map is a first, rough representation, which helps to illustrate the methodology and potentiality of the approach for a dramatic complexity. Obviously the fuzzy map has not to give political sentences. Its aim is to value the casual relationships, their weights and to furnish an instrument in favour of the resolution of the conflicts.

If we must define variables, connections, randomness, the proposed instrument needs cultural and scientific synergies, which are able to express the different points of view, the different analytical "cultures". The logical-mathematicians have "only" the task to define the method that can turn the fuzzy map in an "operative" model, that is able to offer useful instruments for a better analysis of the situation, instruments which will be used in order to propose some solution.

A good fuzzy map is the result of a good team who works together. A team composed by: mathematicians and experts of geopolitics, politics, anti-terrorism, intelligence and of security that is to say of all the "categories" illustrated in the conference "the Glocal Strategies" organized by Ce.A.S. "Centre of the high studies for the fight against politic violence and terrorism (Priverno, Italy, 15/18 May 2002). During this conference this application was presented.

The fuzzy map can be extended thanks to the formulation of other maps, which furnish more details about each single introduced variable. And the game becomes more and more complex…

5. A FUZZY EXPERT SYSTEM FOR THE EVALUATION OF THE DESTABILIZATION LEVEL

The interest of the world-organisms, who are involved in political decisions that may modify the situation in the Middle East area, is really high. The situation is very complex and it is difficult to understand what are the better things to do and then, what road to keep. The logic map, we have designed, gives an idea of who are the "actors" that come on the scene, and what are the influences of the single presence or action. But we need of an instrument able to produce information about the level of destabilization. We desire to have a monitoring way to understand if the level is growing or not and, fixed a threshold of tolerance, if it has reached a danger-level. In every moment, we desire to understand what are the actions that have produced a growth and what is the next action it is necessary to do to obtain its decrease. This instrument should have to work in an automatic way and in real time. This idea produces that it has to be controlled by a computer. However much we may wish to create computers that function like humans, the fact remains that most human reasoning cannot be expressed by mathematical formulae. In other words, as it stands today, computers are great when it comes to the manipulation of data and performing math but, when it comes to fair judgment and expertise, human experts remain unchallenged. Nonetheless, the gap between human and computer reasoning may soon be bridged. The mathematics involved in fuzzy logic has created a silent revolution in the control systems. For these motivations we have thought to use a fuzzy expert system to translate what the map describes, as the implications are linguistic and human understandings are involved. The arrows that connect the single "actors" are expressible in fuzzy rules. For their nature, they are able to transfer the implication between the single variables in an operative way.

Among the situations now located, there are some "obvious" relations that often are crossed and circular. These ones confuse the map. The analysis for the "directions of influence" and the analysis of the relative values derive from the geopolitics analysis, which is "possible" in the historical period in which it was compiled.

"Weak" and "strong" knots emerge, but this weakness-strength is so dynamic that today the values of the map are already changed.

"Central" and "peripheral" knots also exist. They are realities that influence other situation which are on the scenery, or are conditioned by them.

In this map a key point has been located in the destabilization of the macro area, because it represented one of the hot points and the reason of anxiety in the world especially during the days in which the map was compiled.

By its nature it has some loops in which the increasing of some influence may be reinforced or weakened by others, but even by its action. This fact is impossible to translate in a software package, as the loops would carry the program to an "explosion" (in a figurative sense). We have study the map with experts and so, together, we have cut some arrows, to have a model able to produce some result. After this reduction the map has begun a static map.

The initial inputs of this new map are "U.S.A Influence" and "Europe Influence". This obliged simplification has carried to a not consistent reality. The two inputs are not the only initial inputs. So we have decide to change the structure and in figure 3 we have the design of the fuzzy system we have obtained.

The denoted situations in the map can be assembled in many categories: the politic influences which are outside the area, the politic influences which are inside the area, the radicalisms in the both fronts, the military actions and/or terrorist actions.

The inputs are four, two are added to the previous, "Arab Radicalism" and "Islamic Fundamentalism". The addition is due to the fact that the cut arrows let the possibility to some variables to be strengthened, or weakened, to produce, not only an *action,* but even a *reaction.*

Then we have designed the linguistic attributes and the rule-blocks, which connect the initial inputs with the intermediate and outputs variables. The design of the rule-blocks is due to the translation of the strength (plus or minus) of the arrows present in the map.

The output variable, "Macro-Area Destabilization Level", is obtained by the aggregation of three intermediate variables "Palestinian Authority Strength", "Israeli Military Action in the Occupied Territories", "U.S.A. Military Action"

6. THE NUMERICAL EVALUATION AND A SENSIBILITY ANALYSIS

To test the fuzzy system, we have considered that in that moment the European influence was very weak as regards to United States and as regards to the Arabian radicalism; the Palestinian Authority also was very weak and was negatively conditioned by the Israeli presence on the territories and by the progressive asserting of the Arabian-Palestinian radicalism, and so on. We have normalized the inputs range in the interval [0,1]. The experts have translated this information in these numerical values.

U.S.A influence= 0.55   Arab radicalism= 0.48
Islamic Fundamentalism= 0.7   Europe Influence= 0.20

With these four values, as inputs, the experts have decided that a middle level of destabilization should be a correct evaluation.

We have put the same range, [0,1], for the output and the system have produced a value of 0,51. They were satisfied of this replay.

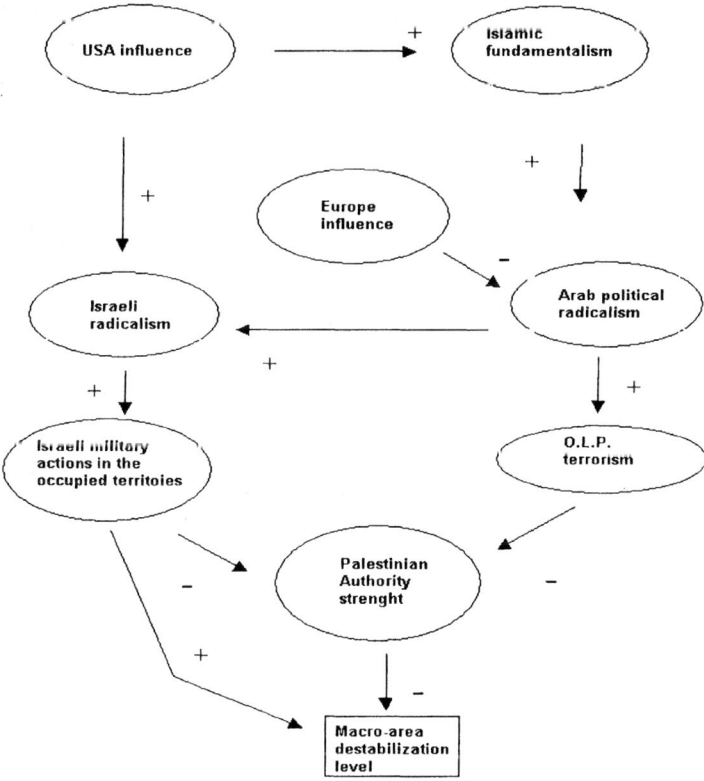

Fig. 2. The logic map without loops

As we have no other values by the experts, to tune the system and to valuate its robustness, we continue our work making a sensibility analysis. We have fixed three of the four inputs and then we have assigned to the last one, values from the first extreme point of the range till the second, with a step of 0,05. We have made this study for all the four inputs and the experts have considered correct all the replays. For brevity we present one of the four ones, that is the case in which the input "Islamic Fundamentalism" is left free to change.

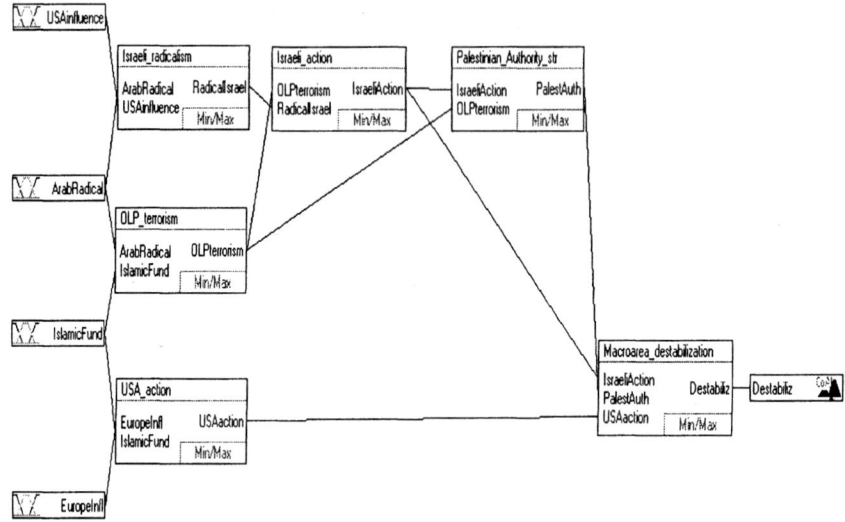

Fig. 3. The system disegn

In the next figure (Fig.4) we show the values that the system assigns to the four intermediate variables and the output variable.

In the following figure, (Fig. 5), we have put in a common diagram the graphs of the six functions.

Looking at the system design, it is possible to see that the intermediate variable "Israeli Radicalism" is constant. This is due to fact that the "Islamic Fundamentalism" input does not influence this variable.

It makes changing in all the other variables, and produces a visible decreasing in the Palestinian Authority strength, as we expect. We agree with the effects on the other variables. They increase in different way. Two of them, "O.L.P. terrorism" and "U.S.A. action" reach their maximum level, while "Israeli military action in the occupied territories reach the value 0.66.

The output value, increases, but does not reach "danger level".

The experts have analysed the performance of the intermediate variables and the output and they decide that the replays are coherent with what they think.

The sensibility analysis for the other variables shows analogous situations, all considered correct by the experts.

7. CONCLUSIONS

We have already said that this map was, and is, a simplification of the complexity of the situation, but it serves to us as an example of the possibility and of the usefulness of a fuzzy approach to the social-political reality.

Is this the panacea useful to resolve all the complex problems? Obviously no, because the complexity doesn't agree with the panacea, with definite solutions, but it is only a scientific approach which tries to decode the complexity dealing with unsettled, dynamic, vague, fuzzy instruments, but effective.

The experts of the sector have been very interested in the approach, but especially in the results. They have decided that these new methods may offer a significant opportunity to fix the "actors" on the scene and to understand their connections either for the influence they do each other, or for the strength the use. The final evaluation may give an useful idea of the level of destabilization and may offer the opportunity to have a monitoring way to control the complex problem of Middle East area. Obviously, not only this design may be enlarge, but this is only one of the possible applications in the security and terrorism field, many others are the complex political situations present in the world. We are working in several others, like, "No Global" movement.

Situation	Islamic Fundamentalism	USA Influence	Europe Influence	Arab political radicalism	Palestinian Authority strength	Israeli military action in the occupied territories	U.S.A action	Israeli radicalism	O.L.P. terrorism	Macro-area destabilization
a	0,00	0,55	0,20	0,48	1,00	0,04	0,27	0,54	0,00	0,29
b	0,05	0,55	0,20	0,48	1,00	0,04	0,27	0,54	0,00	0,29
c	0,10	0,55	0,20	0,48	1,00	0,04	0,27	0,54	0,00	0,29
d	0,15	0,55	0,20	0,48	0,93	0,08	0,29	0,54	0,03	0,31
e	0,20	0,55	0,20	0,48	0,86	0,14	0,33	0,54	0,10	0,33
f	0,25	0,55	0,20	0,48	0,82	0,18	0,37	0,54	0,17	0,34
g	0,30	0,55	0,20	0,48	0,78	0,22	0,41	0,54	0,23	0,36
h	0,35	0,55	0,20	0,48	0,75	0,25	0,44	0,54	0,30	0,35
i	0,40	0,55	0,20	0,48	0,71	0,29	0,48	0,54	0,37	0,34
j	0,45	0,55	0,20	0,48	0,67	0,33	0,53	0,54	0,43	0,34
k	0,50	0,55	0,20	0,48	0,64	0,36	0,60	0,54	0,47	0,35
l	0,55	0,55	0,20	0,48	0,57	0,43	0,65	0,54	0,54	0,38
m	0,60	0,55	0,20	0,48	0,48	0,47	0,69	0,54	0,60	0,43
n	0,65	0,55	0,20	0,48	0,40	0,51	0,72	0,54	0,66	0,48
o	0,70	0,55	0,20	0,48	0,34	0,54	0,76	0,54	0,73	0,51
p	0,75	0,55	0,20	0,48	0,28	0,58	0,80	0,54	0,79	0,51
q	0,80	0,55	0,20	0,48	0,20	0,62	0,83	0,54	0,85	0,51
r	0,85	0,55	0,20	0,48	0,11	0,65	0,90	0,54	0,92	0,53
s	0,90	0,55	0,20	0,48	0,05	0,66	0,93	0,54	0,97	0,52
t	0,95	0,55	0,20	0,48	0,05	0,66	0,93	0,54	0,97	0,52
u	1,00	0,55	0,20	0,48	0,05	0,66	0,93	0,54	0,97	0,52

Fig. 4.

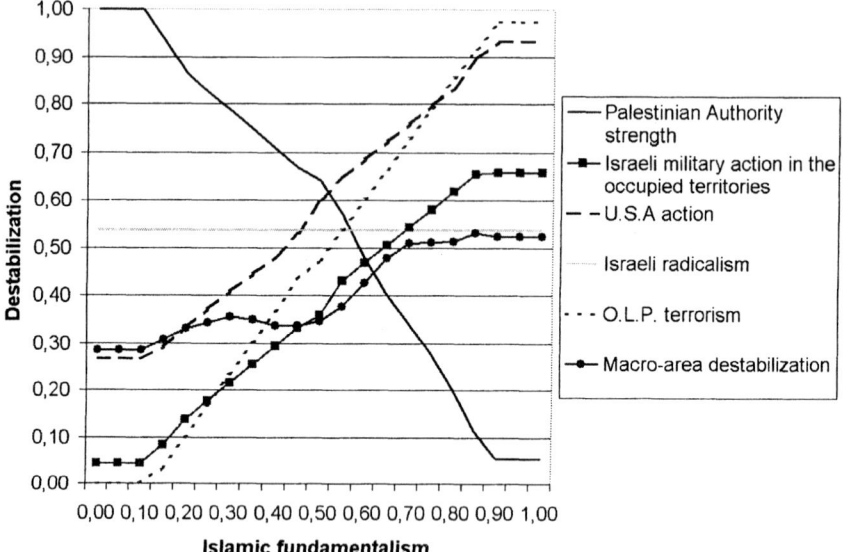

Fig. 5

8. REFERENCES

[1] Atkinson A.C. 1994. 'Fast very robust methods for the detection of multiple outliers'. *JASA* 89, pp. 1329–1339.
[2] G.Bojadziev, M.Bojadziev. 1997. "Fuzzy Logic for Business, Finance and Management", World Scientific Publishing co, Singapore
[3] Dimitrov V. 1998 "Use of Fuzzy Logic when Dealing with Social Complexity" School of Social Ecology, University of Western Sydney
[4] Facchinetti G.: (2001). "Fuzzy Expert Systems: Economic and Financial Applications" In Advanced Computer System J. Soldek and J Pejas eds, 3-26. Kluwer Academic Publishers.
[5] Kasabov N.K. (1996) Foundations of Neural Networks, Fuzzy Systems, and Knowledge Engineering. MIT Press.
[6] Lyotard, J.-F. (1984) "The Postmodern Conditions: A Report of Knowledge", Manchester University Press, Manchester.
[7] Palladino D. 1993 "Sistemi di scelte sociali: il terorema di Arrow" Nuova Secondaria XI, 3,
[8] von Altrock C. (1997). "Fuzzy Logic and neurofuzzy applications in business and finance." Prentice Hall.

A Fuzzy Expert System for Auction Reserve Prices

FRANCESCO FORTE[1], MICHELA MANTOVANI[1],
GISELLA FACCHINETTI[2], GIOVANNI MASTROLEO[2]
[1]*Dept. of Economics, University of Rome "La Sapienza",*
Via del Castro Laurenziano 9, 00161 - Roma. {forte, mantovan}@dep.eco.uniromal.it
[2]*Dept. of Economics, University of Modena and Reggio Emilia.*
Viale Berengario 51, 41100 - Modena. {facchinetti, mastroleo}@unimo@it

Abstract: The paper focuses on the issue of a reliable reserve price: important both for the sellers as for the purchaser. A too high reserve price may discourage the bidding process, but a price too low may damage the sellers. The analysis of the problem shows its high complexity. We suggest an objective methodology of constructing the evaluation of art works, based on a multi-attributes valuation system using a fuzzy expert system. The start point is the use of FM matrix similar to the Boston matrix to assign the work to one of four main categories of authors and art goods: stars, blue chips, portfolios and dogs, questions. For each one of the categories, the second step is the decision tree design. At the basis of these designs there is the belief that four are the main categories of variables, which carry at the final evaluation: artistic values, hedonic values, sociological economic macro-factors, micro-economic factors. These four are not independent variables. So the simple decision trees with four branches become very involved till at the final building which has more then thirty independent variables like the artistic values relate to the artist, to the work, to the artistic current, etc.
The paper is a preliminary effort to apply the Fuzzy Sets Theory to the multi-attributes valuation of art goods. This theory provides a systematic framework to deal with qualitative concepts that can be translated in to quantitative parameters in a complex system of variables only by "fuzzy" relations, because of the intrinsic lack of precision and of uncertainty about the causal relation between sets of the inputs and of outputs. Experts give the ranges of values imputed to the linguistic variables, by reference to the statistics of the past auctions in the international market. The system structure identifies the fuzzy logic inference flow from the input variables to the output variables. The fuzzy inference takes place in rule blocks, which contain the linguistic control rules. The outputs of these rule blocks are linguistic variables. The defuzzification in the output interfaces usually translates them into crisp variables. In this case we propose as output a fuzzy evaluation that produces an interval of values between the minimum and the maximum.

Key words: Input, Output, Linguistic variable, Art market, Multiple Attributes Valuation.

1. INTRODUCTION

According to the best accounting methods as recognised in the European rules, assets valuation, in business corporations, should be done by the two basic principles of prudence: that of prudential assessment of the capital value and that of the continuity of the firm's activity. According to the first prudence criterion, one should avoid an over assessment that deceives the shareholders and the creditors, according to the second one should avoid an under assessment that induces to undue lack of care for the preservation of the asset and the related maintenance expenses and provisions. The same rules seem appropriate as for the assets of a non profit institution, say a Foundation as for its art assets: in order to avoid deception of its supporters and creditors and to avoid lack of care in the preservation of the asset. Clearly the two rules lead to find a "fair value" that it is "in between" the highest and the lowest. The same point of view seems applicable to the basic auction price, for reasons that appear an extension of the above two principles of prudence. Indeed an over assessment here too appears imprudent because may induce some deception: in this case, of the potential purchasers. But an under assessment is imprudent too, because induces to lack of care for the asset, that in this way risks to be undersold.

The consequence of over valuation of assets as for a corporation or a Foundation may bear a loss of credibility, damaging its capability of attracting resources to its activity. The loss of credibility, relating to over assessment of the basic auction prices, may damage their capability of attracting purchasers even for art auction houses. But imprudent under assessment reduces its credibility with potential sellers and thus damages the continuity of its activity. One might argue that under pricing is not damaging, but aside the risk of lack of competition, there is the fact that the valuation by an auction house, with some reputation, is considered an "experts" judgement. The assignment of a low price to a given asset to be sold, normally, is interpreted as an implicit recognition either of the modesty of objective value of that asset or of a weakness of the market demand. On the other hand, over assessment by the auction houses may induce the would be purchasers to desert; and unsold assets may reduce the reputation of the house not only from the point of view of its trustworthiness but also from the point of view of its skill as for the art values.

On the other hand, because the two conflicting prudential criteria lead to a valuation in between, there is the risk of subjective discretion: how to let the customer on the demand and on the offer side to believe that the basic auction value always correspond to a prudent "in between" criterion and that the way to reconcile the two conflicting principles is consistently pursued in a given way?

We believe that this result may be reached combining a systematic methodology of consideration of the variables affecting the art market values, based on a theoretical groundwork (see [17], [18], [23]) supported by empirical research with a mathematical modelling of them that takes in to account the complexity of the factors and the uncertainty relating to their appreciation, that may be identified by the Fuzzy Sets Theory [32]. This theory provides a systematic framework to deal with qualitative concepts that can be translated into quantitative parameters in a complex system of variables only by "fuzzy" relations, because of the intrinsic lack of precision and of uncertainty about the causal relation between sets of the inputs and of outputs.

In this paper we present a fuzzy expert system, which tries to describe, by a decision tree, all the variables involved in the final judgement and all the connections between them. These connections are present in the branches of the tree. This is a typical multi-criteria problem in which, very often, the input are linguistic attributes the experts give and the importance of one information over the others is not always quantified with crisp valuation, but it is more easy to describe them by IF-THEN rules.

The start point is the use of FM matrix similar to the Boston matrix to assign the work to one of four main categories of authors and art goods: stars, blue chips, portfolios and dogs, questions. For each one of the categories, the second step is the decision tree design. At the basis of these designs there is the belief that four are the main categories of variables, which carry at the final evaluation: artistic values, hedonic values, sociological economic macro-factors, and micro-economic factors. These four are not independent variables. So the simple decision trees with four branches become very involved till at the final building which has more then thirty independent variables.

Multi-criteria problems may relate to several problems like decision-making to assignment of a given character, or of a given ranking of value or of a given cardinal quantitative measure like a given economic (monetary) value. Here the problem is not that of deciding what to choose, but how (and how much) to judge a phenomenon. Even more delicate is the task of assigning a quantitative value, as our case of economic valuation of art assets. It appears to us that rather than a crisp value, here, one has to aim to a fuzzy one, to be comprise between a minimum and a maximum, possibly with a small distance among them.

2. THE ART MATRIX, THE STARTING POINT

The starting point of this study is the assignment of the art work to one of four quadrant of a FM art market matrix (FM-AMM) that Forte and Mantovani have devised in analogy the Boston matrix employed to classify the corporations [13]. Unlike the Boston matrix where the income flows are considered together with the changes in capital values, the FM-AMM focuses only on the capital values, because, obviously, the art works normally to not give a consistent flow of monetary income, because their benefits mostly flow to the owners as final consumers or/and to the public directly by low admission tickets or indirectly as "external economies" of various kind. The two quadrants on the left are characterised by high variability of their market values in a greater range of variation. The two quadrants on the right, on the contrary, are characterised by a substantial market values 'stability within a much smaller range of variation. Each quadrant it is divided in sub categories, because they include a block of different linguistic variables, which may be translated in different ranges of values. To identify the stars, the blue chips, the portfolios one shall, first, look to the market prices in auctions in the international free market by the authors of the considered works, taking the top values realised. The values are expressed in euros of constant purchasing power. For authors whose works have never been in auctions in the free art markets or never (or only very rarely for minor pieces) were sold in auctions, the expert has to make the classification by analogy with authors who passed in the auctions. It is clear now that the linguistic classification shall often proceed differently for the authors belonging to different quadrants. This initial distinction implies that the FES does not work with a unique system of parameters as for the translation of inputs of linguistic variables in ranges numerical values.

Table 1: the Art Matrix

I STAR Superstars Stars Starlets	**II BLUE CHIPS** Top chips Blue chips medium Blue chips lower range
III QUESTIONS Possible increase Random Possible decline Lemons	**IV PORTFOLIOS & DOGS** Portfolio-High Portfolio-medium Portfolio-low Portfolio - miscellany Dogs

Value:

STAR: from 500.000 to 40.000.000	BLUE CHIP from 50.000 to 500.000
SUPERSTARS: more than 5.000.000	TOP CHIPS: from 250.000 to 500.000
STARS: from 2.000.000 to 5.000.000	BLUE CHIPS medium from 125 to 250
STARLETS: from 500.000 to 2.000.000	BLUE CHIP low range from 50 to 125
QUESTIONS POSSIBLE Increase: authors whose works are likely to be undervalued. RANDOM: authors with unclear future. POSSIBLE DECLINE: authors whose works are likely to be overvalued. LEMONS: works of dubious authenticity.	PORTFOLIOS and DOGS from 0 to 50.000 PORTFOLIOS- High from 25.000 to 50.000 PORTFOLIO-Medium: from 10.000 to 25.000 PORTFOLIOS- Low from 2.500 to 10.000 PORTFOLIOS -MISCELLANY: less than 2.500 bust not likely to decline DOGS: less than 2.500 likely to further decline

3. THE FUZZY EXPERT SYSTEM DESIGN

A first sketch of the decision tree (Table 2) is born from this idea: the linguistic variables have been studied by borrowing from the current economic analysis and from empirical testing. We have grouped them in four categories of factors, each consisting of three sub categories, distinguishing the exogenous linguistic variables pertaining to the work and his author and the exogenous linguistic variables relating to the political, cultural, economic, sociological and legal "environment".

The following figure shows the whole structure of the fuzzy system including input interfaces, rule blocks and output interfaces.

Table 2

Endogenous variables	1. artistic values	of the author of the work of the artistic movement
	2. edonic values	functional semiologic technical
Exogenous variables	3. socio economic macro-factors	national preference and political factors socio-cultural trends macro economic cycles
	4. market micro economic factors	free or controlled market information flows marketing

Some comments may be, at this point, useful to clarify what we mean by the various linguistic variables under consideration and how enter as inputs in the valuation process.

The expert not according his personal judgement shall identify the artistic variables, about the author and the artistic movement, but according to that of the prevailing judgements, that *presumably determine that of the market.* The concept of "reputation", developed by the economists, in areas different from the artistic one, it is also relevant here. As for the value of the specific work under consideration it should be noted, among others, that normally for the art works of a given (important) author, in a given art movement, there is a product cycle: the beginning has more originality but there may be an upward trend to a peak, after which there is a decline. The date of the work therefore is important and if the works is undated it has, *coeteris paribus,* less value.

Figure 1

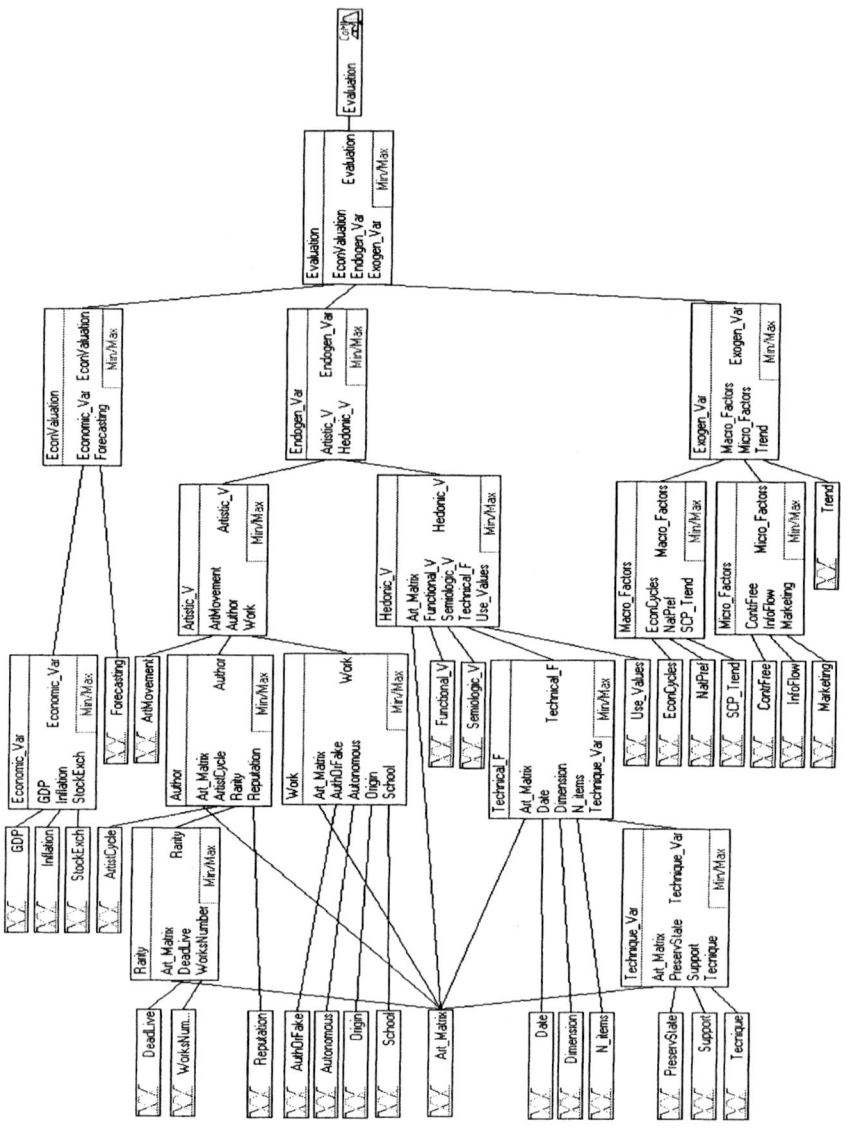

As for the functional factors, we mean first of all the "informational factors": an art work may have had and may still have a function of "information" about figures and facts of religion, history, private life of personalities. In addition, it may be that the artwork had (and may be still has) a practical function as some vases. And this factor may add value, because it may increase the rarity of the artwork. Empirical research on the big data set of the art auction prices may be useful to give a "linguistic" assessment to the group of functional variables that we have named as "semiologic" which pertain to the kind of figures, the colours and similar factors, that seem to obey to some statistical law, at least in relation to certain kinds of works, [19], [21]. Some time, however, these factors are author-related. For instance flowers add value to Van Gogh' paintings. It is probably in the area of technical factors that systematic empirical research is particularly relevant. Forte and Mantovani in [14],[20] have shown that the works of great dimension (those greater than a square meter), generally have values much greater than those of average dimension (those ranging between an half and one square meter) and those of average dimension generally have a value greater than those of small dimension (less than half square meter) in a way that may justify, a first broad approximation, the consideration of the value per square cm, but needs further more specific enquiry in relation to the type of work and artistic movement considered. Another important technical variable is the type of material employed that has effects on the quality and resistance to the atmospheric factors of the work. A third variable, that we have catalogued among the technical ones, because it is mostly an endogenous variable, but one may properly define as a micro economic one, primarily relating to the supply side of the market, has to do with the "rarity" of the considered works. While rarity is primarily an absolute concept pertaining to the supply side, it is also, to an extent, a relative concept pertaining to the demand side of the market. One fact affecting rarity on the demand side, doubtless, it is the appreciation of the good: works of low interest tend to be fungible commodities, so that the fact that there are few pieces of a given author of a given kind does not matter much, because other goods of other authors are considered good substitutes to these works. Bur rarity, viewed on the demand side, has also to do with other factors, affect the preferences, as the peculiarity of the provenance or the fact that in that painting there are details unusual for that author and the like. Factors of imputed rarity that art experts with knowledge of what are the market tastes may be able to detect. A final group of technical factors has to do with the state of preservation and with whether the work is or not signed and whether the signature is or not clearly visible and clearly authentic. Works without these requisites may risk being "lemons".

The macro socio economic factors mostly operate on the demand side, but some have an origin on the supply side. The purchasing power of the demand for the different types of art goods has an obvious effect on their value. And the "tastes" of the purchasers various nations are not indifferent to the nationality of the authors and of the artistic movements. An important degree of nationalism or national fashion here exists and can be easily tested by empirical research. For instance Sorge in a doctor dissertation under the guidance of Forte and Mantovani have found that, as for expressionists, nearly half of the purchase of French authors is done in the French market, where presumably the purchasers or French culture are dominant [22]. The same research by Sorge shows that the average values of the American informal art' works have an average value seven time that of the works of the European informal movements in the same set of market. It likely that this big difference, at least to an to an extent, has to be explained by the different purchasing power in the American market combined with a national preference of the American private and public collectors for the American artists. Socio cultural international trends generally have a strong influence on the demand: "fashions" do matter in arts, as, *mutatis mutandis*, in clothing and internal decoration or architecture. Expert may know, by statistics and occasional empiricism, that, for instance, the trend of the Flemish paintings of the seventeen-century is now up and that the trend of another art movement is now downward. Some time politics and political economy has a strong influence on art trends. Chinese art is experiencing and upward trend in relation to the Chinese political and economic development and the increasing opening of China to the international economic and political community.

Forte and Mantovani have found that for the art market there is a cycle as for the stock market and for the macro economies and that there are a strong relations between the business cycles and the art markets cycles and between the stock exchange cycles and those of the art markets, however with lags and intensity that change according to the type of market: for free art markets these relations are more pronounced both in the time dimension and in the intensity, [15]. Coming to the micro economic factors listed in Table 2, one first must consider for which market the valuation is done. As noted at the beginning, art market values, *ceteris paribus* are greater in the free art markets than in the controlled markets. However after the valuation has been done referring to the free market, if the relevant market is a controlled market a parameter of conversion must be introduced to downgrade it, [12]. Among the micro economic factors is also relevant the information flow, [24]. Forte and Mantovani have tested it by Indices of diffusion of different artists of comparable values, in the international Museums finding an interesting relation between this kind of diffusion and the market value of them, [13]. Temporary shows and other various forms of promotion too have a strong influence on the market values.

Obviously here one must distinguish those that have already been done in the past so that enter in the market value as appreciated by the demand and those that might be done in the future with a likely effect of improvement of the demand and of the trend of the market prices.

As one can see, in our MAVS there are two intermediate steps: one with the aggregation of the endogenous variables and another with the aggregation of the intermediate input thus obtained with the two groups of exogenous variables.

One may dispute this sequence: which, however, in our view it is justified by the different variability and information set of the two classes of variables, the first being more intrinsic to the art work and the art knowledge, the second being more extrinsic and related to macro and micro variations of the political, economic, cultural, legal "environment" and to the knowledge about its behaviour.

4. CONCLUSIONS

This paper presents a first effort on the issue of a reliable reserve price. The idea, surely new, is to reproduce, in a structural way, what the experts do when have to define the price of an artwork. Many are the information they need to make a correct evaluation. All their accumulated experience is translated in the decision tree and in the rule-blocks. This idea is interesting for us, not only for the possible real applications, but as it lets the possibility to hand down to posterity a part of history of art and culture that should be lost if it is transmitted only by mouth. Surely many changes and additions are to be done, the work is only at the beginning.

5. REFERENCES

[1] Candela G. - Benini M., (1997) Produzione e circolazione dell'informazione nel mercato dell'arte Bologna, Clueb.
[2] Candela G. - Scorcu A., (2000) *Economia e mercato della grafica d'arte* Patron Bologna.
[12] Forte F. - Mantovani M., (1998) "L'investimento nell'arte sul mercato internazionale libero e in quello regolamentato" in *Il Risparmio*, n.1.
[13] Forte F. - Mantovani M., (1999 a) "Il patrimonio culturale pubblico;.alcune riflessioni e prime verifiche empiriche", ISAE Roma
[14] Forte F. - Mantovani M., (1999 b) "La valutazione dei beni artistici nel patrimonio delle fondazioni museali" in *Rivista Italiana di Economia, Demografia e Statistica*, vol. LIII, 1999 n. 3
[15] Forte F. - Mantovani M. (1999c) "La convenienza finanziaria dell' investimento in arte" in *Bancaria"* n.7/8
[16] Forte F. - Mantovani M., (2000) "La domanda di grafica: analisi macro economiche dei mercati del disegno e delle stampe", in (Candela G. Scorcu A.)
[17] Frey B. - Pommerhene W. (1991) *Muse e mercati*. Il Mulino, Bologna
[18] Lazzaro E. - Mossetto G., (1997) "Le determinanti dei prezzi delle opere d'arte", in (Candela G. Benini M) *Produzione e circolazione dell'informazione nel mercato dell'arte* Clueb, Bologna
[19] Floch J.M.., (1998) Semiotica, marketing e comunicazione. Dietro i segni le strategie, Franco Angeli, Milano
[20] Mantovani M. - Forte F., (2000) "La domanda di grafica: analisi micro economiche dei mercati del disegno e delle stampe" in (Candela G Scorcu A)
[21] Santagata W., (1998) Simbolo e merce. I mercati dei giovani artisti e le istituzioni dell'arte contemporanea, Il Mulino, Bologna,
[22] Sorge M., (1999) *"La valutazione economica degli espressionisti nei mercati europei"*. Degree thesis. Faculty of Economics. University of Rome La Sapienza.
[23] Throsby D., (1994) "The Production and Consumption of Arts, A View of Cultural Economics", *Journal of Economic Literature*, 32.
[24] Trimarchi M. (1997) "Snodi informativi, costi di transazione e processi di selezione nel sistema dell'arte", in (Candela G. Benini M) Clueb, Bologna
[25] Zadeh L.A., (1975) "The concept of linguistic variable and its applications to approximate reasoning" Parts I, II, III, Inform. Sci. 8, 199-251; 301-357; 9, 43-80.

Vessel traffic optimization using a linear model with fuzzy coefficients

WALDEMAR UCHACZ, ZBIGNIEW PIETRZYKOWSKI
Maritime University of Szczecin, Waly Chrobrego 1-2, 70-500 Szczecin, Poland
e-mail: walu@wsm.szczecin.pl, zbip@wsm.szczecin.pl

Abstract: The paper presents a problem of vessel traffic optimisation with the use of fuzzy linear programming. The Świnoujście-Szczecin fairway has been taken as a practical example. The L-R representation of fuzzy numbers was used for the model description. The interpretation of fuzzy numbers has been presented. As deviations from the fixed values of constraint coefficients have been allowed, the solutions obtained are more realistic. The approach enables a flexible and safer formulation of an optimisation task. The calculations and their results have been presented and interpreted.

Key words: vessel traffic, optimization, fuzzy linear programming

1. INTRODUCTION

The problem of vessel traffic management in narrow fairways can be formulated as the optimization of passage times of vessels in compliance with the regulations in force. This optimization consists of the determination of optimal times of vessels entering the fairway and maintaining proper speeds at particular fairway sections. In reality certain allowance is made for deviations from fixed values of constraint coefficients and variables. This step is necessary to account for variations in the times vessels actually enter the fairway and in the times of passing particular sections by vessels. In such situations one alternative to a classic linear programming problem can be a problem of linear programming with fuzzy coefficients.

2. DESCRIPTION OF A VESSEL TRAFFIC MODEL

Principal assumptions of a linear mathematical model are presented in [6]:
- The fairway is divided into sections, at which the regulations in force are concerned with: permitted minimum and maximum speeds, vessels passing and overtaking,
- Values of admissible speeds depend on vessel parameters (length and draft),
- Criteria for allowed passing and overtaking depend on mutual relations between vessel parameters (lengths and drafts),
- Traffic of vessels on the fairway is determined (i.e. does not undergo optimization, it is only taken into account as a limitation for other vessels).

The following notation has been applied:
T_i, T_j – real time of readiness of vessels i,j to enter the fairway,
t_i, t_j – time of vessels i,j waiting for fairway entry,
m,n – numbers of vessels waiting for fairway passage: i=1,...,n, j=1,...,m
r – number of fairway sections: k=1,...,r,

$f_{k_1}^m$ – function determining the time of reaching the closer limit of k-th passing section,

$f_{k_2}^m$ – function determining the time of reaching the farther limit of the k-th passing section,

$f_{k_1}^w$ – function determining the time of reaching the closer limit of the k-th overtaking section,

$f_{k_2}^w$ – function determining the time of reaching the farther limit of the k-th overtaking section.

The problem of vessel traffic optimization can be brought down to a linear programming (LP) problem, which in a standard form can be presented as follows:

$$\min c^T x \qquad (1)$$

with the constraints:

$$\begin{aligned} Ax \leq b \\ x \geq 0 \end{aligned} \qquad (2)$$

When we assume the minimization of the total waiting time of all ships as an optimization criterion:

$$OF = \min \left(\sum_{i=1}^{n} c_i x_i + \sum_{j=1}^{m} c_j x_j \right) \qquad (3)$$

and a system of constraints:

$$t_i - t_j - Mx_{ijk} \leq f_{k_2}^m (v_i, v_j, k, T_i, T_j)$$

$$t_i - t_j + Mx_{ikj} \geq f_{k_1}^m (v_i, v_j, k, T_i, T_j)$$

$$\sum_{k=1}^{r} x_{ijk} = r - 1 \qquad (4)$$

$$t_i - t_j - My_{ijk} \leq f_{k_2}^w (v_i, v_j, k, T_i, T_j)$$

$$t_i - t_j + My_{ijk} \geq f_{k_1}^w (v_i, v_j, k, T_i, T_j)$$

$$\sum_{k=1}^{r} y_{ijk} = r - 1$$

$$t_i \leq C_{ijk}^1$$

$$t_i \geq C_{ijk}^2$$

$$t_i, t_j \geq 0$$

where: x, y – binary variables,
M – sufficiently large number,
a model is obtained that belongs to a class of mathematical mixed linear integer programming problems. Generally, solving such problems is considered as an NP difficult problem.

In the analyzed model the vector x is the vector of the times of vessels waiting for entering the fairway and the times of vessel passing along particular fairway sections. The vector c includes weight coefficients, while the matrix A and the vector b include coefficients resulting from fairway traffic constraints – e.g. harbour regulations [3]. [5] presents an algorithm of solving the problem by the branch-and-bound method.

The presented mathematical model of vessel traffic optimization contains a system of constraints, which accounts for conditions to be fulfilled while vessels pass or overtake each other and constraints resulting from vessels on the fairway.

One of the alternative areas admissible for n=2, m=3, i.e. numbers of vessels on the opposite course has been chosen as an example of an optimization problem with fuzzy coefficients.

$$OF = \min \left(\sum_{i=1}^{2} t_i + \sum_{j=1}^{3} t_j \right) \qquad (5)$$

$$2{,}28 \leq t_1 - t_3 \leq 4{,}0719$$

$$-0{,}216 \leq t_1 - t_4 \leq 1{,}4161$$

$$1{,}3361 \leq t_1 - t_5 \leq 2{,}553 \tag{6}$$

$$1{,}553 \leq t_2 - t_3 \leq 2{,}888$$
$$-2{,}1038 \leq t_2 - t_4 \leq -0{,}553$$
$$0{,}1161 \leq t_2 - t_5 \leq 1{,}4161$$
$t_i \geq 0$, i=1,...,5 – variables: times of waiting for entering the fairway.

The system has this optimal solution: t_1=2,28, t_2=1,553, t_3=0, t_4=2,106, t_5=0,1369.

Such a solution means that vessels will be passing at the limits of fairway sections where vessel passing is permitted. In reality, both a vessel cannot enter the fairway and move along with accuracy that may result from calculations based on admissible vessel speeds and fairway limits set forth in harbour regulations. If this is so, a model utilizing fuzzy coefficients of constraints will render the situation more realistically. This calls for solving a problem of linear programming with fuzzy coefficients.

3. A PROBLEM OF LINEAR PROGRAMMING WITH FUZZY COEFFICIENTS

An optimization problem formulated in its classical form features strict and sharp relationships concerning both constraints and objective function. Making these relationships less strict, thus allowing a slight non-fulfillment of the constraints enables us to find 'satisfactory' solutions. This is possible by introducing fuzzy coefficients into a classical linear programming problem [2, 4]. A problem of linear programming with fuzzy coefficients has this form:

$$\min \tilde{c}^T x \tag{7}$$

$$\tilde{A}x \lesssim \tilde{b}$$
$$x \geq 0 \tag{8}$$

This problem for n-element vector x (j=1,..., n) and for m constraints (i=1, ..., m) can be written as follows:

$$\text{Min } \tilde{c}_1 x_1 \mp \tilde{c}_2 x_2 \mp \ldots \mp \tilde{c}_n x_n \tag{9}$$

$$\tilde{a}_{i1} x_1 \mp \tilde{a}_{i2} x_2 \mp \ldots \mp \tilde{a}_{in} x_n \lesssim \tilde{b}$$
$$x_j \geq 0 \tag{10}$$

Each of the coefficients in relations (9) and (10) can be presented in the form of a fuzzy number in the L-R representation [1]:

$$\tilde{a}_{ij} = (\underline{a}_{ij}, \overline{a}_{ij}, \underline{\alpha}_{ij}, \overline{\alpha}_{ij})_{LR}$$
$$\tilde{b}_i = (\underline{b}_i, \overline{b}_i, \underline{\beta}_i, \overline{\beta}_i)_{LR} \qquad (11)$$
$$\tilde{c}_j = (\underline{c}_j, \overline{c}_j, \underline{\chi}_j, \overline{\chi}_j)_{LR}$$

Then the left-hand side of the inequality (10) can be written as:

$$\tilde{a}_{i1}x_1 \tilde{+} \tilde{a}_{i2}x_2 \tilde{+} \ldots \tilde{+} \tilde{a}_{in}x_n = (\underline{a}_i(x), \overline{a}_i(x), \underline{\alpha}_i(x), \overline{\alpha}_i(x))_{LR} \qquad (12)$$

where:

$$a_i(x) = \sum_{j=1}^{n} a_{ij} x_j \qquad (13)$$

Then the conditions (constraints) for n-element vector **x** (j=1,..., n) and m constraints (i=1, ..., m) take this form:

$$(\underline{a}_i(x), \overline{a}_i(x), \underline{\alpha}_i(x), \overline{\alpha}_i(x))_{LR} \tilde{\leq} (\underline{b}_i, \overline{b}_i, \underline{\beta}_i, \overline{\beta}_i)_{LR}$$
$$x_j \geq 0 \qquad (14)$$

One of the interpretations of the conditions of inequalities (10) and (14) is that of Rommelfanger [4]. It is assumed that coefficients $\tilde{a}_i$ are trapezoidal numbers, while $\tilde{b}_i$ are triangular numbers with zero left-hand scatter.

Simplifying the shape of the membership function of right-hand sides of constraints by determining their shape only to the right from the core, we can write the fuzzy number $\tilde{b}_i$ in this form:

$$\tilde{b}_i = (b_i, 0, \overline{\beta}_i)_{LR} \qquad (15)$$

This means that there exists a number bi for which the constraint is certainly fulfilled. However, numbers larger than bi, fulfilling the condition to a lesser degree, should also be accounted for.

At the same time each of the numbers $\tilde{a}_i$ can be written as two simpler numbers: left-hand and right-hand trapezoidal numbers $(\tilde{a}_{iL}, \tilde{a}_{iR})$:

$$\tilde{a}_{iL} = (\underline{a}_i, \underline{a}_i)_{LR} \qquad (16)$$

$$\tilde{a}_{iR} = (\bar{a}_i, \bar{\alpha}_i)_{LR} \tag{17}$$

Having defined the fuzzy relation LE:

$$LE(\tilde{a}_{iR}, \tilde{b}_i) = \begin{cases} 1 & \text{for } \bar{a}_i = b_i \wedge \bar{\alpha}_i \leq \bar{\beta}_i \\ \dfrac{b_i - \bar{a}_i}{\max\{b_i - \bar{a}_i, \bar{\alpha}_i - \bar{\beta}_i\}} & \text{for } \bar{a}_i \leq b_i \\ 0 & \text{otherwise} \end{cases} \tag{18}$$

we can interpret the inequality $\tilde{a}_{iR} \lesssim \tilde{b}_i$ as follows:

$$\tilde{a}_{iR} \lesssim \tilde{b}_i \Leftrightarrow LE(\tilde{a}_{iR}, \tilde{b}_i) \geq \varepsilon \tag{19}$$

where: ε - level of aspiration; $\varepsilon \in \langle 0, 1 \rangle$

The inequality (19), taking account for (15) and (16), can be brought to the form

$$b_i - \bar{a}_i \geq 0 \tag{20}$$

The first inequality in (20) is equivalent to sharp (certain) constraints, which makes the approach safe for a decision-maker. Increasing the level of aspiration ε makes the admissible area smaller, while the determined solution is 'safer'.

4. A MATHEMATICAL FUZZY MODEL OF VESSEL TRAFFIC

The model presented in Chapter 1, intended for the optimisation of vessel traffic in the Szczecin-Świnoujście fairway, precisely describes the movement of vessels. The practical implementation of solutions obtained by classical linear programming is very difficult indeed. This results from difficulties in observing the times of vessels entries into the fairway as well as the times of passages at particular sections of the fairway. This makes it necessary to take into account inaccurate waiting times and moments of passing particular fairway sections. That is why it seems natural to formulate an optimisation problem as a linear programming problem with fuzzy coefficients.

One difficulty that appears is that conditions include both smaller-than and larger-than constraints. Consequently, both types of constraints have to be considered. To be more precise, left-hand constraints have to be transformed into right-hand ones.

The optimisation problem described in Chapter 1 has been transformed into a form of a fuzzy linear programming problem.

The passing of a pair of vessels (i,j) at a section k is determined by a pair of constraints with fuzzy coefficients:

$$\tilde{a}_i t_i - \tilde{a}_j t_j \gtreqless \tilde{b}^1_{ijk} \tag{21}$$

$$\tilde{a}_i t_i - \tilde{a}_j t_j \gtreqless \tilde{b}^2_{ijk} \tag{22}$$

The fuzzy numbers are assumed to have trapezoidal form $\tilde{a}_i, \tilde{a}_j$:

$$\begin{aligned}\tilde{a}_i &= (\underline{a}_i, \overline{a}_i, \underline{\alpha}_i, \overline{\alpha}_i)_{LR} \\ \tilde{a}_j &= (\underline{a}_j, \overline{a}_j, \underline{\alpha}_j, \overline{\alpha}_j)_{LR}\end{aligned} \tag{23}$$

while absolute terms of right-hand and left-hand constraints have a triangular representation $\tilde{b}^1_{ijk}, \tilde{b}^2_{ijk}$:

$$\tilde{b}^1_{ijk} = (b^1_{ijk}, \underline{\beta}^1_{ijk}, \overline{\beta}^1_{ijk})_{LR} \tag{24}$$

$$\tilde{b}^2_{ijk} = (b^2_{ijk}, \underline{\beta}^2_{ijk}, \overline{\beta}^2_{ijk})_{LR} \tag{25}$$

Making use of the right-hand representation of fuzzy numbers, the inequality (24) can be transformed into the form of two fuzzy inequalities:

$$\begin{aligned}\overline{a}_i t_i - \overline{a}_j t_j &\leq b^1_{ijk} \\ \overline{a}_i t_i - \overline{a}_j t_j &\leq b^1_{ijk} - \varepsilon(\overline{\alpha}_i t_i - \overline{\alpha}_j t_j - \overline{\beta}^1_{ijk})\end{aligned} \tag{26}$$

By analogy, introducing the left-hand representation of fuzzy numbers in the constraints (22), the fuzzy inequalities can be expressed as a pair of fuzzy constraints:

$$\begin{aligned}-\underline{a}_i t_i + \underline{a}_j t_j &\leq -b^2_{ijk} \\ -\underline{a}_i t_i + \underline{a}_j t_j &\leq -b^2_{ijk} - \varepsilon(\underline{\alpha}_i t_i - \underline{\alpha}_j t_j - \underline{\beta}^2_{ijk})\end{aligned} \tag{27}$$

where ε- level of aspiration indicates a degree to which fuzzy inequalities are fulfilled.

Calculations have been performed using the case presented before, introducing fuzzy values of coefficients a_i, b_i in place of crisp values.

According the presented above non-fuzzy representation of fuzzy inequalities, the constraints (6) used in the example in Chapter 1 have been substituted for 24 'smaller-than' constraints.

The calculated value of objective function (OF) is used as an assessment criterion:

$$OF = f(\varepsilon, \beta)\big|_{\underline{a}, \overline{a}, \underline{\alpha}, \overline{\alpha}} \tag{28}$$

The results are presented in Figures 1a, 1b and 2a, 2b.

The results of solutions of fuzzy problems are worse than those of determined problems. This is due to the introduction of additional constraints, narrowing the area of admissible solutions. The results become worse as the level of aspiration ε increases in the fulfilment of fuzzy inequalities.

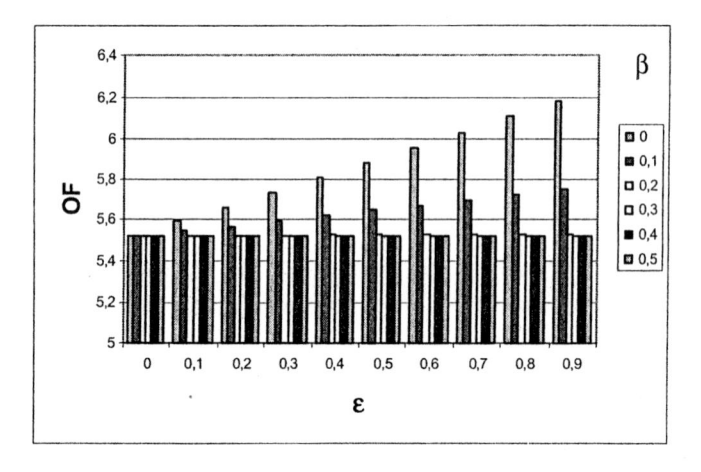

Fig. 1a. Case for $OF = f(\varepsilon, \beta)$, $\underline{a} = 0.9$, $\overline{a} = 1.1$, $\underline{\alpha} = 0.1$, $\overline{\alpha} = 0.1$

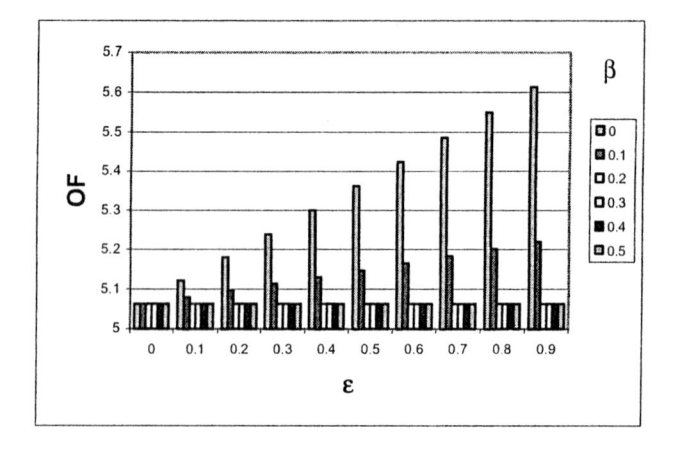

Fig. 1b. Case for $OF = f(\varepsilon, \beta)$, $\underline{a} = 0.8$, $\overline{a} = 1.2$, $\underline{\alpha} = 0.1$, $\overline{\alpha} = 0.1$

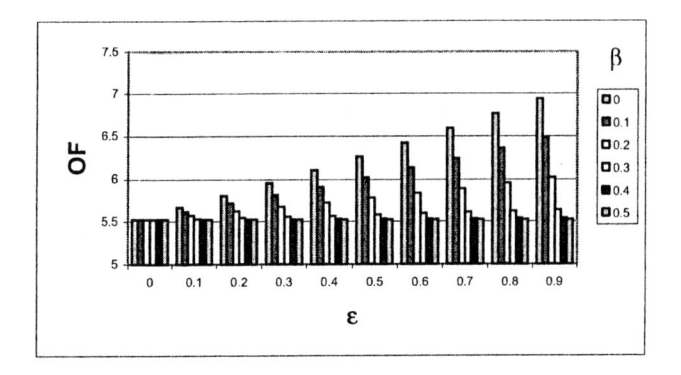

Fig. 2a. Case for $OF = f(\varepsilon, \beta)$, $\underline{a}=0.9, \overline{a}=1.1$, $\underline{\alpha}=0.2$, $\overline{\alpha}=0.2$

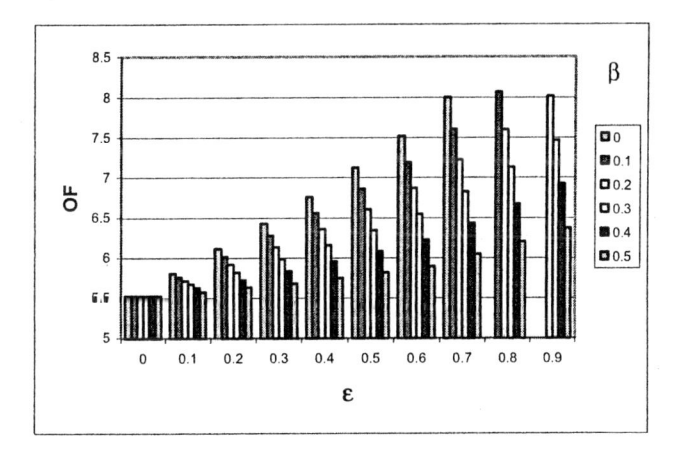

Fig. 2b. Case for $OF = f(\varepsilon, \beta)$, $\underline{a}=0.9, \overline{a}=1.1$, $\underline{\alpha}=0.4$, $\overline{\alpha}=0.4$

The fuzziness of absolute terms of constraints (*b*) means the fuzziness of the time of a vessel reaching the limits of vessels passing section. As the degree of fuzziness increases (increase in β) the value of the objective function decreases.

The fuzziness of coefficients with variables (*a*) means the fuzziness of the time when a vessel enters the fairway. The fuzziness of the value *a* and setting a high level of aspiration results in a lack of admissible solutions. In particular cases, for relatively large values of α, the influence of the limiting component $\varepsilon(\alpha_i t_i - \alpha_j t_j - \beta_{ijk})$ may decrease, which will cause an increase in the value of OF.

5. SUMMARY

The paper presents a problem of vessel traffic optimisation using a method of linear programming with fuzzy coefficients. The case of Szczecin-Świnoujście fairway has been discussed. The L-R representation of fuzzy numbers has been used for the description of constraint coefficients. The form of fuzzy constraints for linear programming problems is necessary in the case when accurate values of constraint coefficients are not known. By transforming fuzzy constraints into non-fuzzy linear constraints we can conventional methods for solving a linear programming problem. The results will depend on the degree of aspiration of fulfilling the fuzzy inequalities. Calculations have been performed. The fuzzy coefficients of constraints have been interpreted. The use of the fuzzy linear programming method has resulted in worse results than in the case of determined problems. This is due to the introduction of additional constraints, narrowing the area of admissible solutions, those corresponding to an assumed level of aspiration ε. The approach presented herein enables a more flexible formulation of an optimisation problem. At the same time allowing for deviations from strict values of constraint coefficients makes the solutions more realistic.

6. REFERENCES

[1] Dubois D., Prade H. 'The mean value of a fuzzy number'. *Fuzzy Sets and Systems* 24, North Holland, pp. 279-300, 1987

[2] Kacprzyk J. 'Fuzzy sets in system analysis'. *PWN*, Warszawa 1986 (in Polish).

[3] *Port Regulations, Instruction N° 10 of the Szczecin Maritime Office Director*, Szczecin, 1993 (in Polish)

[4] Rommelfanger H. 1994. 'Fuzzy Decision Support Systems'. *Springer Verlag*, Berlin (in German)

[5] Uchacz W. 2001. 'Adaptation of the branch-and-bound method for solving vessel traffic optimisation problems', *1st International Congress of Seas and Oceans*. Szczecin, pp. 559-564

[6] Uchacz W., Kwiatek T. 2000. 'Monitoring port regulations and traffic violations on the Szczecin – Świnoujście fairway'. *Annual of Navigation* Gdynia, pp. 143-157

Variable Precision Rough Sets
Evaluation of Human Operator's Decision Model

ALICJA MIESZKOWICZ-ROLKA, LESZEK ROLKA
Rzeszów University of Technology
ul. W. Pola 2, 35-959 Rzeszów, e-mail: alicjamr@prz.rzeszow.pl, leszekr@prz.rzeszow.pl

Abstract: This paper considers the evaluation of human decision model basing on measures of the variable precision rough sets theory. A modified notion of the positive area of classification was used in order to avoid problems in analysis of inconsistent data. Decision tables were generated and investigated in case of control of a dynamic plant (aircraft).

Key words: rough sets, decision model, aircraft control

1. INTRODUCTION

The notion of information system was introduced by Pawlak in the framework of the rough sets theory [3] and used to represent knowledge, commonly expressed in form of a table. The rows of the table correspond with objects of an universe and the columns with attributes of the objects.

Each group of attributes generates an equivalence relation, which allows to classify all elements of the universe and create equivalence classes that contain the objects with the same value of attributes. Such a relation is called the indiscernibility relation.

We obtain a special category of information system - a decision table, when the set of attributes is divided into two distinct subsets: condition attributes C and decision attributes D. The decision table can be analysed by investigating the dependencies between attributes and evaluating the approximation quality or approximation accuracy. Finally one can obtain reducts and generate decision rules, which can be applied in computer control algorithms [2, 3].

However, one has to remark that the most recognised applications of the rough sets theory concerned industrial processes with slow dynamic or static information systems [2, 3]. Unfortunately we can hardly analyse decision tables obtained from control of dynamic plants. This is caused by large sizes of obtained universes. In such a case it is easy to find contradictory decisions. The non deterministic decision rules are always rejected and the calculated value of approximation quality is low.

One could conclude that the human operator controls the process with low determinism, but it is not necessarily true.

The described problems can be avoided by using the approach of variable precision rough sets theory (VPRS), which is more suitable for analysis of dynamic plant control.

2. DECISION MODEL OF HUMAN OPERATOR

We assume that a control action of the human operator is preceded by comparison of information about the required state of the plant, preserved in his memory, with the information about the actual state of the plant. Basing on that comparison and using an inner model the operator takes a decision and then executes a control action.

The control actions of the operator will be expressed in form of a decision table. It is necessary to specify the condition and decision attributes and take into account the lag caused by human factor and the characteristic of the plant. The recorded process data are used to build a decision table, which is the base for obtaining the decision model of the operator.

The application of the modified measures of VPRS [1] makes it possible to determine the consistence of control actions of the operator and to specify his decision model in form of deterministic decision rules. This is done by evaluating the measure k_{AR} (described in the next chapter) that expresses the dependence of decision attributes on condition attributes.

When the value of k_{AR} is nearly equal to 1, then the consistence (determinism) of operator's decisions is large and his decision model is constant. A low value of k_{AR} indicates that the decisions are random and don't depend on the values of condition attributes (assuming a complete set of condition attributes). This means that the operator's abilities to process the information are not correctly formed. One can also detect the importance of particular condition attributes and determine the subset of attributes necessary for identification of the operator's decision model.

3. VARIABLE PRECISION ROUGH SETS

The theory of VPRS is based on a changed relation of set inclusion given in (1) and (2) [5], defined for any nonempty subsets X and Y of the universal set U.

We say that the set X is included in the set Y with an admissible error α

$$X \stackrel{\alpha}{\subseteq} Y \Leftrightarrow e(X,Y) \le \alpha \qquad (1)$$

where:

$$e(X, Y) = 1 - card(X \cap Y)/card(X). \qquad (2)$$

$e(X, Y)$ is called the inclusion error of X in Y.
The value of α should be limited: $0 \le \alpha < 0.5$.

The former proposition leads to a new notion of α-approximation of sets [3].
Let $A = <U, R>$ be an approximation space and $X \subseteq U$ any set,
where: U is a finite set of elements called the universe,
$R \subseteq U \times U$ is a binary relation called the indiscernibility relation.

<u>α-lower approximation</u> of X by R, denoted as $\underline{R}X$ is a set

$$\underline{R}_\alpha X = \{x \in U : [x]_R \stackrel{a}{\subseteq} X\} \tag{3}$$

which is equivalent to

$$\underline{R}_\alpha X = \{x \in U : e([x]_R, X) \le \alpha\}. \tag{4}$$

<u>α-upper approximation</u> of X by R, denoted as $\overline{R}X$ is a set

$$\overline{R}_\alpha X = \{x \in U : e([x]_R, X) \le 1 - \alpha\}. \tag{5}$$

According to the definitions given above we formulated [1], by analogy to original rough sets theory, the notions of the α-lower approximation of a family X^* by R, α-positive area of X^* and γ_R-α-approximation quality of X^* by R.

Let $X^* = \{X_1, X_2, ..., X_n\}$ be a classification of the universe U.

α-positive classification area of X^*, with respect to a set of attributes P, in the system S is defined as follows:

$$Pos_P^a(X^*) = \bigcup_{i=1}^{n} \underline{P}_\alpha(X_i). \tag{6}$$

If $X^* = \{X_1, X_2, ..., X_n\}$ is a classification of the universe U, then

$$\gamma_P^a(X^*) = \frac{card\, Pos_P^a(X^*)}{card\, U} = \frac{\sum_{i=1}^{n} card(\underline{P}_\alpha X_i)}{card\, U} \tag{7}$$

is called <u>α-approximation</u> quality of X^* by P.

In order to analyse a decision table a measure denoted by k_{WZ} for the α-dependence of the decision attributes D on the condition attributes C can be applied:

$$k_{WZ} = \gamma_C^\alpha(D^*) = \frac{\text{card } Pos_C^\alpha(D^*)}{\text{card } U} = \frac{\sum_{i=1}^{m} card(\underline{C}_\alpha D_i)}{\text{card } U} \quad (8)$$

where: $0 \leq k_{WZ} \leq 1$, and $D^* = \{ D_1, D_2, ..., D_m \}$.

We proposed [1] a different definition of the α-positive area of a set X:

$$PosR_\alpha(X) = \{ x \in U: x \in ([x]_R \cap X) \text{ and } e([x]_R, X) \leq \alpha \}. \quad (9)$$

The notion $PosR_\alpha(X)$ can be applied to a family of sets. By using it to equivalence classes obtained from a decision table we get a new measure instead of k_{WZ}, denoted by k_{AR}.

α-approximation quality of D^* by C is expressed as follows:

$$k_{AR} = \frac{\text{card } Pos_C^\alpha(D^*)}{\text{card } U} = \frac{\sum_{i=1}^{n} \sum_{j=1}^{m} \partial_{ij} \cdot card(C_i \cap D_j)}{\text{card } U} \quad (10)$$

where $\partial_{ij} = \begin{cases} 1 & \text{if } e(C_i, D_j) \leq \alpha \\ 0 & \text{otherwise} \end{cases}$

where:
n - number of equivalence classes for decision attributes C,
m - number of equivalence classes for condition attributes D,
α - acceptable inclusion error; $0 \leq \alpha < 0.5$.

4. APPLICATION OF VPRS TO ANALYSIS OF PILOT'S DECISION MODEL

In order to analyse the process of aircraft control by a pilot we must determine the necessary condition and decision attributes.

The first group of condition attributes consists of deviations from required values of selected flight parameters. That flight parameters have to be maintained by the pilot on a fixed level for a given flight phase. The second group contains the changes of the former parameters and this is a source of prognostic information for the pilot.

The decision attributes are deflection angles or changes of deflection angles of the aircraft's control elements.

The values for particular condition attributes are coded as integer numbers e.g. (-3, -2, -1, 0, 1, 2, 3) basing on fixed intervals for deviations from the required values of the parameters. The boundaries of the intervals conform to valid norms or suggestions of experts.

For decision attributes the linguistic values "negative", "zero", "positive" are used.

As an application example of the methods described above an analysis of the task "left turn" is presented, which was realised by a pilot on a flight simulator of the aircraft "Iskra" under conditions with and without turbulence and for the following flight parameters:

- φ_{req} — roll angle,
- H_{req} — altitude,
- Ψ_{rec} — recovery course,
- v_{req} — airspeed.

The set of attributes for the flight phase "left turn" contains 15 condition attributes and 5 decision attributes.

Two kinds of control tasks were considered: multivariable control and stabilisation of a single variable.

In order to analyse the control task of selected variables two methods were used and the results of them were compared:
a) method, which determine the values of k_{AR} for all discrete-time instants (all elements of the universe) for a given decision table,
b) method, which determine the values of k_{AR} for those instants only, were a qualitative change of control occurred.

It was necessary to select condition and decision attributes that, from a point of view of the pilot, are important during control of a given variable.

The results of analysis of control actions are presented in the tables. The control task was to stabilise the roll angle of the aircraft for a required altitude.

Some of the selected condition and decision attributes are described below (with respect to the k-th row of decision table):

$c_1 : \Delta\varphi(k) = \varphi(k) - \varphi_{req}$ deviation of roll angle from the required value,
$c_2 : d\varphi(k) = \varphi(k) - \varphi(k-1)$ change of roll angle,
$c_3 : (\varphi(k) - \varphi(k-1))/T$ rate of change of roll angle,
$c_4 : \Delta\Psi(k) = \Psi(k) - \Psi_{rec}$ deviation from recovery course,
$c_7 : \Delta H(k) = H(k) - H_{req}$ deviation of altitude from the required value,
$c_8 : w(k)$ rate of climb,
$c_9 : dw(k) = w(k) - w(k-1)$ change of rate of climb,
$c_{11} : \Delta dh(k-1) = dh(k) - dh(k-1)$ change of rudder deflection angle at the instant $k-1$,
$c_{12} : dl(k-1)$ deflection angle of ailerons at the instant $k-1$,
$c_{13} : \Delta dl(k-1) = dl(k) - dl(k-1)$ change of ailerons deflection angle at the instant $k-1$,
$d_2 : dl(k)$ deflection angle of ailerons,
$d_3 : \Delta dl(k) = dl(k+1) - dl(k)$ change of ailerons deflection angle.

The coding of values of the attributes c_1, c_4, c_7 was based on mandatory norms for evaluation of the considered flight phase. The values of the attributes c_2, c_9, c_{11}, c_{13}, d_3 were obtained by using a special function. The result of the function depends not directly on the change of a given parameter in one sampling interval, but is calculated taking into account the results of adjacent discrete-time instants. The values of the other attributes were determined by using experimental criteria and considering opinions of experts.

The generated decision table for the multivariable control task is characterised by the results given in the table 1. We can observe that the value of the measure k, defined in the original rough sets theory, was nearly equal to zero in contrast to k_{AR} and k_{WZ}.

Selected condition attributes	Selected decision attributes	k	k_{WZ} $\alpha = 0.2$	k_{AR} $\alpha = 0.2$	Number of el. in universe	Number of determ. rules	Number of non determ. rules
$c_1 \ldots c_{10}$	$d_1 \ldots d_5$	0.079	0.523	0.46	658	42	118
$c_1 \ldots c_{15}$	$d_1 \ldots d_5$	0.137	0.761	0.702	658	66	115

Tab. 1. Analysis of decision table for multivariable control task

The other tables contain results of analysis of decision tables obtained for stabilisation of single variables.

Condition attributes: $c_1, c_2, c_3, c_{12}, c_{13}$. Decision attributes: d_2, d_3.

Method	k	k_{WZ} $\alpha = 0.2$	k_{AR} $\alpha = 0.2$	Number of elements in universe	Number of determ. rules	Number of non determ. rules
a	0.033	0.84	0.798	658	17	38
b	0.762	0.881	0.857	44	17	5

Tab. 2. Analysis of decision table for roll angle stabilisation

Measure $\alpha = 0.2$	Removed attribute (for method b)					
	none	c_1	c_2	c_3	c_{12}	c_{13}
k_{WZ}	0.881	0.786	0.881	0.881	0.81	0.19
k_{AR}	0.857	0.762	0.857	0.857	0.786	0.19

Tab. 3. Analysis of importance of condition attributes for roll angle stabilisation

Condition attributes: c_7, c_8, c_9, c_{11}. Decision attributes: d_1.

Method	k	k_{WZ} $\alpha = 0.2$	k_{AR} $\alpha = 0.2$	Number of elements in universe	Number of determ. rules	Number of non determ. rules
a	0.128	0.894	0.859	658	11	40
b	0.648	0.741	0.722	54	16	11

Tab. 4. Analysis of decision table for altitude stabilisation

Measure $\alpha = 0.2$	Removed attribute (for method b)				
	none	c_7	c_8	c_9	c_{11}
k_{WZ}	0.741	0.741	0.593	0.222	0.0
k_{AR}	0.722	0.722	0.556	0.211	0.0

Tab. 5. Analysis of importance of condition attributes for altitude stabilisation

Condition attributes: c_7, c_8, c_9, c_{11}. Decision attributes: d_1.						
Method	k	k_{WZ} $\alpha = 0.2$	k_{AR} $\alpha = 0.2$	Number of elements in universe	Number of determ. rules	Number of non determ. rules
a	0.003	0.773	0.704	648	9	60
b	0.149	0.394	0.351	94	12	30

Tab. 6. Analysis of decision table for altitude stabilisation under turbulence conditions

Measure $\alpha = 0.2$	Removed attribute (for method b)				
	none	c_7	c_8	c_9	c_{11}
k_{WZ}	0.394	0.394	0.223	0.415	0.0
k_{AR}	0.351	0.351	0.191	0.34	0.0

Tab. 7. Analysis table of importance of condition attributes for altitude stabilisation under turbulence conditions

By analysing the aircraft control process - roll stabilisation (table 2) we can observe a relatively large consistence of pilot's decision rules (greater than 0.8).

The investigation of importance of particular condition attributes (table 3) leads to a conclusion that the lack of the attribute c_{13} (previous change of ailerons deflection angle) would cause a large loss of information for the pilot. The attributes c_1 and c_{12} have a similar importance.

Basing on the evaluated importance of condition attributes we can state, in case of altitude stabilisation (table 5 and 7), that for the generated decision table the attributes: c_8 - rate of climb, c_9 - change of rate of climb and c_{11} – previous change of rudder deflection angle are particularly important. After discarding the attribute c_{11} there would be no apparent dependence between the decisions of the pilot and the conditions, and this is obviously not true.

5. CONCLUSIONS

After analysis of many control tasks realised by pilots on a flight simulator we can state that the variable precision rough sets is a useful method, which allows to characterise the decision model of human operator who controls a dynamic plant. A very important and difficult problem was the correct choice of condition and decision attributes, in order to completely characterise the process of control realised by a human.

The measure k_{AR} could be effectively used for evaluating the consistency of the operator's decision model. The value of k_{AR} was slightly lower than that of k_{WZ}, but the paradox of increase the value of k_{WZ}, after removing condition attributes, was eliminated (table 7).

The value of the measure k, defined in the original rough sets theory, was much lower for the same decision tables. That measure has proved to be too "restrictive" for the presented application.

6. REFERENCES

[1] Mieszkowicz-Rolka A., Rolka L. 2002 'Variable Precision Rough Sets in Analysis of Inconsistent Decision Tables'. Proceedings of 6-th International Conference on Neural Networks and Soft Computing, Zakopane (to appear in Springer Verlag)

[2] Mrózek A. 1989 'Inference models of human operators and their application in computerization of technological objects'. Zeszyty Naukowe Politechniki Śląskiej, Gliwice (in polish)

[3] Pawlak Z. 1991 'Rough Sets. Theoretical Aspects of Reasoning about Data'. Kluwer Academic Publishers, Dordrecht, Boston, London

[4] Słowiński R. ed. 1992 'Intelligent Decision Support. Handbook of Applications and Advances of the Rough Sets'. Kluwer Academic Publishers

[5] Ziarko W. 1992 'Analysis of uncertain information in the framework of variable precision rough sets modelling'. Proceedings of Workshop. Rough Sets. State of art and perspective, Kiekrz

Application of rough sets in the presumptive diagnosis of urinary system diseases

JACEK CZERNIAK, HUBERT ZARZYCKI
*Technical University of Szczecin, Faculty of Computer Science & Information Systems
Institute of Artificial Intelligence & Mathematical Methods
address: ul. Żołnierska 49, 71-210 Szczecin, e-mail: jczerniak@wi.ps.pl, hzarzycki@wi.ps.pl*

Abstract: The main idea of this article is to prepare the model of the expert system, which will perform the presumptive diagnosis of two diseases of urinary system. This is an example of the rough sets theory application to generate the set of decision rules in order to solve a medical problem. The lower and upper approximations of decision concepts and their boundary regions have been formulated here. The quality and accuracy control for approximations of decision concepts family has been provided as well. Also, the absolute reducts of the condition attributes set have been separated. Moreover, the certainty, support and strength factors for all of the rules have been precisely calculated. At the end of the article, the author has also shown the reverse decision algorithm.

Key words: rough sets, decision rules, concept, attribute reduct set, region, certainty factor, support factor, strength factor, decision algorithm.

1. DESCRIPTION OF THE PROBLEM

1.1 Introduction

The main idea of this article is to prepare the algorithm of the expert system, which will perform the presumptive diagnosis of two diseases of urinary system. It will be the example of diagnosing of the acute inflammations of urinary bladder and acute nephritises. For better understanding of the problem let us consider definitions of both diseases given by Manitius.

„*Acute inflammation of urinary bladder is characterised by sudden occurrence of pains in the abdomen region and the urination in form of constant urine pushing, micturition pains and sometimes lack of urine keeping. Temperature of the body is* *rising, however most often not above 38^0C. The excreted urine is turbid and sometimes bloody. At proper treatment, symptoms decay usually within several days. However, there is inclination to returns. At persons with acute inflammation of urinary bladder, we should expect that the illness will turn into protracted form."[1]*

"Acute nephritis of renal pelvis origin occurs considerably more often at women than at men. It begins with sudden fever, which reaches, and sometimes exceeds 40^0C. The fever is accompanied by shivers and one- or both-side lumbar pains, which are sometimes very strong. Symptoms of acute inflammation of urinary bladder appear very often. Quite not infrequently there are nausea and vomiting and spread pains of whole abdomen."[1]

1.2 General decisive diagram

In order to better visualise the research problem let us accept as start point to further considerations, the diagram of expert system with six inputs for data and two decision outputs, which was showed on the picture Fig.1.

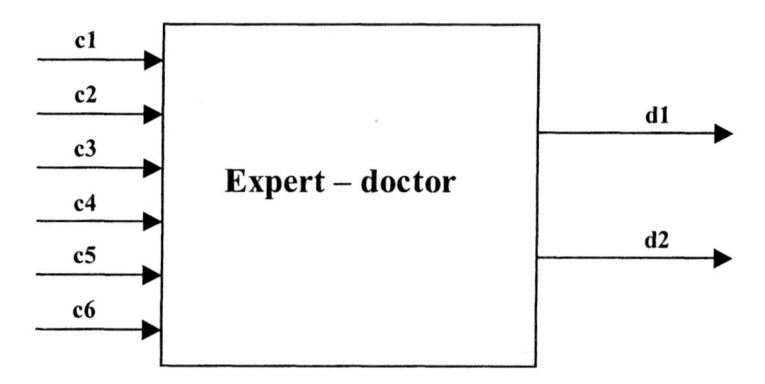

Fig. 1 General decisive diagram of expert system.

1.3 Original database of information

Below there is the full set of experimental data, which in further sections of this article will be processed using the method of rough sets in order to obtain optimum set of decisive equations.[2][6]

Patient	Temperature	Nausea	Lumbar pain	Urine pushing	Micturition pains	Burning of urethra	Inflammation of urinary bladder	Nephritis
Obj.	c1	c2	c3	c4	c5	c6	d1	d2
p1	p	no	no	yes	yes	no	yes	no
p2	w	yes	yes	yes	yes	yes	yes	yes
p3	g	no	yes	yes	no	yes	no	yes
p4	p	no	yes	no	no	no	no	no
p5	w	yes	yes	yes	yes	no	yes	yes
p6	p	no	no	yes	yes	yes	yes	no
p7	w	no	no	no	no	no	no	no
p8	p	no	no	yes	no	no	yes	no
p9	n	no	no	yes	yes	yes	yes	no
p10	n	no	yes	no	no	no	no	no
p11	w	yes	yes	no	yes	no	no	yes
p12	w	no	yes	yes	no	yes	no	yes

Tab. 1 Original information database.

No	Description of attribute	Symbol	Domain
1	Temperature of patient	c1	{ n, p, g, w } n – normal temp. 36^0-37^0C p – subfebrile state 37^0-38^0C g – febrile state 38^0–40^0C w – high fever above 40^0C
2	Occurrence of nausea	c2	{ yes, no }
3	Lumbar pain	c3	{ yes, no }
4	Urine pushing (continuous need for urination)	c4	{ yes, no }
5	Micturition pains	c5	{ yes, no }
6	Burning of urethra, itch, swelling of urethra outlet	c6	{ yes, no }
7	Inflammation of urinary bladder	d1	{ yes, no }
8	Nephritis of renal pelvis origin	d2	{ yes, no }

Tab. 2 The breakdown of input attributes and their values.

2. DETERMINATION OF THE EXPERT MODEL

2.1 Elementary conditional sets

Process of determination of decisive equations set of characteristic for expert should be started from separation of elementary conditional sets. All these sets are shown in the table below.

Obj.	c1	c2	c3	c4	c5	c6	d1	d2	E_i	X_i
p1	p	no	no	yes	yes	no	yes	no	E1	X1
p2	w	yes	yes	yes	yes	yes	yes	yes	E2	X2
p3	g	no	yes	yes	no	yes	no	yes	E3	X3
p4	p	no	yes	no	no	no	no	no	E4	X4
p5	w	yes	yes	yes	yes	no	yes	yes	E5	X2
p6	p	no	no	yes	yes	yes	yes	no	E6	X1
p7	w	no	no	no	no	no	no	no	E7	X4
p8	p	no	no	yes	no	no	yes	no	E8	X1
p9	n	no	no	yes	yes	yes	yes	no	E9	X1
p10	n	no	yes	no	no	no	no	no	E10	X4
p11	w	yes	yes	no	yes	no	no	yes	E11	X3
p12	w	no	yes	yes	no	yes	no	yes	E12	X3

Tab. 3 Elementary conditional sets.

Let us assume, that U is universe of p_i examples. So, we obtain as follows:
U = {p1,p2,p3,p4,p5,p6,p7,p8,p9,p10,p11,p12} card(U) = 12
Set of conditional C attributes. C = {c1,c2,c3,c4,c5,c6}
Family of C * attribute sets, which is C-elementary E_i. $C^* $ = {E1,E2,E3,E4, ... ,E12}
Attribute C-elementary E_i sets.
E1 = {p1}, E2 = {p2}, E3 = {p3}, E4 = {p4}, E5 = {p5}, E6 = {p6}, E7 = {p7},
E8 = {p8}, E9 = {p9}, E10 = {p10}, E11 = {p11}, E12 = {p12}
As it can be seen from above calculations, all elementary E_i sets are singletons.

2.2 Elementary decisive sets (concepts)

The next step to determine the expert model should be concepts fixing, i.e. elementary decisive sets. All these sets are contained in the Tab.3 table. [4][2]
Let us assume, that F is family of decisive concepts X_i.
F = {X1, X2, X3, X4} where;
X1 = {p1, p6, p8, p9}, X2 = {p2, p5}, X3 = {p3, p11, p12}, X4 = {p4, p7, p10}
Let us make an attempt to present decisive concepts X_i in form of logical elementary sums, of attribute sets E_i.
ConceptX1:X1={p1,p6,p8,p9}={p1}U{p6}U{p8}U{p9}={E1}U{E6}U{E8}U{E9}

Concept X2: X2={p2, p5} = {p2} U {p5} = {E2} U {E5}
Concept X3: X3={p3, p11, p12} = {p3}U{p11}U{p12} = {E3}U{E11}U{E12}
Concept X4: X4={p4, p7, p10} = {p4}u{p7}u{p10} = {E4}U{E7}U{E10}

In the next step one should try to restrict the solution, if of course such possibility will exist. One should check it by calculating lower and upper approximations of concepts.

2.3 Lower and upper approximations of concepts and their boundary regions

Lower CX1 approximation of X1 concept in the area of conditional attributes looks like below.
C = {c1,c2,c3,c4,c5,c6}. $\underline{C}$X1 = E1 U E6 U E8 U E9
Upper approximation of X1 concept.

$\overline{CX1}$ = E1 U E6 U E8 U E9 $\overline{CX1} = \underline{C}X1$

Conclusion:
Concept X1 ∈ F is C-distinguishable, which means, that it is distinguishable in relation to set of attributes C = {c1, c2, c3, c4, c5, c6}.
Lower approximation of X2 concept. $\underline{C}$X2 = E2 U E5
Upper approximation of X2 concept.

$\overline{CX2}$ = E2 U E5 $\overline{CX2} = \underline{C}X2$

Conclusion:
Concept X2 ∈ F is C-distinguishable.
Lower approximation of X3 concept. $\underline{C}$X3 = E3 U E11 U E12
Upper approximation of X3 concept.

$\underline{C}$X1= E3 U E11 U E12 $\overline{CX3} = \underline{C}X3$
Conclusion:
Concept X3 ∈ F is C-distinguishable.
Lower approximation of X4 concept. $\underline{C}$X4 = E4 U E7 U E10
Upper approximation of X4 concept.

$\overline{CX1}$ = E4 U E7 U E10 $\overline{CX4} = \underline{C}X4$

Conclusion:
Concept X4 ∈ F is C-distinguishable.
Boundary region $GR(X_i)$ of rough set X_i.
$GR(X_i) = GP(X_i) - DP(X_i)$
$GR(X_1) = GP(X_1) - DP(X_1) = \{\phi\}$ $GR(X_2) = GP(X_2) - DP(X_2) = \{\phi\}$
$GR(X_3) = GP(X_3) - DP(X_3) = \{\phi\}$ $GR(X_4) = GP(X_4) - DP(X_4) = \{\phi\}$
Conclusion :
Due to the fact that for every concept, the boundary region is an empty set, there are no such ranges in the area of attributes, in which deduction is not certain.

2.4 Quality and accuracy of approximation of decisive concepts family in the area of conditional attributes

Continuing the discussion on concepts, let us move to calculations of quality and accuracy of their approximations. The table below contains the breakdown of concepts and their upper and lower approximations.

X_i	card($\underline{C}X_i$)	card($\overline{C}X_i$)
X_1 = {p1, p6, p8, p9}	4	4
X_2 = {p2, p5}	2	2
X_3 = {p3, p11, p12}	3	3
X_4 = {p4, p7, p10}	3	3
Suma	12	12

Tab. 4 List of decisive concepts.

Thus assuming, that $Pos_c(F)$ is C-positive area of F concepts family, we obtain as follows:

card(Pos_c (F)) = card($\underline{C}X_1 + \underline{C}X_2 + \underline{C}X_3 + \underline{C}X_4$) =
card({p1,p2,p3,p4,p5,p6,p7,p8,p9,p10,p11,p12}) = 12
card(U) = 12

$\sum_{X_i \in F}$ card(CX_i) = card(CX_1) + card(CX_2) + card(CX_3) + card(CX_3) = 4+2+3+3 = 12

Now we can calculate C-quality of concepts family approximations from the formula below.

$$\gamma_c(F) = \frac{\text{card}(Pos_c (F))}{\text{card}(U)} = \frac{12}{12} = 1$$

Whereas C-accuracy of concepts family approximations, using the following equation.

$$\beta_c(F) = \frac{\text{card}(Pos_c (F))}{\sum_{xi}\text{card}(\overline{CX_i})} = \frac{12}{12} = 1$$

As results from calculations, all X_i concepts of F family are C-distinguishable. D set of decisive attributes depends completely on set of conditional C attributes ($k = \gamma_c(F) = 1$). It means, that expert, who gave data related to presumptive diagnosis performed an unambiguous classification.

To keep the order and systematic of deduction, let us check C-boundary area F family of X_i sets yet.

$B_{n\tilde{c}}(F) = U_{X_i \in F} B_{n\tilde{c}}X_i$ $B_{n\tilde{c}}(X_i) = \overline{C}X_i - \underline{C}X_i$
$B_{n\tilde{c}}(X_1) = \overline{C}X_1 - \underline{C}X_1 = \{\phi\}$ $B_{n\tilde{c}}(X_2) = \overline{C}X_2 - \underline{C}X_2 = \{\phi\}$
$B_{n\tilde{c}}(X_3) = \overline{C}X_3 - \underline{C}X_3 = \{\phi\}$ $B_{n\tilde{c}}(X_4) = \overline{C}X_4 - \underline{C}X_4 = \{\phi\}$
$B_{n\tilde{c}}(F) = B_{n\tilde{c}}(X_1) U B_{n\tilde{c}}(X_2) U B_{n\tilde{c}}(X_3) U B_{n\tilde{c}}(X_4) = \{\phi\}$

As it is apparent from calculations, C-boundary area of F family is an empty set. The same situation occurs for every X_i set. Conclusions derived from above fact are trivial, so they will not be farther considered.

2.5 Absolute reducts of conditional attributes sets

Results of attempts to remove individual c_i attributes from C sets of conditional attributes illustrates the following table.

Removed conditional attribute	none	c1	c2	c3	c4	c5	c6	c2,c3
Number of distinguishable elementary sets E_i	12	9	12	12	11	11	10	12

Tab. 5 Results of attempts to remove individual attributes.

As it can be seen $\tilde{C} = 12$
If the following equality is valid, then we have a redundant attribute;

$$\widetilde{C - \{c_i\}} = \tilde{C}$$

It concerns for attributes {c2, c3}. Whereas the rest of attributes is absolutely irremovable from C sets, because there is a difference between the indistingshability relation [2][3] of examples originating from reduced set of attributes and the original set of attributes;

$$\widetilde{C - \{c_i\}} \neq \tilde{C}$$

So the absolutely irremovable attributes include { c1, c4, c5, c6 }. So, the absolute core of C attributes set is; CORE(C) = {c1, c4, c5, c6}.

2.6 Relative reducts of conditional attributes sets

The table below shows the list of attributes giving the initial material for further calculations of relative reducts [7].

Let us consider the two following formulas, which we will use to decide whether to remove the attribute or not.

$$\gamma_{\tilde{C}-\{c_i\}}(D^*) = \frac{\text{card}(\text{Pos}_{\tilde{C}-\{c_i\}}(D^*))}{\text{card}(U)} \qquad \gamma_{\tilde{P}}(D^*) = \frac{\text{card}(\text{Pos}_{\tilde{P}}(D^*))}{\text{card}(U)}$$

Decision		Removed C_i conditional attribute						
d_1	d_2	none	c_1	c_2	c_3	c_4	c_5	c_6
no	no	3	3	3	3	3	3	3
no	yes	3	3	3	3	2	3	3
yes	no	4	4	4	4	4	4	4
yes	yes	2	2	2	2	1	2	2

Tab. 6 Initial data for relative reducts of conditional attributes set.

We can officially express two final rules about relative possibility to remove attributes [7]. If the following equality is valid;
$$\text{Pos}_{\tilde{C}-\{c_i\}}(D^*) = \text{Pos}_{\tilde{P}}(D^*) \text{ to } \gamma_{\tilde{C}-\{c_i\}}(D^*) = \gamma_{\tilde{P}}(D^*)$$
then we say, that c_i attribute is removable (D – removable).
However If;
$$\text{Pos}_{\tilde{C}-\{c_i\}}(D^*) \neq \text{Pos}_{\tilde{P}}(D^*) \text{ to } \gamma_{\tilde{C}-\{c_i\}}(D^*) < \gamma_{\tilde{P}}(D^*)$$
Then we say, that c_i attribute is irremovable(D – irremovable).
So because the following equalities are valid;

$$\text{Pos}_{\tilde{C}-\{c_1\}}(D^*) = \text{Pos}_{\tilde{P}}(D^*) \qquad \text{Pos}_{\tilde{C}-\{c_2\}}(D^*) = \text{Pos}_{\tilde{P}}(D^*)$$
$$\text{Pos}_{\tilde{C}-\{c_3\}}(D^*) = \text{Pos}_{\tilde{P}}(D^*) \qquad \text{Pos}_{\tilde{C}-\{c_5\}}(D^*) = \text{Pos}_{\tilde{P}}(D^*)$$
$$\text{Pos}_{\tilde{C}-\{c_4\}}(D^*) = \text{Pos}_{\tilde{P}}(D^*)$$

It means, that attributes c1,c2,c3,c5,c6 are D-removable from set of conditional attributes. Whereas due to the following equality;
$$\text{Pos}_{\tilde{C}-\{c_6\}}(D^*) = \text{Pos}_{\tilde{P}}(D^*)$$

2.7 Relative significance of conditional attributes

On this stage of considerations we can try to list calculated relative significance of conditional attributes. Those calculations are based on the following formula [2]:

$$\delta_{(C,D)}(C_i) = \frac{\gamma_C(D^*) - \gamma_{\tilde{C}-\{c_i\}}(D^*)}{\gamma_C(D^*)} = 1 - \frac{k'}{k}$$

As a consequence, we can find results in Tab.7 table, which shows $\delta_{(C,D)}$ values for each attribute.

Decision		Removed C$_i$ conditional attribute					
d$_1$	d$_2$	c$_1$	c$_2$	c$_3$	c$_4$	c$_5$	c$_6$
no	no	0	0	0	0	0	0
no	yes	0	0	0	0.33	0	0
yes	no	0	0	0	0	0	0
yes	yes	0	0	0	0.5	0	0

Tab. 7 Breakdown of relative significance values of conditional attributes.

Further comments on this list does not seem purposeful.

2.8 Decisive algorithm of the problem and its partition on the well and badly defined part

So, there is full set of decisive rules, which due to previous considerations could be considerably limited.

```
R1:  IF(c1=p)&(c2=n)&(c3=t)&(c4=n)&(c5=n)&(c6=n)THEN(d1=n)&(d2=n)
R2:  IF(c1=w)&(c2=n)&(c3=n)&(c4=n)&(c5=n)&(c6=n)THEN(d1=n)&(d2=n)
R3:  IF(c1=n)&(c2=n)&(c3=t)&(c4=n)&(c5=n)&(c6=n)THEN(d1=n)&(d2=n)
R4:  IF(c1=g)&(c2=n)&(c3=t)&(c4=t)&(c5=n)&(c6=t)THEN(d1=n)&(d2=t)
R5:  IF(c1=w)&(c2=t)&(c3=t)&(c4=n)&(c5=t)&(c6=n)THEN(d1=n)&(d2=t)
R6:  IF(c1=w)&(c2=n)&(c3=t)&(c4=t)&(c5=n)&(c6=t)THEN(d1=n)&(d2=t)
R7:  IF(c1=p)&(c2=n)&(c3=n)&(c4=t)&(c5=t)&(c6=n)THEN(d1=t)&(d2=n)
R8:  IF(c1=p)&(c2=n)&(c3=n)&(c4=t)&(c5=t)&(c6=t)THEN(d1=t)&(d2=n)
R9:  IF(c1=p)&(c2=n)&(c3=n)&(c4=t)&(c5=n)&(c6=n)THEN(d1=t)&(d2=n)
R10: IF(c1=n)&(c2=n)&(c3=n)&(c4=t)&(c5=t)&(c6=t)THEN(d1=t)&(d2=n)
R11: IF(c1=w)&(c2=t)&(c3=t)&(c4=t)&(c5=t)&(c6=t)THEN(d1=t)&(d2=t)
R12: IF(c1=w)&(c2=t)&(c3=t)&(c4=t)&(c5=t)&(c6=n)THEN(d1=t)&(d2=t)
```

As it seems to be purposeful to explain the meaning of the decisive algorithm recorded in this manner, let us do this with the one of decisive rule as an example. So, the Rule R4 has the following meaning:

```
IF
   Temperature      - 380-400        AND
   Nausea           - not present    AND
   Lumbar pain      - present        AND
   Urine pushing    - present        AND
   Micturition pains - not present   AND
   Burning of urethra - present
THEN
   It Is NOT    Inflammation of urinary bladder
   It Is        Nephritis of renal pelvis origin
```

Remaining rules should be unfolded in analogous manner.

At the end of this of section, let us consider also the lower approximations of possible decisions:

$$\underline{\tilde{C}}D_1 = E_4 \cup E_7 \cup E_{10} = \{p_4, p_7, p_{10}\}; \underline{\tilde{C}}D_2 = E_3 \cup E_{11} \cup E_{12} = \{p_3, p_{11}, p_{12}\}$$
$$\underline{\tilde{C}}D_3 = E_1 \cup E_6 \cup E_8 \cup E_9 = \{p_1, p_6, p_8, p_9\}; \underline{\tilde{C}}D_4 = E_2 \cup E_5 = \{p_2, p_5\}$$
$$\text{Pos}_{\tilde{C}}(D^*) = \underline{\tilde{C}}D_1 \cup \underline{\tilde{C}}D_2 \cup \underline{\tilde{C}}D_3 \cup \underline{\tilde{C}}D_4 = \{p_1, p_2, ..., p_{12}\}$$

$$\gamma_{\tilde{C}}(D^*) = \frac{\text{card}(\text{Pos}_{\tilde{C}}(D^*))}{\text{card}(U)} = \frac{12}{12} = 1$$

Due to the fact, that all rules are determinative, the decisive algorithm has been defined well. Because there were no not-determinative rules, so there is no badly defined part as well.

2.9 Support, certainty and strength of each rule

In order to calculate the support of $\Phi \rightarrow \Psi$ rules in S, let us begin, as usual, from recalling of full set of rules.

Reduced table of rules looks like below. Empty places mean, that value of attribute in this place does not influence the output [5].

Rule	c1	c2	c3	c4	c5	c6	d1	d2	Support
Rn1		no		no	no	no	no	no	3
Rn2	g	no	yes	yes	no	yes	no	yes	1
Rn3	w		yes				no	yes	2
Rn4	p	no	no	yes			yes	no	3
Rn5	n	no	no	yes	yes	yes	yes	no	1
Rn6	w	yes	yes	yes	yes		yes	yes	2

Tab. 8 Reduced table of rules.

Before we begin considerations included in this section, the following explanations are worth to be done:
- premise of rule,
- conclusion of rule,
$\Phi \rightarrow \Psi$ - decisive rule,
$\|\Phi\|_S$ - meaning of Φ premise in the S information system.

Support of rules calculated from the following equation, (it is quantity of its meaning in S) amounts to:

$$\text{supp}(\|\Phi \wedge \Psi\|_S) = card(\|\Phi \wedge \Psi\|_S)$$

Certainty (confidence) factor of $\Phi \rightarrow \Psi$ rule defines the frequency of occurrence of objects in S, that have Y conclusion in set of objects having Φ premise.

$$\pi_S(\Psi | \Phi) = p_u(\|\Psi\|_S | \|\Phi\|_S) = \frac{card(\|\Phi \wedge \Psi\|_S)}{card(\|\Phi\|_S)}$$

$Rn1 : \pi_S(\Psi | \Phi) = \frac{3}{3} = 1 \quad Rn2 : \pi_S(\Psi | \Phi) = \frac{1}{1} = 1$

$Rn3 : \pi_S(\Psi | \Phi) = \frac{2}{4} = 0.5 \quad Rn4 : \pi_S(\Psi | \Phi) = \frac{3}{3} = 1$

$Rn5 : \pi_S(\Psi | \Phi) = \frac{1}{1} = 1 \quad Rn6 : \pi_S(\Psi | \Phi) = \frac{2}{2} = 1$

It is necessary to remember, that certainty factor of the rule equals "1" then and only then, when $\Phi \rightarrow \Psi$ is true in S, so when quantity of examples $\Phi \rightarrow \Psi$ in S is equal to the quantity of examples with F premise in S.

The last one from the considered features is strength of $\Phi \rightarrow \Psi$ rule. Strength of rule is calculated from the formula below;

$$\delta_S(\Phi, \Psi) = \frac{\text{supp}(\Phi, \Psi)}{card(U)} = \frac{card(\|\Phi \wedge \Psi\|_S)}{card(U)} = \pi_S(\Phi | \Psi) \bullet \pi_S(\Phi)$$

$$Rn1 : \delta_S(\Phi, \Psi) = \frac{3}{12} = 0.25; Rn2 : \delta_S(\Phi, \Psi) = \frac{1}{12} = 0.08$$
$$Rn3 : \delta_S(\Phi, \Psi) = \frac{2}{12} = 0.16; Rn4 : \delta_S(\Phi, \Psi) = \frac{3}{12} = 0.25$$
$$Rn5 : \delta_S(\Phi, \Psi) = \frac{1}{12} = 0.08; Rn6 : \delta_S(\Phi, \Psi) = \frac{2}{12} = 0.16$$

2.10 Limited decisive algorithm and inverse decisive algorithm

So we can finally formulate the decisive algorithm. It is set of acceptable rules in S, which are independent, covering U-universe and they keep logical cohesion of information system. Limited set of decisive rules Dec(S):

```
Rn1:  IF(c2=n)&(c4=n)&(c5=n)&(c6=n)                    THEN(d1=n)&(d2=n)
Rn2:  IF(c1=g)&(c2=n)&(c3=t)&(c4=t)&(c5=n)&(c6=t)      THEN(d1=n)&(d2=t)
Rn3:  IF(c1=w)&(c3=t)                                   THEN(d1=n)&(d2=t)
Rn4:  IF(c1=p)&(c2=n)&(c3=n)&(c4=t)                     THEN(d1=t)&(d2=n)
Rn5:  IF(c1=n)&(c2=n)&(c3=n)&(c4=t)&(c6=t)              THEN(d1=t)&(d2=n)
Rn6:  IF(c1=w)&(c2=t)&(c3=t)&(c4=t)&(c5=t)              THEN(d1=t)&(d2=t)
```

Due to the fact, that $\Psi \rightarrow \Phi$ rule is called the inverse decisive rule in relation to $\Phi \rightarrow \Psi$ rule, so set of all rules inversions of algorithm Dec(S) is called the inverse algorithm and marked Dec *(S). Set of inverse rules Dec *(S):

```
Rn1*: IF(d1=n)&(d2=n)  THEN  (c2=n)&(c4=n)&(c5=n)&(c6=n)
Rn2*: IF(d1=n)&(d2=t)  THEN  (c1=g)&(c2=n)&(c3=t)&(c4=t)&(c5=n)&(c6=t)
Rn3*: IF(d1=n)&(d2=t)  THEN  (c1=w)&(c3=t)
Rn4*: IF(d1=t)&(d2=n)  THEN  (c1=p)&(c2=n)&(c3=n)&(c4=t)
Rn5*: IF(d1=t)&(d2=n)  THEN  (c1=n)&(c2=n)&(c3=n)&(c4=t)&(c5=t)&(c6=t)
Rn6*: IF(d1=t)&(d2=t)  THEN  (c1=w)&(c2=t)&(c3=t)&(c4=t)&(c5=t)
```

In this manner, we obtained decisive algorithm seen from two points of view, showing expert model, which carries out presumptive diagnosis of acute inflammations of urinary bladder and acute nephritis of renal pelvis origin.

3. REFERENCES

[1] A.Manitius, Co należy wiedzieć o chorobach nerek i dróg moczowych, PZWL, Warszawa 1989, pp. 46,47.
[2] A.Mrózek, L.Płonka, Analiza danych metodą zbiorów przybliżonych, AOW PLJ, Warszawa 1999, pp. 9-47.
[3] W.Ziarko, „Variable Precision Rough Set Model", Journal of Computer and System Sciences, 1993, pp. 39,40,59.
[4] J.Jelonek, K.Krawiec, R.Słowinski, „Rough set reduction of attributes and their domains for neutral networks", Comput. Intell., Vol.11, No.2, 1995, pp. 339-347.
[5] A.Szladow, W.Ziarko, „Rough sets: Working with imperfect data", AI Expert, 1993, pp. 7,36-41.
[6] A.Piegat, Modelowanie i sterowanie rozmyte, AOW EXIT, Warszawa 1999, pp. 24-70.
[7] Q.Shen, A.Choucholas, „Rough set-based dimensionality reduction for supervised and unsupervised learning", Int. J. Appl. Math. C.S., 2001, Vol.11, No.3, pp. 583-601.

Neural Networks and Their Economic Applications

JANUSZ MORAJDA
Cracow University of Economics, Dept. of Computer Science
ul. Rakowicka 27, 31-510 Kraków, Poland, e-mail: eimorajd@cyf-kr.edu.pl

Abstract: The paper outlines basic types of neural networks and presents their selected applications in marketing, finance and other areas of business and economy.

Key words: neural networks, neural modelling, prediction, classification.

1. INTRODUCTION

Artificial neural networks (ANNs, called often simply "neural networks") represent a field of artificial intelligence that has experienced a rapid progress and great popularity among both academics and practitioners. Although ANNs are analogous to non-parametric and non-linear statistical regression models, they have abilities to model non-linear processes with few (or no) assumptions about the character of the system being modelled. This feature turned out to be very useful in business and economic applications, where usually little is known about the nature and dependencies occurring in analysed processes.

The paper briefly characterises the most commonly used kinds of neural networks and presents their selected applications in economy and management.

2. BASIC TYPES OF NEURAL NETWORKS

Multilayer perceptron (MLP)

MLP is probably the most frequently applied type of neural network. It consists of a certain number of neurons (cells) that are grouped in layers (fig. 1a). An input layer transfers and distributes the input data in the network, one or more so called *hidden* layers actually process the information, and an output layer generates network output signals. The data is processed in a feed-forward manner (only in one direction, from input to output) [3, 13, 16, 19].

The neurons of hidden and output layers of MLP generate their output signals y according to the rule (1):

$$y = f\left(\sum_i x_i w_i\right) \quad (1)$$

where x_i is the i-th input signal (incoming to the given neuron), w_i is the *weight* parameter of i-th input connection, and f is so called *activation (transfer) function*. Usually f is a certain non-linear function (e.g. sigmoid or hyperbolic tangent), what allows MLP to model non-linear dependencies in the analysed data.

The development of neural model is based on the network *learning (training)* process. At this stage network weights are iteratively updated during presentation of learning patterns included in the *learning set*. MLP is trained in a *supervised* way, i.e. by comparing the actual network outputs (generated in response to the given input signals) with the correct (desirable) answer values attached to each learning pattern. The goal of learning process is to find a set of weights that minimise sum of (squared) errors (differences between the actual and desired outputs). The most common learning method is the *backpropagation* algorithm [3, 13].

Radial basis function networks (RBF)

The structure of the RBF neural network is in principle the same as the architecture of MLP (fig. 1a), however RBF has always only one hidden layer, and its cells process the data in a different way [13]. Each neuron belonging to the hidden layer calculates the distance between the input vector **x** and its own weight vector **w**, and then applies it as the argument of a symmetric *radial basis function* f (e.g. Gaussian function) to obtain a neuron output value (equation 2).

$$y = f(\|\mathbf{x} - \mathbf{w}\|) \quad (2)$$

The output neurons generate their signals according to equation (1), usually utilising linear f. The learning of RBF is a supervised process.

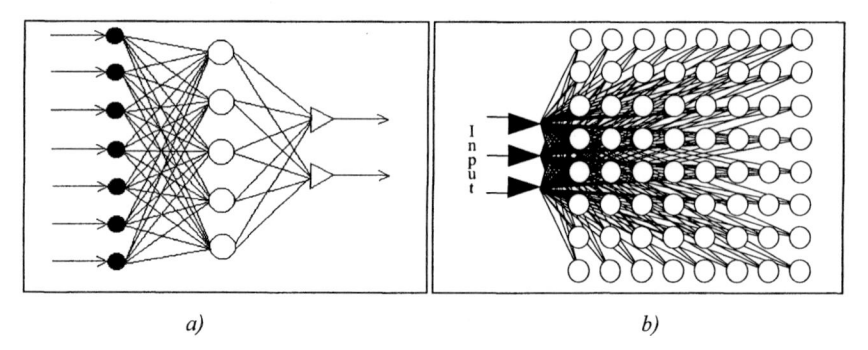

Fig. 1. The structures of neural networks: a) feed-forward (MLP, RBF), b) SOM.

Self-organising maps (SOM, Kohonen networks)

The architecture of SOMs [4, 13, 16, 19] includes two layers: first one only delivers and distributes an input pattern in the network, while the second, organised usually as a 2-dimensional map of neurons, actually process the data (fig. 1b). Each cell in the second layer is connected with all inputs.

The learning procedure of SOM is an *unsupervised* process, i.e. correct (desired) cell output signals are unknown (only input information is utilised for weight modification). When a learning pattern x is delivered, for each map neuron the distance $d = \| w - x \|$ between its weight vector w and vector x is calculated. The neuron having minimal d wins. The weights are modified only for the winner and the cells from its certain neighbourhood; this modification brings w closer to x. The process is iteratively repeated many times for all learning patterns x [3, 4, 13].

SOM is regarded as a tool that perform non-linear transformation of any metric space into 2-dimensional discrete space, and as the method of non-parametric regression that fits *code vectors* (weight vectors) w to the pattern distribution in a feature space. The training process orders the map so as similar patterns are represented by neighbouring neurons on the map. Consequently SOMs are applied to cluster analysis and also to its 2-dimensional visualisation.

3. ECONOMIC APPLICATIONS OF NEURAL NETWORKS

Great many examples of neural networks applications in economy and management have been reported in literature. Below, some selected cases of such applications (based on the author's research) have been presented.

3.1 Marketing data classification (supervised process)

A crucial domain of ANNs utilisation in business and economy is data classification. Principally the knowledge concerning firms or consumers classification is essential in marketing management. Although many statistical methods have been developed, neural networks turned out to be powerful tools in this area [17, 19]. The example below shows the use of supervised neural networks in a process of clients classification in direct marketing, presented by Morajda [12].

Let us consider the company that would like to promote a new product directly by mailing campaign addressed to clients "stored" in the database. In order to reduce mailing costs, the company wants to select only prospective customers, i.e. carry out a process of clients classification onto two classes: prospective and non-prospective. In this task the information about results of previous campaign concerning similar product may be very useful. These data, that include particular consumers characteristics and information about their responding (purchasing the product), could be utilised to supervised neural network learning. The developed neural model, after delivering features of potential client to the network input, generates output signal(s) indicating the selected class.

Table 1 presents the research results of application of three types of neural networks: multilayer perceptron - MLP, radial basis function – RBF and learning vector quantization networks – LVQ (structure of LVQ is similar to SOM, however groups of output neurons are *a priori* assigned to particular classes and weights are modified using a supervised learning algorithm [19]). The 200 records were used for network development (learning and validation) and next 100 records formed the independent test set. Each record included 24 input features describing a client and a binary variable indicating client's class (prospective or non-prospective).

Additionally, for each type of network, there was considered the usefulness of utilisation of principal component analysis (PCA) [3, 9] as a pre-processing tool that ortogonalises input variables and reduces their number (here: from original 24 to 10 after the transformation). Training process for each model has been repeated 9 times starting from different initial conditions (columns P1, ..., P9 in table 1).

Neural model	P1	P2	P3	P4	P5	P6	P7	P8	P9	Mean	Std.dev.	Rule A
MLP without PCA	63	63	64	64	65	64	67	62	59	**63.44**	2.19	63
MLP with PCA	61	61	62	57	59	60	52	50	57	57.67	4.18	58
LVQ without PCA	61	56	58	62	54	60	60	55	62	58.67	3.04	59
LVQ with PCA	56	62	61	59	62	61	60	62	60	60.33	**1.94**	64
RBF without PCA	62	53	61	60	55	61	61	61	66	60.00	3.84	60
RBF with PCA	66	58	69	60	63	61	62	54	62	**61.67**	4.33	64

Tab. 1. Percentage of correctly classified patterns (clients) in the test set, obtained for 6 neural models in 9 training processes P1, ..., P9. Classification rule A performs as a "committee decision" on the basis of the majority of decisions for cases P1 – P9 (see [12]).

Obtained results indicate the usefulness of neural networks in marketing data classification and in other similar issues. It is worth recommending the application of MLP network (without PCA) in such a type of problems.

3.2 Cluster analysis of financial chart patterns (unsupervised process)

In several areas of business and economy there is a need to perform cluster analysis. Although there exists many statistical methods for solving such problems, neural network theory deliver another powerful tool for unsupervised clustering (also enabling visualisation of clusters topology) – self-organising map (section 2).

Many economic applications of SOMs have been reported in literature [14, 19]. Below it has been summarised the research performed by Lula and Morajda in [6], concerning the utilisation of SOM in the clustering of financial chart patterns created by stock quotations.

The research deals with the Polish stock index WIG quotations from 16.04.1991 to 8.11.2000. For each trading day the 20-dimensional pattern including 20 relative index changes (in relation to present quotation) has been constructed. The set of 1918 so obtained patterns has undergone unsupervised clustering process. The information about clusters and their sizes, and also about shapes of typical (representative for particular classes) patterns may be useful for capital market analysis and also for forecasting of stock quotations dynamics.

The graphical representation of the developed SOM (having dimensions 10 x 10), indicating particular clusters with numbers of patterns assigned to particular map neurons, is shown in figure 2.

	1	2	3	4	5	6	7	8	9	10
S1	0	0	29	26	55	0	31	11	0	0
S2	0	0	46	15	37	65	220	10	31	15
S3	78	0	0	10	38	0	23	5	69	0
S4	0	62	0	0	0	0	0	0	2	0
S5	0	21	0	95	0	0	0	0	0	0
S6	92	0	5	0	116	0	0	0	0	0
S7	0	0	129	3	0	0	0	0	0	0
S8	0	0	0	0	14	0	0	0	0	0
S9	130	0	63	0	197	0	77	0	0	0
S10	77	0	0	0	0	11	4	0	6	0

Fig. 2. The picture of developed SOM (10 × 10) with numbers of patterns represented by particular neurons [6]. Coherent shaded areas separated by double lines correspond to identified clusters of quotation chart patterns (13 clusters have been recognized). Weight vector of the neuron representing the greatest number of patterns in a cluster is considered as its typical representative.

The selected typical quotation patterns are shown in figure 3.

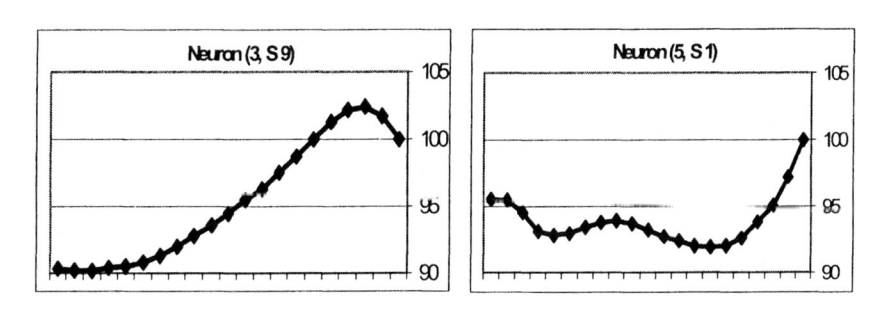

Fig. 3. Two typical patterns represented by neurons (3, S9) and (5, S1) on the SOM (fig. 2).

During the real trading process, early identification of the current pattern or the pattern sequence analysis may be helpful for future quotations prediction.

3.3 Forecasting

3.3.1 Financial prediction and investment strategy creation

Neural networks are often applied to price changes forecasting and trading decision-making in capital markets [14]. Morajda [8] describes an effective ANN utilisation in financial futures trading. The data come from Polish futures contracts market from the 2-years-long period and include 19 input variables and 1 output variable that contain information about the nearest change of the contract quotation.

The research concerned multilayer perceptrons MLP (trained with three different methods: conjugate gradients, backpropagation with weight modification after each *epoch* i.e. whole training set presentation, and backpropagation with weight modification after each pattern), and RBF networks. The learning process has been repeated 10 times for different initial weight values. The results have been compared with effects of linear regression application. Obtained values of RMS (root of mean squared) error for particular models for the validation dataset (average value for 10 training processes and the best result) and for test dataset (best model selected on the basis of validation RMS error) are presented in table 2.

Dataset	MLP conj. gradient alg.	MLP epoch backprop.	MLP pattern backprop.	RBF neural network	Linear regression
Validation – average	1.9787	1.9937	1.9707	2.0869	2.1551
Validation – best	1.9569 *	1.9798	1.9581	2.0450	
Test – best model	2.2235 *	2.2179	2.2471	2.3059	2.4000

Tab. 2. RMS errors of particular models trained for quotation prediction of financial futures.

Table 2 indicates that neural models (especially MLPs) show superior performance to linear methods. The best model selected on the basis of validation error (marked by asterisk *) has also performed very well for the test data. Figure 4 presents the increase of cumulative return during the test period, as a result of use of active trading strategy based on the predictions generated by network (*).

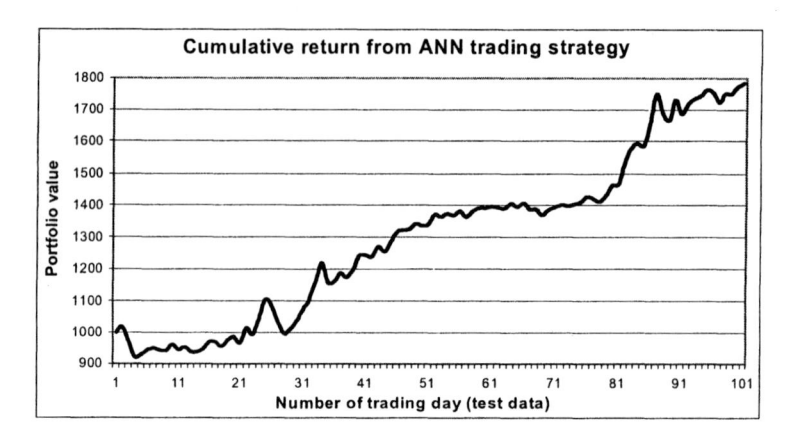

Fig. 4. Cumulative return as a result of trading strategy application, based on MLP (*)

3.3.2 Approximation to probability density functions

Standard ANN applications (like the model shown in section 3.3.1) give only "point" predictions without any information about the probability distribution for the forecasted variable v. Morajda [11] has constructed a neural system, which approximates probability density functions in stock index forecasting. The basic principle consists in reducing the prediction dilemma to the classification problem.

Theoretical background has been worked out by Ruck et al. [15] who show that multilayer perceptron learned with the backpropagation algorithm can approximate (in a mean squared-error sense) the Bayes optimal discriminant function; moreover, in a multiclass discriminant problem MLP output signals can represent *a posteriori* probabilities that given input vector **x** belongs to particular classes.

The idea of a system is based on division of the set of all possible values of predicted variable v into k subsets that determines also classes of input vector **x** – if given value of v belongs to i-th subset then corresponding vector **x** belongs to i-th class. Next, MLP with k outputs corresponding to particular subsets (i.e. classes of input vector **x**) is developed. During the training stage, when a given t-th vector $\mathbf{x}_t$ is delivered to the network input, the output (desired) pattern consists of value 1 assigned to the output indicating proper class of $\mathbf{x}_t$, and values 0 assigned to all other outputs. During the exploitation stage, MLP output signals represent *a posteriori* probabilities for input vector classification, i.e. approximate the probability density function for the variable v.

Figure 5 presents the example of application of such a neural system to Polish stock index WIG prediction (predicted variable v is the next logarithmic daily rate of return of WIG). The MLP with 4 selected input variables (vector **x**) delivering information about current stock index dynamics, 96 hidden units and 12 outputs (corresponding to assumed 12 classes of **x**), has been used. The chart shows approximated distributions of probability density functions for v for 3 test days, compared with empirical distribution for development (training and validation) data.

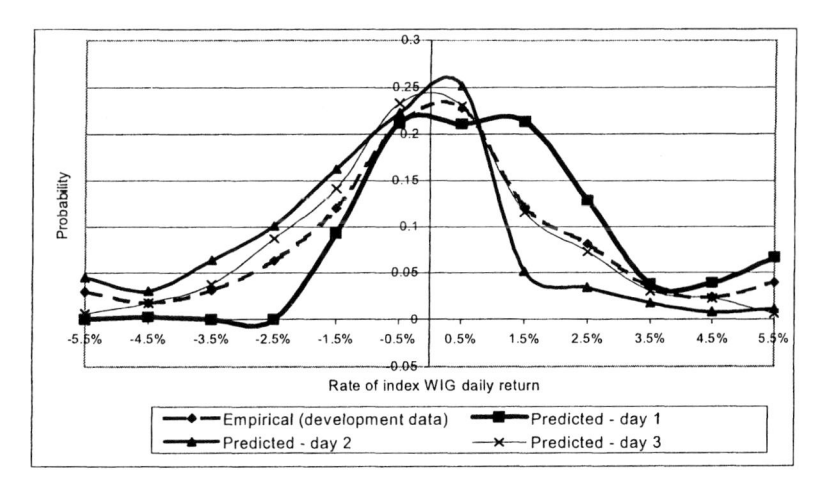

Fig. 5. Predicted approximations of probability density distributions of daily return rate, obtained by the 4-96-12 classification multilayer perceptron for three subsequent test days.

3.3.3 Visual prediction maps

Section 3.2 discusses utilisation of SOMs in financial chart patterns clustering. That method, however, deliver no information about dependencies between particular patterns and corresponding future rates of return in a given financial time series. In [10] Morajda has proposed a modification of SOM that can model such dependencies, moreover, the method can be applied in time series forecasting and its visual analysis. The basic idea consists in the orientation of 2-dimensional map (see fig. 1b and 7) so as the vertical axis represents the future rate of return, while only the horizontal axis represents the feature vector. Consequently subsequent rows of cells on the map are assigned to increasing values of return rates.

The learning procedure for such maps is similar to SOM training (see section 2), however the winning neuron for a given learning input pattern *must* belong to the row representing known value of corresponding return rate. So modified training technique is in principle a supervised learning method. The developed maps allow cluster analysis of financial chart patterns (described in section 3.2) but with additional information about the future rate of return for particular clusters, which is shown on the vertical axis of the map. The method enables also the reconstruction of typical patterns for the clusters connected with given values of return rate.

The developed map can be also effectively utilised in the forecasting process. When a certain pattern **x** is given to the input, the map neurons generate signals indicating distances between vector **x** and their own weight vectors **w**. Cells reacting with low signals "recognise" the pattern **x**. The row of the map, where a neuron generating the lowest signal is placed, indicates the value of return rate forecast. However, the visual (or numerical) analysis of all map signals may deliver more sophisticated possibilities of forecasting and allows the prediction uncertainty evaluation. An example of such a map performance for prediction of Polish stock index WIG for a selected trading day has been shown in figures 6 and 7.

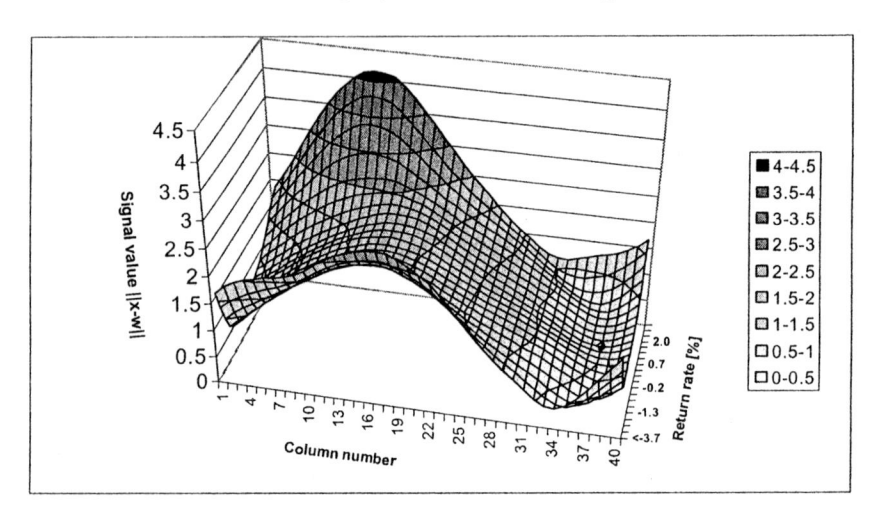

Fig. 6. Three-dimensional visualization of signals distribution of the 40 × 20 map, generated as a response for a given WIG pattern in order to predict its next daily rate of return [10].

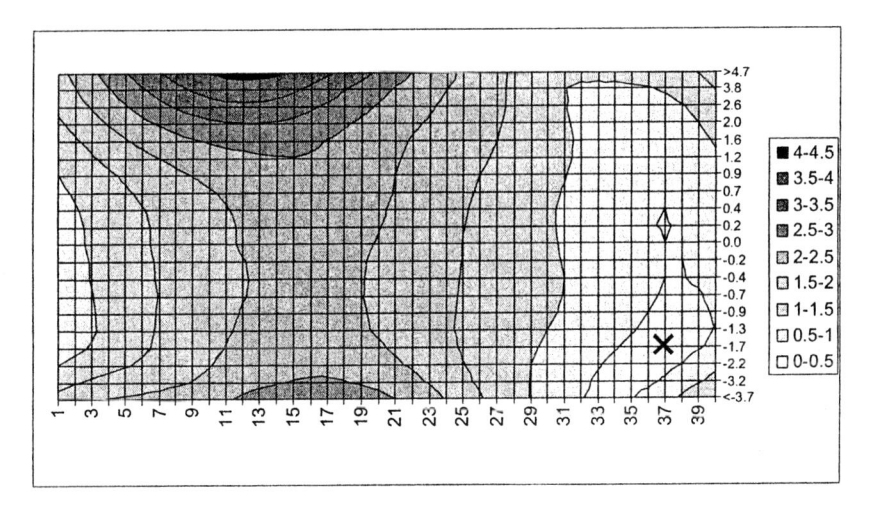

Fig. 7. Two-dimensional visualization of the map. Vertical axis represents daily rates of return for WIG in %. The cross marks neuron generating minimal signal, its corresponding return rate is –1.7%. Actual rate at that day was –4.4%, however map area representing the lowest signal values (0.0 – 0.5) indicates the real possibility of occurrence of such a low return rate.

3.4 Other areas of economic ANN application

The examples above show only a few typical applications of neural networks in business and economy. There are, however, many other domains, where ANNs proved to be useful [5, 7, 14, 18]. The important ones have been listed below:
− corporate mergers prediction [14],
− sales forecasts [17, 19],
− tax control [7],
− bankruptcy prediction [14] and credit granting decision support [18, 19],
− bond rating and stock selection for securities portfolio [14],
− foreign exchange rate prediction [14],
− human resources management [1],
− statistical quality inspection [2],
− real estate market modeling [5].

4. FINAL REMARKS

The submitted examples and obtained research results confirm the usefulness of ANNs in many real problems of economy and management. Neural networks can be perceived and applied as a complementary tools for classical statistical and econometric methodologies. However, due to their abilities to effective, non-parametric modelling of complex, non-linear, poorly identified and noisy objects (like many economic systems), ANNs often function better than classical methods. Consequently, further research on ANNs applications in the mentioned areas of human activity is definitely worth performing.

5. REFERENCES

[1] Collins J.M., Clark M.R. 1993. 'An Application of the Theory of Neural Computation to the Prediction of Workplace Behavior'. Personnel Psychology, 46.
[2] Harston C.T. 1991. 'Business with Neural Networks'. Handbook of Neural Computing Applications, pp. 391-399.
[3] Haykin S., 1994. 'Neural Networks. A Comprehensive Foundation'. Macmillan College Publishing Company, New York.
[4] Kohonen T. 1995. 'Self-organizing Maps'. Springer-Verlag, Berlin.
[5] Lula P. 1999. 'Feed-forward Neural Networks in the Modelling of Economic Phenomena' (in Polish). Cracow University of Economics. Kraków.
[6] Lula P., Morajda J. 2002. 'The Classification of Patterns Occurring in Financial Time Series with Utilization of Kohonen Neural Networks' (in Polish). Scientific Publications, Cracow University of Economics. Kraków - *in printing process*.
[7] Morajda J. 1997. 'Selected Possible Applications of Neural Networks in Economy and Management' (in Polish). Scientific Publications No. 493, Cracow Univ. of Economics.
[8] Morajda J. 2000. 'Neural Networks as Predictive Models in Financial Futures Trading'. Proc. of the 5-th Conference „Neural Networks and Soft Computing", Zakopane.
[9] Morajda J. 2000. 'Principal Components Analysis as a Data Pre-processing Method for Neural Networks' (in Polish). Scientific Publications No. 551, Cracow University of Economics. Kraków.
[10] Morajda J. 2001. 'Modification of Self-organizing Feature Maps for Time Series Modelling' (in Polish). Proc. of XXXVII Conference of Statisticians, Econometricians and Mathematicians of South Poland, Ustroń, Poland - *in printing process*.
[11] Morajda J. 2002. 'Multilayer Perceptrons as Approximations to Probability Density Functions in Time Series Forecasting'. Statistical Review, Warsaw - *in printing process*.
[12] Morajda J. 2002. 'Marketing Data Analysis with Utilization of Neural Networks' (in Polish). Proc. of the Conference "Contemporary methods and means of data processing and transmission", Academy of Insurance, Kielce.
[13] Osowski S. 1996. 'Neural Networks in Algorithmic Depiction' (in Polish) WNT Warsaw
[14] Refenes A.P. (ed.) 1995. 'Neural Networks in the Capital Markets'. Chichester, Wiley.
[15] Ruck D.W., Rogers S.K., Kabrisky M., Oxley M.E., Suter B.W. 1990. 'The Multilayer Perceptron as an Approximation to a Bayes Optimal Discriminant Function'. IEEE Transactions on Neural Networks, vol. 1, no. 4.
[16] Tadeusiewicz R., 1993. 'Neural Networks' (in Polish). AOW RM, Warsaw.
[17] Venugopal V., Baets W. 1994. 'Neural Networks & their Applications in Marketing Management'. Journal of Systems Management, September.
[18] Witkowska D. 1999. 'Artificial Neural Networks in Economic Analyses' (in Polish). Łódź.
[19] Zieliński J.S. (editor) 2000. 'Intelligent Systems in Management – Theory and Practice' (in Polish). PWN, Warsaw.

Application of data with missing attributes in the probability RBF neural network learning and classification

MARCIN PLUCIŃSKI
Faculty of Computer Science and Information Systems, Technical University of Szczecin, ul. Żołnierska 49, PL-71210 Szczecin, e-mail: mplucinski@wi.ps.pl

Abstract: The lack of some attributes in an input vector is a very frequent problem in classification tasks. In the paper there is presented an application of the probability RBF neural network to classification of samples with missing attributes and tuning of the network with incomplete data.

Key words: probabilistic RBF neural network, classification, incomplete data

1. INTRODUCTION

The lack of some attributes in an input vector is a very frequent problem in classification tasks. It concerns many real situations like classification in economy, medicine and technical systems.

The various techniques for dealing with uncertainty are very important [5]. When data have been collected for a particular purpose, known beforehand, it is often possible to minimise, or even completely avoid, the occurrence of missing values in data samples. On the other hand, when data are collected as a by-product of some other activity and subsequently subjected to some sort of data mining operation, missing values are much more likely to be present. In a case of missing attributes there can be found some common solutions in the literature [2,3,4,5].
1. Missing attributes can be substituted by a mean value, most likely value or a static value given by an expert (for example we can decide that all missing attributes should be replaced by 0). Such techniques solve the problem of working and tuning of the classifier. However, very often data samples are incomplete due to the fact that some attributes are too large or too small to measure them. Substituting such attributes by mean value can lead to wrong work of classifier.
2. If an attribute can take only some values, the lack of it can be coded as a special additional value. Sometimes, an extra input (giving an information if the

attribute is present or not) can be added to the classifier. Such solutions increase the complication of the classifier and larger number of inputs makes the process of the classifier tuning harder and longer.
3. Another technique treat unknown input as a special case of uncertain input (input affected by a strong noise process).

In classification systems, missing attributes cause two different problems [2].

1. Classification with missing attributes.
   In that task we have the classifier model F and a vector of input attributes $\vec{X}$ with some known part $\vec{X}^*$ and some unknown part $\vec{X}_u$.

$$\vec{X} = (\vec{X}^*, \vec{X}_u) = (\vec{X}^*, ?)$$

The model has to predict the most probable class for the incomplete input vector: $F(\vec{X}^*, ?) = ?$.

2. Tuning with incomplete data.
   To use all available information during training, it is desirable to make use of all (complete and incomplete) training vectors.

$$?(\vec{X}^*, ?) = class$$

In the paper there will be presented an application of the probability RBF neural network (properly modified) to the both mentioned above tasks.

2. PROBABILISTIC RBF NEURAL NETWORK

The probabilistic RBF neural network [6, 7] works with data set (file) which acts as a learning set for feedforward neural network. Let's assume that classified sample X_i is described by certain set of inputs (attributes). The classification result depends on input values x_{ij}. The data set is defined by samples with known membership to the class and it can take a form (1):

$$\begin{matrix} x_{11} & x_{12} & \ldots & x_{1j} & \ldots & x_{1p} & c_1 \\ x_{21} & x_{22} & \ldots & x_{2j} & \ldots & x_{2p} & c_2 \\ \vdots & \vdots & & \vdots & & \vdots & \vdots \\ x_{i1} & x_{i2} & \ldots & x_{ij} & \ldots & x_{ip} & c_i \\ \vdots & \vdots & & \vdots & & \vdots & \vdots \\ x_{m1} & x_{m2} & \ldots & x_{mj} & \ldots & x_{mp} & c_m \end{matrix} \quad (1)$$

where:

$X_i = [x_{i1}, x_{i2}, \ldots, x_{ip}]$ – the sample i,

x_{ij} – the value of input j for sample i,
c_i – the class which the sample i belongs to,
q – the number of classes,
m – the number of samples,
p – the number of inputs,
$i = 1, \ldots, m$,
$j = 1, \ldots, p$,
$k = 1, \ldots, q$.

The quality of classification first of all depends on taken tuning coefficient, but also on size of the data set, inputs taken into account and their normalisation method.

In the network we must calculate the functions $g_k(\mathbf{X})$ which are the estimate of the probability density function for the class k. Such estimate can be calculated from:

$$g_k(\mathbf{X}) = \frac{1}{n_k \cdot \sigma} \sum_{i=1}^{n_k} W\left(\frac{\mathbf{X} - \mathbf{X}_i^{(k)}}{\sigma}\right). \tag{2}$$

The Gauss function is often used as a W function, so the estimate takes the form:

$$g_k(\mathbf{X}) = \frac{1}{n_k \, \sigma_k^p \cdot (2\pi)^{p/2}} \sum_{i=1}^{n_k} \exp\left(\frac{-\sum_{j=1}^{p}\left(x_j - x_{ij}^{(k)}\right)^2}{2\sigma_k^2}\right), \tag{3}$$

where:

n_k – number of classes classified to the class k,
$x_{ij}^{(k)}$ – samples from the data set classified to the class k,
σ_k – coefficient defining the action range of the Gauss function (for the class k).

Function (3) can be simplified for the classification purpose. If we assume the same value of σ for all classes then the formula (4) can be used:

$$\tilde{g}_k(\mathbf{X}) = \frac{1}{n_k} \sum_{i=1}^{n_k} \exp\left(\frac{-\sum_{j=1}^{p}\left(x_j - x_{ij}^{(k)}\right)^2}{(p\sigma)^2}\right) = \frac{1}{n_k} \sum_{i=1}^{n_k} \exp\left(-c \sum_{j=1}^{p}\left(x_j - x_{ij}^{(k)}\right)^2\right), \tag{4}$$

where: c – tuning coefficient which must be found. As a classification result, the network returns the class for which the value of $\tilde{g}_k(\mathbf{X})$ function is maximum.

Each neuron is described by the Gauss function and its shape depends on the chosen tuning coefficient c. For example, Fig. 1 presents table of 3 samples and shapes and locations of its neurons.

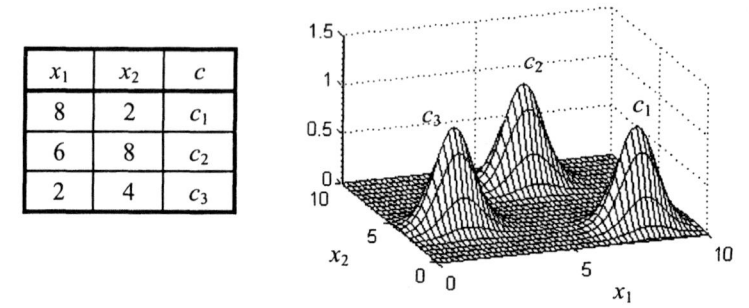

x_1	x_2	c
8	2	c_1
6	8	c_2
2	4	c_3

Fig. 1. Exemplary samples and its neurons

The selection of the tuning coefficient c must be done with a special care. When we choose large enough value of c, the network can correctly classify all samples from the data set, so the overfitting of the network is very easy. In practice, the test file must be created from the data file and as the final value of c we must choose the largest of found values (there is often a number of such values) which assures the minimum classification error of the test file.

If the main data set is small, we can not exclude from it a part of samples to create the test set. Accidentally, some important sample could be excluded and the classifier would work wrong. In such situation a crossvalidation methods can be used. One of the most popular method is "leave one out" method. It consists in leaving one sample from the data set and then in classifying it. Such step must be repeated for all samples and the classification error can be calculated as:

$$e_{cv} = \frac{r_{cv}}{m}, \qquad (5)$$

where: r_{cv} – the number of wrong classified samples. Similarly as above, we choose the largest of found c values which assures the minimum classification error e_{cv}.

3. PROCEEDING WITH INCOMPLETE SAMPLES

3.1 Classification of samples with missing attributes

Let's assume that all samples are complete and we have the classifier model F. Our task is to classify a vector $\vec{X}$ with some known attributes (described by vector $\vec{X}^*$) and some unknown (described by $\vec{X}_u$).

$$\vec{X} = (\vec{X}^*, \vec{X}_u) = (\vec{X}^*, ?)$$

If the dimension of the vector $\vec{X}$ equals p and the dimension of the vector $\vec{X}^*$ equals p^* it occurs [1, 2] the calculations of the function $\tilde{g}_k(X)$ can be done only in the projection of the space R^p onto space R^{p^*}. It means that functions $\tilde{g}_k(X)$ can be calculated only in this dimensions which are available (only for this attributes which are known in classified sample).

3.2 Network tuning with incomplete data

The situation is more complicated when incomplete samples must be used for learning RBF neural network. Let's consider samples analysed earlier but without an attribute x_2 in the last one. Fig. 2 presents table of samples and shapes and locations of its neurons.

Seemingly, the situation is very advantageous and the samples (mostly the last one) should not be treated as less valuable. The third sample "carry" much more information than the complete sample. It shows that if the attribute $x_1=2$ than for any attribute x_2 the sample belongs to the class c_3. The shape of the neuron created for the uncomplete sample is different than the shape of complete sample neurons, Fig. 2.

Why the situation is advantageous only seemingly? Because in many cases, a lack of an attribute doesn't mean that it is not necessary to make a decision which class the sample belongs to. The lack of an attribute is usually caused by the impossibility of the measurement, strong noise or even by ordinary human inattention. From this point of view the third sample has less value than two other and its influence on the network classification process should be less too.

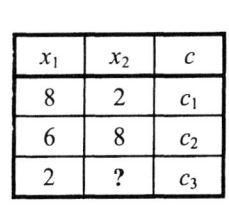

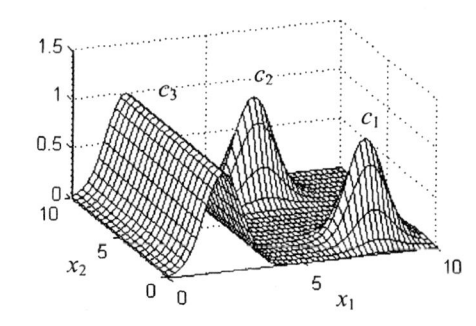

x_1	x_2	c
8	2	c_1
6	8	c_2
2	?	c_3

Fig. 2. Exemplary samples and its neurons

Two additional parameters are added to the original probability RBF neural network to take into account this influence for each sample:

- p_N – neuron width parameter (decrease the neuron width),
- p_R – samples reliability parameter (decrease the neuron height).

Both parameters can take values from the interval <0,1>. RBF neural network calculates for all samples the probability of membership to all possible classes. Modified network does it with the formula:

$$\tilde{g}_k(\mathbf{X}) = \frac{1}{n_k} \sum_{i=1}^{n_k} \exp\left(-c \frac{\sum_{j=1}^{p}\left(x_j - x_{ij}^{(k)}\right)^2}{p_W^{s(i)}}\right) \cdot p_R^{s(i)}, \qquad (6)$$

where: $s(i)$ – the number of missing attributes in the sample. Calculations are made only for this attributes which are known (in the projection of the space R^p onto space R^{p^*}). New coefficients change a shape of a neuron, Fig. 3. If the sample has more missing attributes it is less valuable and in that way, it's influence on the classification result is less too.

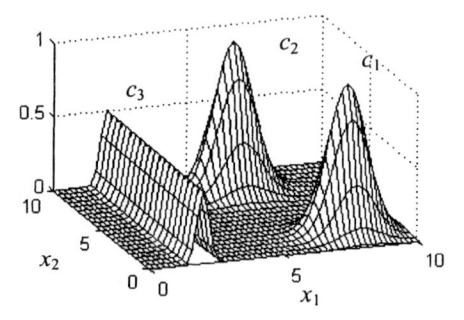

Fig. 3. Exemplary samples and its neurons

4. EXPERIMENTS

In the first experiment the network will be learnt with complete data and next it will be used for classification of incomplete data. The popular benchmark dataset[1] [8] (for diagnosing diabetes of Pima indians) will be used. Each sample has 8 inputs and 1 output which takes the value 0 or 1. The whole dataset includes 768 complete samples.

In the beginning the network should be properly learnt. In the learning process the best value of tuning coefficient $c = 38.6773$ was found. It assures that the dataset

---

[1] All data taken from PROBEN1 – a collection of problems for neural network learning in the realm of pattern classification and function approximation. The benchmark set is available for anonymous FTP from the Neural Bench archive at: ftp.cs.cmu.edu, directory: afs/cs/project/connect/bench/contrib/prechelt, file: proben1.tar.gz.

is classified with the error e_{data} = 10.42% (it means that 80 form 768 samples were classified wrong). Next we will randomly remove some attributes from samples and we will try to classify them. Results are shown in the Tab. 1 and Fig. 4.

In the next experiment the network will be learnt with uncomplete data. As a dataset we will use DIABETES data with 10% of attributes removed. The best coefficients found for such network are: c = 38.6773, p_w = 0.95, p_r = 0.25.

Number of removed attributes	% of removed attributes	Classification error e	
		samples	%
0	0	80	10.42
65	1	86	11.20
311	5	93	12.11
608	10	103	13.41
927	15	117	15.23
1234	20	125	16.28
1516	25	134	17.45
1816	30	148	19.27

Tab.1. Results of classification of uncomplete samples (network learnt with complete data)

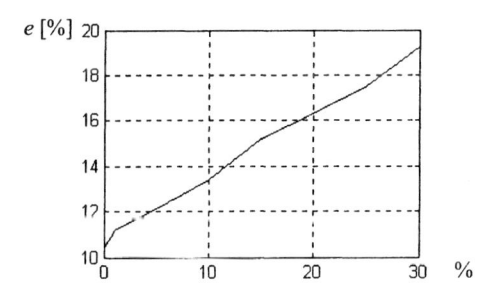

Fig. 4. Classification error with respect to % of removed attributes

Number of removed attributes	% of removed attributes	Classification error e	
		samples	%
0	0	100	13.02
65	1	103	13.41
311	5	109	14.19
608	**10**	**80**	**10.41**
927	15	132	17.19
1234	20	142	18.42
1516	25	157	20.44
1816	30	146	19.01

Tab.2. Results of classification of uncomplete samples (network learnt with uncomplete data)

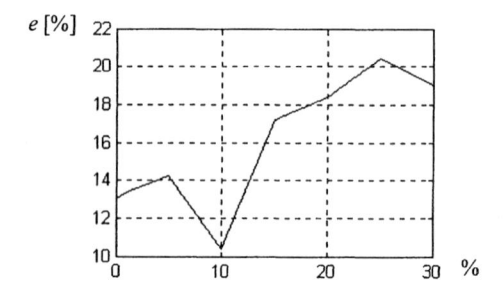

Fig. 5. Classification error with respect to % of removed attributes

Results of classification are shown in the Tab. 2 and Fig. 5. The surface of the crossvalidation error with respect to coefficients p_w and p_r is shown in the Fig. 6. Fig. 6 shows that crossvalidation error takes the minimum value for found coefficients $p_w = 0.95$, $p_r = 0.25$.

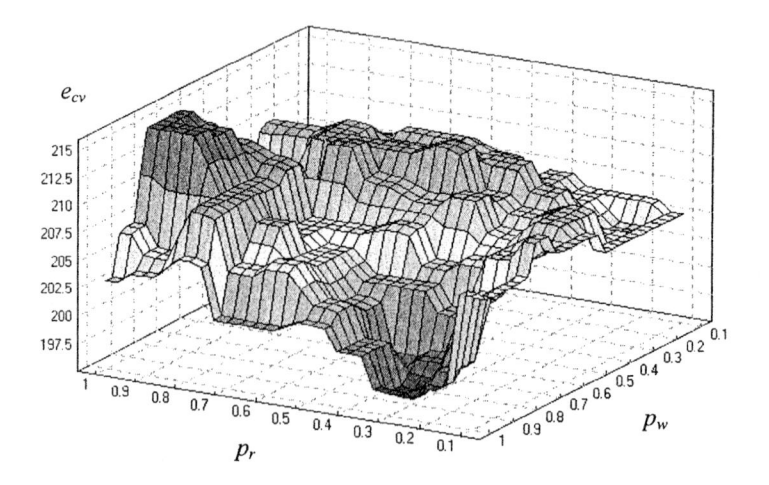

Fig. 6. The surface of the crossvalidation error with respect to coefficients p_w and p_r

In the last experiment we will predict the heart disease [8] on the base of real uncomplete data. The decision is made based on personal data such as: age, sex, smoking habits, subjective patient pain descriptions, and results of various medical examinations such as blood pressure and electro-cardiogram results. Each sample has 12 inputs, 1 output and the whole data set consists of 920 samples.

The best coefficients found for such network are: $c = 23.9883$, $p_w = 0.7$, $p_r = 0.9$. Such network assures data error $e_{data} = 11.19\%$ (125 wrong classified samples) and the minimum crossvalidation error. The exemplary surfaces of the crossvalidation error with respect to coefficients c, p_w and p_r are shown in the Figs. 7 and 8.

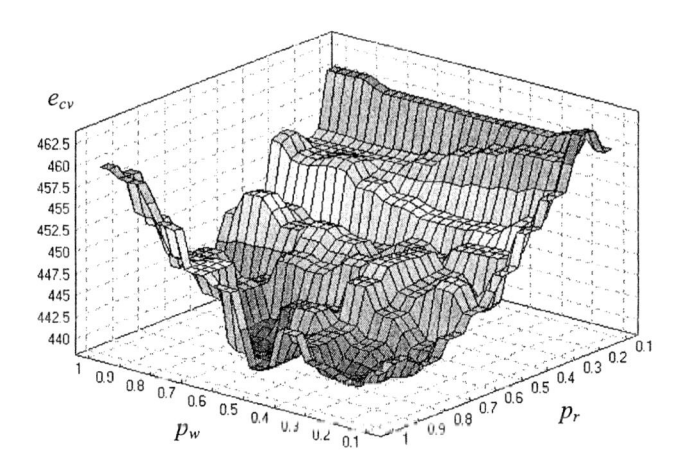

Fig. 7. The surface of the crossvalidation error with respect to coefficients p_w and p_r (section done for $c = 23.9883$) – prediction of heart disease experiment

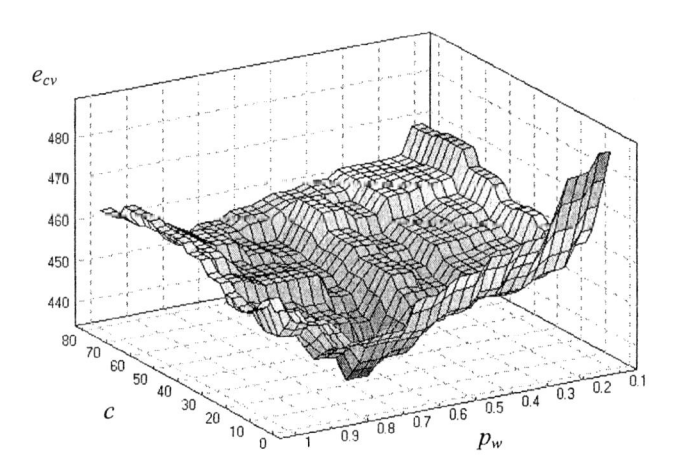

Fig. 8. The surface of the crossvalidation error with respect to coefficients p_w and c (section done for $p_r = 0.9$)

5. CONCLUSION

Proposed modification of the probabilistic RBF neural network occurred very effective solution. The classification quality was comparable with other techniques used for dealing with samples with missing attributes [8].

The main advantage of the modified network is easiness of its learning (only 3 coefficients to tune). The network classifies correctly complete samples and samples with large amount of missing attributes so it is a very good and universal classification tool.

6. REFERENCES

[1] Ahmad S., Tresp V.: Some solutions to the missing feature problem in vision, In: Hanson S.J., Cowan J.D., Giles C.L. (eds), Advances in Neural Information Processing Systems 5, San Mateo, CA, Morgan Kaufman Publishers, 1993
[2] Berthold M.R., Huber K.P.: Missing values and learning of fuzzy rules, International Journal of Uncertainty, Fuzziness and Knowledge-Based Systems, vol. 6, No 2, April 1998
[3] Ghahramani Z., Jordan M.I.: Supervised learning from inclomplete data vis an EM approach, In: Cowan J.D., Tesauro G., Alspector J. (eds), Advances in Neural Information Processing Systems 6, San Mateo, CA, Morgan Kaufman Publishers, 1994
[4] Kim M.W., Arozullah M.: Generalized probabilistic neural network based classi-fiers, International Joint Conference on Neural Networks, Baltimore, 1992
[5] Liu W.Z., White A.P., Thompson S.G., Bramer M.A.: Techniques for dealing with missing values in classification, In: Liu X., Cohen P., Berthold M.R. (eds), Advances in Intelligent Data Analysis, Lecture Notes in Computer Science, pp. 527-536, Springer Verlag, 1997
[6] Masters T.: Sieci neuronowe w praktyce – programowanie w języku C++, Wydawnictwa Naukowo Techniczne, Warszawa, 1996
[7] Pluciński M.: Application of the probabilistic RBF neural network in multidimensional classification problems, Proceedings of the 8th International Conference "Advanced Computer Systems", Mielno, Poland, 17-19 October 2001
[8] Prechelt L.: PROBEN1 – A set of neural network benchmark problems and bench-marking rules, Technical Report, 1994
[9] Tresp V., Neuneier R., Ahmad S.: Efficient methods for dealing with missing data in supervised learning, In: Tesauro G., Touretzky D.S., Leen T.K. (eds), Advances in Neural Information Processing Systems 7, MIT Press, Cambridge MA, 1995

A method of investigating a significance of input variables in non-linear high-dimensional systems

IZABELA REJER[1], ANDRZEJ PIEGAT[2]
[1]University of Szczecin, Mickiewicza 64, Szczecin, Poland,
e-mail: i_rejer@uoo.univ.szczecin.pl
[2]Technical University of Szczecin, Żołnierska 49, Szczecin, Poland,
e-mail: apiegat@wi.ps.pl

Abstract: This article introduces a new method of investigating a significance of input variables in non-linear multi-dimensional systems. The main advantage of the proposed method, in comparison to other widely used methods, is that it allows to investigate the significance of input variables in larger subspaces of analysed system. The article presents not only theoretical basis of the proposed method but also a practical example which aim is to build a ranking of significance for a 19-dimensional system of an unemployment rate in Poland in years 1992 – 1999.

Key words: ranking of input variables, significance of input variables

1. INTRODUCTION

An investigation of significance of input variables in linear systems is a relatively simple task because there are a lot of analytic methods that can be used for dealing with it, for example: Hellwig method, principal component analysis (PCA), linear discrimination and many others. The only problem that can appear during the investigating of significance in linear systems is connected with a possibility of ill conditioning of a matrix of observations [1]. Too small amount of data (in relation to numbers of studied dimensions) or highly correlated input variables can exclude the possibility of calculation of an inverse matrix. But the problem mentioned above is rather easy to identify, therefore it can be said, that building a proper ranking of significance in linear systems is not a difficult task.

Unfortunately the same can not be said about non-linear systems. Of course there are a lot of methods that can be used for investigating the significance of input variables in such systems [2, 3, 4, 5]. However most of them fail when the system is high-dimensional and described via small number of information. The reason for this is that in such systems there is no possibility to build full-input models with a satisfying level of generalisation and regarding to this the examination has to be leaded in small subspaces of the analysed system.

This article introduces a new method of investigating the significance of input variables in non-linear multi-dimensional systems. The main advantage of proposed method is investigating much larger subspaces of analysed system than other broadly used methods. The reason for this is that the ranking of significance in proposed method is based on linear models which can be built by using less data points than non-linear ones.

2. UNEMPLOYMENT RATE IN POLAND

The practical application of proposed method, which will be presented in a further part of this article, refer to building a ranking of importance of macroeconomic factors that could potentially influence on unemployment rate in Poland in years 1992-1999. Eighteen factors (tab. 1) described via 96 monthly pieces of data [6], normalised to range <0, 1>, will be used in this example.

x_i	Factor's name	x_i	Factor's name
x_1	Dollar's rate of exchange	x_{10}	Minimal salaries
x_2	Rate of rediscount	x_{11}	Sold production of industry
x_3	Money supply	x_{12}	Average expanses of households
x_4	Number of graduated	x_{13}	Government income
x_5	Number of workers	x_{14}	Government outcome
x_6	Number of inhabitants	x_{15}	Corporate income tax
x_7	Export	x_{16}	Corporate income
x_8	Number of months	x_{17}	Net corporate profit
x_9	Number of work's offers	x_{18}	Personal income tax

Tab. 1. Factors that could potentially influence on unemployment rate in Poland in years: 1992-1999.

3. DESCRIPTION OF THE METHOD

Proposed method is based on an approximation of multi-dimensional non-linear system by series of local multi-dimensional linear models where each local model describes single subset of data. Succeeding models are building by shifting the time window by fixed amount of data. In a general case a size of the shifting can be arbitrary chosen but one should remember that the closer neighbourhood of the consecutive models, the better rate of approximation of the whole system can be obtained. Obviously in situation when the character of the analysed system is well known the size of the shifting can be chosen in according to an expert knowledge. However, in typical situations when the knowledge about the system is very limited a special caution against choosing too large shifting should be taken into account. The same can be said about the amount of data assumed for every local model. In a general case, the less data will be used for building a local model, the more partial models will be generated, and the better rate of approximation will be obtained. The larger number of local models can help also in showing a time variability of a system, what is particularly essential when the economic systems are under evaluating. However, the amount of data in each local model can not be also too small (comparing to the number of dimensions of the input vector of the system) because that could lead to an overffiting of the model. The approximation described above can be stated by following set of equations:

$$\begin{aligned}
y &= a_{1,0} + a_{1,1}x_1 + a_{1,2}x_2 + \ldots + a_{1,n}x_n & dla \quad t &\in (1,k) \\
y &= a_{2,0} + a_{2,1}x_1 + a_{2,2}x_2 + \ldots + a_{2,n}x_n & dla \quad t &\in (1+i, 1+i+k) \\
y &= a_{3,0} + a_{3,1}x_1 + a_{3,2}x_2 + \ldots + a_{3,n}x_n & dla \quad t &\in (1+2i, 1+2i+k) \\
&\ldots\ldots\ldots\ldots\ldots\ldots\ldots\ldots\ldots\ldots & &\ldots\ldots\ldots\ldots\ldots\ldots \\
y &= a_{m,0} + a_{m,1}x_1 + a_{m,2}x_2 + \ldots + a_{m,n}x_n & dla \quad t &\in (1+mi, 1+mi+k))
\end{aligned} \qquad (1)$$

where:
- n — number of variables,
- m — number of linear local models,
- k — amount of data in single local model,
- i — size of the shifting,
- t — moment in time, $t \in (1\ldots z)$,
- z — amount of data in the whole system,
- y — output variable,
- $x_1\ldots x_n$ — input variables,
- $a_0\ldots a_m$ — vectors of coefficients of local models.

Some graphic examples of using this method in 2 and 3-dimensional systems are shown in the fig. 1 and 2.

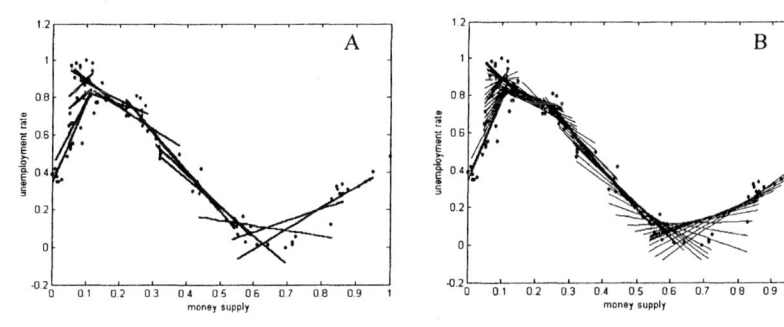

Fig. 1 - An approximation of one-input non-linear system by set of local linear models; the amount of data in each local model: 20; the size of the shifting: A - 5, B - 1.

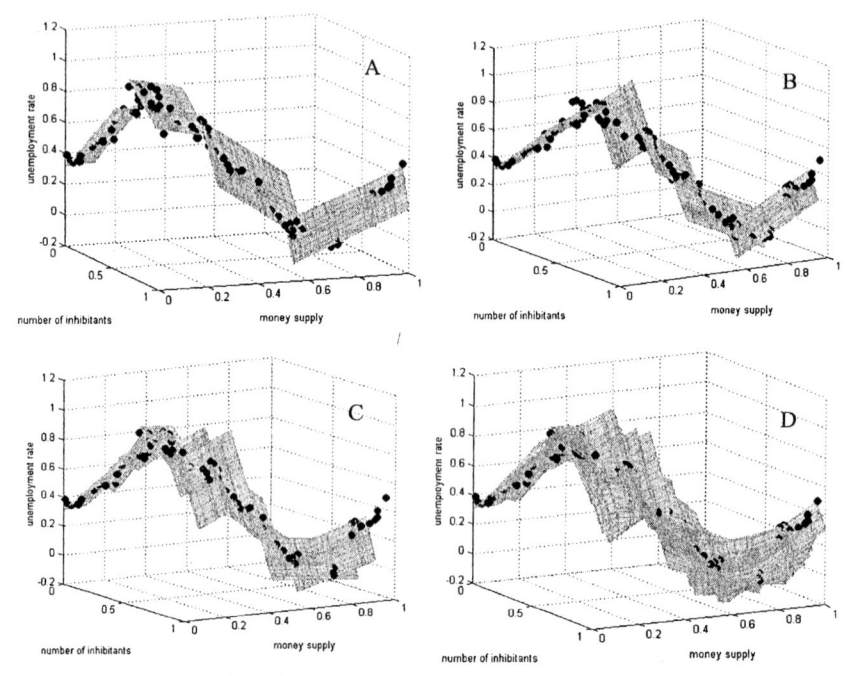

Fig. 2 - An approximation of two-input non-linear system by set of local linear models; the amount of data in each model: 20; the size of the shifting: A – 24, B – 15, C – 8, D - 1.

One can wonder what profits can be gained by describing a non-linear systems via set of linear models. The most important implication of such approach is a possibility of using linear method of estimating the order of importance of input variables in non-linear system. In a single linear model the ranking of significance of input variables can be established by analysing the coefficients of the model, according to the rule: the larger ruthless value of the coefficient, the larger significance of the corresponding variable. That means the information, which is stored in vectors of coefficients of all models, can be used to establish a ranking of significance separately for every single local model. Obviously the ranking of significance can be slightly different in different models. The reason for this is that every model is constructing only for small segment of studied period and the system is not static in time. However the average value of the coefficients should eliminate local deviations and should show the global significance of input variables for a whole period of time. So, the values of significance of input variables in all local models can be used for estimating the global significance by calculating the arithmetic average of linear coefficients of all variables. For example, a global significance of variable x1 will be calculated as average of coefficients corresponding with this variable in all local models (equation 2).

$$ist_{x1} = \frac{1}{m}\sum_{j=1}^{m}|a_{1j}| \qquad (2)$$

(notation like above).

4. CASE STUDY

Proposed method was applied for building a ranking of input variables in a 19-dimensional system of an unemployment rate in Poland that was briefly introduced at the beginning of this article. As the system was supposed to be a time-variable the average significance of the input variables in the whole analysed period was searched. Regarding to lack of apriori knowledge about the rate of nonlinearity of analysed system the parameters of the method were set on such levels that should allow obtaining a high rate of approximation. In according to this the size of the shifting was set to one and the amount of data for each local model was set to 40. On this base 57 local models, placed in 19-dimensional space, were built. Below are three examples of the constructed models:

- model number 1
  y=0.4267+0.3499x_1-0.3565x_2-1.4664x_3+0.2651x_4-0.0419x_5+1.0877x_6-0.2226x_7-0.0973x_8+0.1925x_9+0.0126x_{10}+0.0591x_{11}-0.0392x_{12}+0.0139x_{13}+0.0207x_{14}+0.0549x_{15}-0.0999x_{16}-0.1147x_{17}-0.1653x_{18}
  error: 0.14%
- model number 26
  y=0.8958+0.2183x_1-0.3586x_2-1.4586x_3+0.3664x_4-0.1845x_5+0.1775x_6+0.1106x_7-0.0599x_8-0.0943x_9+0.1166x_{10}-0.3622x_{11}+20.0345x_{12}+0.0139x_{13}+0.0823x_{14}-0.0128x_{15}+0.4057x_{16}-0.0038x_{17}-0.1665x_{18}
  error: 0,17%%
- model number 57
  y=-3.2398+0.2187x_1 0.1664x_2-0.3632x_3+0.4394x_4-0.3476x_5-2.84x_6-0.1923x_7+0.056x_8-0.0325x_9+0.108x_{10}+0.2495x_{11}+0.1787x_{12}+0.001x_{13}+0.0432x_{14}-0.0436x_{15}-0.258x_{16}-0.0886x_{17}-0.1442x_{18}
  error: 0.41%

As it can be observed via the examples of local models presented above the significance of the input variables is not static in time. That confirms the assumption about time-variability of the analysed system. The time-variability of the system can be also presented via charts showing the value of the significance of each variable in succeeding local models (fig. 3). As it can be observed in the fig. 3A the significance of the variable "number of inhabitants" was rather big in the whole analysed period, accept a small gap in the middle of it. The second variable "money supply" (fig. 3B) was also very important in all models but this time the significance was the biggest in the first few models and the smallest in the last ones. Two last charts (fig. 3 C and D) show variables which significance was so small in all models that they rather should not be regarded as the determinants of the unemployment rate in Poland in analysed period.

On the base of all 57 local models 18 vectors of coefficients, informing about significance of individual variables, were obtained. After calculating the average values of coefficients the following ranking of significance was received (tab. 2).

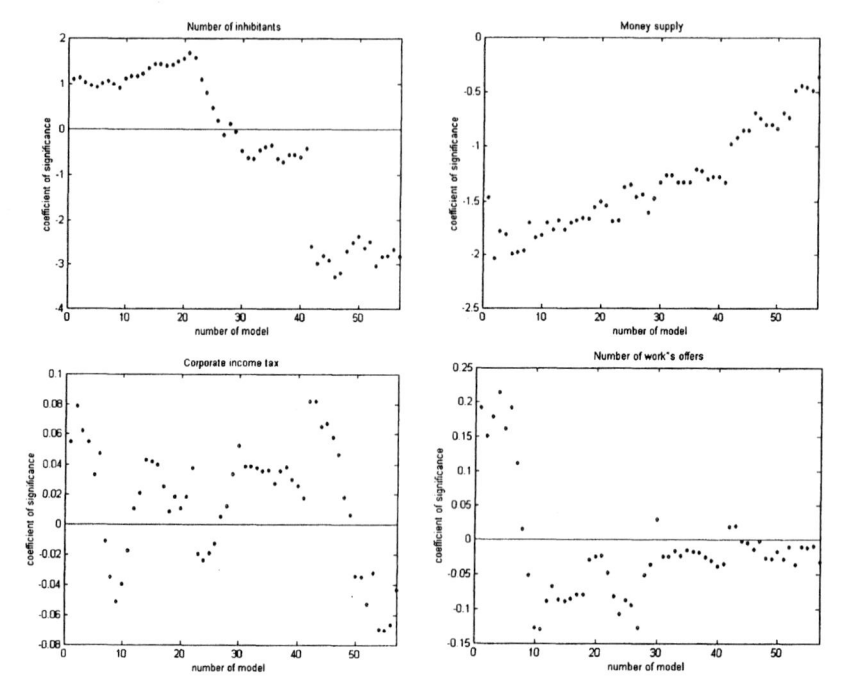

Fig. 3 – The changing significance of the variable in succeeding models; A – number of inhabitants, B – money supply, C - corporate income tax, D – number of work's offers.

Name of variable	Coeff. of signif.	Name of variable	Coeff. of signif.
Number of inhabitants (x_6)	1,4249	Average expanses of households (x_{12})	0,0951
Money supply (x_3)	1,3190	Minimal salaries (x_{10})	0,0895
Rate of rediscount (x_2)	0,4548	Export (x_7)	0,0863
Dollar's rate of exchange (x_1)	0,3426	Personal income tax (x_{18})	0,0841
Number of graduated (x_4)	0,2728	Net corporate profit (x_{17})	0,0770
Corporate income (x_{16})	0,2447	Government outcome (x_{14})	0,0681
Number of workers (x_5)	0,2228	Number of work's offers (x_9)	0,0592
Sold production of industry (x_{11})	0,1970	Government income (x_{13})	0,0419
Number of months (x_8)	0,1134	Corporate income tax (x_{15})	0,0373

Tab. 2. The ranking of importance based on set of linear models.

The input variables which are at the first places of the ranking presented in tab. 2 are mostly in agreement with economic theories and with the general knowledge. First input "number of inhabitants" was pointed by A. Smith and M. Friedman in classical and new classical economic theory. Two next inputs "money supply" and "rate of rediscount" are highly correlated with J. Keynes theory. The fourth variable "dollar's rate of exchange" was underlined in the survey leaded by Polish government and the fifths one "number of graduated" according to the common knowledge, has a great impact on supply of unemployed.

In spite of above explanations, the results of the ranking from tab. 2 were verified by building non-linear model of analysed system. Non-linear neural networks [3, 7, 8] were used as a tool for building this model. The parameters of these networks were as follows:
- flow of signals: one-way,
- architecture of connections between layers: all to all,
- hidden layers: 1 hidden layer with 4 sigmoidal neurons,
- output layer: 1 linear neuron,
- training method: backpropagation algorithm with momentum and changing learning rates,
- testing method: algorithm of generating testing points proposed by authors of this article [9].

To find out which input variables should be introduced to non-linear model of analysed system an inductive approach was used. A criterion determining which variable should be added to the model at every stage of modelling was a minimum average error of the model. During the survey a model with five input variables (tab. 3) and average error equal to 2,21% was obtained. The model was next examined via sensitivity analysis. The results of this analysis were a base of final ranking of input variables of analysed system. This ranking is presented in tab. 3.

Name of variable	Sensitivity
Number of inhabitants	53,18%
Money supply	13,34%
Rate of rediscount	13,23%
Number of graduated	10,63%
Dollar's rate of exchange	9,63%

Tab. 3. The ranking of importance based on non-linear model.

5. CONCLUSION

The results presented in tab. 3 show that the same input variables were introduced to non-linear model as these that were indicated by ranking built via a set of local linear models. The only difference between both rankings lies in opposite order of two last variables. This little inaccuracy of local-linear ranking can be a result of a fact, which was underlined at previous part of the article, that the linear models are only the approximation of a non-linear system. But in spite of this inaccuracy, according to the knowledge of the authors, the proposed method is the only one that allows investigating the importance of input variables with so good results in so high-dimensional system described via so small amount of data.

The proposed method of investigating the importance of input variable via approximation of multi-dimensional non-linear system by sets of multi-dimensional linear models can be very useful in practical application because:
– the amount of data required to use this method is significantly smaller then in other methods – in according to this the proposed method allows to examine bigger subspaces of analysed system,
– the results obtaining via this methods are mostly in agreement with the real ones,
– the linear models which are the base of the method have very stable theoretical background,
– the calculations are very quick and easy to make.

6. REFERENCES

[1] Welfe A. 1998. 'Ekonometria'. Polskie Wydawnictwo Ekonomiczne, Warszawa
[2] Kang S., Isik C., Morphet S. 2002. 'Input Ranking via Statistical Input Sensitivity'. *Conference on Neural Networks and Soft Computing.* Zakopane.
[3] Sung A. H. 1998. 'Ranking importance of input parameters of neural networks'. *Expert Systems with Applications* 15, pp. 405-411.
[4] Liu H., Motoda H. 1998. 'Feature selection for knowledge discovery and data mining'. *Kluwer Academic Publishers.* USA.
[5] Lin Y., Cunningham G.A., A new approach to fuzzy-neural system modeling, *IEEE Transactions on Fuzzy Systems.* vol.3. No.2. pp. 190-198.
[6] Toczy ski T. 01.1992-12.1999. 'Biuletyn Statystyczny GUS' Zakład Wydawnictw Statystycznych. Warszawa.
[7] Masters T. 1996. Practical Neural Network Recipes in C++. *Scientific-Technical Publishing Company,* Warsaw
[8] Demuth H., Beale M., 2000. 'Neural Network Toolbox User's Guide'. *The Math Works Inc.* Natick MA USA.
[9] Rejer I., Piegat A. 2002. How to Test Overfitting When There is not Enough Data for a Testing Set? *Conference on Neural Networks and Soft Computing.* Zakopane.

Evolutionary Algorithm in Problem of Avoidance Collision at Sea

ROMAN ŚMIERZCHALSKI
Gdynia Maritime University, Department of Ship Automation
ul. Morska 83, 81-225, Gdynia, e-mail: roms@am.gdynia.pl

Abstract: In the paper a version of the Evolutionary Planner /Navigator algorithm has been used as a major component of such a decision support system for computing the near optimum trajectory of a ship in given environment. By taking into account certain boundaries of the manoeuvring region, along with navigation obstacles and other moving ships, the problem of avoiding collisions at sea was reduced to a dynamic optimisation task with static and dynamic constrains. The introduction of a time parameter and moving constrains representing the passing ships is the main distinction of the new system. Results of algorithm parameters, having the form obtained using the program for navigation situations are given.

Key words: Evolutionary algorithms, genetic operators, trajectory planning, avoiding collisions at sea.

INTRODUCTION

One of more challenging tasks within the field of dynamic optimisation is planning the trajectory for an object moving in the dynamic environment. A solution to this problem, in which globally optimal solutions are looked for, may find wide applications in numerous issues connected with steering real objects, for instance, for an autonomous robot in changing environment, a ship treated as an object passing areas of changing weather, or a naval ship avoiding obstacles. When solving problems of this kind, a compromise trajectory is searched as a solution, the compromise being reached between costs of the deviation from the assumed trajectory, or the shortest trajectory leading to the assumed target, and the requirement for passing certain static and/or dynamic obstacles in given environment [9]. All trajectories which meet the requirement of passing the objects, fixed or changing their position, compose a set of permissible trajectories. The task of finding optimal trajectory is reduced to the selection of the trajectory, from the above set. The trajectory is optimal with respect to a given target function, representing, for instance minimum trajectory length, its smoothness, or time needed for the target point to be reached. In the case of evolutionary algorithms, the adaptation of the trajectory to the environment is evaluated with respect to an assumed fitness function. The passing trajectory will be configured in a constrained environment using line segments defined by trajectory turning points. Efficiency of the solution search for this problem is connected with the adopted optimisation method. Taking into consideration the type of problem and algorithm efficiency, an evolutionary algorithm was selected as fitting the best the requirements of the trajectory planning task. Evolutionary algorithms [3] [11] [12] [14] have reached good position within the group of optimisation algorithms, and their applicability in this area was confirmed by numerous practical applications. The algorithm is relatively easy for implementation, moreover it can be easily adapted to various types of tasks (continuous or discrete space, with or without constraints, etc.). At the same time it reveals the naturally built-in tendency for searching near optimum solutions. Like for other optimisation algorithms, the use of evolutionary algorithms requires adaptation of their functions to the problem of concern, and selection of a set of parameters to define their action (for instance, the volume of population, representation of individuals, stop criteria, operator modification, type of selection, etc.). In case of dynamic optimisation tasks[7] which have to be solved on-line, a crucial parameter is efficiency of the algorithm. In the evolutionary algorithms is usually defined as the number of necessary evaluations of the fitness function to meet the required objective, which is directly connected with the speed of motion of the population in the direction towards optimum, and resulting computational time.

1. EVOLUTIONARY ALGORITHM

Evolutionary algorithms [4], [5] create a class of algorithms with adaptation random search. Their operation bases on probabilistic methods for creating a population of solutions. In the presented case of the safe trajectory estimation, they are used for creating the population of passing paths, and finding the optimum solution within this population, i.e. the best possible path with respect to the fitness function. The listing below shows an operational concept of the adaptation algorithm estimating the safe trajectory, using the C++ language convention.

Evolutionary_algorithm()
{
  int T; /*T - generation counter variable*/

  T = 0:
  input_data_for_parametrising_operation_of_evolutionary_algorithm();
  input_data_for_defining_environment();
  $P(T)$ = creation_of_initial_chromosome_population();
  building_dynamic_obstacles();
  population_evaluation ($P(T)$);
  while (!= terminating_conditions())

```
    {
T = T + 1;
    Op = operator_selection();
    Par = selection_of_parents_or_parent();
    offspring_creation_and_ introduction( Op, Par );
    building_dynamic_obstacles();
    population_evaluation ( P(T) );
    introduction_of_new_individual();
    selection_of_best_individual ( P(T) );
    }
}
```

The multiple iteration process of transforming and creating new individuals, accompanied by the creation of new populations is carried on until the stop tests in the program are fulfilled.

2. EVOLUTIONARY PROBLEM TO AVOID COLLISION

Formulating the task of estimating the optimum safe trajectory in a well known environment, considered as an evolutionary problem, involves defining the evolutionary steering goal and conditions under which this goal has to be reached.

2.1 Definition of environment and constraints

The kinematic model of the ship motion was applied for estimating the safe trajectory [6] [8]. The dynamics of the ship is taken into account at the phase of steering down the estimated safe trajectory. The ship sails in the environment with natural constraints (lands, canals, shallow waters) or those resulting from formal regulations (traffic restricted zones, fairways, etc.). It is assumed that these constraints are stationary and that they can be defined by polygons - like the way the electronic maps are created. When sailing in a stationary environment, the own ship meets other sailing strange ships - moving targets. Part of these targets are a collision threat, while the rest does not influence the safety of sailing of the own ship.

The degree of the collision threat with dangerous targets is not constant and depends on the approach parameters [1] [2] [13]: D_{CPA} (**D**istance at **C**losest **P**oint of **A**pproach) and T_{CPA} (**T**ime of **C**losest **P**oint of **A**pproach), as well as on the speed ratio of the both ships, and the aspect and bearing of the target. It is assumed that the dangerous target is the target that has appeared in the area of observation and can cross the estimated course of the own ship at a dangerous distance. In the evolutionary task, the targets threatening with a collision are interpreted as moving **dangerous areas** having shapes and speeds corresponding to the moving targets determined by the ARPA system. The shapes of these dangerous areas depend of the safety conditions: an assumed D_{safe} safe distance, speed ratio, and bearing.

The ranges of 5 - 8 N. miles in front of the bow, and 2 - 4 N. miles behind the stern of the ship are assumed. Their actual values depend of the assumed time

horizon. The safe distance is selected by the operator depending on the weather conditions, the sailing area, and the speed of the ship. In the environment model:
- fixed navigation constraints are modelled using convex and concave polygons,
- moving targets are modelled as moving hexagons,
- the dimensions of the own ship are neglected due to small length of the own ship with respect to maximum length of the areas representing the moving targets.

2.2 Planning the trajectory in a collision situation

According to transport plans, the own ship should cover a given route **Ro** in an assumed time. On the other hand, it is to move safely down the given trajectory - i.e it must avoid navigation obstacles and moving targets. Estimating a ship trajectory in a collision situation is a difficult compromise between the above mentioned necessary deviation from the given course and the safety of sailing. Due to these contrasting conditions, this task is reduced to the multi-criterion optimum planning of the passing path, S, which takes into account the safety and economy of the ship motion. The estimation of the own ship trajectory in the collision situation consists in determining the path, S, from the actual beginning point p_{beg_temp} to the actual end point p_{end_temp}. This path has the form of a sequence of elementary line segments s_i ($i = 1, .., n$), linked with each other in turning points (x_i, y_i).

The actual location of the own ship on the route **Ro** makes the actual beginning point $p_{beg\_temp} \in$ **Ro**. The choice of the actual end point, p_{end_temp}, depends on an assumed sensible horizon, or operator decision. This point, however, should also be located on the route **Ro**.

The path S is assumed a safe path S_safe in the permissible space, limited by

$$X = \{ \mathbf{x} \in R^2 : a_i \le x_i \le b_i \text{ for } i=1,2 \} \tag{1}$$

when any of elementary line segments s_i ($i = 1, .., n$) does not cross static constraints O_stat_i ($i = 1,..,k$), and at time instants t determined by current locations of the own ship does not come in contact with moving dangerous areas $O\_dyn(t)_i$ ($i = k+1,..,l$) representing the targets. The space Y is named the safe space when

$$Y = X - \bigcup_{i=1}^{k} O\_stat_i - \bigcup_{i=k+1}^{l} O\_dyn(t)_i \tag{2}$$

The set **S** of paths belonging to the permissible space X is the set **S_safe** of safe paths when

$$\{ \mathbf{S\_safe} \cap \bigcup_{i=1}^{k} O\_stat_i, \mathbf{S\_safe} \cap \bigcup_{i=k+1}^{l} O\_dyn(t)_i \} = \mathbf{0} \tag{3}$$

Paths which cross the restricted areas generated by static and dynamic constrains are called unsafe, or dangerous paths.

The steering goal of the evolutionary task of estimating the own ship trajectory in a collision situation is the search of the set of safe paths, **S_safe,** in the permissible space X, with subsequent selection of the optimum path S_opt from the set **S_safe** with respect to the fitness function determined by the cost of the path.

2.3 Modelling of moving targets

The own ship is assumed to move with a constant speed ϑ along the passing path S from the beginning point (x_0,y_0) to the end point (x_e,y_e), and at the initial instant t_0 the motion of the strange ships - targets is defined as constant. For each target, its motion is represented by the following parameters: bearing, distance, speed, and course, estimated by the ARPA (Automatic Radar Plotting Aid) system. Each paths (individual) is first generated in a random way, and then modified using genetic operators. Next, a set of instantaneous dynamic dangerous areas relating to the targets is attributed to the path by the evolutionary algorithm. The instantaneous locations of these dynamic areas with respect to the passing path depend on time t, determined from the first crossing point (x_{int},y_{int}) between the own ship's path S and the trajectory of the target. The crossing point (x_{int},y_{int}) is the point of the highest collision threat. Having known the length of the line segment from the beginning point, (x_0,y_0), to the crossing point (x_{int},y_{int}) and assuming that the own ship will keep moving with the uniform speed ϑ, it is possible to determine time t which the own ship needs to cover this distance. If the own ship moved with the speed ϑ along the path S, then after time t it would reach exactly the crossing point with the trajectory of the target. After time t, the instantaneous location of the target with respect to the own ship is modelled by the constraint, being the restriction dangerous area with a hexagonal shape. The detailed shape and dimensions of the hexagon depend on the safety conditions given by the operator.

The values assumed in the paper are the following:
- the distance in front of the bow which guarantees avoiding the collision is equal to $3 * D_{safe}$ (in practice, safe distance D_{safe} is taken from the range between 0.5 and 3.0 nautical miles),
- the distance behind the stern is equal to D_{safe},
- the width of the dangerous area on each side of the own ship is chosen with the preference of the ship's passage behind the stern of the target, which depends on the course and bearing of the target.

Moreover, the dimensions of the restricted dangerous area take into consideration the speed rate between the ships. The ship with higher speed is a highest collision threat.

2.4 Population individuals - chromosomes

It was assumed that the passing path S is represented by a single individual - a chromosome. Each individual consists of genes, specified by co-ordinates (x_i,y_i), being the line segment s_i turning points. Linked, the line segments s_i determine the passing path S. All individuals in the population have common beginning and end points. The population consists of m individuals. Each individual, apart from the co-ordinates turning point (x_i, y_i) of the particular line segments is attributed the data int_i informing whether the next segment of the path is safe and whether the turning point does not enter the restricted dangerous areas. The first population is generated in a random way.. The individuals are reproduced by the genetic operators, this reproduction leading to their modification and possible creation of better offsprings.

3. INDIVIDUAL GENETIC OPERATORS

Basing on three basic genetic operations, namely the reproduction, crossover, and mutation, a set of modified operators was developed which execute specific functions used for changing the passing path - the individual, chromosome. This list of operators includes (see: Fig. 1): soft mutation, mutation, adding a gene, swapping gene locations, crossing, smoothing, deleting a gene and individual repairBefore the reproduction of a new individual, the selection of the operator is done in a random way. It is not that all operators can be applied in all situations of individual reproduction. For instance, the operators that add a gene, or repair an individual can be only used for reproducing dangerous paths.

Soft mutation. This operator moves randomly the gene - the turning point of a path line segment, in order to „smooth" the safe trajectory. The operator determines randomly new co-ordinates in a local range in such a manner that the path remains safe.

Mutation. Like the soft mutation, this operator moves randomly the turning point of a path line segment but it is used when dramatic changes, in an arbitrary direction, in the shape of the path are necessary. In the initial phase of the algorithm operation, the range of changes of the turning point co-ordinates has a global character which allows the program to look for totally different paths in a relatively wide range.

Adding a gene. The operation adds a randomly generated turning point to a dangerous path, i.e. the path which comes into contact with one or more constraints. The point on the path in which the new turning point is to be added is also selected randomly.

Crossing. The operator takes two individuals - two parent at paths and creates two offspring paths. In each of the two parent at paths, a crossing point is chosen randomly from the set of available turning points. Due to the different, generally, number of line segments constituting each path, is not necessary to choose the same turning points on both paths with respect to the starting point. Then, the paths swap their cut-off parts. If the selected cut point is located on the dangerous part of the path, it is moved one point forward. The newly generated paths (offspring individuals) may differ in a number of turning points from their parents.

Swapping gene locations. The operation consists in changing the order of two arbitrary turning points in the path. This operation can lead to shortening the path, or making an dangerous path safe.

Smoothing. Smoothing of the safe trajectories is executed by eliminating one turning point in the path.

Deleting a gene. This operation deletes an arbitrary turning point in the path. Two cases of deleting the turning point are considered - for a safe and dangerous paths. The choice of turning point in the dangerous path is done in a random manner, and in the safe path it depends on whether the next line segment is safe.

Individual repair. The dangerous paths, i.e. those which come into contact with at least one of the constraints, are subject to the action of this operator. At a distance d from the crossing point of the path with the constraint, a new turning point is generated, which is the beginning point for the series of line segments by-passing the border. New line segments are created along the border line between the turning points until the new generated by-pass path crosses that being repaired, or exceeds the maximum permissible number of turning points for a single path.

4. SIMULATION STUDIES AND PROGRAMME TESTS IN COLLISION SITUATIONS

In order to test operational correctness of the *on-line* version of programme vTP/N++, certain trajectories were calculated using the both versions and then compared. The test was divided into three phases. In the first phase, passing paths obtained in the *off-line* mode were tested. Then the real motion was studied of the own ship travelling along the assumed trajectory and passing other objects. The level of identity was assessed with which the positions of passed ships – domains were calculated with respect to the own ship. For the *on-line* version, a quality assessment was made for the calculated trajectory on the basis of *on-line* calculations performed after changing parameters of motion of one or more dynamic constraints. The comparison was made for two sample environments characterised by a relatively high level of complexity.

The first case (Fig. 1) presents the situation in which the own ship passes round four islands and four objects moving from different directions and at different speeds. Input parameters for the simulation, in which the population number was equal to 40, are shown in Fig. 1.

Ship trajectory adaptations, made in the *off-line* mode after the own ship has met four moving objects in a collision situation, are shown in Fig. 2, after 500, and 2000 generations, respectively. The solution obtained after 2000 generations made it possible to pass round the islands, at the same time leaving aside the moving objects. Current speeds of the own ship were individually calculated for each trajectory segment which allowed the ship to reach the target point in a safe way and the shortest possible time. The realisation of the proposed trajectory optimised the ship passage cost with respect both to safety and economic conditions, eliminating the risk of excessive approach to the passed objects. It is noteworthy that the results are presented in a relative form, in which the domains of the dynamic constraints are drawn up in positions which they will reach when the own ship is in front of their bows or behind their sterns.

The next phase studies the real motion of the own ship travelling along the assumed trajectory and passing strange objects. This phase makes it possible to assess more accurately the correctness of positions of the passed ships – domains with respect to the own ship. Fig. 3 presents the navigational situation in the real motion after T_i = 10, 20, 30, 40, min (i= 1,..,4). In contrast to the relative presentation (Fig. 2), here the positions of the domains representing dynamic constraints and the position of the own ship on the trajectory are determined after the time which elapsed after the simulation has started (Option „Run" pressed down) to the time instant when the option „real time situation" was started.

The option „real time situation" was implemented in order to stop the motion of all objects for a given time instant and to simulate possible changes in parameters of motion of the domains representing passed objects interpreted as dynamic constraints. Changing parameters of passed objects creates a new navigational situation – a new environment which provokes the adaptation of the ship trajectory calculated in the *off-line* mode. Switching to the *on-line* mode, the system vEP/N++ adapts the *off-line* trajectory version to the new environment, treating the time when the objects were stopped as the starting point of the modified trajectory.

For the test environment, the algorithm switched to the *on-line* mode at $T_2 = 20$ min. Then selected parameters were changed, namely: the course of the object seen in the right part of the screen, which was changed from 45 degrees to 210 degrees, and the speed of motion of the object seen in the upper left part of the screen, changed from 5,2 to 17,6 knots. These changes were dictated by the requirement to observe the operation of the algorithm in extremely complex environment. Fig. 4 (b) shows a newly calculated safe trajectory (generation number = 2000) which has taken into account the above changes. After comparing Fig. 2 and Fig. 4 (b) one can see that the path calculated in the *on-line* mode is similar to the trajectory obtained in the *off-line* mode, with certain differences resulting from trajectory corrections made due to environment changes introduced. This proves operational correctness of the *on-line* version.

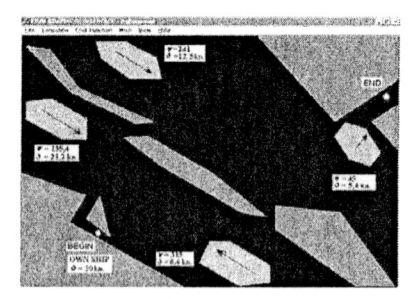

Fig. 1. Test environment for Generation=0. Mode: off-line

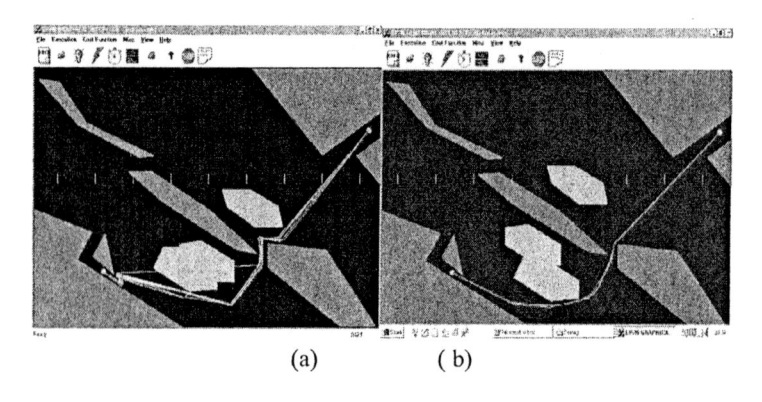

(a)   (b)

Fig. 2. Test environment for (a) Generation=500, (b) Generation=2000. Mode: off-line

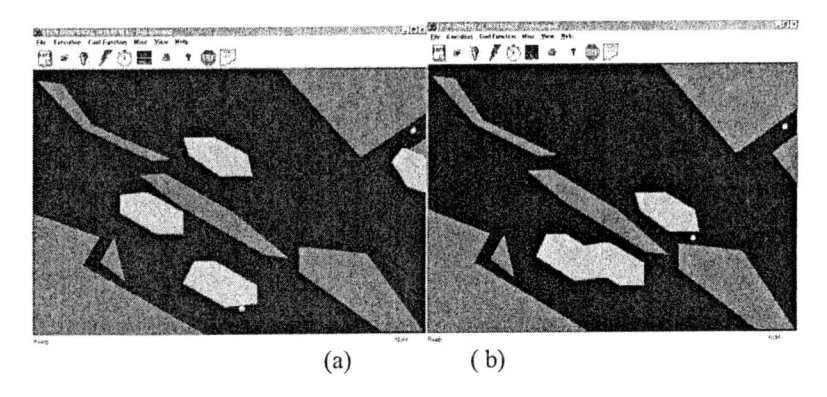

Fig. 3. Test environment, option „Real time situation" for time (a) $T_1 = 20$, (b) $T_2 = 40$ min.

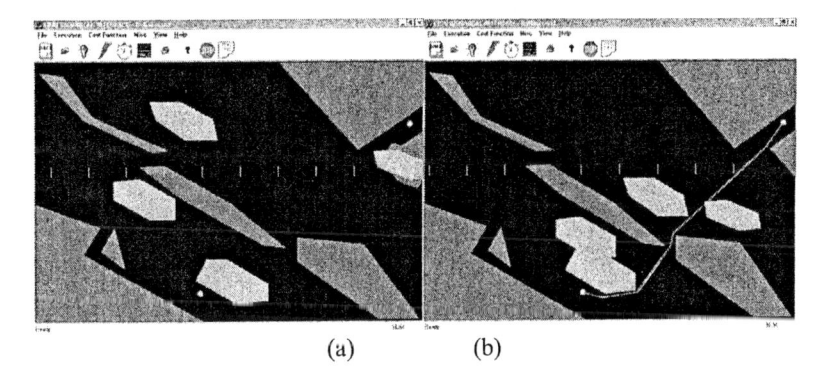

Fig. 4. Test environment for start time $T_1 = 20$ min. (a) Changing parameters of motion of two targets, (b) new optimum trajectory

5. CONCLUSION

The evolutionary system of ship trajectory planning makes it possible to steer the ship in a well known environment both with static, and dynamic navigation constraints, as well as to make adaptation corrections of the ship trajectory in order to follow unforeseeable changes in the situation at sea. The evolutionary method of determining the safe and optimum trajectory in the environment is a new approach to the problem of avoiding collisions at sea. A number of preliminary tests have made it possible to formulate the following conclusions:
- evolutionary algorithms can be effectively used for solving the problem of planning ship trajectory in areas of extensive traffic, like harbour entrances, coastal regions,
- introduction the on-line mode makes it possible to solve the problem in a wider range.

For particular trajectory sections, the actual trajectory is evaluated with which the ship covers this section in order to pass safely and economically all navigational constraints, both fixed and moving.

6. REFERENCES

[1] Burns R. S., An intelligent automatic guidance system for surface ships. Marine Technology and Transportation, Coputational Mechanics Publications, Southampton, Boston 1995, pp. 641-652.
[2] Burns R. S., The aplication of artificial intelligence techniques to modelling and control of surface ships. Eleventh Ship Control Systems Symposium, Coputational Mechanics Publications, Southampton, Boston 1995 Vol. 1, pp. 77-83.
[3] Lin HS, Xiao J, Michalewicz Z, Evolutionary Algorithm for Path Planning in Mobile Robot Environment. Proceeding IEEE Int. Conference of Evolutionary Computation, Orlando, Florida, 1994.
[4] Michalewicz Z, Genetic Algorithms + Data structures = Evolution Programs. Spriger-Verlang, 3rd edition 1996 .
[5] Michalewicz Z, Xiao J, Evaluation of Paths in Evolutionary Planner/Navigator. Proceedings of the International Workshop on Biologically Inspired Evolutionary Systems, Tokyo, Japan 1995 .
[6] Śmierzchalski R, The Decision Support System to Design the Safe Manoeuvre Avoiding Collision at Sea. 14th International Conference Information Systems Analysis and Synthesis, Orlando, USA, 1996.
[7] Śmierzchalski R, Multi-Criterion Modeling the Collision Situation at Sea for Application in Decision Support. 3rd International Symp. on Methods and Models in Automation and Robotics, Miedzyzdroje, Poland 1996.
[8] Śmierzchalski R, Trajectory planning for ship in collision situations at sea by evolutionary computation. 4th IFAC Conference on Manoeuvring and Control of Marine, Brijuni, Creotia, 1997.
[9] Śmierzchalski R, Dynamic Aspect in Evolutionary Computation on Example of Avoiding Collision at Sea. 4th International Symp. on Methods and Models in Automation and Robotics, Międzyzdroje, Poland 1997.
[10] Śmierzchalski R, Evolutionary Guidance System for Ship in Collisions Situation at Sea. 3rd IFAC Conference Intelligent Autonomous Vehicle, Madrid, Spain 1997.
[11] Śmierzchalski R, Michalewicz Z, Adaptive Modeling of a Ship Trajectory in Collision Situations. 2nd IEEE World Congress on Computational Intelligence, Alaska, USA 1998.
[12] Trojanowski K, Michalewicz Z, Planning Path of Mobil Robot (in Polish). 1st Conference Evolutionary Algorithms, Murzasichle, Poland 1998.
[13] Witt NA, Sutton R, Miller KM, Recent Technological Advances in the Control and Guidance of Ship. Journal of Navigation Vol. 47, 1994.
[14] Xiao J, Michalewicz Z, Zhang L, Evolutionary Planner/Navigator: Operator Performance and Self-Tuning. Proceeding IEEE Int. Conference of Evolutionary Computation, Nagoya, Japan 1996.

Improvement and Evaluation of Autonomous Load Distribution Method

YUGO ITO, SHIN-ICHI MIYAZAKI, YOSHINOBU IIIGAMI, SHIN-YA KOBAYASHI
Faculty of Engineering, Ehime University
3 Bunkyou-cho, Matsuyama, Ehime, 790-8577 Japan,
e-mail: ito@koblab.cs.ehime-u.ac.jp, kob@koblab.cs.ehime-u.ac.jp

Abstract: We have proposed "Autonomous Load Distribution Method(ALD)" as one of the load distribution algorithm for multi-computer system. The ALD method requires that node information is reliable in order to distribute load suitably. In this paper, we propose the new ALD method that is appended receiver-initiated function, and apply it on a workstation cluster to compare it with the original method.

Key words: Multi-computer system, Load distribution, Distributed processing, Autonomous system, Receiver-Initiation,

1. INTRODUCTION

With the widespread use of Ethernet and FDDI networking techniques and with the advent of cheap computers for workstations, we can find a user environment in which a large number of computers under the same control are mutually connected by a network in laboratory of universities and office of enterprises. Such systems are named as "multi-computer systems" in this paper.

In a multi-computer system, it is necessary to distribute tasks for efficient utilization of system resources and fast processing. However, since the number of nodes which consists one system is set to hundreds from dozens, it is difficult for each user to grasp all those loads and processing ability, and to distribute tasks appropriately. Therefore, some kinds of methods with which a node distributes load automatically are proposed from the former [1].

We have proposed "Autonomous Load Distribution Algorithm (ALD)" as a load distribution protocol for multi-computer system. It is shown by reference that the ALD method is superior to some methods proposed in the past [2]. To date, we have implemented the ALD method and some other load distribution methods (e.g. sender-initiated algorithms, receiver-initiated algorithms, and combinations of both types). We have evaluated the outcome under some conditions. According to the evaluation result, the ALD method is most effective among them in most cases [2].

In this paper, we propose an additional function to the ALD method for more effectiveness. We implement the new ALD method with the function and the original ALD method on a workstation cluster, and then compare them.

2. AUTONOMOUS LOAD DISTRIBUTION METHOD

In the ALD method, the node where the task execution is required by the user negotiates with the other nodes by peer-to-peer communication (Figure 1). The algorithm of the ALD method consists of the Request Decision Procedure and the Reply Decision Procedure (Figure 2). The detail of these procedures is given below.

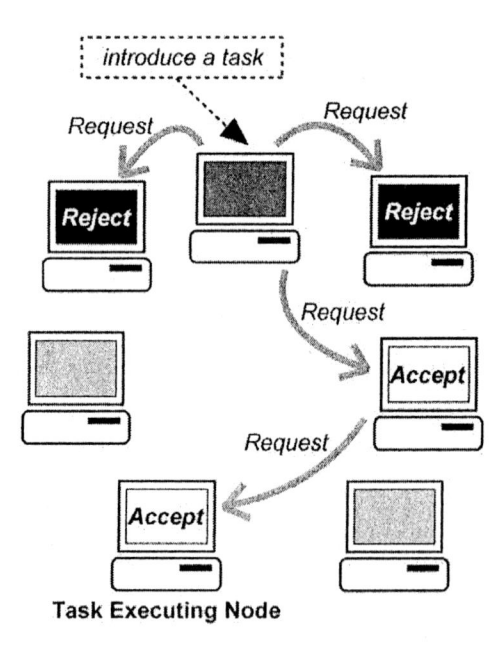

Fig. 1. Autonomous Load Distribution Method

2.1 The Request Decision Procedure

After a node has the task introduced or accepts the request from other node, the node determines whether it should request execution of a task to other nodes or not.

This procedure is called "the request decision procedure". The Request Decision Procedure consists of "Making a list of candidate" and "Negotiating with other nodes". We call the node that requests "requester".

- Making a list of candidates

A node estimates the task processing time by requester itself and other nodes based on the information about the target task (task information) and the information about a requester or other nodes (node information). A list of candidates is obtained by sorting the nodes in incremental order of task processing time. The requester is added to the last of a list. When no node with less estimated task processing time than a requester is found, a requester executes the task.

- Negotiating with other nodes

After making a list of candidates, a requester negotiates to the node which is the head of a list. When the node which is the head of a list is a requester, a requester executes a task, without negotiating. When a node negotiate, at first the requester sends the request message to a negotiation partner. The request message includes the information of the target task, node information, and the task processing time estimated by the requester. The node which received the request message begins reply decision procedure based on the information included in a request message, and appends node information to the result, then returns it. When a result is acceptance, the requestee executes a task. When a result is rejection, the requester negotiates with the next node of a candidate list. Moreover, the requester updates the node information database its own based on the node information included in the request result.

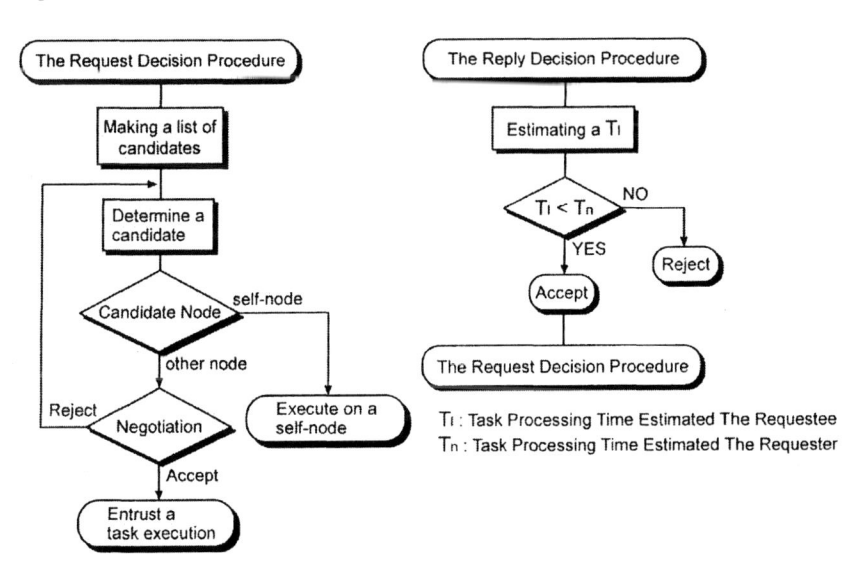

Fig. 2. Algorithms of The ALD method

T_i : Task Processing Time Estimated The Requestee
T_n : Task Processing Time Estimated The Requester

2.2 The Reply Decision Procedure

When a node receives the request message from other node, the node performs the reply decision procedure. Here we call the node requested from the requester "requestee". In this procedure, the requestee estimates the task its own processing time (T_l) is based on the task information included in the request message. As compared with its own task processing time (T_l) and the processing time estimated by requester (T_n), if T_l is shorter than T_n ($T_l < T_n$), the request will be accepted and an acceptance message will be transmitted. Otherwise, then the request is rejected and returns a rejection message.

3. IMPROVEMENT OF THE ALD METHOD

3.1 Adaptive ALD Method

In load distribution, we call the task transmission node which is heavily loaded "the sender". And we call the node which is lightly loaded and receives a task "the receiver".

In the sender-initiated load distribution method, the sender that has a task introduced begins to finds the lightly loaded receiver. The conventional ALD method is categorized into the sender-initiated method. On the other hand, we propose the ALD method which appends the receiver-initiated function how a lightly loaded node tries to find the heavily loaded sender node (Figure 3). We call this new ALD method "adaptive ALD method".

In the adaptive ALD method, sender-initiated function is active only a node has a task introduced. On the other hand, receiver-initiated function is activating when a node becomes lightly loaded. When load of a node becomes lighter than threshold, the node sends "I am lightly loaded" message (IaL message) to heavily loaded node. This message makes information on the heavily loaded node refreshed. This acknowledgement enables the heavily loaded node find an adequate requestee. This is the purpose of the receiver-initiated function. We will show details of receiver-initiated function in the next section.

3.2 Receiver-Initiated Component

We introduce Receiver-initiated component into ALD algorithm. This component consists of two parts. One is threshold calculation and the other is load acknowledgement.

Load of a node becomes lighter just when task has been done on the node. At this time, if the load of the node is lighter than threshold, the node becomes a receiver. In other words, Receiver-initiated component is activated. The receiver sends information of load of itself to the most heavily loaded node. It is key for receiver-initiated function how precise the threshold is. Here we should take notice of that the threshold is not constant, is dependent on conditions of load of others and the node itself. Anyway, in the case of the load of every node is high, the threshold is also high, otherwise, the threshold is low.

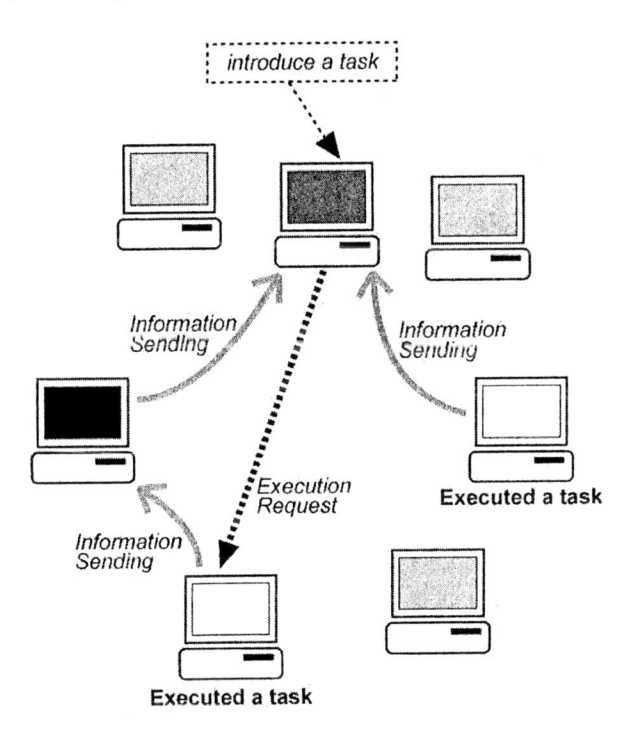

Fig. 3. Adaptive ALD Method

Deciding if load of any node is lower than threshold is determining relative situation of load of the node among all nodes. We will show the algorithm how to determine the relative load of the node.

First, the node calculate load of not only itself and also other by the following equation.

$$LSi = \frac{li+1}{Si} \qquad (1)$$

Here, l_i is load (the number of tasks) at $node_i$, and S_i is the processing power of $node_i$. If the node accept the task to do, load of it increases. This is the reason why 1 is added to l_i in equation (1).

Second, relative load (RL_{local}) is calculated by the equation (2).

$$RLlocal = \frac{LSlocal - LS\min}{LS\max - LSlocal} \qquad (2)$$

Here RL_{local} is in the range from 0 to 1, if the value of RL_{local} is small, it can estimate that the response of the task of a self-node is good. RL ranges from 0 to 1, and also threshold is settled between 0 and 1. If threshold is low, for example 0.1, a few nodes may be receiver. If threshold is high, for example 0.8, many nodes may be receivers. The receiver sends information of load of it to the most heavily loaded node. Of course, the most heavily loaded node is chosen based on local information, in the strict sense, the chosen node is not surely most heavily loaded, but expectantly.

After a node receives a message from the receiver, the node decides if it should relay the message to other node. This decision is done based on the receiver's load informed and load information on the node. This procedure is very similar to the procedure how the receiver does. At first, the node calculates relative load (RL_{org}) of the receiver with informed load information and local load information. And then, if $RL_{local} \leq T_h$ and the most heavily loaded node is not the node itself, the node acknowledges the heavily loaded node recursively.

The algorithm is given below (Figure 4).

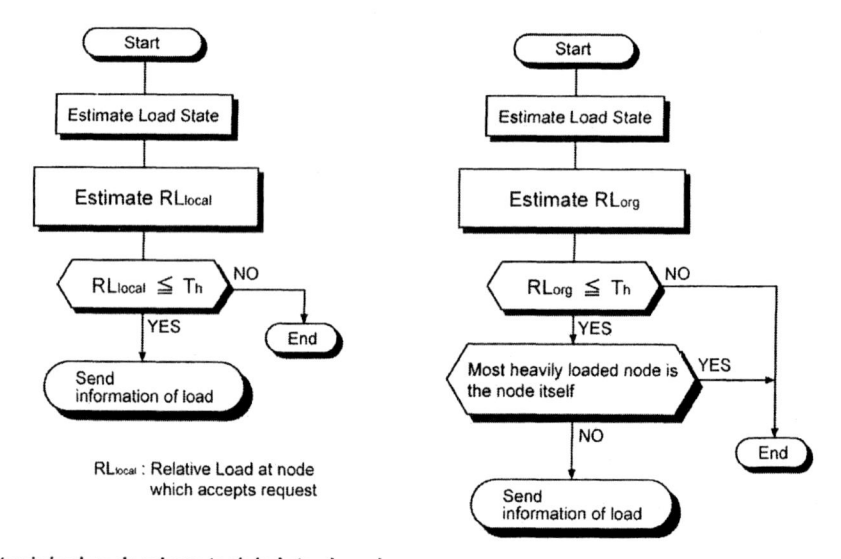

Fig. 4. Algorithm of Receiver-Initiated Component

4. EVALUATION

We implement the conventional ALD method and the improved ALD method on a workstation cluster, and evaluated them on various kinds of conditions.

4.1 Evaluation Conditions

- Implementation of the ALD Method

We implement the conventional ALD method and the improved ALD method on a workstation cluster *FUJITSU AP3000*. The implemented system is constituted by N (={8, 16}) sets of nodes with equal processing power and CPU scheduling on each node is Round-Robin. The high-speed network AP-Net connects those nodes.

A load distribution function consists of an Interface Process, a Negotiation Process, and an Execution Process as shown in a Figure 5. These processes on each node work cooperatively in order to distribute load. Socket system call is used for communication between each process.

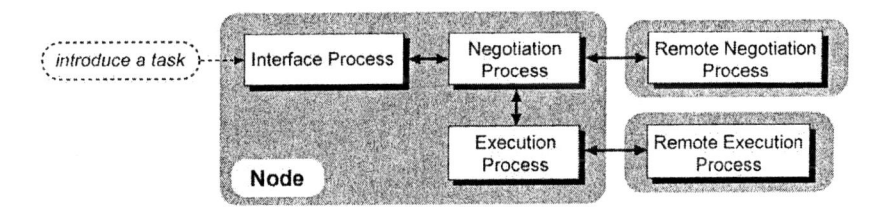

Fig. 5. Process Composition

- System Load

We define the execution time [sec] of a task executed at a node without other processed task as task size. The task to introduce is assumed to be an empty loop program. Moreover, task size follows the exponential distribution and the average arrival interval (average introduction interval) of a task also follows an exponential distribution. Average arrival intervals at nodes where tasks are introduced are equal.

Here, the ratio of the average task size is referred to as $\overline{w}$, and an average arrival interval is referred to as $\overline{t}$, and then $\lambda = \overline{w}/\overline{t}$ is node load. We define the average of the node load in a system as system load.

$$\Lambda = \frac{1}{N}\sum_{i=1}^{n} \lambda i \tag{3}$$

In the above equation, n is the number of nodes ($1 \leq n \leq N$) which are introduced a task. In order to change system load for evaluation, we change the average task arrival interval $\overline{t}$ (and fix the average task size at 5[sec]).

4.2 Comparison with the conventional ALD method

System Load Characteristics

We measured the mean response time according to change the system load Λ on two conditions, the case where a task is introduced partially and where a task is introduced uniformly. The system consisted of 8 nodes in all. (The threshold T_h of the Node Information Sending Decision Procedure was set to $T_h = 0.5$.)

- For Partial Loading
A task is introduced to only one node among all nodes.

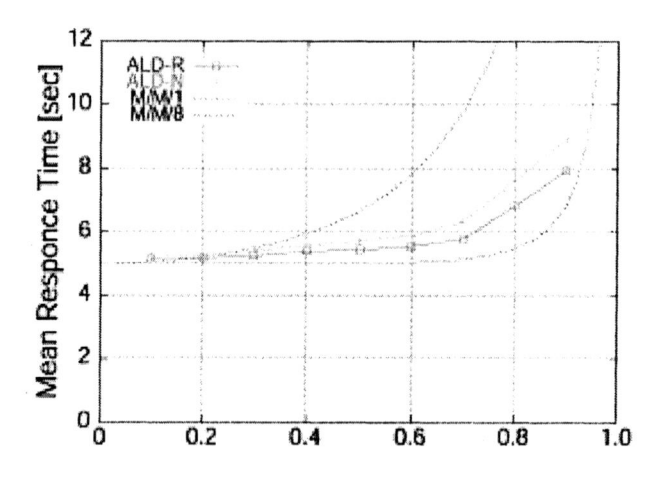

Fig. 7. Mean Response Time

Figure 7 shows Mean Response Time versus System Load Λ. *M/M/1* and *M/M/8* system is also shown Figure 7. *M/M/8* is theoretical limitation of evolution. Sign ALD-R shows the adaptive ALD method, and ALD-N shows the conventional ALD method.

In the case of $\Lambda < 0.6$, both of conventional method and adaptive method increase slightly, and we can not find difference between conventional method and adaptive one. In the case of $\Lambda < 0.6$, both increase gradually according to system load, and adaptive method achieves less response time than conventional.

- For Uniform Loading
We will show the result under condition that tasks are introduced to all nodes evenly, in other words all nodes have same mean arrival interval.

According to Figure 8, the adaptive method is more effective than the conventional method, even when load is uniformly introduced to each node.

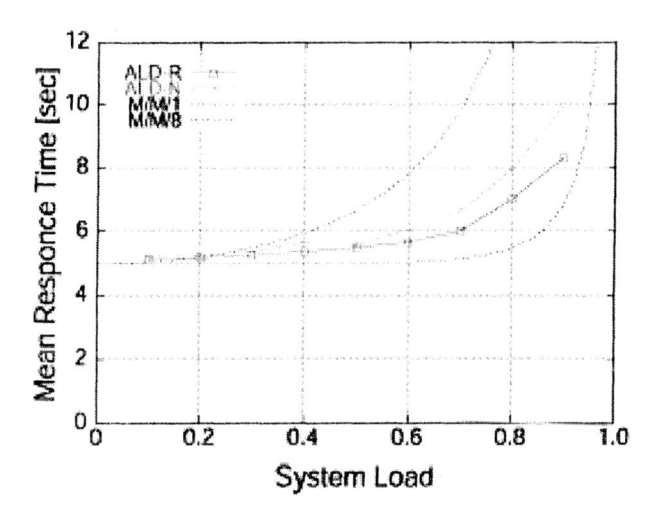

Fig. 8. Mean Response Time

5. CONCLUSION

Some methods for the load distribution in multi-computer system were proposed in the past, and it is already shown that the conventional ALD method which we proposed is superior to those past systems [1][2]. In this paper, we have proposed the adaptive ALD method by adding the receiver-initiated function to the conventional ALD method. The receiver-initiated function enables to refresh the node information not only when negotiation occurs but also when a node becomes lightly loaded. Hence, Node Information retained by each node can be kept more reliable and load distribution is performed more suitably. We evaluated and showed that the improved ALD is superior to the conventional ALD method especially in a heavily loaded condition.

6. REFERENCES

[1] N.G.Shivaratri, P.Krueger, and M.Singhal. 1992. 'Load distributing for locally distributed systems'. *IEEE* Computer, 25, No.12, pp. 33–44.
[2] S.Kobayashi, T.Ogawa, and T.Watanabe 1996. 'Autonomous Load Distribution for Multi Computer Systems (in Japanese)'. *IEICE* D-I, VOL.J79-D-I, NO.11, pp. 903–915.
[3] S.Kobayashi, H.Kimura, and T.Takebe 1993. 'A Load Distribution Method for Multicomputer System Based on Inter computer negotiation'. Proceeding of 1993 Joint Technical Conference on Circuits/System.
[4] S. Miyazaki and S.Kobayashi. 'Improvement of Autonomous Load Distribution Algorithm with Receiver Initiated Mechanism'. *IPSJ* SIG Notes, 2001-DPS-102, pp.139–144.

Idea of the National System of Education and Verification Traffic's Knowledge as a Tool of Traffic Safety Increasing

PRZEMYSŁAW RÓŻEWSKI[1], ANTONI WILIŃSKI[1],
OLEG ZAIKINE[1], KRZYSZTOF GIŻYCKI[2]
[1] *Technical University of Szczecin, Faculty of Computer Science and Information Systems, Zolnierska 49, 71-210, Szczecin, Poland, e-mail: {prozewski, awilinski, ozaikine}@wi.ps.pl*
[2] *WINFOR Research and Development Institute of Advanced Computer Information Technology, Zolnierska 49, 71-210, Szczecin, Poland, e-mail: kgizycki@winfor.pl*

Abstract: Due to large number of the traffic's accidents necessity of immediately traffic safety increasing is appearing. The most reliable way to achieve safety increase of traffic safety is to pay more attention to the driver's education process. The authors introduced the National System of Education and Verification Traffic's Knowledge as a solution of the education issue. The proposed system is based on the up to data computer technologies and ensured the complete education and testing environments. The system is developed for the sake of the European drivers' education standards. The economical factors are under heavy consideration as well as the quality of education's materials. In addition, the idea of the integrated information network of driver's school is discussed.

Key words: Traffic Safety, Information System, Knowledge Management, Internet

1. INTRODUCTION

1.1 General information about project

Nowadays the issue of traffic safety is actual and important problem [14]. In almost every country, especially developing countries, the number of cars is frequently growing. The possibility of traffic's accidents might be depending on the number of cars and drivers' skills. The generally feeling about the safety on the road is close to word: insufficient. The one cannot fight with the statement that the traffic safety is directly depended on the drivers' education level. The better-educated driver usually drive in the safety way. The reason of developing the Computer Information System (CIS) to educated drivers is self- defending [6]. The CIS must support the driver's licence testing as well as the driver's pre-license and post-license education processes.

The authors used the approach, which is based on the achievements of CIS, to develop the National System of Education and Verification Traffic's Knowledge (NSEVTK). The proposed system takes advantages of several state-of-the-art CIS technologies, such as: Dedicated Information Networks, Internet, Distance Learning, Digital TV, new education materials [5]. The wide spectrum of technologies and techniques gives us real possibility to develop system, which contributed to enhance the level of traffic's safety. The selected technologies, solutions allow us to adopt system's functionality to new working conditions and permit the authorized users to control the entire system environment.

1.2 Background

The driver's education time is limited by market and government's arrangement [1]. It is rather impossible to enlarge the driver's education time to period of one year or even half of year. Therefore, the authors tried to use the fixed time (on average: 20 hours of practical and 10 hours of theoretical exercising) in the optimal and efficient way. The best solution is to develop and maintain dynamical adopted system, which bases on the drivers' progress reports, judgments the ability of the licence test passing. However, this clarification seems to be beyond the present technological and first of all financial possibility. The system has to store the each driver's profile and the main criterions should be developed.

The drivers learn how to drive a car in the driver's school (DS). The DS's are usually one-person company; those kind of small-business companies are spread all around the country. The education track is divided into two parts: theoretical and practical. The theoretical part provides the knowledge about the proper road behaviour, road low interpretation, and road signs and lights. The important part of this track is the first aid training under skilled instructor supervision. The practical part is directly responsible for real driver skills, such as the correct judgment of speed, road, and distance according to weather conditions. This type of knowledge (explicit knowledge) is difficult to learn. Only the practical training, repeatedly repeating of exercises, gives opportunity to achieve required level of skills. The idea of standardized European procedure of driver's practical training is wrong, because of differences in driver's culture across the European continent. Even in local society, the road's habits are not the same. The licence course must be adapted to specific circumstances of traffic in current places.

2. NATIONAL SYSTEM OF EDUCATION AND VERIFICATION OF TRAFFIC'S KNOWLEDGE

The authors have projected system, which will be responsible for driver's education track. The proposed system, as mentioned above, is called the National System of Education and Verification Traffic's Knowledge and covers the two of the most important phases of driver's education (Fig.1). The education phase is responsible for the process of made acquired the required practical and theoretical knowledge, including the driving car ability. The verification phase is a final stage of the driver's education track. The practical and theoretical knowledge is evaluated and in case of success, the driver's licence is issued.

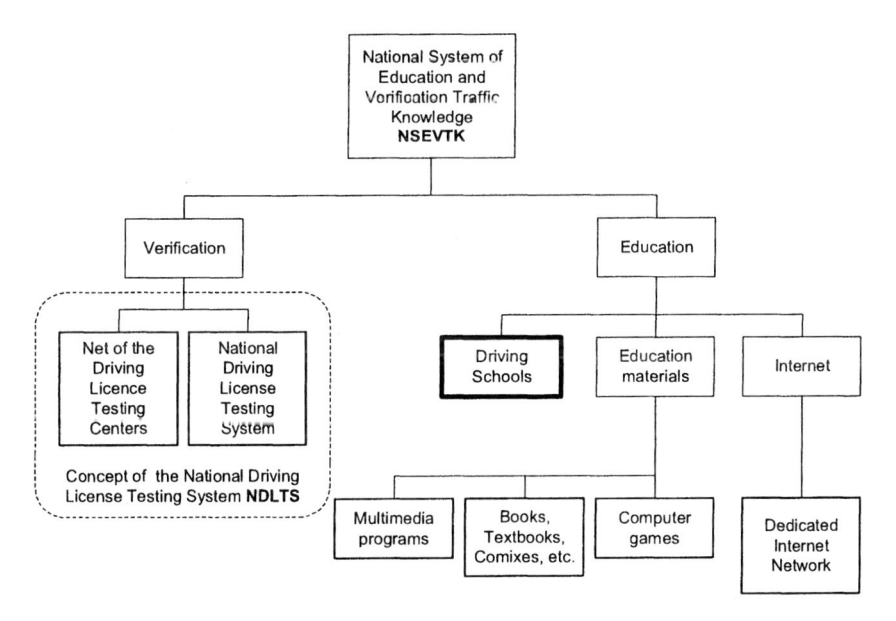

Fig.1 The functional scheme of National System of Education and Verification Traffic's Knowledge

The one must distinguish the special role of the DS, the most important place of driver's education. Other elements are only the helpful part of education process. The main track is always carried by the DS. That is the reason why the great attention is pointed to the DS quality and high standard services.

Let's consider the NSEVTK's functions according to the criterions of the Information System (IS), which was introduced in [7]. The author [7] listed five functions of every IS. Due to the special characteristics of presented system, (the complex character and vast dimension) the authors must narrow the discussed system's elements. The paper analysed only the most important issues in term of traffic safety.

a) Information processing function

Processing function is the main function of each IS. The data is processing in the number of ways during the drivers' education track. We must realize that the data formats and standards are different according to system phase, which we considered. During the learning phase, the system processes the questions of prospective drivers. However, the same system must process the driver's answer for the period of the driving licensee's test.

b) Education and learning functions

The system must be adopted to wide spectrum of potential users [10], The universal characteristic of used tools is taken in consideration on the every decision steps, for example the cognitive project of user's interface system, systems' communicates. The following issue is directly transformed into the contents of the NSEVTK.

The education set of system function can be treated as a system core. The developers should pay special attention to this part of system. The open architecture and restricted control must be supported. The existing technologies can be used along with new education techniques: distance learning, Internet, etc. The proper usage of mentioned systems can create deep education environment, which plays role of safety traffic encouragement.

c) Information system development function

The methodology of system development is important in the implementation and development phase as well as during every day routine [5]. The following factors are fulfilled: needs, problems and users. The adapted development process allows us to proper clarification of system's functionalities.

d) Management and control functions

Some sort of workflow can be recognized from the NSEVTK. The information is transformed into knowledge during each pace of system's time. The human's aspect of system does the control and management tasks very difficult. Very often, the optimal system state is not easy to estimate. The discussed mechanism plays role of feedback, the analysed information give required knowledge about systems' states and can be used to change some systems' parameters. The best way to keep system working is to take care of evolution character of system. The management and control parts of the NSEVTK are multidimensional. The system managers have to deal with quality management, human resources issue, etc. On the distinct management and control's levels, the other types of management's and control's mechanisms are used.

e) Strategy and planning functions

The one can claim that such well defined system might be development only according to control's subsystem outcomes. It is not true. The system functionality should support the ability of long distance strategy (e.g. the special attention can be paid to one of traffic's issues such as speed limitation in the period of Summer).

The last accent of discussion of strategy is issue of the DS. The DS must survive on the free market, which is the main goal of every company. The business should be profitable and lucrative. The profitability can be achieved through control and planning system's functions. The proposed system must combine the good traffic education with the requirements of costs limitation. The system has to avoid the possibility of reduction DS outcomes at the cost of reduction in the area of education track.

3. CONCEPT OF NATIONAL DRIVING LICENCE TESTING SYSTEM

The main task of the National Driving License Testing System (NDLTS) is testing drivers. The operation ranges of system must be national because of required system ability to interaction with other national systems such as: the Department of Motor Vehicles, National Department of State, National System of ID Record, etc. The discussed system has clearly determined his functions: to make available the specific information in specific and deterministic time [12]. The manner of system is specified precisely in the rules of the road and other government's arrangements [1]. The NDLTS can be characterized by following statements:
a) The system is user's oriented, the architecture and selected technology were adapted to specific application.
b) The system exists under rigorous working discipline. Each procedure has been written down and each procedure's violation will be punished according to law.
c) The one can indicate two types of information in the NDLTS: 1) The questions which are used in test; the up-to-date factor is not critical; the changes are rare and small; the amount of question is limited and system can store question in distributed manner. 2) The information about applicants. These types of data have to be immediately sent to central node and be distributed to other national system in the secure manner.
d) The basic logic subsystem is implemented into the system. The logical subsystem is only able to give answer about test's results. The reasons of failure or success are fuzzy and inaccessible. The system is far away from taking advantages of the artificial intelligence and expert system.
e) The practical test, which is the part of driving license test, must be supported.
f) The system was developed to serve and accumulate information. The tasks of processing part of system are limited to management applicants and random generation to question.
g) The system includes sets of subsystems: security subsystem, biometric subsystem, interface subsystem, database subsystem, network subsystem etc. Each of them can be discussed separately.

The wide area project of the NDLTS assumes only one distributed database structure, which central point is connected to the central node [3]. Each Drivers License Testing Centre (DLTC) has his own database, which is used as a main storage element in local node. This database gains possibilities to maintenance test, registration and manager activities in the DLTC. The some numbers of nodes (one can call them - the security network access points) make available several services such as: secure connection to national network, service support, etc. These nodes do not need any computer facilities; the network equipments are only necessary. These types of nodes are situated in each capital of province or big agglomeration. In condition of optimisation access to resources, this structure can be more optimal. However, in the cities or towns is the biggest accumulation of the telecommunication network, thus this places were selected as the security network access points.

The central node gains access to the central server, which has always up-to-date question database. Only this server is able to allow other servers to access to national network. All traffic between the NDLTS and other national or government systems is captured and stored. A main supervisor can obtain statistics about status and current situation of each DLTC's in any time and he doesn't have to call local database in the selected DLTC.

The NDLTS consists some numbers of the local's nodes. Each of the NDLTS's nodes is situated in the DLTC. Typical DLTC is made up of three independent rooms. Office, when the one can register himself, test room with infrastructure ready to carry test and special room with main server (Fig.2).

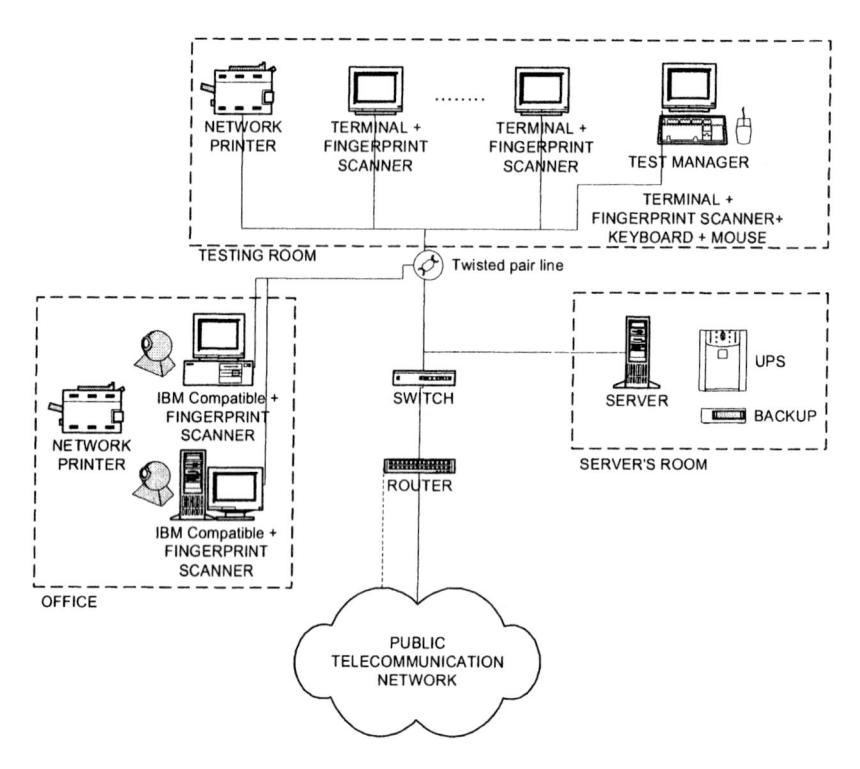

Fig.2 Typical structure of Drivers License Testing Centre

4. TRAFFIC'S EDUCATION MATERIALS

The amazing popularity of the computer as a communication and entertainment devices gives limitless possibility to convey the new attractive contents to drivers [2], [8], [11]. The important thing is the universal character of material; even experienced driver should be able to find new interesting information. The target group is widening to whole driver's society.

The education materials can appear in a number of forms [16]. From books and textbooks, the education materials evolved to multimedia programs. The multimedia programs join several types of media: video, text, music, sound (included background voices), computer's graphic and animation. Based on hypertext mechanism the most recent content arises in the new way [2].

The typical example of multimedia program, which has the set of required features, is the traffic encyclopaedia created by WINFOR (the original Polish name: *Encyklopedia Ruchu Drogowego*) [15]. The most important feature seems to be the complex approach to subject built into the multimedia form. This product consists of, among other things, the rule of the road with expert comments, whole branch of traffic's sings and lights. The professionals discussed typical road situations and provided the correct road behaviours. The significant part of product was devoted to the first aid training. Almost the same attention was paid to the car's exploitation and construction.

The next traffic's knowledge source can be the digital TV. An advantage of this medium is a large audience and working interaction modes. The digital TV environment opens a large number of viewers to the distance learning technologies (e.g. Open Traffic's University). The functionalities of the digital TV are on the similar level as Internet in case of traffic education [16]. The live driving lessons can be great entertainment and education tool in the same time.

The targets group of our system should not be limited only to the driver's society. The traffic education must start as soon as possible. The children and teenagers are the same member of traffic as other peoples. If we want to cover this market's group, our offer should be specially prepared. The best solution is to use a computer games as knowledge's carrier [15]. The computer games developed in the proper way learn correct road behaviours as well as give a great fun.

5. WINFORNET AS AN EXAMPLE OF THE DEDICATED INTERNET'S ENVIRONMENT

The idea of the Dedicated Internet's Environment (DIE) was originally developed by WINFOR (Research and Development Institute of Advanced Computer Information Technology) [4], [15]. The DIE is a system of exchange information and data essential to carry the DS such as: the way of preparation and presentation the DS market offers, way of communication with clients, way of company management, way of preparation and carry out the education track. WINFORNET is an initiative, which wants to enlarge the typical DS education's standard. It is possible when the DS's professionals realized that the information workflow is the most important factor of the modern information society [13], [9]. The communications one to one, B2B (business to business), one to group are powerful market tools. The world history gives evidences that the organized group can do much more then single person e.g. credit's negotiation with bank.

Without doubts the most important elements of each DS is the education track. WINFORNET allows theirs members to immediately access to the best education materials. The quality of materials is guaranteed by large number of members; the each education material can be evaluated in the fast and efficient way. On demand information, search engines, access to database is main features of typical Intranet network.

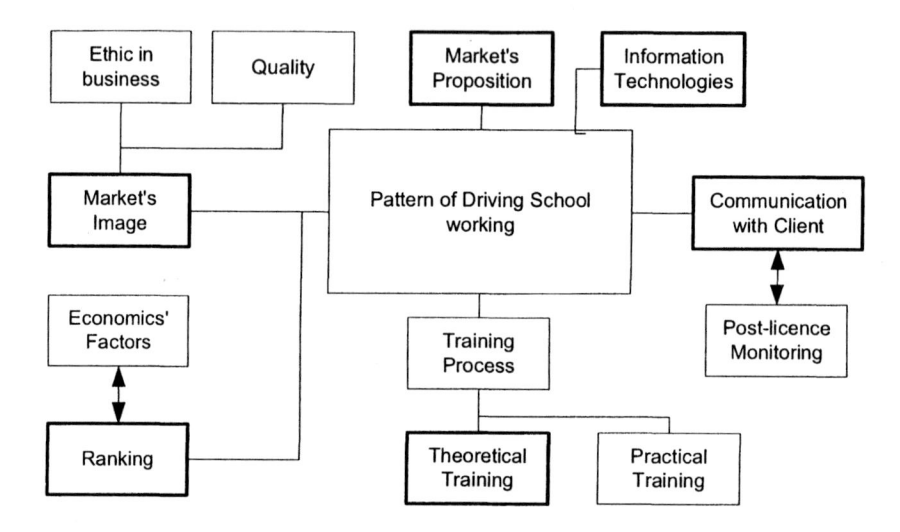

Fig.3 Scheme of the pattern of driving school working

The figure above (Fig.3) presents the typical elements of representative member of WINFORNET network. The special care, which is taken into school image and communication with clients, appears immediately. The bolted blocks can be supported by the WINFORNET network. The DS creates some market offers, the CIS technologies transfer offers to clients. The communication channels have already been established (fax, email, phone, etc.). The business's ethic forced the DS to take a position on WINFORNET standards and guidelines. The DS ranking can be used as best information about current DS market's position and image's builder. The special subsystem can handle access between the driver's society and wealthy WINFOORNET resources.

6. CONCLUSION

The NSEVTK is a huge system. It consists of two main parts: education and verification. The second one can be handling only on the government's level, however the first one is only the DS issue. The verification system (based on the new CIS systems e.g. the biometric identification system) allows drivers society to work with fair and clear-cut way. On the contrary, to wrong imagination about the NSEVTK can force the system diversification. The system must take control over whole driver's education process and the licence's test is the final stage cannot be considered separately. The traffic knowledge is related with traffic's safety in the obvious way.

The new possible function of the NSEVTK is appearing last time. The post-licence monitoring is a way to achieve the new level of traffic's education. The DS takes care about his clients long after the licence test. The help services can be served as the phone hot line, special course (e.g. preparing to driving under the winter conditions), periodic first aid training and so on.

7. ACKNOWLEDGE

Several people have contributed to the ideas reported in this paper. The crew of WINFOR have done and will be doing an enormous works with the development of traffic education materials. The idea of WINFORNET was created and maintained by some members of WINFOR Institute. The Fig.3 was taken from WINFOR blueprints about WINFORNET.

The special thanks go to Mrs. Emma Kushtina, who devoted her time and effort to endless discussion about the CIS problems.

8. REFERENCES

[1] American Association of Motor Vehicle Administrators 2000 'AAMVA National Standard for the Driver License AAMVA DL/ID-2000' United States
[2] Bolter J., Grusin R., 1999, 'Remediation- understanding new media'. The MIT press, Cambridge.
[3] Buras K. 2002 'Wykorzystanie internetu do współpracy centrali z placowka terenowa', MA thesis, supervised by Professor A.Wilinski, Technical University of Szczecin, Faculty of Computer Science and Information Systems, Szczecin, Poland
[4] Gizycki K.,2002 'Produkty i uslugi informatyczne sieci WINFOR', 4th meeting of Polish Federation of Driving Schools, Szczecin, Poland
[5] Hawryszkiewycz I.T.1997 'Designing the Networked Enterprise', Artech House, Boston, Massachusetts,
[6] Jarosz S. 2002 'Projekt ogolnokrajowego systemu ewidencjonowania i monitorowania procesow szkolenia, pozyskiwania i posiadania prawa jazdy', MA thesis, supervised by Professor A.Wilinski, Technical University of Szczecin, Faculty of Computer Science and Information Systems, Szczecin, Poland,
[7] Jayaratna, N.1994 'Understanding and Evaluating Methodologies'; NIMSAD: A Systemic Framework, Maidenhead: McGraw-Hill
[8] Różewski P, Kushtina E. 2001 'Knowledge base approach to courseware design in distance learning', IX-th International Conference KDS-2001, St.-Petersburg 2001, Russia
[9] Tadausiewicz R. 2001 'Możliwości wykorzystania Internetu w edukacji' The Polish Science Academy. Part XLIV/1, 2001, p. 106 -110 "Internet jako narzędzie edukacyjne na tle idei społeczeństwa informacyjnego" Technical training in School, nr 2/3
[10] Tadausiewicz R. 2000 'Virtual Learning on the Base of Experiments in Computer Aided Teaching at the University or Mining and Metallurgy'. Proceedings of EUNIS 2000 Conference Towards Virtual Universities, Poznan.

[11] Zaikin O, Kushtina E, Enlund N 2001, 'A knowledge base approach to courseware design for distance learning', Proceedings of the 7th Conference of European University Information Systems EUNIS'01, Humboldt-University, Berlin, Germany
[12] Zaikine O, Różewski P, Kusthina E. 2000 'Analiza wykorzystania sieci telekomunikacyjnych w zastosowaniach nauczania na odległosc', The Poznans Telecomunication Workshop 2000, Technical University of Poznan, Poznań, Poland,
[13] Zaikine O, Różewski P, Kusthina E. Tadusiewicz R. 2002 'Distance Learning Organization based on General Knowledge Model', Proceedings of the 8th Conference of European University Information Systems EUNIS'02, University of Porto, Portugal,
[14] WINFOR Institute 2001-2002 'Drogowskaz' monthly issued periodical of driving schools
[15] Research and Development Institute of Advanced Computer Information Technology www.winfor.pl
[16] The major Polish Internet website about traffic: www.prawojazdy.com.pl

Distribution of Resources by Means of Multi-Agent Simulation Based on Incomplete Information

EDWARD NAWARECKI, GRZEGORZ DOBROWOLSKI,
MAREK KISIEL-DOROHINICKI
University of Mining and Metallurgy
al. Mickiewicza 30, 30-059 Kraków, Poland, e-mail: nawar@agh.edu.pl

Abstract: In the paper agent-based simulation is proposed as a convenient and efficient tool for solving problems of distribution and transportation of resources under incomplete and uncertain information. The model of the appropriate system is presented with special emphasis on flow of information that accompanies the distribution of resources but, in fact, proves decisive for its efficiency. Selected experiments are reported together with their interpretation and some general remarks.

Key words: agent-based simulation, transportation systems

1. INTRODUCTION

Let us consider an interesting class of discrete optimisation problems that often occur in management and control of production processes [1, 2], and concentrate on distribution and transportation of resources based on incomplete and uncertain information about availability or demand. A verbal description of a reference problem for this class is as follows. Active objects that represent suppliers and consumers of some resource(s) are located in some environment. Each is described by the amount of resource in disposal or value of demand, respectively. The availability and demand of particular resource(s) can change in the course of a distribution process. So does the information about potential suppliers and consumers. Moreover, this information may be incomplete and uncertain.

The core of the problem is to *rationally* realise the distribution of resources based on continually gathered information. According to practical indications one may assume that inquiry as well as transfer of resources entails some kind of expenses. In such a situation rationally realising the process of distribution (quasi-optimisation) means possibly fulfilling the suppliers' and consumers' goals when lowering the cost and efficiently utilising the available information. Solving the problem can be done be means of simulation, yet designing the appropriate model needs several additional assumptions and postulates to be formulated.

It seems that agent-based simulation [3] is a convenient and efficient tool to deal with the problem described above. Results obtained for load balancing of multi-processor structure [4] or others [5] may justify the proposed approach.

The paper is organised as follows. The model (based on the agent paradigm) that represents the reference problem is proposed in sections 2–4. Section 5 describes how to build and realise simulation scenarios. Selected results of experiments and their interpretation are reported in section 6. The whole is closed with some remarks on the presented method and its potential applicability.

2. AGENT-BASED SIMULATION OF RESOURCE DISTRIBUTION

The proposed simulation model built as a multi-agent system [3, 5] consists of an environment and agents that operate in it. The state of the environment and agents changes in consecutive steps and depends on the agents' activity.

Coherent graph $G(V,B)$ where V is a set of nodes and B — a set of arcs constitutes a base for the **environment**. Suppliers and consumers are located in nodes of the graph. They are represented by amount of resources available R_v^+ and demanded R_v^- in particular node $v \in V$. The arcs define transportation routes of given length d_{jk}, $j,k \in V$. Transport is allowed in both directions.

Agents are autonomous entities that are able to make decisions and realise actions. Each agent's basic activity is the transportation of resources from nodes occupied by suppliers to those occupied by consumers. At the same time each agent is equipped with information processing abilities so that transportation tasks are realised more efficiently. These abilities consist in communication with nodes that behave like information centres

Agents can both stay in nodes or move along arcs of the graph. The agents' activities of decision-making and communication take place only in nodes. Movement of an agent is an effect of its autonomous decision and is characterised by the velocity and mass of the transported resource. Index $i = 1,2,...,i_{max}$ is used to point at a particular agent.

The state of the system changes dynamically and so its characteristic quantities are functions of time. The system is event-driven and thus the changes occur only in particular moments of time due to the nature of the agents' activities. Let us introduce discrete variable $n \in [0,T]$ that represents these moments along the system run (in some cases time horizon T can be a subject of external constraint).

3. MODELLING THE FLOW OF INFORMATION

The state of an agent is defined by the amount of energy $E_{a_i}(n)$ and information $I_{a_i}(n)$ it posses:

$$a_i(n) = \{E_{a_i}(n), I_{a_i}(n)\} \tag{1}$$

The information state of an agent (its knowledge) is formed by three groups of data:

$$I_{a_i}(n) = \{G_{a_i}(n), R^+_{a_i}(n), R^-_{a_i}(n)\} \tag{2}$$

Consecutive elements describe: $G_{a_i}(n) \subset G$ – a sub-graph containing nodes explored by agent a_i until n; $R^+_{a_i}(n)$, $R^-_{a_i}(n)$ – amount of resources available and demanded, respectively, in the nodes of $G_{a_i}(n)$.

The state of a node is defined by amount of resources available or demanded and information $I_{v_j}(n)$ it retains:

$$v_j(n) = \{R^+_j(n), R^-_j(n), I_{v_j}(n)\} \tag{3}$$

The information accessible in a node is defined in a similar way as above (index v_j indicates a node not an agent):

$$I_{v_j}(n) = \{G_{v_j}, R^+_{v_j}(n), R^-_{v_j}(n)\} \tag{4}$$

The only difference is that an agent gathers information when visiting consecutive nodes, while a node gets it from passing agents.

An important feature of the described model is a rule that the information about a node (its resources) can be known only in some vicinity, which is determined by a parameter called *radius of informing* defined as length of the shortest path between a given node and these that can hold information about it. This rule reflects availability of information and influences complexity of decision algorithms of agents (a number of variants analysed).

Reliability of information is another mechanism introduced to the model. *Reliability function* is used to describe deterioration of information in the course of time. Exponential dependency is assumed here that allows for interpretation of the function as the probability that the information is true.

Because agents are the only carriers of information, their velocity of moving in the graph determines the speed of information propagation.

4. AGENT'S DECISION-MAKING PROCESS

Decision-making means for an agent a choice (based on its current state) from among the following strategies: interchange of information, transfer of resources (completing an order), and movement. These possible strategies are shown schematically in Figure 1.

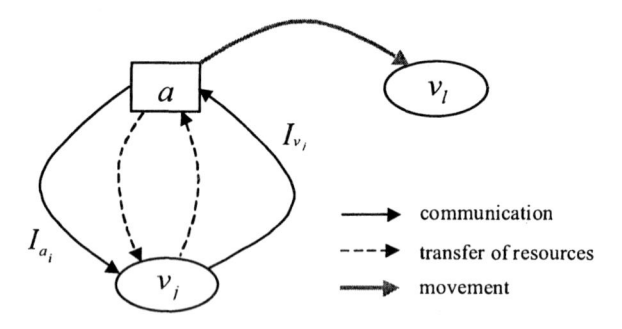

Fig. 1. The possible strategies of agent a_i in node v_j

Organisation of a multi-agent system is based on introducing a special kind of resource called *energy* [5]. An acting agent aims at maximising its energy. At the same time the total amount of energy (sum of energy of all agents) can be used for evaluation of effectiveness of the system.

Thus the main decision factor for an agent is the amount of possessed energy, which at *n*-th simulation step is calculated as:

$$E_{a_i}(n) = E_{a_i}(0) + \sum_n (e^i_{sa}(n) - e^i_{bu}(n) - e^i_{tr}(n) - e^i_{in}(n)) \qquad (5)$$

According to the above, energy is increased as an effect of the sale of resources, while an agent spends energy for: buying resources, transportation, and communication. It is assumed that e^i_{sa}, e^i_{bu}, e^i_{tr} are proportional to the amount of resources; e^i_{tr} depends on the transportation distance also; e^i_{in} – on the number of accesses to the information available in a node or transfers of information in the opposite direction.

An agent takes up a transferring order if it has enough energy to move along the appropriate path (from the node of the supplier to that of the consumer) Moreover, the agent must have additional energy to get to the starting node if necessary. Thus:

$$E_{a_i}(n) \geq e^i_{tr}(n)(d_{sc}W + d_{0s}) \qquad (6)$$

where *W* stands for the amount of transported resources; d_{sc}, d_{0s} – transportation and access paths (length), respectively. Having the order completed, the agent is rewarded with the amount of energy that is proportional to the amount of resources and length of the path.

If an agent cannot transport or communicate it waits for an occasion (new offer that occurs to be feasible). Moreover, an agent can suspend an action if the information about possible orders is not reliable enough.

The sketched above decision-making algorithm is, in fact, augmented with procedures that are necessary for realisation of the chosen strategy. There are procedures of: searching for a path in the graph, evaluating possible alternative orders, etc. that will not be discussed here for the sake of conciseness of the paper.

5. SIMULATION SYSTEM DESIGN ISSUES

The described model of the decentralised transportation-information system equipped with detailed procedures necessary for implementation was used in series of simulation experiments. Procedures of executing and stopping a simulation run, monitoring the behaviour of the system and its elements are of the most importance.

Stopping a simulation run occurs under one of the following conditions:
- fall of total energy in the system $E(n)$ beneath some permissible level E_{min};

$$E(n) = \sum_{a_i} E_{a_i}(n) \le E_{min} \qquad (7)$$

- reaching time horizon T;
- achievement of satisfactory level of supply R_{min}^-.

$$R^-(n) = \sum_{v_j} R_{v_j}^-(n) \le R_{min}^- \qquad (8)$$

Monitoring is carried out for all variables of the model. The most essential are:
- total energy in the system $E(n)$;
- average intensity of transportation $W(n)$ calculated on the base of the total amount of resources transported by agents $W_{a_i}(n)$ at the given moment of time;

$$W(n) = \frac{1}{i_{max}} \sum_{a_i} W_{a_i}(n) \qquad (9)$$

- number of active agents that transport resources at the moment;
- average time of realisation of an order;
- total cost of communication or transportation, etc.

The course of an experiment consists of two phases: a generation of a model and a simulation run. In the first phase a graph (environment) and scenario of availability and demand of resources are generated. The graph is built of the given numbers of nodes and arcs but coordinates of each node and the way they are joined are set at random. Locations of suppliers, consumers, availability and demand of resources as well as moments of time when orders arise are generated at random also.

Behaviour of the system is assumed to be event-driven, and so does a simulation run. Appearance of availability or demand is immediately known at a node it happens. Next agents propagate this information moving across the graph. Simultaneously, each agent may decide to undertake some order it knows about and begin transporting resources.

A simulation run is controlled be a number of parameters. The most important are the following: load capacity of an agent, radius of informing, velocity of an agent when moving across a graph and a parameter that defines deterioration of agent's knowledge.

6. EXPERIMENTAL RESULTS

A reach scenario of experiments has been carried out that aimed at testing the model and investigating its main features. Beneath selected results that deal with information aspect of the model and its behaviour are reported. Moreover, the results seem to be characteristic for the presented approach to the processes under consideration and the agent-based technique used.

Radius of informing seems to be one of more important parameters of the model. The influence of it on time the system needs to complete 95% of the total supply (R_{min} in Eq. (8)) is shown in Figure 2. The curves illustrate three chosen cases that group generated scenarios of the same number of agents and nodes of a graph. These parameters are different for the cases while the average distance between neighbouring nodes stays the same.

It can be observed that the dependency is stabilised over some value of the radius. In each case it is about 2-3 times the average distance between nodes. The observation indicates that unlimited increasing of the radius can only cause loss of efficiency (the amount of related information and processing time increase).

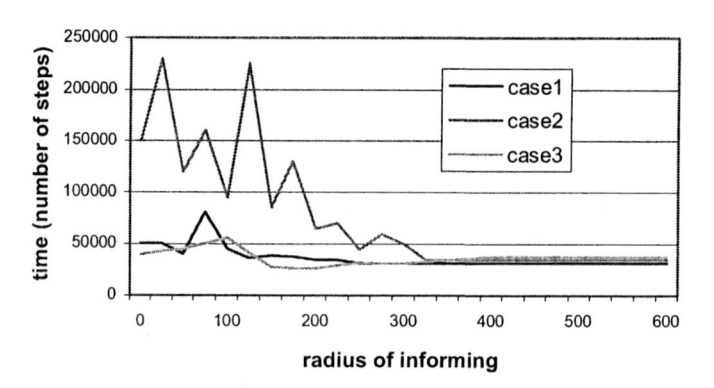

Fig. 2. Influence of value of the radius of informing on completion time for 3 different cases

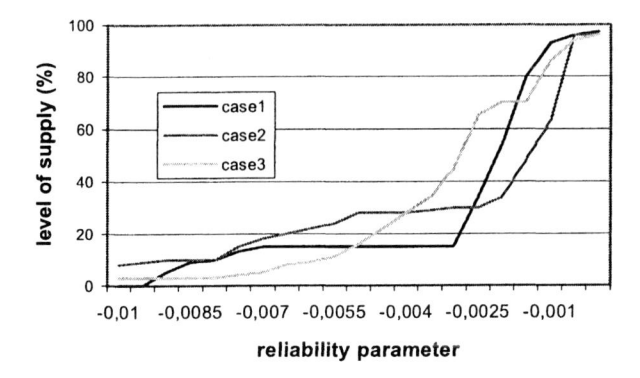

Fig. 3 Relationship between the reliability parameter and level of supply for 3 different cases

Reliability of information is another parameter that characterises information features of the system. The results obtained for the settled time horizon (see Fig. 3) confirm an intuitive idea that the better information is available in the system the more effective are the activities of agents. The analysed cases are generated in the same way as for the experiment described above.

The observed tendency is the same for all the cases but the exact shapes of the curves are different. It leads to the conclusion that the reliability parameter ought to be analyzed together with the number of agents and nodes.

It is worthwhile to point out that **velocity of agents** (that dictates intensity of information propagation) plays similar role in the model. Experiments show that the velocity (as the radius of informing) also discloses a boundary value. The time of completion is stable above that value.

The experiments reported in the paper have been generated on the assumption that process of appearance of resources and demand is stationary. Allowing for changes of parameters of that process can influence the observed boundary values of the radius of informing, reliability parameter or velocity of agents.

7. CONCLUSION

The presented model due to a number of arbitrary and simplifying assumptions has rather academic character, yet it reflects some aspects of reality that has been usually neglected so far. In particular, putting together information aspects and direct physical functioning of considered processes seems to be important.

Other characteristic feature of the approach is the depiction of complete decentralisation of decision-making. It is gained by application of the agent paradigm in modelling and simulation, and, in consequence, some elements of the agent-based technology. Such approach makes it easier to take into consideration other aspects of the system activity (e.g. information as in the reported case). Examination of the model shows also that a rational behaviour of a decentralised system is possible even under deep autonomy of its elements.

Preliminary results of experiments indicate a promising method of analysing interrelations between physical and information aspects of systems. Such analysis can be very useful or even indispensable for designing real transportation, supply, and production systems.

8. REFERENCES

[1] Zaikin O. 2002. 'Queuing Modelling of Supply Chain in Intelligent Production'. Wydział Informatyki, Politechnika Szczecińska, Poland.
[2] Buzacott J., Shanthikumar J. 1993. 'Modelling and Analysis of Manufacturing systems'. Wiley & Sons, N.Y.
[3] Weiss G. (ed.). 1999. 'Multiagent Systems: A Modern Approach to Distributed Artifcial Intelligence'. The MIT Press.
[4] Cetnarowicz K., Nawarecki E. 1995. Système d'exploitation décentralisé réalisé à l'aide de systèmes multi-agents. Troisième Journées Francophone sur l'Intelligence Artificielle Distribuée et les Systèmes Multi-agents. St Baldoph, France.
[5] Dobrowolski G., Kisiel-Dorohinicki M., Nawarecki E. 2002. Dual nature of mass multi-agent systems. *Systems Science*, 27(3):77–96.

A multi-agent approach to modeling and simulation of transport on demand problem

PABLO GRUER[1], VINCENT HILAIRE[1],
JAROSLAW KOZLAK[1,2], ABDER KOUKAM[1]
[1] *Systems and Transports Laboratory/Computer Science Department, Technical University of Belfort-Montbelliard, 90010 Belfort Cedex, France*
[2] *Department of Computer Science, AGH University of Mining and Metallurgy, Al. Mickiewicza 30, 30-059 Krakow, Poland*
e-mail: kozlak@agh.edu.pl

Abstract: This document focuses on a model of multi-agent system for simulation of transport on demand. The system performs efficient allocation of vehicles to dynamically incoming transport orders. The advantages of a multi-agent approach in comparison to the traditional operational research approaches and a short overview of the works in the multi-agent domain on the problem of transport planning and scheduling are given.

Key words: multi-agent systems, contract-net protocol, freight transportation,

1. INTRODUCTION

The transport services become nowadays more and more important. Goods and services have to be delivered to required place on the timely manner. The company should be able to realize the transport orders as economically as possible to be competitive on the market. It is possible to distinguish two general groups of transport services. The first are fast, customized and personalized services, facilitating the movement of people and small packages, offered by taxi companies, car location companies, and also employers transport and transport on demand. In the second group may be placed an international transport of big shipment for long distances, often using different means of transport. It is accomplished by special shipping companies, which deliver express packages or by big transport and shipping companies. In both cases an important problem is a dynamical changing of environment. The change of schedule may be necessary because of new incoming orders.

The operational research and the multi-agent systems research domains are interested in analysis of the transport problem. Dynamic and urgent changes of the state of the system (new transport orders, uncertain knowledge, necessity of rescheduling of orders) resulting that the methods of operational research, giving the centralized algorithm solving the problem, are difficult to apply and have to be adopted to this situation. The multi-agent systems models are designed to work in dynamic-changing environment, intending to apply the emergent solutions of problems. The fundamental properties of multi-agent systems and distributed AI make them to be good tools for the research on the complex logistic and transportation problems.

Several multi-agent applications for transport planning and scheduling have been realized and here we want to mention only some of them. **MARS** system is a simulator, which "models cooperative order scheduling within a society of shipping companies" [1,2]. According to the main ideas of multi-agent approach, the global solution emerges as a result of local strategies and actions of individual agents. **Teletruck** is a real system, realized in cooperation with transport truck company. Each transport operator agent is an active software agent, which is able to communicate and cooperate with the others agents. The vehicles are realized as holonic agent societies, which are controlled by special type of agent. The agents are applied for the modeling of all the objects from transport domain like trucks, drivers, trailers and load species [4].

We aim to create a multi-agent system supporting multimodal transport company planning and scheduling. Sub-optimal solution will be searched using a market equilibrium theory, evolutionary computations and neural networks approach. The simplified model described in this paper represents the functioning of company, which offers a transport on demand service. Taxi company may be considered as an example. The goal of the system is an efficient allocation of transport tasks to possessed vehicles. The structure of the paper is as follows: in Section 2, the principles of our system model are presented. The specification approach is given in section 3. Section 4 contains the description of multi-agent system model, the last section concludes and plans on future works.

2. GENERAL DESCRIPTION OF THE SYSTEM

The system is composed of:
- **environment** which has a form of communication network (see section 4.1)
- **shipping company** performing the customer's orders represented by company-agent (see section 4.3).
- set of vehicles belonged to company, they are represented by **vehicle-agents** located in different nodes of communication network (see section 4.4).

Transport network is represented as a weighted directed graph. The nodes are the points where the roads fork, where the vehicles wait for orders and starting or ending points of package transfer. With each node its name/identifier and co-ordinates describing its location is associated. The links represent the roads. With each link a weight describing the time necessary for its traversing is associated. The packages are transported between the nodes specified in the order. It is assumed that at a given time each vehicle is located in a place of the graph (in node or in the middle of traversing a link).

We make several simplifications in this model:
- each vehicle is able to carry simultaneously only one package;
- after loading the package, it has to be delivered to the destination point; the transshipment between vehicles is not considered;
- only one shipping company is taken into consideration.

The transport orders are randomly generated (or taken from prepared list of orders) and delivered to the transport company. Transport company informs its vehicles when an order has arrived. The vehicles decide if the realization of this order is profitable for them and these, which consider it as profitable send realization offers to the company. The company chooses the best from a point of view of its preferences among them and allocates the task of order realization to it. This order allocation is realized using contract-net protocol.

To make possible the realization of incoming orders or to increase the efficiency of the vehicles (to limit waiting times and moving times to loading points) the necessity of change of the preliminary schedule may appear. This reschedule may be done by exchange/transfer of orders by vehicles using an auction protocol. If this solution does not bring a success, then a company tries to reallocate the orders among its vehicles.

3. FORMAL SPECIFICATION

Our specification approach uses an organizational model which is based on three interrelated concepts: role, interaction and organization. Roles are generic behaviors. These behaviors can interact between themselves to form interaction patterns. Such a pattern which group generic behaviors and their interactions is an organization. Organizations are thus description of coordination structures. Coordination occurs between roles as interaction happen. In this context, an agent is only specified as an active communicative entity which plays roles.

In order to specify MAS described with the role/organization meta-model we build a framework based upon Object-Z and state charts. In fact, the composition process is an integration, state charts are integrated in Object-Z classes. We have then classes which have a reactive part which can react to their environment. This framework is composed of a set of such classes which specify all meta-model concepts: role, interaction and organization. Since classes use a formal language, each concept is given a formal semantic. The framework provides specifiers with a structured approach committed to the organizational model.

We have chosen to use a multi-formalisms approach in order to deal with complexity by applying formalisms to problem aspects for which they are best suited and to prove properties with proofs rules and transformation techniques available in a specific formalism. Moreover, we have defined an operational semantics which allows the animation and verification of our specification.

In the specification phase, the system is viewed as an organization which federates a set of interacting roles. Roles are generic behaviors. These behaviors can interact mutually according to interaction pattern.

Such a pattern which groups generic behaviors and their interactions constitutes an organization. Organizations are thus descriptions of coordination structures. Coordination occurs between roles as and when interactions take place. The design phase consists of two steps, namely agentification and architectural design. Agentification assigns roles to agents.

Interactions between roles identified in the organizational model allow to define the interaction between agents which play these roles. In fact agents instantiate an organization (roles and interactions) when they exhibit behaviors defined by the organization's roles and when they interact following the organization interactions. An agent may instantiate one or more roles and a role may be instantiated by one or more agents. For specifying MAS described with the role-interaction-organization metamodel we build a framework written with a formalism which is a composition of Object Z and state charts. The whole composition mechanism is described in [6]. For the sake of clarity we will only sketch this mechanism. In order to compose Object Z classes and state charts one can write a class with a schema including a state chart. This state chart specifies the behavior of the class. Our choice is to use Object Z to specify the transformational aspects and state charts to specify the reactive aspects. Object Z extends Z with object oriented specification support. The basic construct is the class which encapsulates state schema with all the operation schemas which may affect its variables.

4. SYSTEM MODEL

The system is described at two levels. The first one is an organization level, which contains description of roles. The roles performed by the agents are roles in contract-net protocol (manager or contractor), they are described in section 4.1. The second one - an agent level (see sections 4.2, 4.3, 4.4 and 4.5) - describes the environment, the agents and the interactions among them.

4.1 Organization level

The two classes Scheduler and Vehicle specify Scheduler and Vehicle roles. The first line CNETNode states that each role inherits from a role which integrates Contract Net aspects. These aspects won't be described here due to lack of space. The sub-schema which follows specify the attributes of each class.

Scheduler is specified by a function, locations, which maps Vehicle to Location on the network. It is also specified by orders which is the set of all orders sent to this Scheduler. Eventually, allocated is a function which maps a subset of orders to Vehicle and which represents the orders assigned to company vehicles. The sub-schema behavior specifies with a state chart the behavior of the Scheduler. It consists in waiting for an order and as soon as an order arrives manages offers to vehicle (with the contract net protocol). If an agreement is reached it waits for the order to be finalized. If no agreement is reached it returns to idle state. The calculateGoal function calculates the *g* value as defined in section 4.3.

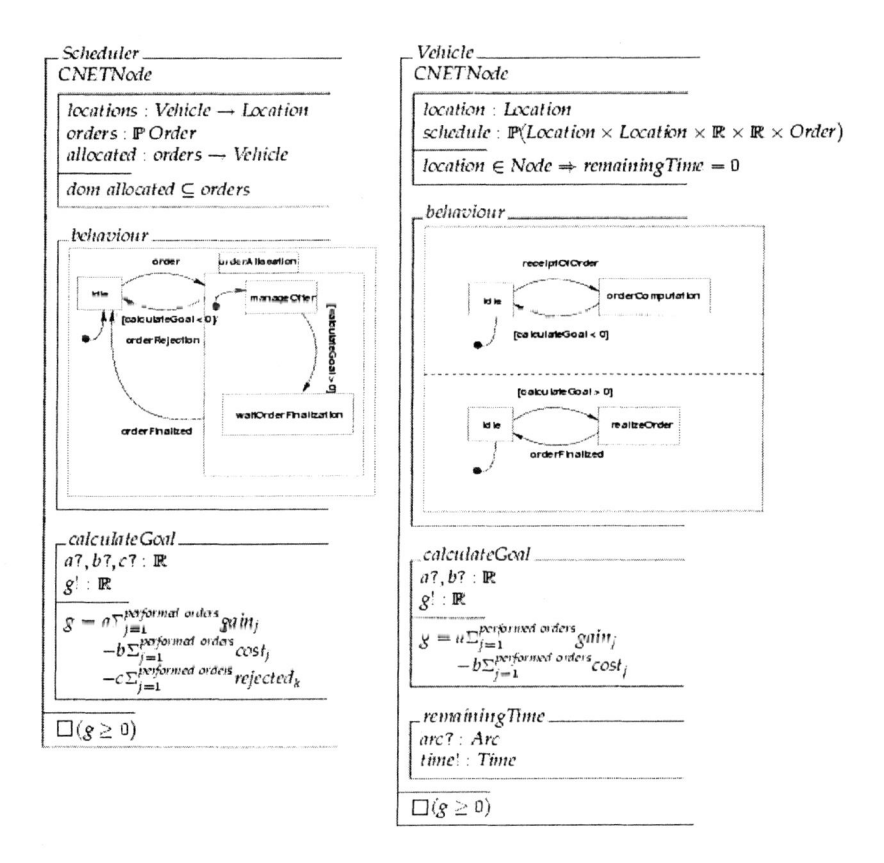

Fig 1. Formal description of roles in the system

Vehicle is specified by a current location and a schedule which is defined in section 4.4. The behavior of each Vehicle is defined by a parallel execution (dashed line) of two processes which are: computation of order costs and order realizations. The calculateGoal function is defined before and the remainingTime function calculates the time remaining on the current location if it is an Arc.

4.2 Environment

Transport network is represented as a directed graph TN (N, E), where N is set of nodes and E is set of arcs respectively. Nodes represent the location. They may be the start or destination point of the goods transfer. With each node V_i is associated a pair (x$_i$, y$_i$), where x$_i$ and y$_i$ are coordinates on the map. Each arc E$_i$ is described by time period tp$_i$, which informs how much time the vehicle needs to traverse it

4.3 Agent company

Actually, there is only one company-agent in the system, but an introduction of several ones in a future is planned. Company agent receives shipping orders and allocates them to the vehicle agents. It fulfills the role of *Scheduler*.

The company agent CA is represented as a touple (KE,KV,OI,OA,g), where: KE - knowledge about the environment (information concerning the transport-network structure, its nodes and arcs), KV - knowledge about the vehicles (information where its vehicles are placed), OI – set of incoming orders, OA- set of allocated orders, g – goal function

Incoming orders. An incoming order (**OI$_i$**) for realization by the fleet of agent-vehicles is represented by a touple OI$_i$ = (NS$_i$,NE$_i$, tl$_i$, td$_i$, c$_i$), where: NS$_i$ - start node, NE$_i$ - end node, tl$_i$ loading time, td$_i$ – delivering time, c$_i$ – gain for order realization.

Allocated orders. An allocated order OA$_i$ is represented as a pair (AV$_i$, O$_i$), where: AV$_i$ - identyfier of agent-vehicle A$_i$, O$_i$ – a transport order, which is allocated to vehicle A$_i$.

Goals. The goal of a company is the realization of all (or at least as high part as possible) of received transport orders with the lowest possible additional costs. The additional costs are the consequences of necessity of moving a vehicle to the loading point. The goal of the company is represented by a goal function and a company should do to maximize its value. The function goal g$_i$ is expressed by the following equation:

$$g_i = a \sum_{j=1}^{\text{performed orders}} gain_j - b \sum_{j=1}^{\text{performed orders}} \cos t_j - c \sum_{k=1}^{\text{rejected orders}} rejected_k \qquad (1)$$

where gain$_j$ – profit after order *j* realization, cost$_j$ – cost of order *j* realization, rejected$_j$ – cost of either rejection or not realization of order, *a, b, c* – coefficients.

Actions. Agent company is able to perform the following actions:
- *Receipt of order.* Agent receives a transport order. A new transport order is added to the incoming orders list.
- *Order allocation.* The message with the information about a transport order is sent to the vehicles. The vehicles answer sending messages with the condition of order realization.
- *Order finalization.* The company receives the confirmation from agent-vehicle that it has realized an order. The value of goal function is changed and the order is removed from allocated order list.
- *Order rejection.* The company is not able to realize an order and decides to reject it. It may by done just after receipt of an order or when the company notices that realization of allocated order is no longer possible. The value of goal function is changed. If the order was allocated, it has to be removed from the list of allocated orders.

4.4 Vehicle agents

Agent-vehicle (A_i) represents a mean of transport with a driver and fulfils the role of *vehicle* defined on the organization level. In this model it may represent a cab. The agent A_i is represented as a touple (l_i, t_i, S_i, K_i, g_i) where l_i – current location (a node or an arc), t_i – the remaining amount of time needed for vehicle to traverse the rest of the arc; S_i - schedule, $S_i = \{s_i\}$, where s_i= (starting location, ending location, loading time, delivering time, order identifier) - one from among loading time and delivering time may be set undefined, K_i. – agent knowledge, g_i – value of goal function, which is expressed by the following equation.

$$g_i = a \sum_{j=1}^{\substack{performed \\ orders}} gain_j - b \sum_{j=1}^{\substack{performed \\ orders}} \cos t_j \qquad (2)$$

where: $gain_j$ – payment received for the realization of orders, in simple case represented by the weights of arcs traversed by the vehicle agent with a package (agent has to choose the shortest possible route), $cost_j$ – cost of realization of orders, in simple case represented by the weights of arcs which agent-vehicle has to traverse to reach a loading point, a, b - coefficients

Actions. The agent-vehicle can perform the following actions:
- *Move to node.* The vehicle starts to traverse a neighboring arc to reach a given node.
- *Load.* A package is loaded to the vehicle.
- *Unload* A package is unloaded from the vehicle
- *Offer order realization* The vehicle receives the information about the order realization from agent-company. It analyzes if the order realization is feasible; which path (chain of arcs) the vehicle has to traverse to realize an order and how the order realization affects on the value of goal function.
- *Drop order.* The realization of order is not feasible.
- *Trade order.* The vehicle passes the order realization to another vehicle.
- *Receive decision about order realization.* The vehicle receives information from agent-company concerning the allocation of order to a vehicle.

4.5 Protocol of order realization

A vehicle is assigned to realization of order using Contract Net protocol [5]:
- Company receives transport order.
- Company announces the order to agent-vehicles.
- Agent-vehicles analyze the situation and check the feasibility of order and the influence of order realization to value of their goal functions. Considering these conditions they decide about sending offers of task realization to agent-company. Offers contain information about increasing of global time needed for arriving to the loading points. (The goal is to minimize the time needed for

arriving to the loading points) and quantity of realized and allocated orders during last period of time.
- The agent-company chooses an agent-vehicle, which will realize the order.

There is a situation possible, that no agent has offered the realization of task. Then, an agent may be selected from among all agent-vehicles, which are feasible to realize a task, even if it will decrease the value of their goal functions. If none such exists, than the rescheduling and replanning is necessary. We intend to realize these actions by optimizing plans of agents using evolutionary algorithms.

5. CONCLUSIONS AND FUTURE WORKS

In this paper we have presented a formal specification of the system. Afterwards, we intend to make the experiments with different expressions of agents' goal functions. Our intention is to introduce additional elements to make an analysis of multi-modal transport possible.
- *Different agents capabilities.* Maximal possible carrying capacity of vehicles and additional features of packages (size and weight), different means of transport (and the arcs are accessible to only one class of vehicles) and different features of vehicles (like maximal speed, carrying capacity)
- *Different types of arcs.* The arc will be associated not only with the time of traverse but also with the costs, which can be different for different types of vehicles.
- *Negotiations among the agents.* The several different vehicles may cooperate with each other to realize one transport order and a shipment may be reloaded between several means of transport.

Negotiations among the agents. The several different vehicles may cooperate with each other to realize one transport order and a shipment may be reloaded between several means of transport.

6. REFERENCES

[1] Klaus Fischer, Jörg P. Müller, Markus Pischel, Darius Schier, „A Model For Cooperative Transportation Scheduling", *Proceedings of the First International Conference on Multiagent Systems*, 1995
[2] Klaus Fischer, Jörg P. Müller, Markus Pischel, „Cooperative Transportation Scheduling: an Application Domain for DAI", *Applied Artificial Intelligence*, vol.10, pp.1-33, 1996
[3] Hans-Jürgen Bürckert, Klaus Fischer, Gero Vierke, *"Transportation Scheduling with Holonic MAS. The TeleTruck Approach", ,"* Proc. 3rd Int'l Conf. Practical Applications of Intelligent Agents and Multiagents, PAAM'98, 1998.
[4] Jörg Böcker, Jürgen Lind, Bernd Zirkler, *"Using a multi-agent approach to optimize the train coupling and sharing system",* European Journal of Operational Research 134(2001) 242-252
[5] R. Smith. "The contract net protocol: High-level communication and control in distributed problem solver" IEEE *Transactions on Computers*, 29(12):1104--1113, December 1980.
[6] V. Hilaire, "Vers une approche de specification, de prototypage et de verification de Systèmes Multi-Agents", PhD thesis, UTBM, 2000

Practical realization of modelling an airplane for an intelligent tutoring system

OREST POPOV[1], ANNA BARCZ[2],
PIOTR PIELA[2], TOMASZ SOBCZAK[2]
*Faculty of Computer Science and Information Systems, Technical University of Szczecin,
ul. Żołnierska 49, 71-210 Szczecin, Poland, fax (+48 91) 487 64 39*
[1] *tel. (+48 91) 449 55 12, e-mail: popov@wi.ps.pl*
[2] *tel. (+48 91) 449 55 84, e-mail: abarcz@wi.ps.pl, ppiela@wi.ps.pl, tsobczak@wi.ps.pl*

Abstract: This paper describes the general design and an example of practical realization of the simulation system for a light airplane, created as a part of an intelligent tutoring system for civil aviation. The choice of appropriate hardware and software means for such a simulation system is also discussed. Proposed structure of the simulation system is based on two independent modules: the simulation kernel and the user interface. The kernel performs all the flight dynamics computations as well as simulates functioning of the onboard systems, while the user interface provides the user with a three-dimensional view on the airplane's cabin and the outside scenery. Both modules communicate with each other as well as with the other parts of an intelligent tutoring system through the network, which makes the proposed simulation system a suitable tool for use in distance learning.

Key words: simulation system, intelligent tutoring system, modelling, desktop flight simulator

1. INTRODUCTION

Today, when computer technology is rapidly developing, traditional tutoring systems are being more and more often replaced by intelligent systems, which take advantage of all the possibilities offered by contemporary computers. A choice of an intelligent tutoring system (ITS) allows first of all decreasing the costs of an educational process. Besides such a system makes this process more flexible allowing e.g. for repeating of certain exercises according to the trainee's progress. Additionally the use of multimedia exerting an influence on a couple of senses simultaneously increases the rate of absorbing the knowledge by the student.

The technology used by intelligent tutoring systems especially in the field of the network communication makes them adequate for distance learning where the student is separated by a distance from the instructor or other learners.

The specificity of distance learning demands from the ITS that some requirements be met. Firstly such a system is expected to work in the client-server architecture where a server co-ordinates the tutoring process and collects data about students' progress. In such a client-server architecture it is important to allow the use of different operating systems or hardware for the students' workstations therefore the client applications should be easy to port to another platforms. Finally a reliable and efficient communication protocol is essential for functioning of such a system.

One of the main domains where an ITS can find application is the process of training the flying personnel where the issue of costs and safety is especially emphasized. The main part of ITS used in aviation is a simulation system (fig. 1) which can be either a full flight simulator (FS) with a motion system or a less complicated system like part task trainer (PTT) or cockpit procedure trainer (CPT) depending on the tasks that are to be learned. Such a simulation system is usually created for a specific aircraft type and is expected to reproduce in a realistic way its dynamics and onboard systems' functioning. With recent improvement in hardware and software it becomes clear that realization of a simulation system, which can be a viable alternative for a PTT driven by a high-end professional workstation is possible with a low-cost personal computer (PC). For such a simulation system based on a PC a name of desktop flight simulator (DFS) will be used.

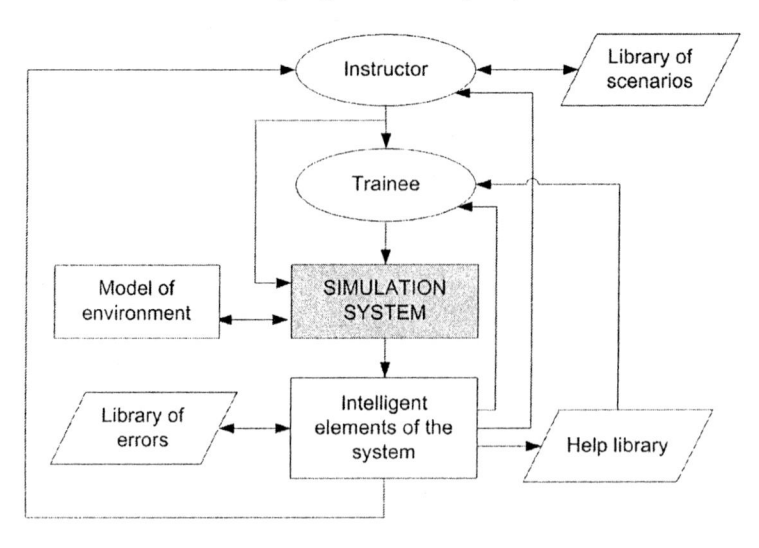

Fig. 1. Example structure of an ITS used in aviation [1]

Such a simulation system is being developed within the confines of ASIMIL project being a part of 5th Framework Programme, II Thematic Programme "Information Society Technologies".

This DFS has been designed for SOCATA TB 20 Trinidad, which is a single-engine touring airplane designed for single pilot operation.

2. COMPUTER TECHNOLOGY AVAILABLE FOR DFS

A variety of hardware and software means can be used for creating a DFS implementation. In this paragraph will be discussed the choice of those means which on one hand will be dictated by the requirements mentioned above and on the other hand will be limited by the economical issues.

A human-in-the-loop simulation has high requirements for the generation of graphics. The issues of providing high quality images at rapid frame rates and responding quickly to the user's actions are crucial to the training process. Contemporary graphics cards used in desktop computers offer possibility of generating realistic three-dimensional images which are often comparable to those generated by professional graphic workstations. Most of those cards come with hardware accelerated industry standard (OpenGL) drivers for Windows and Linux [2].

OpenGL originally released by SGI in 1992 is an official industry standard for programming both 2D and 3D graphics. It has implementations (e.g. Mesa) for most available operating systems therefore allowing for the development of graphics components across an impressively wide range of platforms [3]. Such a development is even easier with the use of GLUT (OpenGL Utility Toolkit) library which implements a portable windowing API for OpenGL allowing for porting applications to a range of platforms without the need of changing the source code. The GLUT library has bindings for the C, C++, FORTRAN and Ada programming languages and its source code is freely available.

DirectX is a set of APIs developed by Microsoft that enables programmers to write programs that access hardware features of a computer without knowing exactly what hardware will be installed on the machine where the program eventually runs. In particular, DirectX lets multimedia applications take advantage of hardware acceleration features supported by graphics accelerators. Direct3D is a part of DirectX responsible for manipulating and displaying 3-dimensional objects. It has become an unofficial standard competing with OpenGL on the personal computers' market.

3. ARCHITECTURE OF DFS

The proposed DFS implementation is divided into two independent parts: modelling subsystem (simulation kernel) and cockpit subsystem (user interface) that communicate with each other using the TCP/IP network protocol [4]. Such an approach to the implementation allows to easier incorporate it into a distributed system like a distance learning environment with the possibility of simultaneous work of many independent cockpit subsystems with a single modelling subsystem which communicates directly with the server of ITS (fig. 3).

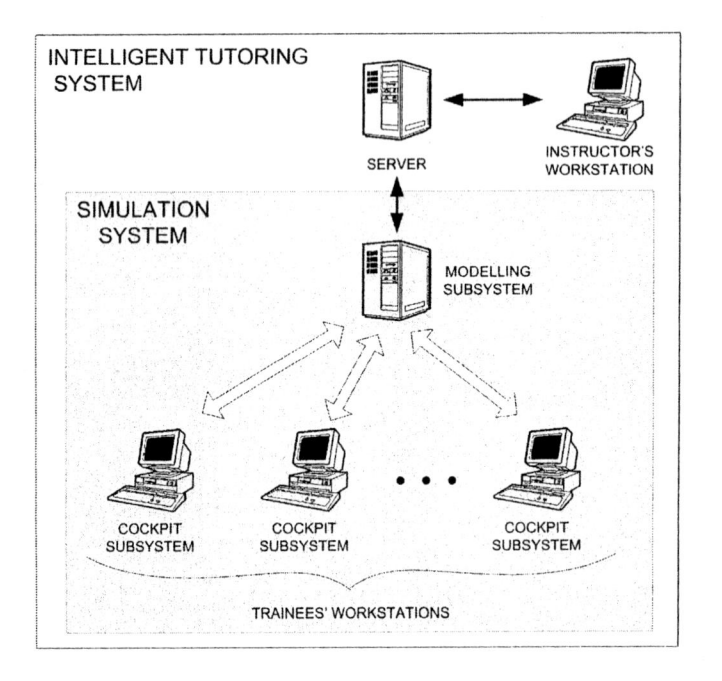

Fig. 2. Proposed simulation system in a distributed ITS [1]

3.1 Simulation kernel

Mathematical model

The model of aircraft's dynamics is based on the set of known non-linear differential equations (1), which describe the motion of a rigid body with six degrees of freedom [5].

$$m(\frac{\partial V}{\partial t} + \Omega \times V) = F$$
$$\frac{\partial (I \cdot \Omega)}{\partial t} + \Omega \times (I \cdot \Omega) = M \tag{1}$$

Where V – velocity vector at the centre of gravity, Ω - angular velocity vector about c.g., F – total external force vector, M – total external moment vector and I – inertia tensor of the rigid body.

The mathematical model allows simulating all stages of the flight - from the ground manoeuvres and take-off up to the landing.

Model of the atmosphere is based on International Standard Atmosphere (IAS).

Algorithm

The general algorithm of the modelling subsystem is presented on fig. 3. Complete equations of motion for the airplane are being solved in real-time in the main loop.

This loop is executed 500 times per second. After each 25 executions (20 times per second) is called the cockpit function that exchanges messages with the user interface and other parts of the ITS. The main loop is divided into 4 modules, which are described below.

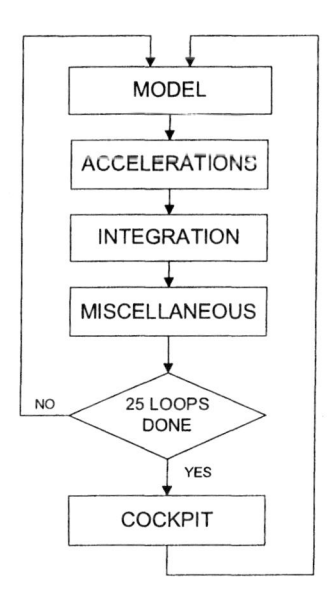

Fig. 3. General algorithm of the simulation kernel

MODEL module:
- AERO – Finding the control surfaces deflections according to the position of controls; estimation of aerodynamic forces and moments coefficients; calculation of aerodynamic forces' and moments' values.
- ENGINE – Estimation of the manifold pressure based on the value of atmospheric pressure and the position of throttle lever; calculation of the fuel flow and engine's power (based on manifold pressure and engine speed); correction of the calculated power based on the values of: mixture ratio, air temperature and magnetos selection; modelling of the starter; estimation of temperatures of exhaust gases and the cylinder head; estimation of oil temperature and pressure based on engine's speed and temperature; calculation of propeller's thrust based on the values of power coefficient and advance ratio; correction of the engine speed based on propeller lever's position and propeller power; modelling the change of propeller blade angle; calculation of the values of propulsion force and moment.

- **LANDING GEAR** – Finding the position and velocity of each wheel in reference to the ground; calculation of the reaction force and friction coefficient for each wheel; calculation of the total value of undercarriage force and moment; the same computations for the contour points of the airframe in case of their accidental contact with the ground.
- **SYSTEMS** – Modelling of various onboard systems: retracting and extending of the flaps and undercarriage; turning on and off the indicator lights, sounds and alarms; calculation of indications of the flight and engine instruments based on real values of the indicated parameters and instrument errors.

ACCELERATIONS module: calculation of the sum of all forces and moments acting on the airplane; determining the linear and angular accelerations in Earth coordinate system, gravity loads and then linear and angular accelerations in aircraft coordinate system.
INTEGRATION module: finding the linear and angular velocities in aircraft and Earth coordinate systems; building the transformation matrix for aircraft and Earth coordinate systems; finding the values of Euler angles, geocentric longitude and latitude.
MISCELLANEOUS module: determining the longitude and latitude of the aircraft as well as the groundspeed and airspeed in aircraft and Earth coordinates; finding the values of the angle of attack, sideslip angle and flight-path angles; calculation of the values of local gravity and atmospheric parameters; finding the position in reference to the ground.

The simulation kernel is written in ANSI C programming language which for its speed and efficiency in using the hardware resources is the most suitable language for an application which works interactively in real-time with a huge amount of computations running each second. The simulation kernel works under Linux OS.

3.2 User interface

Algorithm

The general structure of the user interface subsystem is based on the callback mechanism provided by GLUT library that executes appropriate user's function each time a specific condition like resizing the window, moving the mouse or pressing a key occurs. Below are described all the actions taken in each of the callback functions.

IDLE (executed in a loop when none of the remaining conditions occurs) - receiving messages from the modelling subsystem; playing (or stopping) appropriate sounds if necessary; checking the state of the control device (e.g. joystick); sending messages to the modelling subsystem; shutting down the user interface if necessary; notifying the callback mechanism that the display needs redrawing after updating the airplane's position.
DISPLAY (executed each time the display needs updating) - drawing all of the cockpit elements and the airplane's 3D model depending on the view chosen by the user; drawing the outside scenery.

RESHAPE (executed when the size of the display changes) - setting appropriate field of view for the camera.
KEYBOARD (executed when some alphanumeric key is pressed) - changing the state of appropriate controls (flaps lever, landing gear lever, etc.).
SPECIAL (executed when some of the special keys is pressed) - changing views; switching between full-screen and windowed mode.
MOUSE (executed when some of the mouse buttons are pressed or released) - selecting appropriate cockpit elements (switches, levers, knobs, etc.).
MOTION (executed when the mouse is moved with some of the buttons pressed) - changing the state of the selected cockpit element.
PASSIVE MOTION (executed when the mouse is moved with no button pressed) – „looking around" in the cockpit.

Sounds and alarms

In order to achieve a higher level of realism in reproducing the behaviour of the airplane some sound effects have been implemented. These include e.g. the engine, extending and retracting of the landing gear and flaps, stall and landing gear warnings.

Control devices

The simulation process is controlled by means of joystick, mouse and keyboard. The mouse is used for controlling all the switches, knobs, levers and other elements of the cockpit by clicking and dragging. The right mouse button is used for checking the indication of an instrument or the position of a control in order to pass those values to other elements of the ITS. With the mouse pointer moved to one of the screen borders the user can "look around" changing the present view.

User interface design

For each element of the cabin have been created three-dimensional models of its static and movable parts. The position and orientation of each movable object is calculated according to data received from the simulation kernel. On fig. 4. are shown the elements comprising the structure of UI 5934 altimeter's model used in the current version of the user interface (fig. 5).

The user interface offers the possibility of changing between a wide range of different views including views from the pilot's seat, co-pilot's seat, control tower and outside of the airplane. On the pictures below are shown some typical views used during the simulation.

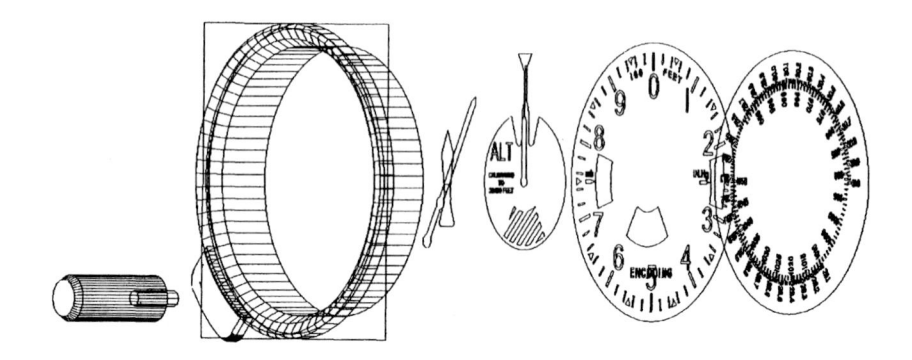

Fig. 4. Construction of an example instrument's model.

Fig. 5. Rendered model of UI 5934 altimeter.

4. CONCLUSIONS AND PLANS

In this paper an approach to create a simulation system for an airplane is presented. The distributed architecture and portable software make this system an ideal tool for use in distance learning and intelligent tutoring systems. Earlier however such a model must be subjected to verification, which in a case of a model based on non-linear equations is a complicated process based mostly on the authors' experience and pilots' opinions on the model's conformity to the real airplane's behaviour.

As an attempt to simplify this verification process the use of a set of linear models is being considered. Such an approach would allow utilizing some regular mathematical methods based on testing the structural properties.

In the next phase of the software development the emphasis will be placed on improving the modelling of atmospheric phenomena (rain, snow, icing, etc.) and their influence on the airplane's dynamics together with appropriate visual and sound effects. The cockpit will have a modular structure allowing the user to easily change its elements (especially the avionics systems).

Fig 6. View from the pilot's seat.

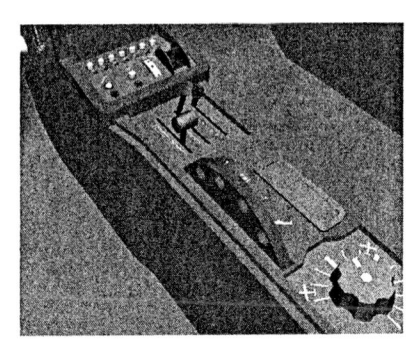

Fig. 7. The cabin interior.

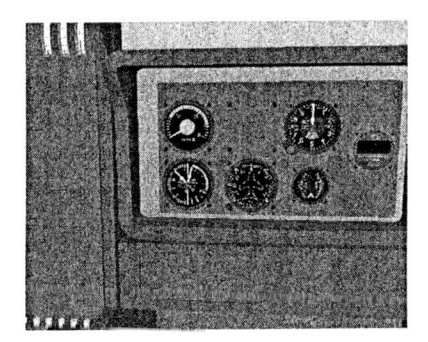

Fig.8. View from the co-pilot's seat.

Fig. 9. View from the outside.

5. REFERENCES

[1] Popov O., Barcz A., Piela p., Sobczak T., Problem of the flight simulation in computer-based training systems for civil aviation, Proceedings of the 6th International Conference Intelligent Tutoring Systems, Workshop Simulation Based Training, Biarritz 2002, France
[2] Kelty L., Beckett P., Zalcman L., Desktop Simulation., SimTecT 99, March 1999
[3] www.opengl.org
[4] Popov O., Barcz A., Piela P., Sobczak T., Design of DFS, Proceedings of ASIMIL, 2001
[5] Etkin B., Dynamics of flight, John Wiley, New York 1959

Model of Natural Language Communication System for Virtual Market of Services

PIOTR PECHMANN, JERZY SOŁDEK
Faculty of Computer Science & Information Systems, Technical University of Szczecin
Zolnierska 49, 70-210 Szczecin, Poland, e-mail: ppechmann@wi.ps.pl

Abstract: Using a natural language in communication with a computer system can greatly facilitate the access to computer services for an average user. This paper presents a model of such communication system based on results of our own research of semantic analysis and sentence generation in Polish language that can be used in a human-computer dialogue.

Described here are multi-agent system structures and specified agent functions related to communication based on natural language. Achievability of the proposed system of the virtual market of services and functions intended for agents are also discussed.

The plans for the future work and research that aim at constructing a prototype of the system of the multi-agent virtual market of services with the capacity for natural language communication between client and service system are discussed in the conclusion.

Key words: communication in natural language, multi-agent systems, e-commerce.

1. INTRODUCTION

In today's world computer systems are becoming more and more indispensable in every field of human life and activity. As the result, using them becomes necessary for people who have little or no experience with computers. For those people, mastering formalised language of communication with the system turns out to be very difficult or even impossible. They cannot formulate queries based on such a language and find it difficult to understand the answers given by the system. Additional trouble comes from the fact that different computer systems realising similar functions use different communication languages. Thus a person using more than one system has to learn the language of each one.

This situation is clearly visible on the market of services offered in the virtual space of the Internet – the means of communication with systems offering the services is one of the greatest barriers in taking advantage of them. Many of people who have little or no computer experience say that it is too difficult to master.

From the point of view of an average user, the best solution would be equipping the systems with the capacity to communicate with the user in natural language. Not only is such a language familiar to the user, but it also contains a vast range of means enabling the user to freely describe the problem to be solved.

The key to realisation of such systems for any chosen natural language, Polish for example, is developing effective algorithms of syntax and semantic analysis of utterances formulated in that language, which is one of the fundamental problems of natural language processing [1]. Only after recognising the meaning of an utterance is it possible to interpret it and cause a desired response of the computer system. Another problem to be solved is generating natural language sentences that are the computer system's answers in the dialogue [2].

For last few years communication in Polish natural language with computer systems has been the subject of research at the Faculty of Computer Science & Information Systems at the Technical University of Szczecin. The goal of this research has been twofold: creating methods of effective semantic analysis and generation of sentences used during communication process and a formalised model of description of sentence semantics. The end results of that research have been an original, heuristic method of object-oriented syntactic-semantic analysis of simple sentences in Polish language [3, 4] and a model of description of semantics of such sentences in the form called *object representation of semantics* (ORS) [4]. This method has been successfully applied in a prototype of a system translating database queries formulated in Polish natural language into queries formulated in SQL language.

The next step would be developing the already existing methods and models into a generalised model of a system allowing the user to communicate in a natural language with different classes of computer systems. In the solution presented in this paper, the task of providing the natural language interface between the user and a computer system is realised by autonomous, intelligent agent systems. Such systems proved to be realisable and highly effective in the task classes whose complexity is comparable to the problems in question [5, 6, 7].

The proposed model is presented in section 2 of this paper. The general structure and functions of the agent-based system conducting a dialogue on behalf of the user as well as an agent-based interface of the service system, which "understands" ORS, are described. The technical means chosen for realisation of the prototype of the model are presented in section 3.

In conclusion (section 4), the achievability of the implementation of the model of the natural language communication system as a multi-agent system has been discussed. The section also presents the scope and direction of further work necessary for building a functioning prototype of multi-agent system of virtual market of services with communication based on Polish natural language.

2. THE MODEL OF COMMUNICATION SYSTEM

The Virtual Market of Services (VMS) is a virtual space that enables those who offer and those who are recipients of various services (i.e. who are the users of the system) to find one another and to communicate. The means used for realising these two VMS key functions (i.e. searching and communicating) are defined in the model of communication system.

In the proposed model two different types of agent-based systems cooperate:
 a) *Proxy Agents* (PA) whose task is to communicate with the user in natural language and to order on his behalf services to be performed by *Agent-based Service Systems*.
 b) *Agent-based Service Systems* (ASS), offering remote access to different kinds of services such as booking tickets, buying goods or obtaining information from databases.

The following two types of servers also belong to the system.
a) *Registration servers*, performing two tasks: keeping ASS registers (catalogues) in order to enable proxy agents to find ASS's that offer services required by the user as well as registering PA's for the purpose of verification of their identity.
b) *DLD Servers*, providing proxy agents with *domain lexicons definitions* (DLD) containing information used in the process of semantic analysis of orders given by the user.

One of the most important principles of the proposed model is enabling the user to communicate with service systems using natural language. The language of PA–ASS communication is also based on a natural language – it is ORS of sentences that are the orders, messages, questions and answers exchanged between PA and ASS systems.

The general scheme of communication process based on these principles can be illustrated as follows (fig. 1):
1) The user gives the proxy agent an order, expressing it in the form of a natural language sentence.
2) The proxy agent:
 − performs the semantic analysis of the order and generates object-oriented representation of its semantics [4],
 − identifies or chooses an ASS for which the order is meant,
 − sends ORS of the order to the appropriate ASS.
3) Agent-based service system processes the order and generates a reply in the ORS form, which it sends to the proxy agent.
4) Based on the received ORS, the proxy agent generates for the user a message in the natural language.

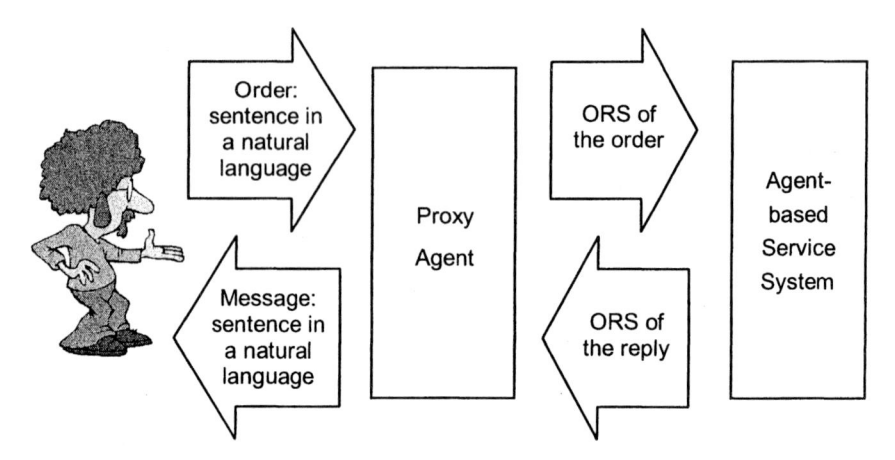

Fig. 1. The general scheme of communication process between the user, PA and ASS

Every proxy agent can communicate with many ASS's at the same time. Also every agent-based service system can simultaneously receive orders from and give replies to many proxy agents.

2.1 Model of the proxy agent

The proxy agent represents and acts on behalf of the client on the virtual market of services. It performs a function of a personal assistant, and proxy for the user in the process of ordering services from agent-based service systems. It communicates with its user using a natural language.

The analysis of the tasks that should be realised by a proxy agent shows five subsystems that can be differentiated within its model (fig. 2). The main functions of these subsystems are:

The proxy agent represents and acts on behalf of the client on the virtual market of services. It performs a function of a personal assistant, and proxy for the user in the process of ordering services from agent-based service systems. It communicates with its user using a natural language.

The analysis of the tasks that should be realised by a proxy agent shows five subsystems that can be differentiated within its model (fig. 2). The main functions of these subsystems are:
– semantic sentence analysis (SSA),
– choice and registration of agent systems (CRAS),
– dialog session support (DSS),
– network communication support (NCS),
– sentence generation (SG).

Tasks realised by the aforementioned subsystems and the way these tasks are performed are presented in the following subsections.

2.1.1 Semantic sentence analysis

This subsystem performs semantic analysis of sentences in a natural language, which the user directs to the VMS system.

The analysis is performed using the method of *object-oriented semantic analysis* that consists of two stages:
- in the first stage, a syntactic-semantic analysis of the sentence is performed using *the syntax matrix matching method* [3];
- in the second stage, a formal description of the sentence meaning in the form of the *object representation of semantics* (ORS) is generated [4].

The information required by the SSA subsystem to "understand" the meaning of a given order and to generate the description of this meaning in the ORS from is provided to the proxy agent as a set of appropriate lexicons [3,4]. In the proposed model such sets are constructed separately for defined and usually narrow subject domains of dialogue that might be conducted by the user with a proxy agent. The particular subject domains are related to the classes of services offered by an ASS, for example, the services offered by the restaurants or different classes of rental services. For each such ASS class, and what goes along with it, for the subject of the dialogue in a natural language specific for such a class, a separate set of lexicons called *domain lexicons definitions* (DLD) is constructed.

The subsystem of semantic analysis gets only those DLD's which it needs to understand the user's orders related to the classes of services the user wants to order using the discussed system. DLD's are acquired by the SSA subsystem from a special server called *DLD server* in two situations:
- in the process of the initial personalization of a proxy agent, when the user specifies what classes of service systems he or she is interested in, for example, restaurants or video rentals;
- in a situation when the user uses an unknown word in his or her order: the sentence is sent to the DLD server, which, based on further analysis, determines which DLD's are relevant to the order's subject and sends them to the SSA subsystem.

In the ORS model the meaning of a sentence is specified using a set of two kinds of entities called *semantic objects* and *semantic relations*.

Semantic objects represent people, things or concepts about whom something is stated in the sentence. There are two types of semantic objects that have been differentiated in the model: *main objects*, which correspond to complements on the syntactic-semantic level, and *attributive objects*, which represent qualifiers and adverbial qualifiers in the ORS.

The description of each semantic object contains two things. The first is the list of *simple attributes* of the object. Simple attribute can represent such features as, for example, colour in the case of objects designating material things, or a family name in the case of objects designating persons.

The second thing is the description of *semantic roles* performed by the object in the sentence. It can be a role performed by the main object in the semantic relation, or a role performed by an attributive object, which is describing different features of the semantic relation or another semantic object.

Semantic relations correspond in ORS to the predicate of a sentence and describe the relationship and dependencies between main objects (i.e. complements) of the sentence. The description of the semantic relation contains the list of semantic objects being in that relation and the list of objects, which are qualifiers of the relation.

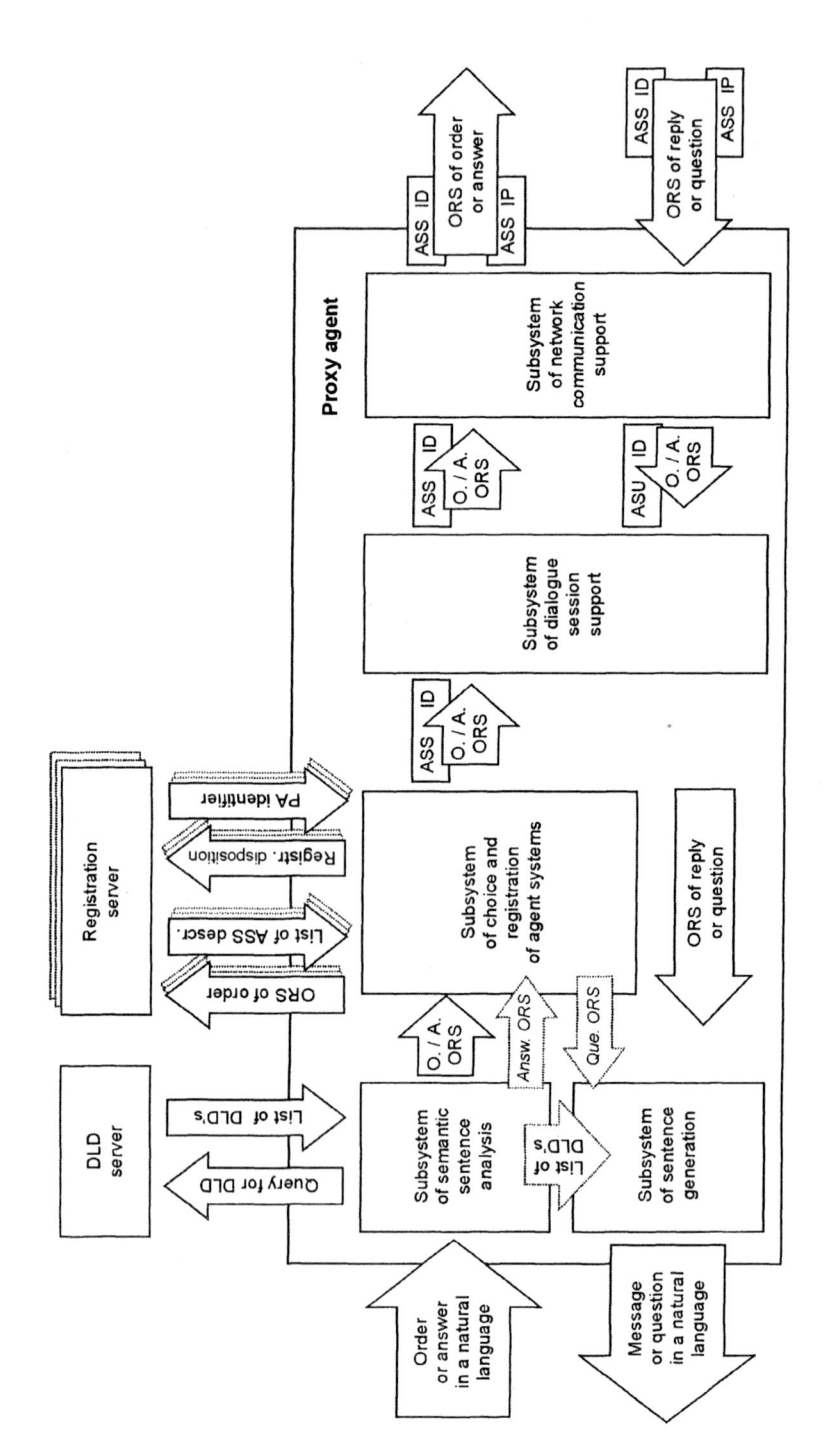

Fig. 2. The model of a proxy agent

For example, the meaning of the sentence "Reserve two places in KFC restaurant next Friday" could be presented in ORS form in the following way (the tables show ORS in a simplified way):

ORS ID	Semantic relation	Main objects: *role_id*: object_ors_id	Attributive objects: *role_id*: object_ors_id	Language representation
R1	To reserve	*object*: O1	*place*: O2 *time*: O3	"reserve"

ORS ID	Semantic object	Simple attributes: *type*: value	Language representation
O1	Place	*number*: Two	"two places"
O2	Restaurant	*name*: "KFC"	"in KFC"
O3	Friday	*feature*: Next	"next Friday"

The meaning of the order recognised and specified in the ORS form by the SSA subsystem is sent to the CRAS subsystem.

2.1.2 Choice and registration of agent systems

As stated above the proxy agent can communicate with many service systems and order them different sorts of tasks on the behalf of its user.

Giving the user an opportunity to communicate with a proxy agent in the most natural way, which resembles the way he or she would communicate with a human assistant as closely as possible, has been one of the most important principles in creating the presented model. If a human assistant is efficient and understands the order he or she should know who should be ordered to perform the task.

That is the main goal of CRAS subsystem – based on analysis of the ORS of the order, making the decision which ASS should be given that order.

Searching for and choosing the appropriate ASS is carried out during the process of comparing ORS of the order with *ORS schemes*, the list of which is a part of ASS description. Each scheme contains information on the key elements of an order's ORS that making it possible to determine for which ASS the order is meant.

In case of orders not precise enough (for example: "Order a pizza" that does not define a pizzeria the pizza should be delivered from) several ASS of the same class (i.e. restaurant / pizzeria) could be determined as the result of comparison. In such case, CRAS subsystem must make the order more precise. In order to do that it conducts a dialogue with the user (in the natural language) asking questions about, for example, the preferred location of the restaurant or its name.

As shown, in order to determine and choose an ASS, the proxy agent must have its description. ASS descriptions can be obtained from *registration servers*. ASS provides a registration server with its description during the registration process. The registration server gives a unique identifier (ASS ID) to each of the registered ASS, which is then used at different stages of PA–ASS communication.

The proxy agent acquires the ASS description or a group of such descriptions in two situations:
- in the process of the initial personalization, when the user specifies which classes of services systems he or she is interested in;
- in a situation, when based on the descriptions of ASS's already registered in the CRAS subsystem the choice of ASS cannot be made; in such a situation the ORS of the user's order is sent to the registration server (or servers), which analyses the ORS and returns the list of descriptions of ASS's, matching the order ("in server's opinion").

The situation resembles the DLD acquisition process by the SSA subsystem.

Another essential task realised by the CRAS subsystem is registering the proxy agent on the registration servers. That registration is indispensable for realisation of the PA identity verification procedures by the ASS systems. The procedures are defined in the model of the security system that is a part of the global model of VMS system.

2.1.3 Dialogue sessions support

After choosing the appropriate ASS the CRAS subsystem sends ORS of the user's order to the *dialogue sessions support* subsystem.

The task of the DSS subsystem is to follow the user–PA–ASS dialogue. The first goal of such a process is freeing the user from the necessity of answering a question answers to which might be known to the proxy agent.

An example of that can be questions about the user's personal data or questions that can be answered based on the knowledge of user's preferences such as his or her favourite pizza ingredients or wine brand. Depending on the built-in intelligence level, the *user preference profile* may be created during the process of the initial agent personalization or developed adaptively based on observing dialogue sessions.

The second goal is facilitating the communication process by receiving some information from the ASS in advance. That could be, for example, the price of a pizza or the brief description of a film in from the video rental the user wants to.

In a situation when the user requests that information, it would have already been available, and so waiting for the ASS answers would not be necessary.

The third goal is to recognize the point when an agreement completes the negotiations between the user and an ASS, and to order making the payment for the service to the payment service server.

2.1.4 Network communication support

The task of this subsystem is supporting the direct network communication with the service systems. The model assumes that the subsystem should be able to communicate with many ASS at the same time.

Communication with each service system is carried out in separate sessions corresponding to the dialogue sessions. The subsystem receives the ORS of an order from the DSS subsystem together with the identifier of the ASS to which the ORS should be sent. If it is the first call for a given ASS, the subsystem determines the network address of that ASS and initiates a new communication session.

Then the subsystem supports the exchange of orders, questions and answers that are sent between DSS subsystem and the ASS. The session may be finished by the DSS subsystem or the service system.

2.1.5 Sentence generation

The last of subsystems making up the proxy agent is the *sentence generation* subsystem.

Its task is generating sentences in natural language based on the description of their meaning described using the ORS. These sentences can be questions and replies given by an ASS as well as questions put to the user by the CRAS subsystem.

Analogous to the subsystem of sentence semantic analysis, also sentence generation subsystem must be equipped with appropriate lexicons. The lexicons for SG subsystem are also organised into DLD packages created for the same subject domains as in case of sentence analysis. DLD packages for the SG subsystem are also provided by DLD servers; the acquisition of these packages is performed simultaneously with the acquisition of DLD by SSA subsystem.

2.2 Model of agent-based service system

In case of agent-based service systems the model defines only these ASS subsystems that constitute interface for the VMS system; the group of those subsystems is called *VMS interface*. Thus for any given ASS the subsystems realising its business functions are only expected to be integrated with that interface.

VMS interface can be considered an autonomous agent (in fact it is a group of agents) that makes available the services on the virtual market on behalf of ASS. Using an analogy to the traditional market, we could say that VMS interface is a dealer of services offered by the ASS.

The general model of agent-based service system is shown in the figure 3. Based on results of the analysis of the tasks of VMS interface, subsystems performing the following functions can be differentiated within the model:
- verification and network communication support (VNCS),
- ORS interpretation (ORS-I),
- ORS generation (ORS-G),
- dialogue session support (DSS),
- registration of agent systems (RAS)

2.2.1 Verification and network communication support

VNCS subsystem supports the direct communication with the proxy agents. It works similarly to its corresponding item in the PA model. Also, in case of ASS, it is assumed that the subsystem should be able to communicate with many PA's at the same time. Communication with each proxy agent is conducted in separate sessions that consist of orders, questions and replies exchanged by the ASS and a given proxy agent.

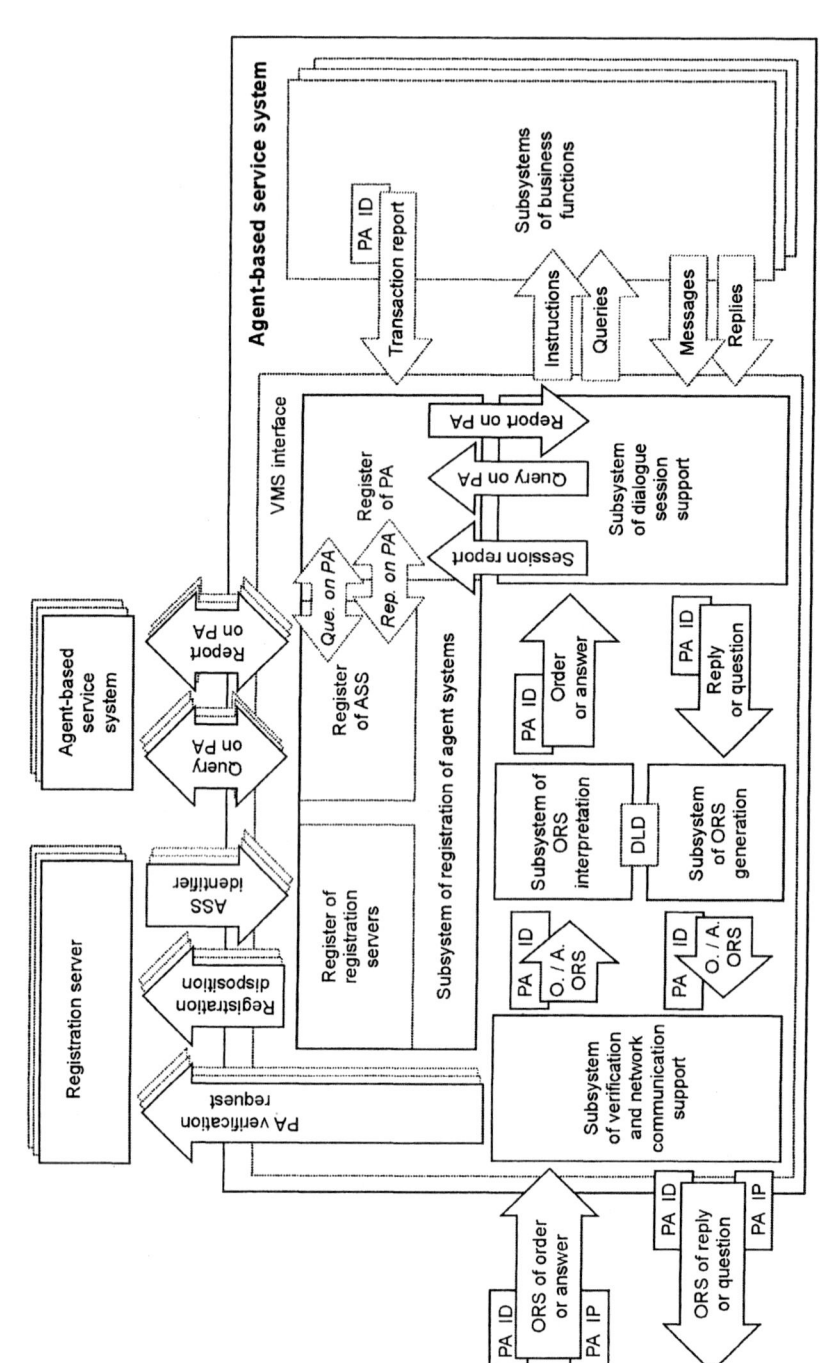

Fig. 3. The model of an agent-based service system

The second task performed by VNCS is verifying the identity of a proxy agent. The PA is verified by the registration servers in answer to a request given by the VNCS subsystem. The model of VMS security system proposes a few verification procedures, which differ in their verification capacity. Depending on the security policy applied for a given ASS, the VNCS subsystem can select one or more of these methods to verify PA identity.

2.2.2 ORS interpretation and generation

The task of ORS-I subsystem is translating an ORS into instructions and messages expressed in the language of internal communication of a service system.

Similarly, the task of ORS-G subsystem is generating ORS corresponding to the reply messages and questions directed to the proxy agent.

ORS interpretation and generation are performed based on the DLD prepared for a subject domain corresponding to the class of services offered by a given ASS. In the ASS model there is no need for DLD acquisition because the subject domain for every ASS is known and defined in advance – thus the appropriate DLD can be added to the ASS during the construction of its VMS interface.

2.2.3 Dialogue session support

DSS subsystem is the most important one in the VMS interface. Its task is administering the process of complete acquisition of the orders given by proxy agents. This task can be divided into two parts:
- obtaining complete information on the order details and data related to the person ordering the service from the proxy agent.
- sending a complete set of instructions required to perform the task to ASS business subsystems.

The kind and amount of information on an order and the person ordering the service as well as the set of instructions for business subsystems obviously depend on the kind of service offered by a given ASS. In case of reservation service, it could be, for example, the information required to reserve a table in a restaurant or a room in a hotel, while in case of an Internet store, it would be information necessary for shipping the ordered article and accepting the charges using the method chosen by the customer. Hence, the detailed scheme of process of an order acquisition may vary depending on the type of the service, so it has not been precisely defined in the proposed model. The general scheme of the process looks as follows.

After receiving a message initiating ordering process from a proxy agent, the DSS subsystem opens a separate dialogue session for that process, and then attempts to verify the proxy agent. The verification is carried out based on *proxy agent profiles*. The profiles are stored in the *proxy agents register* managed by the RAS subsystem.

The exact form of the profile also depends on the type of service offered by an ASS. Generally, a profile may contain two groups of information. The first group is the personal data of the person who orders the service necessary for the realisation of that order. The second group could be information contained in a client profile that had been built based on the history of prior orders. That information may be used, for example, for determining the discount rate to be offered to the client, depending on the number and value of prior purchases, as well as client reliability.

After carrying out client verification, the DSS subsystem conducts a dialog with the proxy agent trying to obtain the details of the order, and, if necessary, the client's personal data required for the transaction.

After receiving all the needed information, the subsystem ends the session and performs two operations:
- it gives the business subsystems all the data and instructions required for completing the order,
- it sends a report on a dialogue session to the RAS, based on which, the RSA subsystem updates the client profile.

2.2.4 Registration of agent system

The RAS subsystem realises two tasks:
- it registers the ASS on the registration servers,
- it administers the register of proxy agents.

The model of the VMS system presupposes the existence of many independent registration servers. A company running a service system would have a choice as to which server (or servers) to be registered on. The addresses of all chosen servers are stored on the *registration servers register*. ASS receives a unique identifier on each server it is registered on.

The RAS subsystem administers a register of proxy agents, which contains profiles of these agents. In the model, it's not the *client's* but *the agent profile* since the data used in creating the profile can be unambiguously bound only to the PA identifier. Thus for the identity verification purposes, it's not only possible, but also advisable that one PA is registered on a few different registration servers. So, one PA can have a couple different identifiers. In addition, one client can use more than one proxy agent.

The PA profile is mainly created based on the reports from dialogue sessions provided by the DSS subsystem. However, a possibility of using two additional information sources is assumed in the model.

The first source might be the transaction reports provided by ASS business subsystems. Such a report can contain the data pertinent to assessing client's reliability, such as information on late payments, etc.

The second source of information assumed in the model is other ASS systems. It can happen that the ASS would receive an order given by an unknown PA. In order to enable the ASS to verify such a proxy agent, the model has been equipped with capacity to exchange information regarding PA through ASS groups.

In case the RAS subsystem receives a query on an PA that has an unknown identifier, it can forward it to the other group members and possibly receive information on that PA from those ASS's that have already done some services for that PA.

ASS groups do not have a formal character – the company that owns a given ASS makes the decision what information may be exchanged with what ASS.

3. ISSUES OF CONSTRUCTING THE MODEL'S PROTOTYPE

The current research leads to the implementation of the proposed model and verification of its functionality by running various tests on the prototype.

It has been decided that the models of all the subsystems will be implemented in Java as JavaBeans modules. The convincing argument here is the richness of resources that Java has to offer for developers of agent-based [8] and network systems as well as a possibility of uncomplicated and easy application of developed JavaBeans modules for creating further PA and ASS systems.

A preliminary selection for the technology and realisation platform for VMS interfaces has been made. It has been decided to test two options.

In the first option particular subsystems would be implemented as group of servelets ran at the Tomcat server [11].

In the second option the interface would be realised in EJB technology using one of the two OpenSource application servers: OpenEJB [12] or JBoss [13].

Databases containing DLD's lexicons and registers of the RAS subsystem will be managed and made accessible by OpenSource mySQL system [14].

Two methods for sending ORS between the agents have been selected.

Because the model does not impose any implementation requirements the agent systems may be realised in different technologies (the VMS system is heterogeneous in its principle). Thus, XML language and HTTP protocol, standard in such cases, have been chosen to realise the main channel of communication between agents.

When both communicating systems are implemented in Java, the object containing ORS can be sent between the agents (trough HTTP protocol) using the serialisation mechanism, thus simplifying and optimising communication process.

The progress of realisation of particular module prototypes varies. Semantic analysis module for queries in Polish natural language has been completed. It implements the SMMM method for the basic set of syntax elements that are parts of simple sentences in Polish language as well as ORSC method for ORS construction.

Domain lexicons for selected vocabulary in the area of queries to ophthalmology information databases have been also constructed. The preliminary tests run on the prototype confirmed usefulness of the proposed method of semantic analysis of queries in Polish natural language.

The works on the module generating sentences in Polish language based on ORS describing their meaning are being conducted. Algorithms for generating phrases that correspond to particular logical parts of a sentence are in the process of development and modification.

The works on the details of the model of VWS interface being the part of proxy agent are in the advanced stage.

Also, some projects aimed at creating ASS prototypes for chosen classes of services are on the way. During the first stage ASS's will be developed for:
- SQL and object-oriented (JDO standard) ophthalmologic databases,
- expert system with rule-based reasoning,
- car rental system.

The most advanced are the works on a system translating ORS into queries in SQL that is the basis of ASS serving the access to the SQL databases. Prototype of such a system is implemented almost in its entirety. The works on other ASS listed here are currently in the stage of creating detailed OSD subsystem models realising functions specific for given type of service.

4. CONCLUSION

The model of system of communication in natural language with computer systems that is presented here is based on results of research on the processes of semantic analysis and generation of sentences in Polish language, which can be used in a human-computer communication. Other formal aspects of natural language processing in a computer system such as a model of describing sentence semantics in the object-oriented form called ORS as well as a model of the process of translating ORS into SQL questions have been also researched. The developed solutions were implemented and verified in the prototype of a system translating database queries expressed in Polish natural language into queries expressed in SQL.

Tests run on the prototype show that the developed model can be successfully implemented into an autonomously operating multi-agent system. The further work will thus be directed at implementing the model in the form of a functional multi-agent prototype of a system of virtual market of services using the communication based on Polish natural language.

The issue of technical achievability of such a prototype has been described in section 3. The analysis of possibilities offered by modern technologies and standards such as EJB, servelets, or XML confirmed the achievability of a fully functional service systems as well as proxy agents.

The issue that must be still worked out is models of process of interpretation (or translation) of ORS of queries (orders) for different classes of service systems. Such models for selected systems are being currently worked on within the framework of master degree projects that are conducted under the academic guidance of this paper's authors.

Another problem is building of multi-agent systems for automated service realisation. There exist feasible solutions for some application classes. For relatively simple services such as sales transactions, renting cars, medical service for patients, which do not require the agent to apply advanced intelligence forms, there are working model examples [6, 7]. More complex applications require using negotiations rules and adapting agent's activity to the environment changes. That makes it necessary to create knowledge basis and to use learning and adaptations methods [9, 10].

The virtual market for services considered by the authors would contain not only such simple services as car rentals but also more complex ones. The services will be implemented in stages starting with the simple ones. However, the basic problem that should be solved right at the beginning, regardless of the class of service being performed by an ASS, is the implementation of a fully functional communication based on semantics description of sentences in natural language into an ASS.

5. REFERENCES

[1] Dobryjanowicz E. 1992. 'Wybrane metody analizy składniowej'. *Akademicka Oficyna Wydawnicza RM.* (in Polish)
[2] Mykowiecka A. 1992. 'Metody generowania tekstów'. *Akademicka Oficyna Wydawnicza RM.* (in Polish)
[3] Pechmann P. 2000. 'Syntax Analysis of Sentences in Polish Language with the Syntax Matrix Matching Method'. *Proceedings of the 7th International Conference "Advanced Computer Systems 2000"*
[4] Pałczyński M., Pechmann P. 2001. 'Constructing Object Representation Of Semantics For A Query In Polish Natural Language Using The ORSC Method'. *Proceedings of the 8th International Conference "Advanced Computer Systems 2001"*
[5] Gozdek M., Sołdek J. 2001. 'Heterogeniczna platforma agentowa zorientowana na zastosowanie agentów w organizacjach wirtualnych oparta na AgentBuilder'. *Materiały VI Sesji Naukowej Informatyki.* Szczecin, 67-75 (in Polish)
[6] Karacapilidis N., Moraitis P. 2001. 'Building an Agent-Mediated Electronic Commerce System with Decision Analysis Features'. *Decision Support Systems.* No. 32, 53-69
[7] Miranda P., Aquilar J. 2002. 'A Multiagent Telemedicine System'. *Applied Artificial Intelligence.* No. 16, 159-172
[8] Bigus J.P., Bigus J. 1998. 'Constructing Intelligent Agents with Java'. *John Wiley & Sons.*
[9] Ren Z., Anumba C.J., Ugwu O.O. 2002. 'Negotiation in a Multi-agent System for Construction Claims Negotiation'. *Applied Artificial Intelligence*, No. 16, 359-394
[10] Bonarini A. 2001. 'Evolutionary Learning, Reinforcement Learning and Fuzzy Rules for Knowledge Acquisition in Agent-Based Systems'. *Proceedings of the IEEE*, Vol. 89, No. 9, 1334-1346
[11] Tomcat server project: http://jakarta.apache.org/tomcat/
[12] OpenEJB project: http://openejb.sourceforge.net/
[13] JBoss project: http://www.jboss.org/
[14] mySQL project: http://www.mysql.com/

Models of Integration in Decision Support Systems

BOŻENA ŚMIAŁKOWSKA
Technical University of Szczecin, Faculty of Computer Science & Information System,
49 Żołnierska st., 71-210 Szczecin, Poland, e-mail: bsmialkowska@wi.ps.pl

Abstract: This article presents an overall characteristics of methods aiming at integration of enterprise's management information systems and decision support systems. The above overview has provided the base for demonstration of Author's own method ensuring higher degree information availability in decision process and management. The method presented is based on virtual data warehouse concept with a database of decision modelling methods and database of models.

Key words: Integration in management information system, data warehouse system, virtual data warehouse system, decision support system, DSS.

1. INTRODUCTION

Among numerous criteria and quality requirements of computer information systems employed in companies, enterprises or institutions, the basic one is to provide high grade information availability to system users. Ensuring high grade availability information at the level of supporting tactic or strategic decisions is not an easy task for information systems at an enterprise. One of the factors influencing the high grade information availability for the purposes of supporting tactic or strategic decision process is the integration of information systems. The integration of information systems employed in a company, enterprise or institution can be connected with necessity to apply many various information technology methods and techniques, concerning various application aspects and cases. Nowadays, we can speak about to called software-hardware platforms, forming a base for information systems in a company. On the other hand, the integration can refer to constructing of a common, functionally homologous database – then it is understood as so called data integration. When speaking about enterprise computerization, in most cases an integration is understood as consolidation of company's existing applications (programs, systems) into an individual consistent integrity. The most recent trend in integration for companies is so called business process integration.

Among the main reasons of integration lack in company's information systems are the following:
- no integration concept while implementing information systems in a company,
- technological variety of non- integrated systems, fundamental for company operation in terms of methods, tools, software-hardware, user systems, operating systems etc.,
- spatial distribution of applications and application related databases,
- variety of software tools (utilities) to run company's branch information systems,
- non-uniformity of standards applied in company's systems implementations,
- variety of end application user interfaces,
- applications produced in executive code, disabling any further modifications.

This article, beside presenting a review of methods and models of application integration for an arbitrary company, presents a new, Author's own method, model, integration concept for the purpose of building up decision support systems. The integration method presented can be successfully applied while constructing Execution Information Systems (EIS), Management Information Systems (MIS) or Knowledge Discovery in databases (KDD).

2. GENERAL CHARACTERISTICS OF DECISION SUPPORT SYSTEMS

The decision process usually requires an access to relevant data and information, at proper time and in a desired form to enable solutions of actual problems arising from organizing procedures, with respect to diversified complexity of the decisions, problems and tasks. Decision makers often make their decisions using special methods and models, starting from simple calculation models using computer calculation sheets, through optimal models and up to pareto- or sub-optimal models.

The data providing high information availability usually cover the process history, facts, events, organization states as well as predictions on future states of organisation and its external conditions.

Nowadays, the information on company's state is valuable while the costs of information report preparation, particularly in collective (aggregated) forms, or the current costs of system maintenance are very high. Those high costs are often unbearable without automation (in full or in part) of retrieval processes or report building processes, to generate more or less aggregated information reports.

Integration and knowledge constitute two particularly significant elements in decision processes where tactic or strategic decisions are concerned and the decisions are made in risk and uncertainty conditions, at determined or undetermined random circumstances, affecting the decisions to be made.

DSS systems require interactive access to data and models, which would enable to solve specific decisive situations although would not provide automatic solutions using only the computer itself. And in that circumstances the role of a user appears particularly essential; a user can interactively participate in creating model solutions to elaborate final decisions and ways of their accomplishment.

3. REVIEW OF INTEGRATION METHODS IN COMPANY'S INFORMATION SYSTEMS

The integration in management systems, execution information systems and decision support systems has been practically implemented at the levels of data and applications. The following methods should be distinguished:
- construction of integrated company's systems starting from beginning phase (data integration and application integration);
- construction of application bridges and special dedicated systems (application interaction without data integration or with data integration in part);
- distributed, federation or multidimensional database systems (data integration and partial application integration);
- data markets and warehouses (data integration and construction of dedicated applications for needs of company's decision makers and top management staff).

The examples of integration methods involving construction of special integrated systems from the beginning phase, are the implemented systems of MRP class or the same known as ERP class systems. Evolution of that class systems has proved that the construction of large integrated systems isn't that simple. Usually, such an undertaking involves high costs within a relatively long period of time in conditions of undefined variability of environment and variability of information technologies as well as variability in functions, mission, company's targets, management methods and administration. Practice confirms also that implementation of "large" systems appears more difficult, using other methods, often incurring additional costs due to the risks arising while accomplishing the undertakings. However, it does not mean that such a method of integration is ineffective if there are examples of correct implementation of MRP/ERP class systems, having been successfully implemented and used.

Nevertheless, not all the companies can afford (in term of costs and time) such a way of information system integration.

The attempts of company's information system integration for the purposes of management, decision support and administration of the company using the method of construction the bridges among existing company's systems, have proved to give effective results in certain individual cases. However, method of bridge constructing disables to use model principles, versatility, standardisation or unification. An interesting example among the above integration method conceptions is J. Ochman's concept or J. Becker's design [1]. Both the designs concern integration at the level of problem subsystems and partial registration subsystems.

However, in case a company, due to various reasons, has not built up an integrated system providing function integration, using any of the two method described above, the company usually tried to provide data integration using

database technologies. Database system integration (distributed, federation or multi-dimensional databases) does not guarantee total integration, particularly in terms of application integration. It often appeared that the management and tactic or strategic decision support is difficult due to the following:
- diversified software-hardware environments used to build up transaction (operation) related information systems;
- application of diversified database management systems;
- implementation of diversified data models in operating (traditional, transaction or subject oriented) databases;
- creation of company's subject oriented database (opersting) systems in different periods of company's life;
- employing diversified technologies in subject oriented systems, e.g. certain subject oriented systems (such as payroll system, production reconsillation system, inventory registration & management system, fixed assets system, etc.) were designed using old technologies while other systems used later technologies.

Additionally, the implementation of federation, distributed or multidimensional databases requires (induce) high investment and organization arrangements to construct such systems. In many cases the construction of federation, distributed or multidimensional databases is impossible, since their main existing databases, to be subject to integration, operate on old inefficient utility and technologies usually insufficiently documented.

New designs basing on new database technologies can induce additional interference to systems used before. Implementation of the innovative integrating solutions is not typical as well. It requires large commitment in term of both the methodical approach and practical actions not only from computer staff but also existing (from before integration) database users. Similarly as in case of bridge construction method the solutions based on database system integration method exclude standardisation, unification or simple transfer.

The latest integration method addressed to management, administration and decision support systems is the method based on construction of so called data markets or data warehouses.

A data warehouse should contain pure, verified and properly aggregated data. The data purity denotes that the same data are recorded with one and only one method. Usually, the transaction systems based on operating database systems, being used to construct the data warehouses on, make use of different data record forms. For example, an subject oriented (operating) database system can use symbols K and M to denote sex while the other systems can use symbols 0 and X or 0 and 1.

When the elementary data from the operating database system is recorded (transferred) to a data warehouse it is aggregated in such a way that in the data warehouse it is referred to in one and only one way. The data stored in a data warehouse have to be correct. The errors appearing in operating databases remain there until certain external corrective actions occur (eg. storno document in financial – accounting system). Similarly as in databases, the data warehouses can contain incomplete information. Special procedures are necessary to ensure that the data being recorded to a data warehouse have been verified, corrected and up-dated. The information available from an operating database has to be correct at the moment it is accessed. The case of a data warehouse is different. The information in the data warehouse is appropriate at a certain moment however not necessarily immediately. In most cases the information is entirely appropriate (correct) at the time it is being stored in the data warehouse. The time horizon of data maintained in data warehouses is usually 5 up to 10 years. In case of the operating databases the time horizon typically covers 60-90 days. In a data warehouse the data are arranged in such a way that a data reference key always contains a time unit (e.g. day, week, etc). Moreover, the information once has been correctly recorded in data warehouse, it cannot be updated. The data in operating databases are not necessarily maintained on the same medium. On the other hand, the data warehouse software provides each data user accessible through the data warehouse can be retrieved in identical form and using identical method. It should be noticed that a key problem to be solved while designing a data warehouse is an appropriate "granularity" of data, determining the data particulars. Selection of the appropriate granulity is connected with selection of an appropriate time chronon (basic unit – the smallest) since time is the main information dimension in both the decision process and the data warehouse. The source data stored in operating (subject oriented) systems are usually the most detailed data while the data warehouse should provide access to history data and aggregated data. It is necessary to design such a data warehouse where the data are aggregated properly and adequately to the needs of users. If the transfer, transformation, aggregation and up-dating of data in a data warehouse are performed correctly the users may concentrate on data usage but not their reliability or compatibility. Nowadays, the integrated decision support system and company's strategy management are designed not only on base of data warehouse technology as that.

The other information technologies interconnected one with another and with the data warehouse, are employed additionally, e.g.:
- data processing methods, reporting and result presentation methods as well as On-line Analytical Processing (OLAP), ROLAP (relational OLAP), MOLAP (multidimensional OLAP), HOLAP (Hybrid data OLAP) or DOLAP (desktop OLAP), etc. [4];
- specialized query languages for data warehouses, where besides the typical queries to database also the queries with fuzzy index values would be possible;
- methods of information retrieval through data penetration, i.e. data-drilling based on drill-down analysis, drill-up analysis or slicing & dicing analysis;
- methods of knowledge retrieval from data (data mining).

The methods of data processing and query languages are necessary elements of user's commands to be accomplished within information system, most often on interactive basis, instructing the system to perform calculation, analysis, forecasts or presentations inevitable in decision process.

The data warehouses allow their users to retrieve the essential and needed information, from larger or smaller or more or less chaotic data collection at the time the information is necessary, as well as in form convenient for analysis (e.g. synthetical-analytical info, graphical presentation, forecast info, etc.) despite source information involved in results comes from different sources, in different format, various time granulity, etc. The data retrieved and discovery from data warehouse and presented to users or decision makers are most often of multidimensional character, dependant on many facts and many various dimensions.

The facts and dimensions, usually described with their attributes arranged in arrays, form a data model of the scheme compatible with a non-normalized relational, hierarchical, multidimensional model or star, cube or snow-flake model [2], [3], [4]. Those models provide a relatively fart data access and data aggregation meeting user's needs.

However, the practical applications of the datawarehouse systems are not free from defects. In fact, only such solutions are implemented where the data warehouses with a fixed (stiff) defined (global and aggregated) data model can be used to integrate data in a coherent entirety only on base of the structures and sources feeding the data warehouses (operating databases), without considering methods variable in time or strategic management models or the methods of acquiring the knowledge on risks to be taken, methods of solution finding basing only on event history. An essential task of integrated data warehouse system it to provide the users with simulation of potentially possible cases and variants of solutions in strategy selection process. Moreover, to enable them to find the best possible decisions, often through learning process while operating the data warehouse system.

A data warehouse system or virtual data warehouse system [5] seems the method providing better solution of information feeder in strategic decision process. The data warehouse or virtual data warehouse fed with results from tests based on decision models taken from a repository database containing methods and models describing company's strategy management. The new method concept has been presented in the following paragraph of this article.

4. MODEL OF DECISION SUPPORT SYSTEM WITH VIRTUAL DATA WAREHOUSE AND DATABASE OF METHODS AND MODELS

The majority of data contained in a data warehouse, as pointed out in related publications [2], [3], [4] and [5], is the information transferred from operating databases. The data inserted to a data warehouse can be the virtual data (i.e. the data not necessarily reflecting the actual company's activity states), coming from analysis carried out, simulations, result forecasts, learning process, etc.

The company's strategy can change in time so the virtual data warehouse should enable modification of information structure (structure dynamics), modification of methods (e.q. rationality calculation) and models (criteria dynamics, model structure dynamics, decision support information retrieval method dynamics).

Therefore, to provide full integration there should be possible to store additional data in a data warehouse, being the results of:
- model calculations, simulations, modelling and model testing;
- benchmarks;

- analysis of successive decision process steps;
- forecasts and analysis necessary for various methods of company's operation improvement and management methods;
- information on data structures at the arbitrary data hierarchy levels (metadata changeable in time), including features enabling structure adaptation to current information needs of a user.

Such an "expanded" data warehouse is usually called [5] a virtual data warehouse. It is not only a system integrated with operating databases but a system containing the knowledge acquired during construction, creation, testing and application of models in strategic or tactic decision process.

The main elements of an integrated information system (incorporating knowledge items) as described above, supporting the management process, in particular at the strategic management level, are the following:
- modelling methods concerning construction, verification, simulation, optimisation and application of mathematical models, econometric models or other models;
- methods of information retrieval and presentation as well as methods of knowledge extraction;
- methods of modelling result materialization (permanent, virtual or temporary "storing");
- repository of methods and models, supporting the company's strategic and tactic management;
- data warehouse or virtual data warehouse;
- virtual facts, dimensions and attributes (database of modelling results) being subject to materialization (storing, recording) in a data warehouse; the data collected during learning process and knowledge attainment by a decision maker/user;
- operating (subject oriented) databases, including the incorporated data scheme;
- methods of transfer, conversion, transposition, and aggregation of data from operating database systems.

The interconnection among the elements has been presented in graph form in Fig. 1.

The main elements of an integrated system presented above, besides the typical components of data warehouse systems, is an additional repository (database) of company's strategy management models and the modelling methods. The additional elements should enable such procedures to follow that the mapping of certain reality or ideas – user's ideas – would be accomplished. The procedures can be supported with information collecting and knowledge collecting, concerning the reality and reality element functions.

The models of company's management at tactic and strategy levels have been the subject of numerous research and scientific works, worth mentioning here. One of the most popular model classes are the econometric balance models or optimisation models, usually operating on numerous criteria and restrictions imposed by balance models as well as defined quantitative or fuzzy criteria and restrictions. One of the model groups is a group of system expansion models. They are so called prediction models simulating system's behaviour for the time $t = K + 1$, basing on observation set for moments $t = 1, 2, ..., K$. Furthermore, the examples of such models are the geometric expansion models, herd models, expotential growth models, etc. Additionally, when the criteria, balance equations or restraints of static models are changed to other static or dynamic characteristics, the strategy selection can be made also using the optimisation models, sub-optimisation models, pareto-optimisation models or dynamic models.

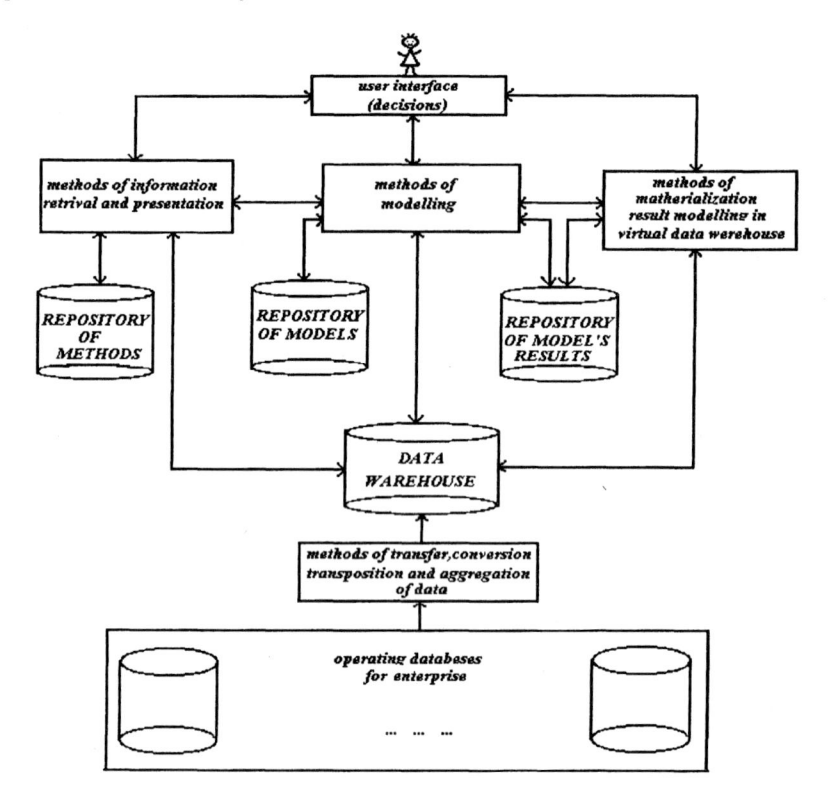

Fig. 1. DSS system concept, company's strategic decision support system with data warehouse.

A model allows a user to make his/her decisions repeatedly, duplicable, giving a single solution or recommending a certain set of decisions, and so on. Full classification of models possibly contained in model repository (database) exceeds the frames of this article and the above discussion in only illustration of a problem of model selection possibilities for the purposes of company's strategy management. The major feature of the integration concept presented herein is the application of object oriented technologies, knowledge collecting and adaptation of (virtual) data warehouse features to meet the information needs in range of company's strategy management issues in time near to the real-time approach. A base for adaptation method is the existence of special class of objects – models under symbolic name models_ strategies_ type (each model from the model database belongs directly or indirectly to that object class).

The methods of that class, using polymorphism feature, provide the universal functions determining the real-time demand for information from data warehouse or virtual data warehouse (e.g. get_ parameters method) and delivering information necessary to feed the strategy management models selected by the user. The calculation models selected interactively by the user, where the said models are the sub-classes of models_ strategies_ type class, basing on the data from (virtual) data warehouse can subsequently feed the same data warehouse with information – the knowledge attained from management models – on base of feedback feeding. Moreover, the said models can record facts and virtual dimensions to the data warehouse (e. g. methods: *save_ virtual_ fact*, used to store the facts attained from a model or *save_ virtual_ dim*, used to store information in form of dimensions of a data warehouse concerned). The virtual facts and dimensions stored in a data warehouse (defined with corresponding rules as the facts and dimensions in the data warehouse) can be used by users depending on their needs as well as materialized (using special methods: *material_ fact* or *material_ dim*). The data (facts or dimensions) having been materialized are further on recognised in the data warehouse in the same way as all other facts or dimensions, i.e. stored there through the data transfer from operating databases. In that case the data warehouse, in fact the virtual data warehouse, would store the virtual facts and dimensions besides the basic facts and dimensions of data warehouse.

The virtual facts and dimensions would be the basis in the supporting process of decisions based on decisive modelling.

5. PREREQUISITES FOR DSS SYSTEM INTEGRATION WITH DATA WAREHOUSE

The main requirement for integration of DSS system with a data warehouse, in the method presented herein, is a positive balance of demand coverage at the moment a user requires for, in range – of information required by methods of modelling the facts, dimensions, states, events and processes occurring in the company, using the features and functions of information retrieval from virtual data warehouse.

The above condition can be expressed with the following formula:

$$\forall_M \forall_{t \in \Re} P_M(t) \subseteq I_{HD}(t) \tag{1}$$

where:
M – an arbitrary model in modelling process;
$P_M(t)$ – information demand for model M at time moment t;
$I_{H,D}(t)$ – possibility to receive information at time t for model M;
$\Re$ – real numbers set.

It is also possible to define the integrity condition for decision support system in more general form, as follows:

$$\forall_M \forall_{t \in \Re} \ \mu(I_{HD}(t)) - \mu(P_M(t)) \geq 0 \tag{2}$$

where: μ – additional parameter denoting the unit of information demanded and attainable in modelling process.

6. SUMMARY

The method presented in this article is an integrated model where a user – decision maker has not only the typical information retrieval mechanisms offered by data warehouse available, but additionally the following:
- to verify current and future states of the company in an interactive way, making use of a great variety of models for prediction, verification or planning as well as decisive modelling;
- to materialize model solutions in virtual data warehouse if the model solutions require so and a user finds them promising in the process of making or verifying the decision.

The materialization of modelling results enables to feed and enrich the virtual data warehouse, at user's discretion. Moreover, the users enrich their knowledge with potential after effects of their decisions that might be made on base of decisive modelling or situational modelling process. The concept presented is then the concept of integrated and flexible and user-need-adaptable system at the level of strategic decisions of global significance.

The system presented has been based on an open approach concept, providing the possibilities to supplement the database of methods and models with new methods and models as soon as the latter have been included in the decision process or have been developed or have had their applicability rules defined.

7. REFERENCES

[1] Becker J. 2002. 'Integracja danych w systemie rachunkowości transakcyjnej'. *Rozprawa doktorska. Politechnika Szczecińska, Szczecin*
[2] Poe V., Klauer P., Brobst S. 2000. ' Tworzenie hurtowni danych'. *WNT, Warszawa*
[3] Sturm J. 2000. 'Hurtownia danych Microsoft SQL Serwer 7.0. Przewodnik techniczny.' *Microsoft Press, Warszawa*
[4] Śmiałkowska B. 2001. 'Effective methods of temporal data representation in data warehouse systems'. *Advance Computer System,* Kluwer Academic Publishers
[5] Śmiałkowska B. 2002. 'Metoda adaptacyjnego zarządzania strategią firmy z zastosowaniem wirtualnej hurtowni danych'. *Prace IBS PAN, Warszawa*
[6] Bazewicz M. 1993. 'Wstęp do systemów informatycznych i reprezentacji wiedzy'. *Wrocław AE*

Object Classification and Recognition using Toeplitz Matrices

KHALID SAEED
Faculty of Computer Science, Bialystok University of Technology,
Wiejska 45A, 15-351 Bialystok, Poland, 1 e-mail: aidabt@ii.pb.bialystok.pl

Abstract: A new object-classifying algorithm is presented in this paper. The algorithm is based on the theory of Toeplitz matrices and their characteristic minimal eigenvalues. The derived Toeplitz forms are applied to verify the projected views of the given images for recognition. Experiments are carried out for some selected standard letters of twelve different font styles. The results are good and encouraging for algorithm extension to apply on other applications like handwritten script, spoken-letter image and varieties of geometrical patterns including views of three dimensional objects for the sake of classification and recognition.

Key words: Object Feature Extract; Classification; Recognition.

1. INTRODUCTION

Despite many efforts to solve the problem of object recognition [1,2,3,4,5,6], there still are no perfect solutions. The aim of this work is to show a new way of feature description and classification. This new approach presents an extension and combination of the works in [1,2]. The percentage of error in the process of classification is maximally reduced. A number of experiments were carried out on scripts as examples of simple objects [7]. However, the possible applications of the theory are not limited to this particular case. There are experiments on recognizing entire words [8] and other kinds of geometrical shapes [9,10]. Also there are current applications on speech analysis and recognition [11,12]. The newness in the work of this paper is the combination of both theories, namely, the applications of Toeplitz matrices [1] and the basic ideas of projection approach [2]. Moreover, the object feature points, forming the input data to Toeplitz forms, are extracted in a completely new way. This is done by considering the views of the object image in its two-dimensional shape. The views are either top and down or right and left, or sometimes both, as far as it is necessary. Then the image description is evaluated either through the Cartesian *x* and *y* coordinates, or by the polar form. Both representations give the possibility of forming a rational function. The polar form is beyond the aim of this paper and is considered in [12]. When considering the Cartesian representation, the numerator polynomial will have its coefficients defined by the *x*-coordinates, while the denominator polynomial coefficients are taken from the *y*-coordinates. Then the rational function is expanded into its Taylor series, whose coefficients form the basic elements of Toeplitz matrices. The main research steps of the whole theory had been published, among others, in [1,9,13,14] while the theory together with its current application for the view-based classification is given here for the first time in its extended version after presenting the simulation of the theory with the given below examples in [7]. Before considering these examples, let us have a general idea about the mathematical part of the algorithmic model.

2. THEORETICAL ASPECTS

According to the method given in [14], examined object-features are described by the following rational function:

$$H(s) = \frac{P(s)}{Q(s)} \qquad (1)$$

where *P(s)* and *Q(s)* are *n*-degree polynomials in the complex variable *s* whose coefficients are the coordinates of the feature points, which are treated as pairs of complex numbers $s_i = x_i + jy_i$ with $i = 1, 2, 3..., n$, *n* being the number of points considered. Therefore,

$$H(s) = \frac{x_0 + x_1 s + x_2 s^2 + ... + x_n s^n}{y_0 + y_1 s + y_2 s^2 + ... + y_n s^n} \qquad (2)$$

Then the following bilinear transformation is applied:

$$s = \frac{1-z}{1+z} \qquad (3)$$

resulting in another rational function *H(z)*.

In the next step the coefficients of Taylor's series for *H(z)* are calculated and used to create Toeplitz matrices. Determinants of these matrices are formed to calculate minimal eigenvalues.

Taylor series:

$$T(z) = c_0 + c_1 z + c_2 z^2 + \ldots + c_n z^n + \ldots \qquad (4)$$

where

$$c_i = \frac{1}{x_0^{i+1}} \begin{vmatrix} y_i & x_1 & x_2 & \ldots & x_i \\ y_{i-1} & x_0 & x_1 & \ldots & x_{i-1} \\ y_{i-2} & 0 & x_0 & \ldots & x_{i-2} \\ y_{i-3} & 0 & 0 & \ldots & \ldots \\ \ldots & \ldots & \ldots & \ldots & x_1 \\ y_0 & 0 & 0 & \ldots & x_0 \end{vmatrix} \qquad (5)$$

for $i = 0, 1, 2, \ldots, n$.

The determinants of Toeplitz matrices are evaluated from the coefficients of Taylor series. They have the following form:

$$D_i = \begin{vmatrix} c_0 & c_1 & c_2 & \ldots & c_i \\ c_1 & c_0 & c_1 & \ldots & c_{i-1} \\ c_2 & c_1 & c_0 & \ldots & c_{i-2} \\ \ldots & \ldots & \ldots & \ldots & \ldots \\ c_i & c_{i-1} & c_{i-2} & \ldots & c_0 \end{vmatrix}, \quad i = 0, 1, 2, \ldots, n \qquad (6)$$

From the minimal eigenvalues and let $\lambda_{\min}\{D_i\} = \lambda_{\min_i} = \lambda_i$ for i = 0, 1, 2, ..., n. Then the following feature vector is evaluated:

$$V = (\lambda_0, \lambda_1, \lambda_2, \ldots, \lambda_n) \qquad (7)$$

Eq.(7) presents the input data passed to the calculating algorithms for next evaluation and graph representation for the sake of comparison and hence recognition. The characteristic behavior of this equation lies in the fact, that it forms a monotonically non-increasing series whose limit has something common with the minimal value of the rational function in Eq.(2) with $s = jy$. Here, we are interested in the curve behavior for object description, while the series limit approached when the condition $|\lambda_i - \lambda_{i+1}| \leq \varepsilon$ is satisfied, is of most significant and essential meaning, but in other applications [10,14].

3. ALGORITHMS AND EXPERIMENTS

The algorithm starts with imaging or bitmapping the object two-dimensional image. The first step is to choose the characteristic points. To accomplish this goal, top and down views are evaluated. The view is a set of pixels that belong to the character contour and have a coordinate *y* for a given coordinate *x*, forming a pair of numbers simply represented by the complex number $s_i = x_i + jy_i$, as defined above.

As an example describing the shape of an object, consider three handwritten capital letters viewed according to the algorithm (Fig. 1).

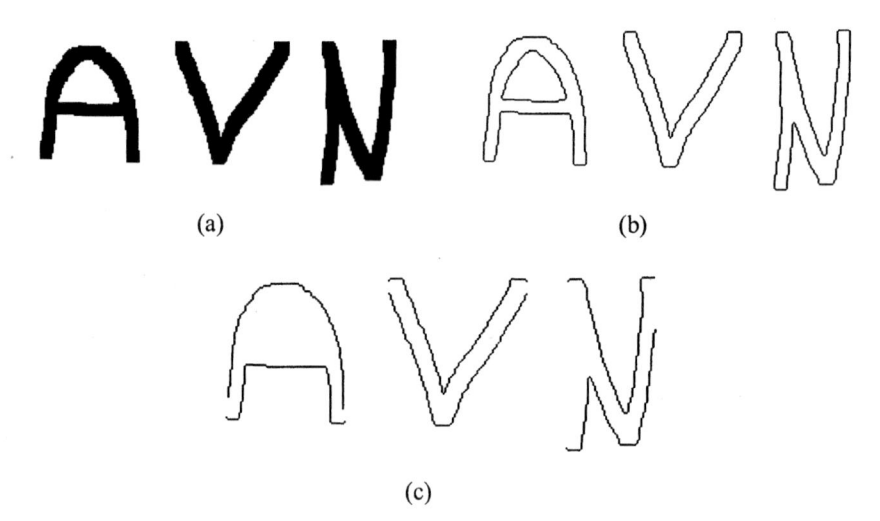

Fig. 1. Concept of views. (a) Hypothetical handwritten letters, (b) the same letters thinned to contour, (c) their top and down views

Next, after choosing the characteristic points from views, the distances of these points from upper side of surrounding rectangle are calculated. The sequence formed from such values is a description of the view and is used to construct the rational function *H(s)* in *Eq.* (2). In addition, *x* coordinates of projected points are included.

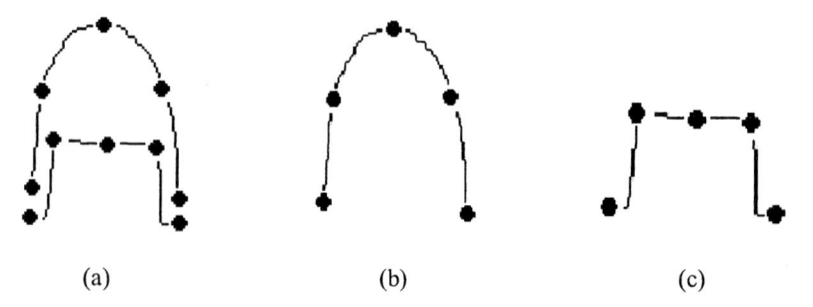

Fig. 2. Projection of characteristic points of the letter A: (a) both views, (b) top and (c) down.

Figure 2 shows how the projection of characteristic points is done. For the upper (top) view, the result is the following vector:

$$(y_1^U, y_2^U, y_3^U, y_4^U, y_5^U) \qquad (8)$$

where y_i^U are the distances of the top view point, which have coordinates given by $x = x_i$, $i = 1,2,3, ..., n$ from the upper side of the surrounding rectangle.

Similarly, for the down view:

$$(y_1^D, y_2^D, y_3^D, y_4^D, y_5^D) \qquad (9)$$

where y_i^D are the distances of down view points, which have coordinates given by $y = y_i$, $i = 1,2,3, ..., n$ from the upper side of surrounding rectangle.

A method of choosing characteristic points and their values may vary. In our experiments we used five points (n = 5) equally spaced on the x axis.

After calculating distance vectors, we can move to build the rational function $H(s)$.

Experiments were carried out for different ways of evaluating the rational function $H(s)$, they are:

(1) Polynomial $Q(s)$ is formed using y_i distance vector constructed from the upper and down views, $P(s)$ is formed from the vector of x values:

$$H_U(s) = \frac{x_0 + x_1 s + x_2 s^2 + ... + x_n s^n}{y_0^U + y_1^U s + y_2^U s^2 + ... + y_n^U s^n} \qquad (10)$$

$$H_D(s) = \frac{x_0 + x_1 s + x_2 s^2 + ... + x_n s^n}{y_0^D + y_1^D s + y_2^D s^2 + ... + y_n^D s^n} \qquad (11)$$

(2) Polynomial $P(s)$ is formed using also y_i distance vector evaluated for the upper and down views, while $Q(s)$ is formed from the vector containing x values:

$$H_U(s) = \frac{y_0^U + y_1^U s + y_2^U s^2 + ... + y_n^U s^n}{x_0 + x_1 s + x_2 s^2 + ... + x_n s^n} \qquad (12)$$

$$H_D(s) = \frac{y_0^D + y_1^D s + y_2^D s^2 + ... + y_n^D s^n}{x_0 + x_1 s + x_2 s^2 + ... + x_n s^n} \qquad (13)$$

(3) Polynomial *P(s)* is formed using y_i distance vector evaluated from the down view, *Q(s)* is formed using y_i distance vector evaluated for the top view:

$$H(s) = \frac{y_0^D + y_1^D s + y_2^D s^2 + \ldots + y_n^D s^n}{y_0^U + y_1^U s + y_2^U s^2 + \ldots + y_n^U s^n} \quad (14)$$

as a result we get one function describing the whole letter.

(4) Polynomial *Q(s)* is formed using y_i distance vector evaluated from the down view, *P(s)* is formed using y_i distance vector evaluated from the top view:

$$H(s) = \frac{y_0^U + y_1^U s + y_2^U s^2 + \ldots + y_n^U s^n}{y_0^D + y_1^D s + y_2^D s^2 + \ldots + y_n^D s^n} \quad (15)$$

Then, according to the theory in [1,14], the feature vector is calculated and used in classification process.

4. RESULTS

Experiments were carried out for letters *A*, *V*, *N* and *O* written using twelve different font styles. Five characteristic points were projected from both views. For each letter the 30-degree Taylor series was calculated, which gave 30-element feature vector. The following graphs present eigenvalues for all letters taking 6 curves of each one. The first one shows results achieved by applying rational function in *Eq.*(10).

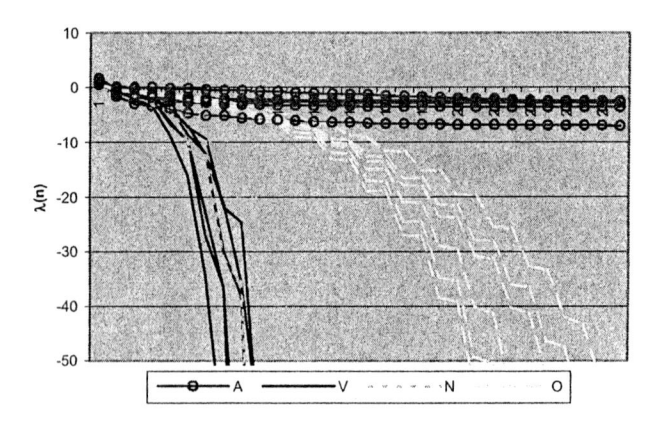

Fig. 3. The graph of minimal eigenvalues for the rational function in *Eq.*(10).

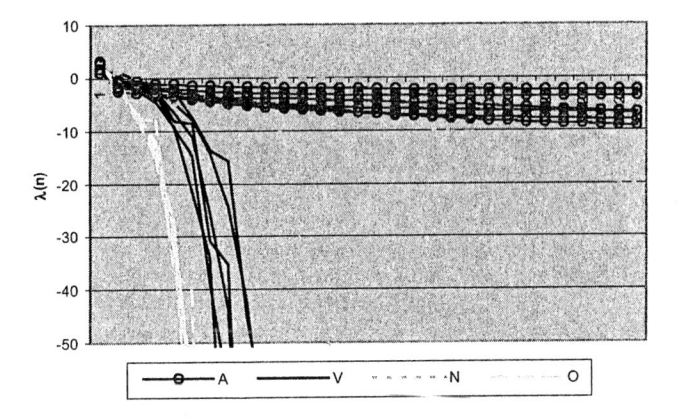

Fig. 4. The graph of minimal eigenvalues for the rational function in *Eq.*(11).

As can be seen from the above graphs, the feature vectors (minimal eigenvalues vectors) can be easily distinguished. The fact, that characteristics of *N* and *V* for the top view, *V* and *O* or *A* and *N* for the down view overlap, isn't crucial, because for classification purpose, vectors from both views are used, which allow us to recognize them. Besides, this effect is easy to understand. For example, characteristics of top views of letters *N* and *V* are almost the same, so the results should be similar.

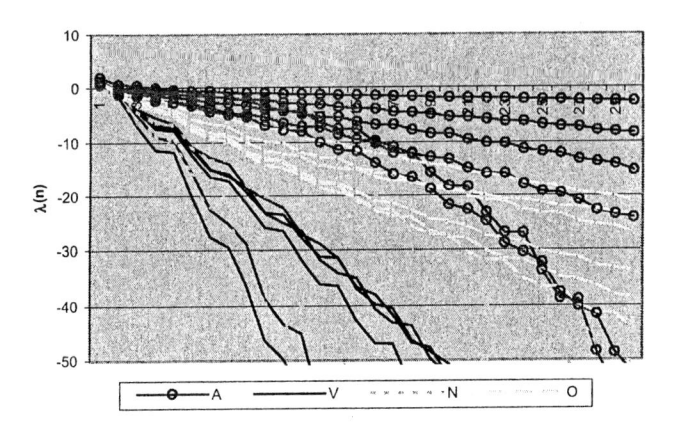

Fig. 5. The graph of minimal eigenvalues for the rational function in *Eq.*(12).

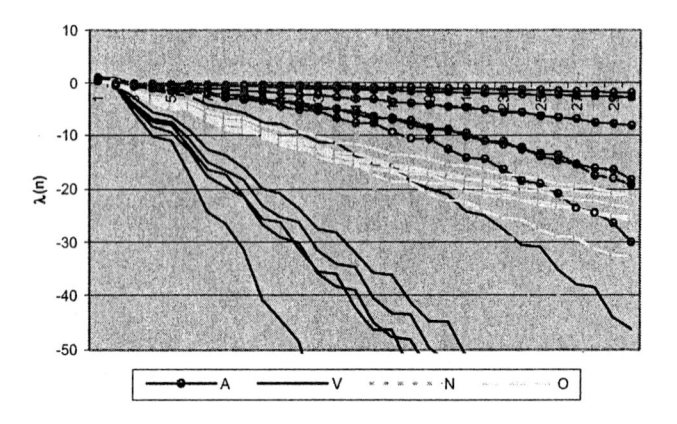

Fig. 6. The graph of minimal eigenvalues for the rational function in *Eq.*(13).

The results presented in Fig. 5 and Fig. 6 aren't as good as the previous ones in Fig. 3 and 4. The effect of overlapping is greater and the characteristics for single character aren't concentrated. However, they are grouping in clusters so they can also be separated.

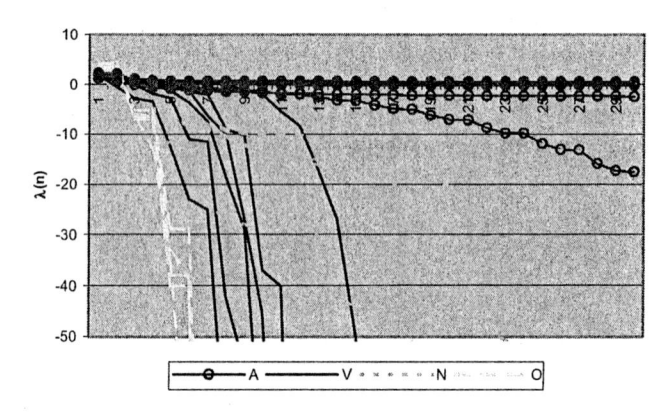

Fig. 7. The graph of minimal eigenvalues for the rational function in *Eq.*(14).

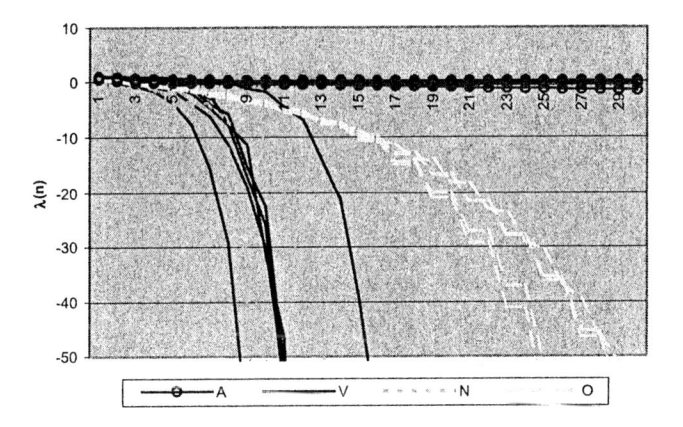

Fig. 8. The graph of minimal eigenvalues for the rational function in *Eq.*(15).

5. CONCLUSIONS AND FUTURE PLANS

The results are good and encouraging to further work. The author's research group has done more experiments on other letters. Some of the letters cannot be recognized by tracing only top and down views (for example, *E* and *Z*) – that is why we are analyzing the left and right views, as well. The next future work step is to test the approach on distorted characters, other languages scripts and spoken letters. In fact, continuous research has been provided on the possible application of the theory of Toeplitz forms and projection approaches and methods in object verification [10] and speech recognition [11,12]. The practical results proved the high efficiency of the method and the Toeplitz-based approach for object classification and recognition. A general comparison with some other known methods [3,4,5,6,15] showed that the algorithm is as good as a number of them, but still more practical and faster in realization than some of them.

6. ACKNOWLEDGEMENT

This work was supported by the Rector of Bialystok University of Technology (grant number W/II/3/01). The author would like to thank his assistants Marcin Adamski and Marek Tabędzki who had helped in the computer implementation.

7. REFERENCES

[1] K. Saeed, "Computer Graphics Analysis: A Criterion for Image Feature Extraction and Recognition." Volume 10, Issue 2, 2001, pp. 185-194, MGV - International Journal on Machine Graphics and Vision, Institute of Computer Science, Polish Academy of Sciences, Warsaw.
[2] K. Saeed, "A Projection Approach for Arabic Handwritten Characters Recognition," New Trends and Approaches in Computational Intelligence, Springer-Verlag, Kosice, Slovakia 2000.
[3] M. Ghuwar, "Modeling and Recognition of Arabic Scripts, " Ph.D. Thesis, Institute of Computer Science, Polish Academy of Sciences, Warsaw, 1997.
[4] D. Burr, "Experiments on Neural Net Recognition of Spoken and Written Text, " IEEE Transactions on Acoustics, Speech, and Signal Proc., Vol.36, No.7, July 1988.
[5] M. Dehgham, K. Faez, "Handwritten Farsi Character Recognition Using Evolutionary Fuzzy Clustering, " Proceedings of Eusipco'98, 9th European Signal Processing Conference, Sep. 8-11, pp. 423-426, Rhodes, Greece 1998.
[6] P. Zabawa,"Automatic Recognition of Handwritten Letters Based on The Parsing of Indexed Graphs," Monograph 172, Technical University of Cracow, Cracow 1994.
[7] K. Saeed, M. Tabędzki, M. Adamski, "A New Approach for Object-Feature Extract and Recognition," 9th International Conference on Advanced Computer Systems – ACS'02, pp.389-397, 23-25 October, Miedzyzdroje 2002.
[8] I. Andruszkiewicz, "Experimental Algorithm on Polish Hand-written Scripts Retrieving," MSc Thesis, Faculty of Computer Science, Bialystok University of Technology, Bialystok 2002.
[9] K. Saeed, "Efficient Method for On-Line Signature Verification," Proceedings of the International Conference on Computer Vision and Graphics - ICCVG'02, Volume 2, 25-29 September, Zakopane, 2002.
[10] K. Saeed, "A New Approach in Image Classification," Accepted for publication and presentation in Proc. 5th International Conference on Digital Signal Processing and its Applications – IEEE/DSPA'03, Moscow 2003.
[11] K. Saeed, M. Kozłowski, A. Kaczanowski, "Metoda do Rozpoznawania Obrazów Akustycznych Izolowanych Liter Mowy," Zeszyty Politechniki Białostockiej, I-1/2002, pp.181-207, Białystok 2002.
[12] K. Saeed, "A Toeplitz-Matrix-Based System for Spoken-Letter Recognition," 10th CAIP Int. Conference on Computer Analysis of Images and Patterns, 25-27 August, Groningen 2003.
[13] K. Saeed, A. Dardzinska, "Language Processing: Word Recognition without Segmentation," JASIST - Journal of the American Society for Information Science and Technology, Volume 52, Issue 14, 2001, pp. 1275-1279, John Wiley and Sons.
[14] K. Saeed, "On The Realization of Digital Filters," Proc. The 1st International Conference on Digital Signal Processing and its Applications – IEEE/DSPA'98, Vol. I, pp. 141-143, Moscow, 1998.
[15] Vel, O. de, S. Aeberhard, "Object Recognition Using Random Image-Lines," Proc. of Image and Vision Computing, Volume 18, pp. 193-198, Elsevier 2000.

Chapter 2

Computer Security and Safety

A Propositional Logic for Access Control Policy in Distributed Systems

MIROSŁAW KURKOWSKI[1], JERZY PEJAŚ[2]

[1] *Institute of Mathematics & Computer Science, Pedagogical University of Częstochowa, Al. Armii Krajowej 13/15, 42-200 Częstochowa, Poland, phone, fax (+48 14) 3612269, e-mail: m.kurkowski@wsp.czest.pl*
[2] *Faculty of Computer Science & Information Systems, Department of Programming Techniques, Technical University of Szczecin, 49, Żołnierska st., 71-210 Szczecin, Poland, phone (+48 91) 4495662, fax. +4891 4876439, e-mail: jerzy.pejas@wi.ps.pl*

Abstract: The goal of this paper is to pursue a proposal of the logic-based model for interpreting the basic events and properties of the distributed access control systems. We provide a convenient formal language, an axiomatic inference system, a model of computation, and semantics. We prove some important properties of this logic and show how our logical language can express some access control policies proposed so far.

Key words: access control, security policy, logic-based security model, public key certificate, attribute certificate, public key infrastructure

1. INTRODUCTION

Access control is a key issue for the security of distributed systems and plays an important role in the security of many organizations (Massacci [MAS97]). To guarantee the security of distributed systems many concerns need to be addressed. Among others authorization is the most important. The problem of authorization can be divided into two related subproblems: representations and evaluation. Representation refers to the specification of authorization requirements, while evaluation refers to the actual determination of the authorities of subjects, which the authorization requirements are given.

It is obvious that each distributed access control system should contain an information protection subsystem, which must be based on precisely defined mathematical models for controlling access to this information. In the paper we consider a new information protection model (security model) derived form a discretionary security model (see S. Castano, et al. [CFM94]). Our model provides a formal reasoning method for a discretionary model (we believe that also for other models, e.g. role based access control) and defines logic to express discretionary policies and finds a decision method, which can be used to verify in a direct, and automatic way the consistency or the logical consequences of an access policy.

The model defines a set of privileges, requests and properties, which allow eliminating the access matrix control (ACL) and define the local, decentralized access policy. This can be made because of introducing certificates (Pejas [Pej02]) that convey identity, use conditions and attributes. Such approach locates also our model into the category of certificate-based access control models (Herzberg, et al. [HMM00]). The certificate-based access control is aimed at specifying security policies for access to resources from untrusted sources, e.g. over the Internet. Trust has long been tied to authorization: *"Access control consists in deciding whether the agent that makes a statement is trusted on this statement; for example, a user may be trusted (hence obeyed) when he says that his files should be deleted."* (Abadi et al. [ABL93]).

On one hand certificates make the security model more flexible and usefull in distributed environment, but on the other it is difficult to answer the question whether some action are proper in our model. Hence a decision method is very important. This method, based on atomic formulas and the model of computation can be used for checking whether the access policy is consistent, or whether a particular desired property is a logical consequence of our model or not.

Recently, the work on logic-based access models and certificate-based authorization has been intensified. Formal reasoning techniques about security models and access policy specifications have been presented in Abadi [ABL93], Li, et al [LGF99], Bertino et al. [BFB99], Jajoda, et al. [JSS97], Massacci [MAS97]. These models are usually based on the modal logic and require people to be good logicians and cannot be automated in a simple way. The logic-based approaches are driven by the need to analyze the policy specification, but generally fail to directly map to an implementation and are not easily interpreted by humans.

Our main goal is to develop the logic and the formal language that can be used for building a security policy specification and for checking any computer system security. In this paper security is defined as an intrinsic system property. Intuitively, it means a system with total security to be a system that will not allow information flow between its users. Therefore, a system is said to be secure under a specific security policy if all of its operations confirm to an ideal secure system except those permitted in the security policy. We show how to express the basic security rules in our logic and how to authorize properly defined requests.

The logic we propose is power expressive and allows building and using the simple expressions even with qualifiers. Because of this our logic is atomic finite and has similar expressiveness as the first order logic. We believe that logic and decision methods based on such logic can be used in the design and verification phase of any access control systems.

2. SYNTAX

In this section we introduce the language of our logic. We give the construction of formulas, axiomatic inference system and basic syntactic concepts.

Definition 1. Let $S_P = \{P_U, P_1, P_2, ..., P_{n_P}\}$ be a set of symbols representing subject (principals, processes, computers, servers, etc.) in a computer network. The set S_P contains a distinguished special element P_U representing the super user.

Definition 2. Let $S_K = \{K_1, K_2, ..., K_{n_K}\}$ be a set of symbols representing asymmetric cryptographic keys.

Definition 3. Let $S_O = \{O_1, O_2, ..., O_{n_O}\}$ be a set of symbols representing objects in a computer network (for example files).

Definition 4. Let $S_T = \{T_{+K}, T_{-K}, T_{+A}, T_{-A}, T_{+T}, T_{-T}, T_{+R}, T_{-R}, T_{+P}, T_{-P}, T_{+O}, T_{-O}\}$ be a set of symbols representing privileges of subjects. This set S_T consists of the following privileges:

1) T_{+K} - of giving the subject an asymmetric cryptographic key,
2) T_{-K} - of taking from subject an asymmetric cryptographic key,
3) T_{+A} - of giving the subject an attribute,
4) T_{-A} - of taking from the subject an attribute,
5) T_{+T} - of giving the subject a privilege,
6) T_{-T} - of taking from the subject a privilege,
7) T_{+R} - of giving the subject an access right to the object,
8) T_{-R} - of taking from the subject an access right to the object,
9) T_{+P} - of creating a subject,
10) T_{-P} - of deleting a subject,
11) T_{+O} - of creating an object,
12) T_{-O} - of deleting an object.

Definition 5. Let $S_R = \{R_O, R_C, R_Z, R_D, R_W\}$ be a set of symbols representing access rights to the objects. The set S_T consists of the following access rights:

1) R_O - owner of an object,
2) R_C - reading an object,
3) R_Z - modifying an object,
4) R_D - writing an object,
5) R_W - executing an object.

Definition 6. Let $S_A = \{A_1, A_2, ..., A_{n_A}\}$ be a set of symbols representing subject's attributes.

We assume, that numbers $n_P, n_K, n_O, n_T, n_R, n_A$ are large enough to bound computer nets sizes. Furthermore, we see (like Bell, et al. [BLP74]) the creation/removal of the object/subject as activation/deactivation of the unused/used object/subject symbol.

Definition 7. Let $S = S_P \cup S_K \cup S_O \cup S_T \cup S_R \cup S_A$ be a set of primitive terms.

Definition 8. We introduce the following predicate symbols:

1) $GiveKey \subseteq S_P \times S_K \times S_Q \times S_K$,
2) $GiveAttrib \subseteq S_P \times S_K \times S_Q \times S_A$,
3) $GivePriv \subseteq S_P \times S_K \times S_Q \times S_T$,
4) $GiveRight \subseteq S_P \times S_K \times S_P \times S_O \times S_R$,
5) $GiveObRight \subseteq S_P \times S_K \times S_O \times S_R \times S_A$,
6) $Md \subseteq S_P \times S_K \times S_P \cup S_O$,
7) $TAwKey \subseteq S_P \times S_K \times S_Q \times S_K$,
8) $TAwAttrib \subseteq S_P \times S_K \times S_Q \times S_A$,
9) $TAwPriv \subseteq S_P \times S_K \times S_Q \times S_T$,
10) $TAwRight \subseteq S_P \times S_K \times S_P \times S_O \times S_R$,
11) $TAwObRight \subseteq S_P \times S_K \times S_O \times S_R \times S_A$,
12) $Del \subseteq S_P \times S_K \times S_P \cup S_O$.

We also define a set of formulas by induction. We first define Φ_{At} a set of atomic formulas. We also give intended interpretations of atomic formulas.

Definition 9. Let Φ_{At} be a smallest set such that:

1) If $P, Q \in S_P$ and $K_1, K_2 \in S_K$, then $GiveKey(P, K_1, Q, K_2) \in \Phi_{At}$. ($GiveKey(P, K_1, Q, K_2)$ is an atomic formula with the intended interpretation: *The subject P, possessing an asymmetric key K_1 gave the subject Q the key K_2. To give the key, automatically means issuing the key certificate. The certificate is valid until it is revoked.*)

2) If $P, Q \in S_P$, $K \in S_K$ and $A \in S_A$, then $GiveAttrib(P, K, Q, A) \in \Phi_{At}$. ($GiveAttrib(P, K, Q, A)$ is an atomic formula with the intended interpretation: *The subject P, possessing an asymmetric key K has given the subject Q the right to use the attribute A. To give this right, automatically means issuing the attribute certificate. The certificate is valid until it is revoked.*)

3) If $P, Q \in S_P$, $K \in S_K$ and $T \in S_T$, then $GivePriv(P, K, Q, T) \in \Phi_{At}$. ($GivePriv(P, K, Q, T)$ is an atomic formula with the intended interpretation: *The subject P, possessing an asymmetric key K has given the subject Q the right to use the privilege T. To give this privilege, automatically means issuing the certificate for this privilege. The certificate is valid until it is revoked.*)

4) If $P, Q \in S_P$, $K \in S_K$, $O \in S_O$ and $R \in S_R$, then $GiveRight(P, K, Q, O, R) \in \Phi_{At}$. ($GiveRight(P, K, Q, O, R)$ is an atomic formula with the intended interpretation: *The subject P, possessing an asymmetric key K has given the subject Q the access right R to the object O.*)

5) If $P \in S_P$, $K \in S_K$, $O \in S_O$, $R \in S_R$ and $A \in S_A$, then $GiveObRight(P, K, O, R, A) \in \Phi_{At}$. ($GiveObRight(P, K, O, R, A)$ is an atomic formula with the intended interpretation: *The subject P, possessing an asymmetric key K has stated that the condition of using the object O with the access right R was the possessing of the attribute A by any subject. The statement is valid until it is revoked.*)

6) If $P, Q \in S_P$, $K \in S_K$ and $O \in S_O$, then $Md(P, K, Q) \in \Phi_{At}$ and $Md(P, K, O) \in \Phi_{At}$. ($Md(P, K, Q) \subset \Phi_{At}$ and $Md(P, K, O) \in \Phi_{At}$ are atomic formulas with their intended interpretation: *The subject P, possessing an asymmetric key K has created the subject Q or the object O, respectively.*)

7) If $P, Q \in S_P$ and $K_1, K_2 \in S_K$, then $TAwKey(P, K_1, Q, K_2) \in \Phi_{At}$. ($TAwKey(P, K_1, Q, K_2)$ is an atomic formula with the intended interpretation: *The subject P, possessing an asymmetric key K_1 has revoked the key K_2 of the subject Q. The key revocation automatically means adding this key to the key revocation list.*)

8) If $P, Q \in S_P$, $K \in S_K$ and $A \in S_A$, then $TAwAttrib(P, K, Q, A) \in \Phi_{At}$. ($TAwAttrib(P, K, Q, A)$ is an atomic formula with the intended interpretation: *The subject P, possessing an asymmetric key K has taken from the subject Q the right to use the attribute A. To take away this rights, automatically means adding the attribute to the attribute revocation list.*)

9) If $P, Q \in S_P$, $K \in S_K$ and $T \in S_T$, then $TAwPriv(P, K, Q, T) \in \Phi_{At}$. ($TAwPriv(P, K, Q, T)$ is an atomic formula with the intended interpretation: *The subject P, possessing an asymmetric key K has taken from the subject Q the right to use the privilege T. To taking away this rights, automatically means adding the privilege to the privilege revocation list.*)

10) If $P, Q \in S_P$, $K \in S_K$, $O \in S_O$, and $R \in S_R$, then $TAwRight(P, K, Q, O, R) \in \Phi_{At}$. ($TAwRight(P, K, Q, O, R)$ is an atomic formula with the intended interpretation: *The subject P, possessing an asymmetric key K has taken from the subject Q the access right R to that object O.*)

11) If $P \in S_P$, $K \in S_K$, $O \in S_O$, $R \in S_R$ and $A \in S_A$, then $TAwObRight(P, K, O, R, A) \in \Phi_{At}$. ($TAwObRight(P, K, O, R, A)$ is an atomic formula with the intended interpretation: *The subject P, possessing an asymmetric key K has revoked the condition of using the object O with the access right R and the attribute A possessed by any subject.*

12) If $P, Q \in S_P$, $K \in S_K$ and $O \in S_O$, then $Del(P, K, Q) \in \Phi_{At}$ and $Del(P, K, O) \in \Phi_{At}$. ($Del(P, K, Q) \in \Phi_{At}$ and $Del(P, K, O) \in \Phi_{At}$ are atomic

formulas with their intended interpretation: *The subject P, possessing an asymmetric key K has deleted the subject Q (the object O)).*

We also define the set of all formulas.
Definition 10. Let Φ be a smallest set satisfying the following conditions:
1) $\Phi_{At} \subseteq \Phi$,
2) If $\alpha, \beta \in \Phi$, then $\neg\alpha, \alpha \wedge \beta, \alpha \vee \beta, \alpha \rightarrow \beta, \alpha \leftrightarrow \beta \in \Phi$.

3. AXIOMATIC SYSTEM

Now we introduce an axiomatic system of our logic: the inference rule and the set of axioms.

The rule. In our system we have only one inference rule, the *modus ponens* rule: $r_o \subseteq (\Phi \times \Phi) \times \Phi$.

$$(r_o) : \frac{\alpha, \alpha \rightarrow \beta}{\beta}.$$

Axioms. We take as axioms all substitutions of our formulas into classical tautologies and few following formulas:

A1. $TAwKey(P, K_1, Q, K_2) \rightarrow \bigvee_{U \in S_P} \bigvee_{K_U \in S_K} GetKey(U, K_U, Q, K_2)$,

A2. $TAwPriv(P, K, Q, T) \rightarrow \bigvee_{U \in S_P} \bigvee_{K_U \in S_K} GetPriv(U, K_U, Q, T)$,

A3. $TAwAttrib(P, K, Q, A) \rightarrow \bigvee_{U \in S_P} \bigvee_{K_U \in S_K} GetAttrib(U, K_U, Q, A)$,

A4. $TAwRight(P, K, O, R, A) \rightarrow \bigvee_{U \in S_P} \bigvee_{K_U \in S_K} GetRight(U, K_U, O, R, A)$.

By *Ax* we denote the set of all axioms.
Definition 11. Let Θ be an axiomatic system such that $\Theta = (\{r_o\}, Ax)$.

Definition 12. By a formal proof of the formula α under the system Θ we mean the finite sequence of formulas such that: the formula α is the last one in this sequence and every formula is either an axiom or a conclusion by the *modus ponens* rule from earlier concluded formulas.

Definition 13. By $Cn(\{r_o\}, Ax)$ we mean a set of all provable formulas in our system Θ.

The set $Cn(\{r_o\}, Ax \cup X)$, where X is an arbitrary subset of Φ, we denote by $Cn_\Theta(X)$.

Definition 14. By a theory we mean a set of formulas such that $X = Cn_\Theta(X)$.
Definition 15. A set of formulas X is called consistent iff $Cn_\Theta(X) \neq \Phi$.

4 MODEL OF COMPUTATION

Now we introduce the mathematical model representing the reality of computer network in the access control problem point of view.

Definition 16. Let $P_U, P_1, P_2, ..., P_{n_p}$ denote subjects (users) of the computer net. (Used below K, T, R, O denote, due to the our logical language, keys, privileges, rights and objects in real network.)

Definition 17. Each network user is allowed to perform the following actions:
1) (P, K_1 *givekey* Q, K_2) – the subject P, possessing an asymmetric key K_1 gives the subject Q the key K_2.
2) (P, K *giveattrib* Q, A) – the subject P, possessing an asymmetric key K gives the subject Q the right to use the attribute A.
3) (P, K *givepriv* Q, T) – the subject P, possessing an asymmetric key K gives the subject Q the right to use the privilege T.
4) (P, K *giveright* Q, O, R) – the subject P, possessing an asymmetric key K_1 gives the subject Q the access right R to the object O
5) (P, K *giveobright* O, R, A) – the subject P, possessing an asymmetric key K states that the condition of using the object O with the access right R is the possessing the attribute A by any subject.
6) (P, K *md* Q) - the subject P, possessing an asymmetric key K creates the subject Q.
7) (P, K *md* O) - the subject P, possessing an asymmetric key K creates the object O.
8) (P, K_1 *tawkey* Q, K_2) – the subject P, possessing an asymmetric key K_1 takes from the subject Q the key K_2.
9) (P, K *tawattrib* Q, A) – the subject P, possessing an asymmetric key K takes from the subject Q the right to use the attribute A.
10) (P, K *tawpriv* Q, T) – the subject P, possessing an asymmetric key K takes from the subject Q the right to use the privilege T.
11) (P, K *tawright* Q, O, R) – the subject P, possessing an asymmetric key K takes from the subject Q the access right R to the object O.
12) (P, K *del* Q) - The subject P, possessing an asymmetric key K deletes the subject Q.
13) (P, K *tawobright* O, R, A) – the subject P, possessing an asymmetric key K revokes the condition of using the object O with the access right R and the attribute A possessed by any subject.
14) (P, K *del* O) - The subject P, possessing an asymmetric key K deleted the object O.
15) () – an empty action.

We denote actions by α.

Definition 18. By a local history of user P_m (m=U, 1, 2, ... ,n_P) in the moment k we mean a sequence of actions $(\alpha_1, \alpha_2, ..., \alpha_k)$ executed by the user. Number k indicates the time instance (discrete time) by which P_m has performed these actions above. The local history of user P_m we denote by ζ_m^k. We distinguish the time instance $k = 0$, in which all users local histories are empty sequences. To simplify we assume that all clocks in the network are synchronized.

Definition 19. A global history in the moment k of users is a sequence of all local histories $\zeta^k = \zeta_1^k, \zeta_2^k, ... \zeta_{n_p}^k$.

Definition 20. Each user P_m in any instant k has:

1) LP_m^k - the set that states the subject activeness. This set is empty in the moment $k = 0$. After the execution of the action (P, K *md* P_m) to the set is added the element „+". After the execution of the action (P, K *del* P_m) it becomes empty. After executing the action (P, K *del* P_m) all contents of all the following sets are deleted. For any moment k the set LP_U^k is not empty.

2) K_m^k - the set of asymmetric cryptographic keys (keys certificates) that P_m knows at the moment k. K_m^k consists of triples (P,K_1,K_2). For $m \neq U$ the set K_m^k for $m \neq U$ is empty in the moment $k = 0$. After executing the actions like (P, K_1 *givekey* P_m, K_2) or (P, K_1 *tawkey* P_m, K_2) each of the sets K_m^{k+1} is enlarged or decreased with the adequate triple. In the moment $k = 0$ the set K_U^1 contains a key K_U.

3) A_m^k - the set of attributes (attribute certificates) that P_m has in the moment k. A_m^k consists of triples (P,K,A). The set A_m^k is empty in the moment $k = 0$. After executing the actions like (P, K *giveattrib* P_m, A) or (P, K *tawattrib* P_m, A) each of the sets A_m^{k+1} is enlarged or decreased with the adequate triple.

4) T_m^k - the set of privileges (privileges certificates) that P_m has in the moment k. T_m^k consists of triples (P,K,T). For $m \neq U$ the set T_m^k is empty in the moment $k = 0$. After executing the actions like (P, K *givepriv* P_m, T) or (P, K *tawpriv* P_m, T) each of the sets T_m^{k+1} is enlarged or decreased with the adequate triple. The set T_U^1 contains the all privileges.

5) RP_m^k - the set of access rights to objects that P_m has in the moment k. RP_m^k consists of quadruples (P, K, O, R). This set is empty in the moment $k = 0$. After executing the actions like (P, K *giveright* P_m, O, R) or (P, K *tawright* P_m, O, R) each of the sets RP_m^{k+1} is enlarged or decreased with the adequate quadruple.

Definition 21. A local state of user P_m in the instant k consists of

1) the local history ζ_m^k,
2) the activeness set LP_m^k,
3) the set of keys K_m^k,
4) the set of attributes A_m^k,
5) the set of privilege T_m^k,
6) the set of access rights RP_m^k.

We denote local states of users in the moment k by s_m^k.

Definition 22. A global state of users in the moment k is a sequence of local users states $s^k = s_1^k, s_2^k, ..., s_{n_p}^k$.

Definition 23. Each object O_n in any time instant k has:

1) LO_m^k - the set that states the object activeness. This set is empty in the moment $k = 0$. After the execution of the action (P, K *md* O_n) to the set is added the element „+". After the execution of the action (P, K *del* O_n) it becomes empty. After executing the action (P, K *del* O_n) all contents of the following set are deleted.
2) RO_m^k - the set stating the conditions of use of the object O_n with given access rights in the moment k. RO_m^k consists of quadruples (P,K,R,A). The set RO_m^k is empty in the moment $k = 0$. After executing the actions like (P, K *giveobright* O_n, R, A) or (P, K *tawobright* O_n, R, A) each of the sets RO_m^{k+1} is enlarged or decreased with the adequate quadruples.

Definition 24. By a local object state o^k in the moment k we mean a sequence of pairs $o^k = ((RO_1^k, LO_1^k), (RO_2^k, LO_2^k), ..., (RO_{n_0}^k, LO_{n_0}^k))$.

Definition 25. By a global system state so^k we mean a pair $so^k = (s^k, o^k)$.

Definition 26. A run η is any sequence of global system states $\eta = (so^1, so^2, ..., so^n, ..)$.

Definition 27. A run η we call correct if it satisfies the following conditions:
1) If (P, K_1 *tawkey* Q, K_2) is the action in the local history of user P executed in the moment k, then (P, K_1 *givekey* Q, K_2) is the action in the same history executed in moment l, such that $l < k$.
2) If (P, K *tawattrib* Q, A) is the action in the local history of user P executed in the moment k, then (P, K *giveattrib* Q, A) is the action in the same history executed in moment l, such that $l < k$.
3) If (P, K *tawpriv* Q, T) is the action in the local history of user P executed in the moment k, then (P, K *givepriv* Q, T) is the action in the same history executed in moment l, such that $l < k$.
4) If (P, K *tawright* O, R, A) is the action in the local history of user P executed in the moment k, then (P, K_1 *giveright* O, R, A) is the action in the same history executed in moment l, such that $l < k$.

Definition 28. By a system point we mean a pair (η, k), where η is an arbitrary correct run and k any time instant. (The point (η, k) should be understood as the global state so^k in the run η).

5. SEMANTICS

Now we give semantics of our logic.

Definition 29. The truth of formula α at a system point (η, k) is defined by induction on the structure of α.

For atomic formulas:
1. $(\eta, k) \models GiveKey(P, K_1, P_m, K_2)$ iff $(P, K_1, K_2) \in K_m^l$ for some $l \le k$,

2. $(\eta,k) \models GiveAttrib(P,K,P_m,A)$ iff $(P,K,A) \in A_m^l$ for some $l \leq k$,

3. $(\eta,k) \models GivePriv(P,K,P_m,T)$ iff $(P,K,T) \in T_m^l$ for some $l \leq k$,

4. $(\eta,k) \models GiveRight(P,K,Q,O,R)$ iff $(P,K,O,R) \in RP_m^l$ for some $l \leq k$,

5. $(\eta,k) \models GiveObRight(P,K,O,R,A)$ iff $(P,K,R,A) \in RO_m^l$ for some $l \leq k$,

6. $(\eta,k) \models Md(P,K,Q)$ iff $LP_m^l \neq \emptyset$ for some $l \leq k$,

7. $(\eta,k) \models Md(P,K,O)$ iff $LO_m^l \neq \emptyset$ for some $l \leq k$,

8. $(\eta,k) \models TAwKey(P,K_1,P_m,K_2)$ iff

$(P,K_1,K_2) \notin K_m^s$ and $(P,K_1,K_2) \in K_m^l$ for some $l < s \leq k$.

9. $(\eta,k) \models TAwPriv(P,K,P_m,T)$ iff

$(P,K,A) \notin A_m^s$ and $(P,K,A) \in A_m^l$ for some $l < s \leq k$.

10. $(\eta,k) \models TAwPriv(P,K,P_m,T)$ iff

$(P,K,T) \notin T_m^s$ and $(P,K,T) \in T_m^l$ for some $l < s \leq k$.

11. $(\eta,k) \models TAwRight(P,K,Q,O_n,R)$ iff

$(P,K,Q,R) \notin RP_m^s$ and $(P,K,Q,R) \in RP_m^l$ for some $l < s \leq k$.

12. $(\eta,k) \models TAwObRight(P,K,O_n,R,A)$ iff

$(P,K,R,A) \notin RO_m^s$ and $(P,K,R,A) \in RO_m^l$ for some $l < s \leq k$.

13. $(\eta,k) \models Del(P,K,Q)$ iff

$LP_m^s \neq \emptyset$ and $LP_m^l = \emptyset$ for some $s < l \leq k$,

14. $(\eta,k) \models Del(P,K,O)$ iff

$LO_m^s \neq \emptyset$ and $LO_m^l = \emptyset$ for some $s < l \leq k$.

For another formulas:

15. $(\eta,k) \models \neg\alpha$ iff non $(\eta,k) \models \alpha$,

16. $(\eta,k) \models \alpha \wedge \beta$ iff $(\eta,k) \models \alpha$ and $(\eta,k) \models \beta$,

17. $(\eta,k) \models \alpha \vee \beta$ iff $(\eta,k) \models \alpha$ or $(\eta,k) \models \beta$.

Definition 30. A formula α is a tautology iff for any system point (η,k) is $(\eta,k) \models \alpha$.

Definition 31. A system point (η,k) is called a model for a set X iff all formulas of X holds in (η,k).

Definition 32. A formula α is called a semantical consequence of set X ($X \models \alpha$) iff for any system point (η,k), if (η,k) is a model for X, then $(\eta,k) \models \alpha$ too.

6. COMPLETENESS AND DECIDABILITY

In this section we show the basic logical properties of our logic. We prove the completeness following the main ideas due to Tarski and Lindenbaum (see [TMR53]).

Lemma 1. For any consistent theory X ($X \neq \Phi$, $X = Cn_\Theta(X)$) there exists a theory Y such that:
1) $X \subseteq Y$,
2) $Y \neq \Phi$,
3) $Y = Cn_\Theta(Y)$
4) $\forall_{\alpha \in \Phi} (\alpha \in Y \vee \neg \alpha \in Y)$.

Lemma 2. Every consistent theory has a model.

Theorem 1. If X is any set on formulas, then:

$$\alpha \in Cn_\Theta(\{r_0\}, Ax \cup X) \quad \text{iff} \quad X \mid\!\!-\alpha.$$

Theorem 2. There exists an algorithm stating if any formula is satisfiable (tautology) or not.

7. APPLICATIONS

Due to atomic formulas (section 2) and axioms from section 3 we can express both a simple and a complex security objective.

Example 1. Some possession rules

In many cases a local state of user is strongly associated with the keys, attributes and privileges in her or his hands. For example formula „Q has a key K" ($Q \neq P_U$) could be written as follows:

$$HKey(Q,K) \leftrightarrow^{df} \bigvee_{P_1 \in S_P} \bigvee_{K_1 \in S_K} GiveKey(P_1, K_1, Q, K) \wedge \bigwedge_{P_2 \in S_P} \bigwedge_{K_2 \in S_K} \neg TAwKey(P_2, K_2, Q, K)$$

This formula means: „Q has a key K iff there is some subject possessing some key which confirms that the key K belongs to subject Q and nobody revoked this key.

Similar formulas could be defined for cases of an attribute and a privilege:

$$HAttrib(Q, A) \leftrightarrow^{df} \bigvee_{P_1 \in S_P} \bigvee_{K_1 \in S_K} GiveAttrib(P_1, K_1, Q, A) \wedge \bigwedge_{P_2 \in S_P} \bigwedge_{K_2 \in S_K} \neg TAwAttrib(P_2, K_2, Q, A)$$

$$HPriv(Q,T) \leftrightarrow^{df} \bigvee_{P_1 \in S_P} \bigvee_{K_1 \in S_K} GivePriv(P_1, K_1, Q, T) \wedge \bigwedge_{P_2 \in S_P} \bigwedge_{K_2 \in S_K} \neg TAwPriv(P_2, K_2, Q, T)$$

Example 2. Confirmation of existence

It is possible to define formulas which can be treated as a validation of existence some subject ($Q \neq P_U$) or object in the distributed computer system:

$$Exist(Q) \leftrightarrow^{df} \bigvee_{P_1 \in S_P} \bigvee_{K_1 \in S_K} Md(P_1, K_1, Q) \land \bigwedge_{P_2 \in S_P} \bigwedge_{K_2 \in S_K} \neg Del(P_2, K_2, Q)$$

$$Exist(O) \leftrightarrow^{df} \bigvee_{P_1 \in S_P} \bigvee_{K_1 \in S_K} Md(P_1, K_1, O) \land \bigwedge_{P_2 \in S_P} \bigwedge_{K_2 \in S_K} \neg Del(P_2, K_2, O)$$

Example 3. Necessary conditions for the operation execution

Some operation can be executed in the case only when there are met the predefined necessary condition(s). For example, the subject can use her or his privilege but first of all the privilege must be in the possession of this subject:

$$\bigwedge_{Q \in S_P} \bigwedge_{K_1, K_2 \in S_K} \left[GiveKey(P, K_1, Q, K_2) \rightarrow HPriv(P, T_{+K}) \right]$$

The formula above means that necessary condition for giving the keys is the possession of privilege for such operation.

Another formula says that the subject P with the key K_1 can issue the certificates but firstly she or he must possess the key K_1 issued by any authorized subject:

$$\bigwedge_{Q \in S_P} \bigwedge_{K_2 \in S_K} \left[GiveKey(P, K_1, Q, K_2) \rightarrow HKey(P, K_1) \right]$$

Or necessary conditions declaring that the subject before being able to do something must exists:

$$\bigwedge_{Q, P \in S_P} \bigwedge_{A \in S_A} \left[TAwAttrib(P, K, Q, A) \rightarrow (Exist(P) \land Exist(Q)) \right]$$

Example 4. Uniqueness of some resources

We can also require the resources to be in unique manner assigned to a subject, e.g. nobody besides the subject Q has the key K:

$$\bigwedge_{Q, P \in S_P} \bigwedge_{K \in S_K} \left[HKey(P, K) \rightarrow \neg HKey(Q, K) \right]$$

Or, the subject P_1 has granted the key K to the subject Q only:

$$\bigwedge_{P_1, P_2, Q \in S_P} \bigwedge_{K_1, K_2, K \in S_K} \left[GiveKey(P_1, K_1, Q, K) \rightarrow \neg GiveKey(P_2, K_2, Q, K) \right]$$

The formulas of types counted above can be added to any access policy specification. They describe the initial system state values and the conditions of the system to be secure.

We can also define a more complex policy specification, which allows us to state authorization specifications. An authorization specification is a collection of rules whose evaluation determines, for each access request that can be submitted, whether the requested access must be granted or denied. For example the standard discretionary access policy states that some object can be red only by those subjects, which are in possession of reading access rights to this object. This requirement can be improve in our logic and formally defined as on Fig.1. The formulas presented on this figure express the following sentence in natural language: *"The object O can read by any subject S if and only if subject S has the key K issued by the subject P_1 and the read access attribute generated by the subject P_2"*.

Authorization rules like these on Fig.1 are the expressions of security policies; they determine the system behavior at run time. In a closed policy only explicitly authorized accesses are allowed. In an open policy accesses that are not explicitly forbidden are allowed. A closed policy allows an access if there exists a positive authorization for it, and denies it otherwise. Similarly, an open policy denies an access if there exists a negative authorization for it and allows it otherwise.

The classical closed/open policies can be simulated in our language by allowing only positive or negative authorization policies to be specified mutually exclusive. The combined use of both positive and negative policies brings to the problem of potential inconsistencies when both a positive and a negative policy apply to the same access (Lupu, et al. [LSL99]), and are not solved by us yet.

Initial conditions:

$$\bigwedge_{U \in S_P} \bigwedge_{K_Q, K_U \in S_K} \left[GiveKey(Q, K_Q, U, K_U) \to HPriv(Q, T_{+K}) \right]$$

$$\bigwedge_{U \in S_P} \bigwedge_{K_U \in S_K} \left[GiveKey(Q, K_1, U, K_U) \to HKey(Q, K_1) \right]$$

$$\bigwedge_{U \in S_P} \bigwedge_{K_Q \in S_K} \bigwedge_{O \in S_O} \bigwedge_{R \in S_R} \left[GiveRight(Q, K_Q, U, O, R) \to HPriv(Q, T_{+R}) \right]$$

Policy conditions:

$KeyGiveBy(P, K, Q) \leftrightarrow^{df} \bigvee_{K_Q \in S_K} GiveKey(Q, K_Q, P, K) \land \bigwedge_{U \in S_P} \bigwedge_{K_U \in S_K} \neg TAwKey(U, K_U, P, K)$

$ReadRGiveBy(P, O, R_C, V) \leftrightarrow^{df} \bigvee_{K_V \in S_K} GiveRight(V, K_V, P, O, R_C) \land \bigwedge_{U \in S_P} \bigwedge_{K_U \in S_K} \neg TAwRight(U, K_U, P, O, R_C)$

$ReadCond(P, O) \leftrightarrow^{df} \bigvee_{P_1 \in S_P} KeyGiveBy(P, K, P_1) \land \bigvee_{P_2 \in S_P} ReadRGiveBy(P, O, R_C, P_2)$

Fig.1 An example of more complex policy specification and access authorization

8. CONCLUSIONS AND FUTURE WORK

Formal logic is mostly used in the specification of security policies. In this paper we have proposed a logical language for the specification of authorizations on which such policy specification can be based. The language allows users to specify, together with the authorizations, the policy according to which access control must be enforced. Different policies can be specified on different objects, according to the needs of the users.

We have illustrated how security specifications are stated in our language and shown initially how different control policies can be represented. We have also stated consistency and completeness constraints that security specifications are required to obey. The major advantage of our approach is that it can be used to specify different access control policies that can all coexist in the same system and be enforced by the same security server.

Our paper leaves space for further work. A first issue we plan to investigate concerns administrative policies. In this paper we have made the assumption that the security administrator states all specifications. The users can extend the model to the consideration of administrative policies regulating the insertion of the different rules.

There are many polices which cannot be directly specified in our logic. In particular this concerns the other policy types such as the mandatory (Bell, et al. [BLP74], Pejas [Pej02]) or role-based (Sandhu, et al. [SFK00]) access policies. However it is believed that some statements extended with additional atomic formulas can express the majority of these.

Another issue we want to solve is the simultaneously coexistence both positive and negative authorization policies (compare Damianou [DNC02]) in our logic. The conflicts between these two types of authorization policies should be avoided by using the tri-value algebra to prioritize policies when they are combined (Ribeiro et al. [RZF01])

Our future plans include also the problems of the integration with alternative security mechanisms. If all polices are defined in terms of our logic then reasoning is relatively straightforward as the ones have common semantics and a strong formal backing. When policies from other services are combined, reasoning is more difficult. However, we think two solutions can be applied. First, as our logic is an expressive language it is often the case that alternative policies may be written in our logic. Second, even if this does not aid existing implementation it greatly simplifies reasoning about interacting policies (compare Hayton [HAY96]).

The authors would like to thank Małgorzata Berezowska for help at work with the text.

9. REFERENCES

[ABL93] **Abadi, M., M. Burrows, B. Lampson and G. Plotkin** *A Calculus for Access Control in Distributed Systems* ACM Transactions on Programming Languages and Systems, vol. 4(15), pp. 706-734, September 1993.

[BLP74] **Bell D.E., LaPadula L.J.** *Secure computer systems: mathematical foundations and model*, Technical Report M74-244, The MITRE Corp., Bedford, MA, 1974

[BFB99] **Bertino E., Ferrari E., Buccafurri F., Rullo P.** *A Logical Framework for Reasoning on Data Access Control Policies*, Proceeding of the 12th IEEE Computer Security Workshop, IEEE Computer Society Press, July 1999

[CFM94] **Castano S., Fugini M.G., Martella G., Samarati P.** *Database security*, Addison-Wesley Publishing Company, New York 1994.

[DNC02] **Damianou N.C.** *A Policy Framework for Management of Distributed Systems*, PhD Thesis, Imperial College of Science, Technology and Medicine University of London Department of Computing, London 2002

[HAY96] **Hayton R.** *OASIS An Open Architecture for Secure Interworking Services*, PhD Thesis, University of Cambridge, 1996

[HMM00] **Herzberg A., Mass Y., Michaeli J., Naor D., Ravid Y.** *Access Control Meets Public Key Infrastructure, Or: Assigning Roles to Strangers*, Security & Privacy, 2000

[JSS97] **Jajodia S., Samarati P., Subrahmanian V. S.** *A Logical Language for Expressing Authorizations*, In Proceedings of the IEEE Symposium on Security and Privacy, pp. 31-42, May 4-7, 1997.

[LGF99] **Li N., Grosof B. N., Feigenbaum J.** *A Logic-based knowledge Representation for Authorization with Delegation*, IBM Research Report, RC 21492, May 99

[LSL99] **Lupu E. C., Sloman M. S.** *Conflicts in Policy-Based Distributed Systems Management*, in IEEE Transactions on Software Engineering - Special Issue on Inconsistency Management, vol. 25(6), pp. 852-869, November 1999.

[MAS97] **Massacci F.** *Reasoning about security: a logic and a Decision Method for Role-Based Access Control*, Springer Verlag, 1997

[PEJ02] **Pejaś J.** *Multilevel Lattice-Based Authorization in Distributed Supervisory and Control Systems*, in Advanced Computer Systems, J. Sołdek and J. Pejas (eds), Kluwer Academic Publishers, Boston/Dordrecht/London, 2002

[TMR53] **Tarski A., Mostowski A., Robinson R.**, *Undecidable theories*, North Holland 1953.

[RZF01] **Ribeiro, C., Zuquete A., Ferreira P.** *SPL: An access control language for security policies with complex constraints*, in Proceedings of the Network and Distributed System Security Symposium (NDSS'01), San Diego, California, February 2001.

[SFK00] **Sandhu, R., Ferraiolo D., Kuhn R.** *The NIST Model for Role-Based Access Control: Towards A Unified Standard*, in Proceedings of the 5th ACM Workshop on Role-Based Access Control, Berlin, Germany, pp. 47-61, 26-28 July 2000.

Certificate-Based Access Control Policies Description Language

JERZY PEJAŚ
Faculty of Computer Science & Information Systems, Department of Programming Techniques, Technical University of Szczecin, 49, Żołnierska st., 71-210 Szczecin, Poland, phone (148 91) 4495662, fax, +4891 4876439, e-mail: jerzy.pejas@wi.ps.pl

Abstract: The paper contains the proposal of the access control policy description language to support security and management of distributed systems. This policy language is based on a declarative, object-oriented Ponder language presented in Damianou [DDL00]. The language is flexible, expressive and extensible to cover the wide range of requirements implied by the current distributed systems paradigms. The additional extensions included into Ponder allow us to implement a certificate-based access control system, which formally has been specified by Kurkowski, et. al. [KUP02].

Key words: access control, security policy, logic-based security model, Ponder language, public key certificate, attribute certificate, public key infrastructure

1. INTRODUCTION

Management of very large, inter-organizational distributed systems cannot be centralized; it must be distributed to reflect the distribution of the system being managed. If we assume, that resources are assigned to physically or logically different domains (treated like distributed hierarchical directories) and managed by different administrators or owners and co-owners of these resources, then within each domain must exist mechanism, which enforces the realization of particular access policy to resources of this domain. It is rather obvious that such access control policy should be time varying. However, this implies also that verification of a subject's membership in domains cannot be based on a trusted centralized server. Furthermore, very often applications such as e-commerce and other Internet-enabled services require connectivity between entities that do not know each other. In such situations, the traditional assumptions for establishing and enforcing access control do not hold; subjects of requests can be remote, previously unknown users, making the separation between authentication and access control difficult.

A possible solution to this problem is to verify of whether or not credentials (see section 3) submitted by some subject can be used to establish properties of their holder (e.g. identity, accreditation) and meet simultaneously the predefined conditions, which allow him or her for the required access. The credentials are based on digitally signed documents, which convey identity, use conditions, attributes, privileges, etc.

A major drawback of existing access control systems is that they have all been developed with a specific access control policy in mind. This means that all protection requirements (i.e., accesses to be allowed or denied) must be specified in terms of the policy enforced by the system (Jajoda, et al. [JSS97]). Hence, the need is evident for a policy language to support the specification of access control and other management policies.

Recent proposals on policy based management of networks and distributed systems provide promising solutions to these problems (see Damianou [DNC02]). They include a trend towards languages able to express different access control policies in a single framework in order to provide a common mechanism able to enforce multiple policies.

There are many ways to divide the discussion on the various policy specification approaches (e.g. Damianou [DNC02]). One of them includes logic-based languages (Abadi, et al. [ABL93], Barker [BAR00], Jajoda [JSS97], Hayton, et al. [HAY98]), high-level policy languages (OASIS [OAS01], Ribeiro, et al. [RZF01]) and work on specification of trust (Blaze, et al. [BFL96], Blaze, et al. [BFIM99], Johnson [JMT98]).

Our main area of interest is to develop the policy language which can be aimed at specifying certificate-based trust policies for access to resources from un-trusted sources e.g. over the Internet. Some proposal of such logic-based language is presented in the work of Kurkowski, et al. [KUP02]. This language can be used mainly to analyzing the policy specification, but can be also directly mapped to an implementation. This paper outlines that such mapping can be done. Furthermore, we show that logic-based access control rules presented by Kurkowski [KUP02] can be expressed in a high level formulation of Ponder language (Damianou, et al. [DDL00], Damianou [DNC02]) and easily interchangeable, and both human and machine-readable.

2. PONDER POLICY SPECIFICATION LANGUAGE

Ponder[1] is a declarative, object-oriented language for specifying security policies with role-based access control, as well as general-purpose management policies for specifying what actions are carried out when specific events occur within

---

[1] This description of Ponder language specification is based on works of Damianou, et al. [DDL00] and Dulay [DLS01].

the system or what resources to allocate under specific conditions. Unlike many other policy specification notations, Ponder supports typed policy specifications.

Ponder has four basic policy types: **authorizations, obligations, refrains** and **delegations** and three composite policy types: **roles, relationships** and **management structures** that are used to compose policies (Damianou [DNC02]). Ponder also has a number of supporting abstractions that are used to define policies: **domains** for hierarchically grouping managed objects, **events** for triggering obligation policies, and **constraints** for controlling the enforcement of policies at runtime.

In the rest part of the paper we particularly interested in a modifications of the Ponder authorization policies. This policy allows us to define two types of authorization policies: positive and negative. A positive authorization defines the actions that subjects are permitted to perform on target objects. A negative authorization policy specifies the actions that subjects are forbidden to perform on target objects. Authorization policies are implemented on the target host by an access control component.

```
inst ( auth+ | auth- ) policyName {
"}"
    subject [<type>] domain-Scope-Expression ;
    target  [<type>] domain-Scope-Expression ;
    action action-list ;
    [when constraint-Expression ; ]
"}"
}
```

Figure 1. Authorization policy syntax (source: Damianou [DNC02])

The primary Ponder syntax of an authorization policy is shown in Figure 1. Everything in bold is a language keyword in the figures presenting the syntax. Choices are enclosed in round brackets ( ) separated by |, optional elements are specified with square brackets [ ] and repetition is specified with braces "{" "}". Constraints are optional in all types of policies and can be specified to limit the applicability of policies based on time or values of the attributes of the objects to which the policy refers. Note that the subject and target elements can optionally include the interface specification reference within the specified domain-scope-expression on which the policy applies.

The implementation of a logic-based policy access control description language, considered in the work of Kurkowski, et al. [KUP02], needs the minor modifications of Ponder language. In particular, these modifications concern the syntax of an authorization policy (see Figure 2).

We added three new key words into the Ponder syntax: credentials, use-conditions and signature. The credentials are data used to establish the claimed identity of a subject, his or her attributes, privileges and access rights as well. The credentials in mind should compose the set of parameters, which allow an access control component to verify whether there are fulfilled all use conditions of the target in question. Optionally, this subject whom the origin of this policy belongs can digitally sign the defined access authorization policy. The digital signature is the guarantee of the policy authenticity and its integrity. This feature is especially valuable in the case of management policy used for distributed resources.

Putting into the policy definition the information about credentials and use-conditions we are able to solve two essential problems of the certificate-based access control systems: (a) the list of private accreditation information provided to a grantee by a grantor, and of which a grantee subsequently proves possession, thereby establishing the subject's identity and his or her access permission to a target, and (b) the list of requirements which should be fulfilled prior to the target is made accessible to the requester according to his or her demand (see section 4).

```
inst ( auth+ | auth- ) policyName {
"}"
    subject [<type>] domain-Scope-Expression
    [credentials credentials-lists;]
    target [<type>] domain-Scope-Expression ;
    [useConditions use-condition-Cert;]
    action action-list;
    [when constraint-Expression ; ]
"}"
    [signature: digital-signature]
}
```

Figure 2. Modified authorization policy syntax

3. CERTIFICATE-BASED ACCESS CONTROL

In open widely distributed information systems (like Internet) for many applications or servers we need to control access to users and entities not known in advance. The application or server may not be able to authenticate these users or to specify authorizations for them (with respect to their identity). The traditional separation between authentication and access control cannot be applied in this context. *"A possible solution to this problem is represented by the use of digital certificates (or credentials), representing statements certified by given entities (e.g., certification authorities), which can be used to establish properties of their holder (such as identity, accreditation, or authorizations)"* (Samarati [SDC01]).

The subject provides the credentials to an application or a server when this one requests performing a particular task. If submitted credentials are sufficient in the sense of the enforced access control policy then the request is allowed and realized; in other case the request is denied.

Definition 1. A *credential* (sometimes also called *signed capabilities*, see Nikander [NIK99], Pejas [PEJ02]), or *authorization certificate*, is a digitally signed piece of information that assigns a subject, usually represented in the form of a cryptographic public key, one or more *permissions*, which allow the subject to perform specified actions on one or more specified objects in a target system). We distinguish five types of credentials (compare Kurkowski, et al. [KUP02]):
1) GiveKey(**grantor**=P, **grantorKeySN**=K_1, **grantee**=Q, **granteeKeySN**=K_2) – the **public key certificate** of the key with the serial number K_2 owned by the subject (grantee) Q and issued by the subject (grantor) P, possessing a public

key with the serial number K_1; the certificate is valid in some predefined period or until is revoked.
2) GiveAttrib(**grantor**=P, **grantorKeySN**=K, **grantee**=Q, **attribs**=set A) – the **attribute certificate** for the set of the attributes A owned by (or granted to) the subject (grantee) Q and issued by the subject (grantor) P, possessing a public key with the serial number K; the certificate is valid in some predefined period or until is revoked.
3) GivePriv(**grantor**=P, **grantorKeySN**=K, **grantee**=Q, **privs**=set T) – the **privilege certificate** for the set of the privileges T owned by (or granted to) the subject (grantee) Q and issued by the subject (grantor) P, possessing a public key with the serial number K; the certificate is valid in some predefined period or until is revoked.
4) GiveRight(**grantor**=P, **grantorKeySN**=K, **grantee**=Q, **objects**=set O, **rights**=set R) – the **access right certificate** for the set of the access rights R to the objects O granted to the subject (grantee) Q and issued by the subject (grantor) P, possessing a public key with the serial number K; the certificate is valid in some predefined period or until is revoked.
5) Md(**grantor**=P, **grantorKeySN**=K, **objects/subjects**=set X) – the **object/subject creation certificate** which is the evidence of objects/subjects X creation issued by the subject (grantor) P, possessing a public key with the serial number K; the certificate is valid in some predefined period or until is revoked; the loss of a certificate validity period or its revocation means the removal of the objects/subjects.

Definition 2. A *use-condition certificate* contains digitally signed conditions that must be satisfied by a user before being given access to a resource. The use-conditions usually must follow some access control policy and are defined by the stakeholder(s) (the resource owner(s)). We use the following notation:

*GiveObRight(grantor=P, grantorKeySN=K, object=O, rights=set R, attribs=set A) – the **use-condition certificate** saying that the access to the object O in the modes R is allowed to any subject, possessing the attributes A; the certificate is issued by the subject (grantor) P, possessing a public key with the serial number K and is valid in some predefined period or until is revoked.*

Each certificate created according to Definition 1 and 2 contains the serial number. It must be unique for each certificate issued by a given grantor (i.e., the grantor name and serial number identify a unique certificate).

We assume the separate classes represent the types of certificates built-in extended Ponder syntax. The names of credentials and use-condition certificates (see Definition 1 and 2) correspond also with names of classes and their parametric constructors. Definitions 1 and 2 omit the description of destructors; their syntax and semantic can be found in the work of Kurkowski, et al. [KUP02].

Example 1: Objects (instances) of the class *GiveKey*.
Assume we want to create object that conforms to the public key certificate of the subject called "Jan Kowalski"; this certificate is issued by the subject "Certum Level IV":

```
string q= "Jan Kowalski", p="Certum Level IV";
int qn=12345678, pn=986347862;
credentials cert = GiveKey(grantor=p, grantorKeySN=pn,
                          grantee=q, granteeKeySN=qn);
```

*Above notation describes the creation of a single object named **cert**, searching the certificate repository of the subject **p** or the domain of subject **q** for the certificate with predefined parameters, gathering the certificate attributes and their storing as the attributes of the object **cert**. Hence, e.g. the notation **cert.notBefore** means the date on which the certificate validity period begins.*

*If both of formal parameters representing the certificate serial numbers have been omitted then in response we have received all certificates (even those which have been revoked) of subject **q**. These certificates have been issued by subject **p** and digitally signed by using any of private keys being in the sole possession of this subject.*

```
string q= "Jan Kowalski", p="Certum Level IV";
credentials set cert = GiveKey(grantor=p, grantee=q);
```

*The usage of the key word **set** is essential in above example because this notation provides the assurances that object **cert** is the set of certificates (maybe with one element only). When this key word is omitted then it means we are interested in receiving any key public certificate being in possession of subject q and issued by the subject p.*

Definition 3. *Permission defines one or more objects and an action or a set of actions that the subject may perform on the object. An action or a set of action depends on privileges of subject, access rights to the objects and subject's attributes.*

Let ***B*** is the set of all possible current permissions such that a subject $s \in S_P$ is allowed to make one or more action(s) $a \in Actions$ to an object $o \in S_O$. For the purposes of this paper, we assume that a set of actions is defined as below.

Definition 4. Let *Actions* be a set of symbols representing actions approachable in certificate-based access control system. We assume this set ***Actions*** contains the following actions (Kurkowski, et al. [KUP02]):
1) givekey(**grantor**=P, **grantorKeySN**=K_1, **grantee**=Q, **granteeKey**=K_2) – the subject (grantor) P, possessing a public key with the serial number K_1 gives the subject (grantee) Q the public key certificate for the key K_2.
2) giveattrib(**grantor**=P, **grantorKeySN**=K, **grantee**=Q, **attribs**=set A) – the subject (grantor) P, possessing a public key with the serial number K gives the subject (grantee) Q the right to use the set of attributes A.
3) givepriv(**grantor**=P, **grantorKeySN**=K, **grantee**=Q, **privs**=set T) – the subject (grantor) P, possessing a public key with the serial number K gives the subject (grantee) Q the right to use the set of privileges A.
4) giveright(**grantor**=P, **grantorKeySN**=K, **grantee**=Q, **objects**=set O, **rights**=set R) – the subject (grantor) P, possessing a public key with the serial number K gives the subject (grantee) Q the access rights R to the objects A.

5) giveobright(**grantor**=P, **grantorKeySN**=K, **object**=O, **rights**=set R, **attribs**=set A) – the subject (grantor) P, possessing a public key with the serial number K states that the condition of using the object O with the access rights R is the possessing the attributes A by any subject.
6) md(**grantor**=P, **grantorKeySN**=K, **objects/subjects**=set X) – the subject (grantor) P, possessing a public key with the serial number K creates the objects/subjects Q.

The certificate is created as a result of use any above counted actions. The name of this certificate agrees with the name of action (see Definitions 1 and 2). The Definition 5 omits the description of the certificate revocation and removal of objects/subjects. The syntax and semantic of these actions is specified in the work of Kurkowski, et al. [KUP02].

The issuing grantor signs the message with its private key and thus the certificate is the grantor's signed assertion that a particular credential or use-condition belongs to a specific subject or object. However, the trust to this binding must be verified. To verify the certificate (binding) we must:
- define the trusted grantor (root grantor) and obtain its credentials or use-conditions certificate,
- obtain all the necessary additional certificates and revocation status information,
- build the chain of credentials or use-condition certificates starting from a certificate issued by the trust root and ending with the certificate issued to the subject of interest to the verifier,
- verify whether each certificate in the chain can be processed to obtain via a chaining of signature key bindings,
- none of the certificates in the chain is expired,
- none of the certificates in the chain is issued without permission,
- none of the certificates in the chain is revoked.

The verification is the complex problem rather and in our system is realized by methods, which are built-in standard Ponder classes, named **subject** or **target**. It means that methods defined below are calling for an object (instance) of this class.

Definition 5. Each verifier is allowed to perform the following methods for validating a chain of certificates:
1) Q.GiveValidKey(**grantor**=P, **grantorKeySN**=K, **granteeKeySN**=K_2, **rootGrantor**=Rg) – the method, which: (1) is calling for the subject (grantee) Q possessing a public key with the serial number K_2 and gets its public key certificate issued by the subject (grantor) P, possessing a public key with the serial number K, (2) checks the certificate validity relatively to root grantor Rg; if successful, the methods returns the one or more valid certificates possessed by subject Q.
2) Q.GiveValidAttrib(**grantor**=P, **grantorKeySN**=K, **attribs**=set A, **rootGrantor**=Rg) – the method, which: (1) is calling for the subject (grantee) Q possessing a set of attributes A and gets its attribute certificates issued by the subject (grantor) P, possessing a public key with the serial number K, (2) checks

the certificate validity relatively to root grantor Rg; if successful, the methods returns the one or more valid certificates possessed by subject Q.
3) Q.GiveValidPriv(**grantor**=P, **grantorKeySN**=K, **privs**=set T, **rootGrantor**=Rg) – the method, which: (1) is calling for the subject (grantee) Q possessing a set of privileges T and gets its privileges certificates issued by the subject (grantor) P, possessing a public key with the serial number K, (2) checks the certificate validity relatively to root grantor Rg; if successful, the methods returns the one or more valid certificates possessed by subject Q.
4) Q.GiveValidRight(**grantor**=P, **grantorKeySN**=K, **objects**=set O, **rights**=set R, **rootGrantor**=Rg) – the method, which: (1) is calling for the subject (grantee) Q possessing a set of the access rights R to the objects O and gets its access right certificates issued by the subject (grantor) P, possessing a public key with the serial number K, (2) checks the certificate validity relatively to root grantor Rg; if successful, the methods returns the one or more valid certificates possessed by subject Q.
5) O.GiveValidObRight(**grantor**=P, **grantorKeySN**=K, **rights**=set R, **attribs**=set A, **rootGrantor**=Rg) – the method, which: (1) is calling for the object (grantee) O accessible in the modes R by any subject, possessing the attributes A and gets its use-condition certificates issued by the subject (grantor) P, possessing a public key with the serial number K, (2) checks the certificate validity relatively to root grantor Rg; if successful, the methods returns the one or more valid certificates associated with the object O.
6) X.ValidMd(**grantor**=P, **grantorKeySN**=K, **rootGrantor**=Rg) – the method, which: (1) is calling for the object/subject X and gets its evidence of creation issued by the subject P, possessing a public key with the serial number K, (2) checks the certificate validity relatively to root grantor Rg; if successful, the methods returns the one or more valid certificates associated with the object/subject X.

4. APPLICATIONS

The deployment model that was needed to implement the Ponder language concepts has been entrusted the enforcement of policies to one or more enforcement agents, i.e. for authorization policies each target's access controller. The subject communicates with the target through interchange the access control rules expressed in Ponder language. Due to the new features added to the Ponder language this interchange must be a little change. Each subject, communicating with some target protected by some policy, should know the rights to approach this target. The need for the trust negotiation issues and strategies that a party can apply to select credentials to submit to the opponent party in a negotiation is obvious. Two distinct credential release strategies can be applied: eager and parsimonious (Yu, et. al. [YMW00]). First, the subject turns over all his or her credentials if the release policy for them is satisfied, without waiting for the credentials to be requested. Second, parsimonious parties only release credentials upon explicit request by the server (avoiding unnecessary releases). These two strategies of being realized can be enforced due to distinct differencing the credentials and use-conditions certificates associated with subject and target, respectively. The subject and target can communicate each other without disclosing possible sensitive information on which the access decision is taken.

Below we show some examples of certificate-based access control, which show direct declaration of policy instances using the modified authorization policy syntax.

```
inst auth+ keyCertIssuer {
   subject s=/NetworkAdmin;
   target <SubAdmin> p=/Nregion/RegAdmin;
   action givekey(grantor=s, grantorKeySN=s.serialNumbery,
                 grantee=p, granteekey=p.key);
}
```

Figure 3. Positive authorization policy for the certificate public key creation

The policy **keyCertIssuer** is saying, that members of the **NetworkAdmin** domain are authorized to issue the public key certificate to any target (subject) of type **PolicyT** in the **Nregion/RegAdmin** domain. Note there is no one credentials and use-conditions which constrain the authorization; this indicates the use of the authorization policy to issue the certificates by each subject form **NetworkAdmin** domain to each subject form **Nregion/RegAdmin** domain.

```
inst auth- printServerAccess {
   subject s = Employees;
   credentials set a = s.GiveValidAttrib()
   target f = Servers/PrintServer;
   action *; // all actions
   when a.getRole() = "Security Officer";
}
```

Figure 4. An example of negative authorization policy

Figure 4 illustrates the usage of the negative authorization policy. In this policy **Employees** cannot print any information on **PrintSerwer** if they are in the role of Security Officer. Note the role of the subject is based on attribute certificate and checked in the constraint.

The number of the subjects, which are permitted to create the certificates and fulfill the requirements of policy **keyCertIssuer,** (see Figure 3) can be reduced to exactly one subject such as this defined in the public key certificate (see Figure 5).

Prior to grant the subject possessing the distinguished name **"/C=PL/O=PS Szczecin/CN=Admin"** the permission of giving the public key certificate to any subject form **/Nregion/RegAdmin** domain, the access controller checks in advance if this subject has the valid public certificate (one or more) issued by the subject identified by name **r** and the valid privilege certificate for giving any subject a public key certificate, as well. If these conditions are all met (additionally the serial number of the public key certificate is equal to value of variable **sn**), then the access controller authorizes the subject's right for giving the public key certificates. Data needed in the process for the creation of a certificate are approachable as the attributes of two objects **p** and **q**, placed there after the initial processing of the request received form the subject **p**. Note that the policy **rootIssuer** is digitally signed by the subject, which is possessing the public key certificate uniquely identified by hashID (the hash value of subject public key) or by the pair (issuer, serialNumber) of the certificate in question.

```
inst auth+ rootIssuer {
   string r="/C=PL/O=Unizeto CERTUM/CN=Certum Level IV";
   int sn=2731982764164;
   subject p="/C=PL/O=PS Szczecin/CN=Admin";
   credentials set c=p.GiveValidKey(issuer=r, grantorKeySN=sn);
   target <SubAdmin> q = /Nregion/RegAdmin;
   action givekey();
   when c.serialNumber = 148392475893

 signature: /value=0x26734FD6E8A6435B3cd/alg=sha1WithRsa
            /hashID=2344dc4fa23ca332b
            /issuer="/C=PL/O=Unizeto CERTUM/CN=Certum Level IV"
            /serialNumber=238990275928326
}
```

Figure 5. Positive authorization policy with constrains for the certificate public key creation

The modified authorization policy syntax allows us to define more complex policy specification like this taken form Kurkowski, et al. [KUP02]: *"The object O can be read by any subject S if and only if subject S has the key K issued by the subject P_1 (i.e. /C=PL/O=PS Szczecin/CN=PS Admin) and the read access attribute generated by the subject P_2 (named /C=PL/O=PS Szczecin/CN=WI Admin)"*.

```
inst auth+ ReadAuth {
   string   r = "/C=PL/O=PS Szczecin/CN=PS Admin",
            tpk = "/C=PL/O=Unizeto CERTUM/CN=Certum CA";
            ari = "/C=PL/O=PS Szczecin/CN=WI Admin";
   subject s=/users/financeDept;
   credentials set c = s.GiveValidKey(grantor=r,
                                       rootGrantor=tpk),
                   a = s.GiveValidAttrib(),
                   p = s.GiveValidRight(grantor=ari,
                                         rights = "read");
   target f = /file/payroll;
   useConditon set u = f.giveObRight(grantor="Kowal",
                                      access="read")
   action f.read();
   when p.right() in u.right() && u.issuer() = f.getOwner() &&
        a.attr() in u.attrib();
}
```

Figure 6. Positive authorization policy for reading an object

It is worthy of comparison the policy **ReadAuth** (see Figure 6) and the policy **pureReadAuth**, which one has been written in pure Ponder language (see Figure 7).

```
inst auth+ pureReadAuth {
   subject s=/users/financeDept;
   target f = /file/payroll;
   action f.read;
}
```

Figure 7. Pure Ponder authorization policy for reading an object

The policy **pureReadAuth** allows any subject from **/users/financeDept** domain to read any file from **/file/payroll** domain. Compared to this, the credentials and use-condition used in the specification of the policy **ReadAuth** limit the group of the files users only to those subjects, which can submit the additional, exactly defined permissions.

5. CONCLUSIONS AND FUTURE WORK

In the paper we show that proposal of logic language for certificate-based access control, specified in the work of Kurkowski, et al. [KUP02], can be rather simply implemented in the high-level policy languages. Two approaches can be applied: either implementing the language from the beginning or using some existing language. We have chosen the second approach, introducing the necessary modification into the syntax of Ponder language.

The modifications, which have been proposed, concern mainly the syntax of an authorization policy. Ponder language has three other basic policy types (e.g. Dulay, et al. DLS01]): obligations, refrains and delegations and three composite policy types: roles, relationships and management structures that are used to compose policies. The analysis of logic language of Kurkowski, et al. [KUP02] shows, that it is possible to resign the part of Ponder policy types. An example is the delegation policy, which is often used in access control systems to cater for temporary transfer of permissions between users. A user's ability to delegate permissions can be tightly controlled by credentials especially by those, which concern attribute certificates, privilege certificates and access rights certificates, and allow cascaded delegation of access rights.

Our working draft for Ponder modification proposals needs to be developed further. In particular, this concerns the works for simplicity and usability of Ponder syntax and their adjustment to the need of the certificate-based access policy. The expressive power of Ponder language should be also applied to the integration with alternative security access policies. We believe, that in particular, it is possible to integrate the Ponder language with mandatory access policies, using the mechanisms described in the work of Pejas [PEJ02].

6. ACKNOLEDGMENTS

The author would like to thank Miroslaw Kurkowski who has contributed a great deal to the work presented in this paper, with his useful comments and advice.

7. REFERENCES

[ABL93] **Abadi, M., M. Burrows, B. Lampson and G. Plotkin** *A Calculus for Access Control in Distributed Systems* ACM Transactions on Programming Languages and Systems, vol. 4(15), pp. 706-734, September 1993.

[BAR00] **Barker S.** *Security Policy Specification in Logic*, in Proceedings of the International Conference on Artificial Intelligence (ICAI00), Las Vegas, Nevada, USA, pp. 143-148, 26-29 June 2000.

[BFL96] **Blaze M., J. Feigenbaum, J. Lacy** *Decetralized Trust Management*, in Proc.1996 IEEE Synposium on Security and Privacy, pp.164-173, Oakland, CA, May 1996, IEEE Computer Society Press

[BFIM99] **Blaze, J. Feigenbaum, J. Ioannidis,, A.D. Keromytis** *The Role of Trust Management in Distributed Systems Security*, in *Secure Internet Pogramming: Security Issues for Mobile and Distributed Objects*, ed. Jan Vitek and Ch. Jensen, Springer-Verlag Inc, pp. 185 – 210, New York, 1999.

[DDL00] **Damianou N., N. Dulay, E. Lupu and M. Sloman** *Ponder: A Language for Specifying Security and Management Policies for Distributed Systems. The Language Specification - Version 2.3* Research Report DoC 2000/1, Imperial College of Science Technology and Medicine, Department of Computing, London, 20 October 2000.

[DNC02] **Damianou N.C.** *A Policy Framework for Management of Distributed Systems*, PhD Thesis, Imperial College of Science, Technology and Medicine University of London Department of Computing, London 2002

[DLS01] **Dulay N., E. Lupu, M. Sloman, N. Damianou** *A Policy Deployment Model for the Ponder Language*, an extended version of paper in Proc. IEEE/IFIP International Symposium on Integrated Network Management (IM'2001), Seattle, May 2001, IEEE Press.

[HAY98] **Hayton, R. J., J. M. Bacon, K. Moody** *Access Control in an Open Distributed Environment*, in Proceedings of the IEEE Symposium on Security and Privacy, Oakland, California, U.S.A., pp. 3-14, May 1998.

[JSS97] **Jajodia S., Samarati P., Subrahmanian V. S.** *A Logical Language for Expressing Authorizations*, In Proceedings of the IEEE Symposium on Security and Privacy, pp. 31-42, May 4-7, 1997

[JMT98] **Johnston W., S. Mudumbai, M. Thompson** *Authorization and Attribute Certificates for Widely Distributed Access Control*, IEEE 7th International Workshops on Enabling Technologies: Infrastructure for Collaborative Enterprises, WETICE '98

[KUP02] **Kurkowski M., J. Pejaś** *A Propositional Logic for Access Control in Distributed Systems*, 9th International Conference on Advanced Computer Systems, 23-25 October 2002, Międzyzdroje, Poland

[NIK99] **Nikander P.** *An Architecture for Authorization and Delegation in Distributed Object-Oriented Agent Systems*, PhD Thesis, Helsinki University of Technology, Department of Computer Science, Telecommunications Software and Multimedia Laboratory, FI-02015 TKK, Espoo, Finland, 1999

[OAS01] OASIS (Organization for the Advancement of Structured Information Standards) *XACML language proposal, version 0.8*, available from http://www.oasis-open.org/committees/xacml, 10 January 2002.

[PEJ02] **Pejaś J.** *Multilevel Lattice-Based Authorization in Distributed Supervisory and Control Systems*, in Advanced Computer Systems, ed. by J. Sołdek, J. Pejas, Kluwer Academic Publishers, Boston/Dordrecht/London, 2002

[RZF01] **Ribeiro, C., Zuquete A., Ferreira P.** *SPL: An access control language for security policies with complex constraints*, in Proceedings of the Network and Distributed System Security Symposium (NDSS'01), San Diego, California, February 2001.

[SDC01] **Samarati P., S. De Capitani di Vimercati** *Access Control: Policies, Models, and Mechanisms*, in Foundations of Security Analysis and Design, R. Focardi and R. Gorrieri (eds), LNCS 2171, Springer-Verlag, 2001

[YMW00] **Yu T., X. Ma, M. Winslett** *An efficient complete strategy for automated trust negotiation over the internet*, in Proceedings of 7th ACM Computer and Communication Security, Athens, Greece, November 2000.

Encryption using two-dimensional cellular automata with applications

MARIAN SREBRNY[1], PIOTR SUCH[2]
[1] *University of Commerce, Kielce, Poland and Institute of Computer Science, Polish Academy of Sciences, marians@ipipan.waw.pl*
[2] *University of Commerce, Kielce, Poland, piotr@wsh-kielce.edu.pl*

Abstract: A new symmetric cryptosystem is presented, based on two-dimensional cellular automata. Enciphering uses both left- and right-toggle rules. Enhanced cryptographic power is obtained by designing some simple geometric transformations on squares of bits of information. As an application, a software system „IPI Protect" is presented which integrates with MS Word for protecting the documents against unauthorized modifications while allowing free viewing and printing.

Key words: cryptography, security, symmetric cryptosystem, cellular automata.

1. INTRODUCTION

Cellular automata, CA, were introduced by John von Neumann [9]. Conway [10] presented the game of Life, a famous automaton self-reproducing its own structure. Cellular automata have an important application in implementation of logical operations [5]. The cellular automata provide a mathematical model of concurrent computations; i.e., with many concurrently executed operations. In the literature they are compared and contrasted with Turing machines modeling sequential computations; i.e., with a single operation in each step, step by step, linearly.

In mid-eighties Stephen Wolfram [12] applied the cellular automata in cryptology. Following that pioneering paper, Howard Gutowitz [3] constructed an interesting cryptosystem based on one-dimensional cellular automata. Gutowitz introduced the concept of left- and right-toggle rules in order to deal with non one-to-one transitions occurring possibly during the work of an automaton.

In this paper we propose a new cryptosystem following some ideas of Gutowitz and using some results of J.Kari [4]. The encryption/decryption algorithm uses two-dimensional cellular automata. We present its main functional description. Last but not least, we give its application as program „IPI protect" for protecting MS Word documents against unauthorized modifications.

2. BASIC CONCEPTS

One can think of a cellular automaton as a one or more dimensional array, with entries possibly written down in its cells. The entries are in the form of bits (zero or one). One can speak of a local state, i.e. the state of a single cell, or of a global state, meaning the state of all the cells of a given automaton.

| 0 | 1 | 1 | 1 | 0 | 0 | 0 | 0 |

Fig. 1. An example of a cellular automaton and its states.

Automata function by changing their states. A transition to a next state takes place according to the transition *rules*. A rule transforms state t_i of a cell to state t_{i+1}. A rule can be thought of as a table that determines the next step state of a cell depending on the current states of the neighboring cells. A rule can be treated as a local function changing the state of a single cell, or as a global function changing all the cells at once in each step.

In order to determine the next state a rule looks at the neighboring cells and takes their sates as its input. A system of those cells is called a *neighborhood*. In the case of one-dimensional automata a neighborhood is defined as the number of cells left and right from the central cell.

Fig. 2. An example of a neighborhood in dimension 1: one cell from the left and one from the right hand side.

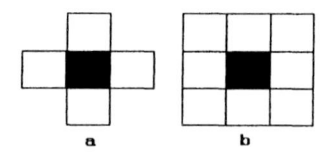

Fig. 3. Examples of neighborhoods for 2D automata.

A transition rule for one cell to its next state can be given in the form of a table.

The rule of Table 1 is called *rule 105*, since its outcome (the third column) is a binary representation of number 105. For this type of neighborhood there are 256 rules (because with 8 bits of the outcome one can write all the integers from 0 to 255). The rules can be reversible or not reversible. If one can determine the value of the central bit knowing only the outcome bit then such a rule is called reversible. Rule 105 is reversible. In the case when the last entry of the table was 0, we would have got *rule 104*, which is not reversible. For each combination 1x1 (where x denotes an unknown central bit), we have always 0 as the outcome for both lines 6 and 8.

000	→	0
001	→	1
010	→	1
011	→	0
100	→	1
101	→	0
110	→	0
111	→	1

Tab. 1. An example of rule 105 for 1D automata with neighborhood of radius 1.

3. CRYPTOGRAPHY WITH CELLULAR AUTOMATA

Here are some of the most important properties of the cellular automata from the standpoint of their use for data encryption.

Parallel computations. In order to deal with large documents of text or large streams of data, the encryption algorithms need to be able to perform parallel computations. The cellular automata can do it. Practically, in a single step (instance of time) one can obtain a transition to the next state of all the cells simultaneously.

Simple computations. All the actions of the cellular automata are performed on the set of binary digits {0,1}. These are just changing the states of particular cells. There is no integer arithmetic, no addition or multiplication in the course of execution of the cellular automata operations.

Irreversible rules. Using such rules increases cryptographic power of the algorithms based on the cellular automata. In the case of two-dimensional automata, the computational complexity of the executed operations becomes so large that the reversibility of the rules problem becomes undecidable (Kari [4]). That is, there does not exist any computable procedure, which in general, i.e., for a given rule, can return its reversed rule.

Hashing information. Changing a bit at a single cell gives avalanche effect. In a few steps the changed bit forces changes of all the other bits of the state of the automaton. One can still accelerate this process by using neighborhoods of higher dimension.

All the above properties of the cellular automata give enough of motivation and hope for cryptosystems of very high quality. These days many researchers work on applications of the cellular automata to encryption/decryption but also to pseudo random number generation ([11]) and to generation of message digests ([8]). Finally, let us mention that intensive research has revealed successful lines of attacks on some cryptosystems based on one-dimensional cellular automata ([6], [1] and [2]).

4. ENCRYPTION WITH 2-DIMENSIONAL CELLULAR AUTOMATA

In this section we give some details of the proposed new encryption/decryption algorithm. We build on some earlier ideas of Howard Gutowitz [3]. Gutowitz introduced the concept of a *left-* or *right-toggle rule*. It can be described by the following formulas:

$$1-s_i^t = F(1-s_{i-r}^t, \ldots, s_i^t, \ldots s_{i+r}^t)$$

Formula 1. Left-toggle rule.

$$1-s_i^t = F(s_{i-r}^t, \ldots, s_i^t, \ldots 1-s_{i+r}^t)$$

Formula 2. Right-toggle rule.

In other words, a change of the most distant bit of the neighborhood always causes a change of the central bit. The following tables illustrate that principle.

$\{s_{i-r}^t, s_i^t, s_{i+r}^t\}$	$s_i^{t+1}(30)$
000	0
001	1
010	1
011	1
100	1
101	0
110	0
111	0

000 --> 0
100 --> 1

001 --> 1
101 --> 0

010 --> 1
110 --> 0

011 --> 1
111 --> 0

Tab. 2. Rule 30 in comparative setting.

Rule 30 is a left-toggle rule. The first part of the Table 2 shows the transition for each combination of the neighborhood and the central bit. On the right hand side the lines of the same table have been coupled to show that a change of the (underlined) left bit of the input always causes a change of the output – either from 0 to 1 as in the first and third couple or from 1 to 0 as in the second and fourth couple.

The algorithm proposed in this paper has the following four basic properties:
- three automata are used, two of those are irreversible;
- a neighborhood has a special single toggling bit standing out;
- a symmetric key, which contains identifiers of the transition rules;
- certain geometric transformations give extra dissipation of data.

The proposed enciphering algorithm works on a 2D cellular automaton of size 32x8 bits. Two auxiliary automata of size 2x8 and 32x8 contribute to the course of work of the main one introducing non-uniqueness factor to the algorithm. In a single run (execution) of the algorithm 32 ASCII characters are enciphered. One can increase the size of those automata. However, this means also bigger number of rules, hence bigger size of the key.

The automata used in our algorithm can be graphically shown as in Fig. 4, where the auxiliary automata CALink and CATop provide some data necessary for the algorithm execution but the enciphering itself is performed within automaton CACrypt.

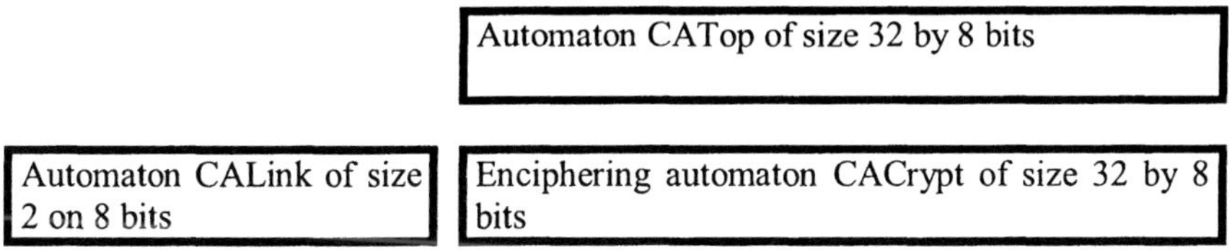

| Automaton CATop of size 32 by 8 bits |

| Automaton CALink of size 2 on 8 bits | Enciphering automaton CACrypt of size 32 by 8 bits |

Fig. 4. Graphic system of the automata.

An overview of our algorithm follows. It processes plaintext blocks of 32 bytes and produces ciphertext blocks of the same size (32 bytes). The algorithm is run as many times as many blocks there are. In case of uneven filling of the input blocks, the last block is completed with the space characters. Plaintext is written into CACrypt cells as an initial state. ASCII characters are entered in columns in their binary representation. The initial states of CALink and CATop are taken from the key, as well as the rules for all the three automata.

The first computation is to find the vectors of all the states of automata CALink and CATop in the current run of the algorithm. Using the rules and the 9-bit neighborhoods those automata make 32 steps. In each of them, a new state is computed and saved in the arrays called the vectors of states. This completes pre-computations.

Enciphering is done in a loop 32 times. A single loop consists of three steps: ciphering phase, toggling phase and dissipation.

In ciphering phase, for each cell of CACrypt, a 7-bit neighborhood is used. For the first two column we take a part of the neighborhood from automaton CALink. Applying the rule of CACrypt appropriate for a given column we determine a new state for a given cell. Deciphering is performed in the reverse way.

The goal of the toggle phase is to change the states of CACrypt by applying data from CATop. 8-bit neighborhood is determined now, while the central cell does not count. The state of the central cell is taken from CACrypt. These data determine which rule of CATop is applied. Its output is written to the cell (of CACrypt) as its next state.

The dissipation phase is realized by rotating squares of bits of size 2x2 in automaton CACrypt. The key rules of CACrypt provide information on how many times each square is to be turned round and in which direction – left or right. The bits contained in the rules are read in packets of three. The first two bits determine the number of turns for the corresponding square; the third bit prompts the direction. All the squares of CACrypt are turned round when the loop is executed 32 times. Moreover, always before an even turn the net of squares is shifted one position left and down.

When the three phases are complete, CATop and CALink get their next state written from the vectors of states. The next iteration of the main loop starts off. When the loop is over the data written eventually in CACrypt are written to the output bit stream. Some details are given below.

A pseudo code of this algorithm may be given as follows:

procedure Enciphering
INPUT: 32 byte plaintext; initial state of CATop (1...32 bytes); initial state of CALink (1...2 bytes), rules of CACrypt (1...32 of 2*128 bit vectors); rules of CALink (1...2 of 2*512 bit vectors); rules of CATop (1...32 of 2*512 bit vectors)
OUTPUT: 32-byte ciphertext

//setup of the auxiliary automata
generate the vectors of states for automata CALink and CATop
//the main loop of the algorithm
for k:=1 **to** 32 **do**
    begin
  //enciphering phase
  for x:=1 **to** 32 **do**
    for y:= 1 **to** 8 **do**
    begin
      compute the next state of cell (x,y) in automaton CACrypt using CALink (see below)
    end
  //toggle phase
  for x:=1 **to** 32 **do**
    for y:= 1 **to** 8 **do**
    begin
      join the neighborhood from CATop with that of CACrypt for cell (x,y) and determine the next state of cell (x,y) of CACrypt
    end
  //dissipation phase
  Rotate the squares
  set to the next one the state of CALink copying it from the vector of states
  set to the next one the state of CATop copying it from the vector of states
end

The deciphering algorithm looks like very similar. Everything happens in the reversed direction than in the enciphering case. (See below.)

Enciphering phase

In the enciphering phase we use neighborhoods of the shape shown at Fig. 5 below.

These neighborhoods are used with the right-toggle rules. The toggling bit is that of the right-most cell. The same bit and cell are meant as central here; shown in black.

The key used in this phase consists of 32 rules used as left-toggle ones. This is a symmetric key. Since a neighborhood consists of 7 bits we have 128 combinations. Thus each rule can be represented in the form of a table of 7x128 of bits and a vector of 1x128 bits. In order to simplify generation of a key and for simplicity of presentation the rules are given in the form shown at Fig. 6 below.

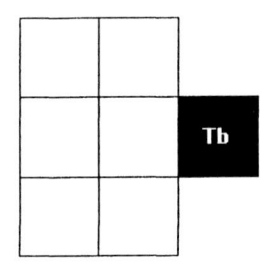

Fig. 5. A neighborhood used for enciphering.

line	Neighborhood	Tb	Output of the rule
1	0 0 0 0 0 0	0	1
	0 0 0 0 0 0	1	0
2	0 0 0 0 0 1	1	0
	0 0 0 0 0 1	0	1
	. . . . . .		
64	1 1 1 1 1 1	1	0
	1 1 1 1 1 1	0	1

Fig. 6. A system of bits in one rule.

Here a neighborhood is shown in the form of a 1-dimesional vector of 6 bits. The consecutive two lines are grouped together with their two toggling bits in random order. That is, the first of them is chosen at random and the second is complementary. The toggling bits (Tb) are shown in their own column. The output of the rule is also obtained as the bit complement to the toggling bit. Due to this form of graphic presentation one has to keep in the key only the vector of output values. The toggling bits and the table of neighborhoods can be generated on-the-fly during an execution of the algorithm.

The actions in the phase of enciphering a single cell of automaton CACrypt can be listed as follows:
1. input the 6 bits of the neighborhood of the cell to be encrypted without the toggling bit (e.g., those 6 bits give number 35, read top-down line after line);
2. look-up in the rule (for this column in the key) the line indexed by those 6 bits. (E.g., we get lines 70 and 71);
3. out of those two lines choose that one in which the rule output is the same as the value of the toggling bit Tb in the currently considered neighborhood;
4. as the next state of the cell to be encrypted write down the value of Tb of the above chosen line.

The actions in the phase of deciphering a single cell of automaton CACrypt can be listed as follows:

1. input 6 bits of the neighborhood of the cell to be deciphered but without the cell to be deciphered (e.g., those 6 bits give number 35);
2. find out these lines of the rule that are indexed by the above 6 bits. (E.g., for 35 we get lines 70 and 71);
3. out of those two lines choose that one in which the value of Tb is equal to the value of Tb taken from automaton of the currently considered neighborhood;
4. as the value of the next state of this cell write down the value of the rule of the line chosen above.

All those actions are shown in Figure 7 below.

CACrypt initial state

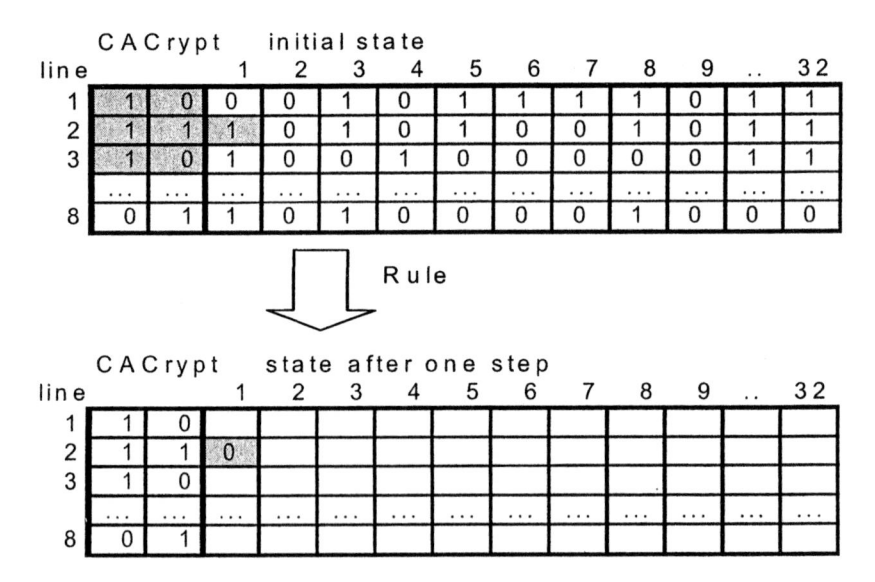

line	1	2	3	4	5	6	7	8	9	..	32
1	1	0	0	0	1	0	1	1	1	1	0	1	1
2	1	1	1	0	1	0	1	0	0	1	0	1	1
3	1	0	1	0	0	1	0	0	0	0	0	1	1
...	...	...	...	...	...	...	...	...	...	...	...	...	...
8	0	1	1	0	1	0	0	0	0	1	0	0	0

⇩ Rule

CACrypt state after one step

line	1	2	3	4	5	6	7	8	9	..	32
1	1	0											
2	1	1	0										
3	1	0											
...	...	...	...										
8	0	1											

Fig. 7. Enciphering of a single cell.

The initial values of the first two columns are treated by using automaton CALink starting the enciphering phase. CALink is of size 2x8 bits. Its initial state and its transition rules come from the key. Its neighborhoods are of the shape shown in Figure 3b. Since the neighborhoods have size bigger than CALink itself, the outside bits are to be taken from the other end of the automaton CALink or CACrypt, respectively. For instance, the neighborhood of cell (1,1) is formed by the following cells: (2,8)(1,8)(2,8)(2,1)(*1,1*)(2,1)(2,2)(1,2)(2,2). For each such neighborhood, the next state of cell (1,1) is determined by the transition rules from the key. The rules for automaton CALink are constructed just like those of CACrypt. It uses 2 rules, each of length 512 bits.

The following actions make a transition to the next state of a single cell of automaton CALink (Tb is the bit of the central cell here):
1. input the central bit and the eight bits of the neighborhood (9 bits together);
2. find the output of the rule line indexed by those 9 bits;
3. write the above output value to the central cell as its next state.

Automaton CALink is irreversible. It is a consequence of loosing the state of the cells of a given neighborhood while passing to the next state. State s_i^{t+1} of a cell at time instance t+1 is computed from the states of a neighborhood at time t. In order to reconstruct the state of time t from that of time t+1 one needs to know the states s_i^t of the appropriate neighborhoods. Those have been lost, however.

At the deciphering phase we use the states s_i^{31}, s_i^{30},... s_i^0 of CALink automaton. This is possible due to storing all the states of CALink in the vector of states. Before running the deciphering algorithm we set CALink at state s_i^0. We write the cells of CALink into the vector of states, then we compute s_i^1 and we write it into the vector state. We repeat this until we get all the 32 states of CALink. In the deciphering phase we use that vector of states instead of recovering the previous state of the automaton.

The toggle phases

The second part of the algorithm consists of changing the states of all the cells of automaton CACrypt. To this end we use CATop automaton. Its goal is to generate the bits of some auxiliary neighborhoods, which are of the shape shown in Figure 3b. For instance, in order to compute the next state of cell (4,3), see Figure 8, for automaton CACrypt one executes the following steps:
- input the neighborhood of cell (4,3) from CATop automaton;
- input the current state of cell (4,3) from CACrypt;
- apply the transition rules of automaton CATop to compute the next state of that neighborhood.

CATop (fragment of the automaton)   CACrypt (fragment of the automaton)

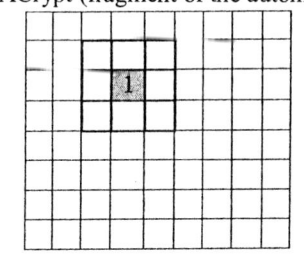

Fig. 8. Composition of a neighborhood.

Automaton CATop has 32 rules of length 512 bits each. The rules are constructed just like those of CACrypt. CATop acts just like CALink. In the deciphering phase, just like within automaton CALink, the vector of states is constructed at the beginning of executing the algorithm, and stored for later use as input to reconstruct the former states of CACrypt.

Taken together, there are 32 steps of automata CALink and CATop at the beginning of a run of the algorithm. The states calculated within those steps are stored in the auxiliary tables until they are needed in CACrypt in the enciphering phase.

The dissipation phase

The third part of the algorithm consists of some geometric transformations on the squares of size 2x2 for further dissipation of data. We chop the tape of automaton CACrypt into a net of squares as shown in Figure 9. Within each square of the net the bits are turned round left or right. The direction is taken from the key. The number of turns is taken from the key too. In this case each square can be turned round 0, 1 or 2 times without repetitions. Turning a square round twice to the right gives the same effect as two turns two the left.

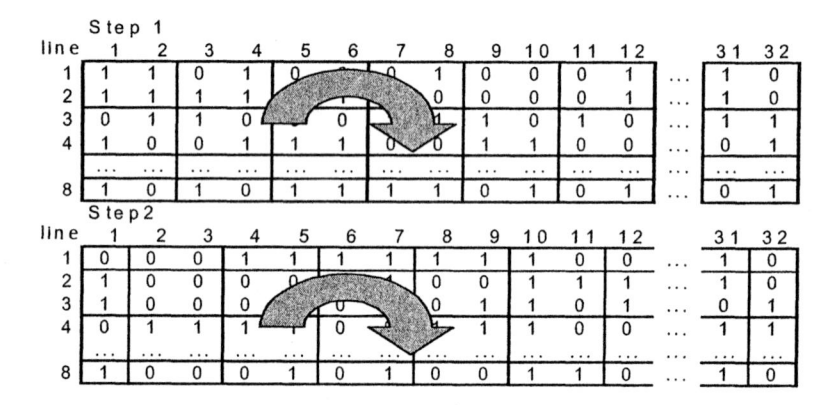

Step 1

line	1	2	3	4	5	6	7	8	9	10	11	12	...	31	32
1	1	1	0	1	0	0	1	0	0	0	1	...	1	0
2	1	1	1	1			0	0	0	0	1	...	1	0
3	0	1	1	0	0		1	0	1	0	...	1	1
4	1	0	0	1	1	1	0	0	1	1	0	0	...	0	1
...	...	...	...	...	...	...	...	...	...	...	...	...	...	...
8	1	0	1	0	1	1	1	1	0	1	0	1	...	0	1

Step 2

line	1	2	3	4	5	6	7	8	9	10	11	12	...	31	32
1	0	0	0	1	1	1	1	1	1	1	0	0	...	1	0
2	1	0	0	0			0	0	1	1	1	...	1	0
3	1	0	0	0		0	1	0	1	...	0	1
4	0	1	1	1	0		1	1	0	0	...	1	1
...	...	...	...	...	...	...	...	...	...	...	...	...	...	...
8	1	0	0	0	1	0	1	0	0	1	1	0	...	1	0

Fig. 9. A net of squares to turn round.

This method is enhanced in every step by shifting the net of squares alternately by vector of length 0 and by vector [(0,0),(1,-1)], where the origin of the axis system is at the upper left corner of the automaton. This gives rise to a possibility that the upper left bit can be turned over even to the lower right corner, for instance.

In the deciphering phase the same geometric transformations are executed in the reversed way.

The key consists of the following three components:
1. Two rules and initial states of automaton CALink. Each of the rules is given in the form of two vectors of 2^9=512 bits each.
2. 32 rules of automaton CACrypt, one rule for each column. Each of the rules consists of two vectors of 2^7=128 bits each.
3. 32 rules and initial states of automaton CATop. Each of the two rules is in the form of two vectors of 2^9=512 each.

Each rule consists of two vectors: the first is a list of the values of toggle-bits, the second is a list of the output values of the rule.

This completes our brief presentation of the main lines of our algorithm of encryption/decryption using two-dimensional cellular automata. This algorithm has been implemented in a program named „IPI Protect" available at [13].

5. AN APPLICATION: PROGRAM „IPI PROTECT"

Main motivation for this program was to provide a reliable tool for encryption and protection of MS Word documents against unauthorized modifications. The program has the following properties:
- protects documents with encryption using 2D cellular automata;
- uses a symmetric key;
- provides password protected authorization rights to documents;
- integrates with MS Word software;
- enables using a built-in key as well as a key stored on a disc (e.g., a chip card).

An ultimate goal of this tool is to extend the options providing enhanced protection of access rights to MS Word documents. „IPI Protect" serves the following four extra protection rights.
- the right to open a given document in MS Word. Checking this option gives full control over the document to the current user. Checking it off enables choosing the options described below. To this end a new extra program RTF Viewer was written and added to MS Word;
- the right to print;
- the right to save changes;
- the right to copy. Choosing this option enables copying the document body to the clipboard.

Depending on the key – built-in or external - one can decrease or increase the security level. As usually, a symmetric key needs special care for storage on a dedicated chip card or just a diskette. Using a built-in symmetric key enables delivering the document in its enciphered version through an open communication channel; e.g., by e-mail. In this case a secure channel must be used to exchange the access key.

The program consists of three files: IPICAConv, whose goal is to integrate with MS Word and provide a new saving format; IPICA.dll, which contains our enciphering algorithm and some extra form sheets; program RTFView which displays the documents with switched off options of any modification whatsoever.

In Figure 10 we show a general scheme of „IPI Protect".

6. CONCLUSION

Applying two-dimensional cellular automata for encryption is a new proposal, as far as we know. The algorithm presented here can be implemented on multi-processor machines, thus giving much better efficiency. Using the irreversible rules to generate the extra link bits gives an extra enhanced cryptographic power. Very simple geometric transformations on the squares of bits seem to give an effect similar to substitutions, resembling so-called S-boxes. (See [13].)

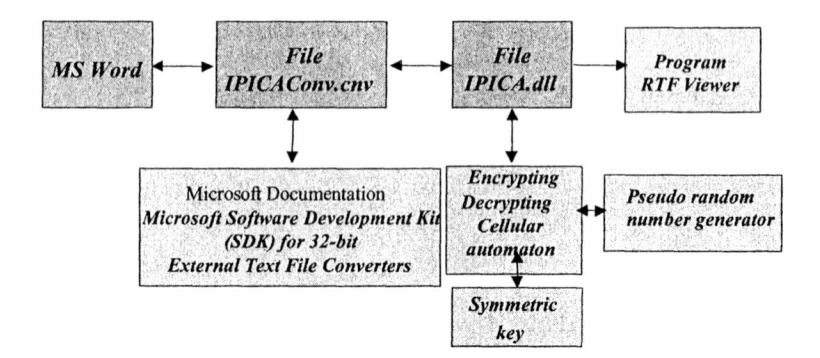

Fig. 10. A functional scheme of „IPI Protect".

As for future work we would like to announce some attempts of refining the algorithm in order to get the highest possible quality of our cryptosystem while keeping very high speed of its execution. The question of resistance of the proposed cryptosystem against different kinds of possible attacks (cryptoanalysis) needs further research.

7. REFERENCES

[1] P.H. Bardell, Analysis of Cellular Automata Used as Pseudorandom Pattern Generators, *Proceedings of 1990 International Test Conference*, pp. 762-768
[2] J. Daeman, R. Govaerts, and J. Vandewalle, A Framework for the Design of One-Way Hash Functions Including Cryptanalysis of Damgård's One-Way Function Based on Cellular Automata, *Advances in Cryptology-ASIACRYPT'91 Proceedings*, Springer-Verlag, 1993, pp. 82-96
[3] H. Gutowitz, *Cryptography with Dynamical Systems*, Laboratoire d'Electronique Paris, France, July 25, 1996
[4] J. Kari, Reversibility of 2D Cellular Automata is Undecidable, *Physica D* 45 (1990), pp. 379-385
[5] K. Kułakowski, *Automaty komórkowe*, AGH w Krakowie, Ośrodek edukacji niestacjonarnej, Kraków 2000 (in Polish)
[6] W. Meier and O. Staffelbach, Analysis of Pseudo Random Sequences Generated by Cellular Automata, *Advances in Cryptology – EUROCRYPT '91 Proceedings*, Springer-Verlag, 1991, pp. 186-199
[7] A. Menezes, P. van Oorschot, and S. Vanstone, *Handbook of Applied Cryptography*, CRC Press, 1996
[8] M. Mihajlevic, Y. Zheng and H. Imai, *A Fast Cryptographic Hash Function Based on Linear Cellular Automata over GF(q)*, Mathematical Institute, Serb. Acad. Sci. & Arts, Kneza Mihaila 35, Belgrade, Yugoslavia
[9] J. von Neumann, *Theory of self-reproducing automata*, Urbana University of Illinois Press, 1966
[10] P. Sarkar, A Brief History of Cellular Automata, ACM Computing Surveys Volume 32, Issue 1 (2000), pp. 80-107

[11] M. Tomassini, M. Sipper, M. Zolla, M. Perrenoud, Generating high-quality random numbers in parallel by cellular automata, *Future Generation Computer Systems* 16 (1999), pp. 291–305
[12] S. Wolfram, Cryptography with Cellular Automata, www.stephenwolfram.com; also in: *Advances in Cryptology: Crypto'85 Proceedings*, Lecture Notes in Comp Science, 218, Springer-Verlag, 1986, 429-432
[13] http://www.wsh-kielce.edu.pl/~piotr

Secure data storing in a pool of vulnerable servers[1]

MARCIN GOGOLEWSKI[2], MIROSŁAW KUTYŁOWSKI[3]

[2] *Cryptology Centre, Department of Mathematics and Computer Science, Adam Mickiewicz University, Umultowska 87, 61-614 Poznań, Poland, marcing@amu.edu.pl*
[3] *Institute of Mathematics, Wrocław University of Technology, Wybrzeże Wyspiańskiego 27, 50-370 Wrocław, Poland, mirekk@im.pwr.wroc.pl*

Abstract: Secure storing of data is a much more challenging task than encryption with a secret key. These data can be destroyed (for instance through overwriting) either by an external adversary or by the administrator of the data server. If such an attack is deployed only occasionally, for a well chosen data, then a hardware fault can be blamed for the loss of data. Therefore effective countermeasures are to be deployed.
In order to elude the threat described one may store multiple copies of data in a pool of data servers. However, in order to limit the costs, the number of copies must be limited. Again, this provides a chance for an adversary to attack only the few servers actually storing the copies of data relevant for him.
In this paper we design a simple and elegant method for secure storing of encrypted data based on Rackoff-Simon onion protocol used previously against traffic analysis. Our protocol works in an environment where the servers and the clients communicate through a shared communication channel which provides anonymity of the sender (such as an Ethernet bus). The protocol uses only standard symmetric and asymmetric encryption schemes. The protocol presented in this paper guarantees that
(a) the user alone chooses where the data is stored, the number of copies can be determined immediately before storing the data,
(b) the server storing the data has no knowledge about other servers storing the same data,
(c) consistency: either all or no copy of the data is stored by the honest servers (i.e. the servers not overrun by an adversary),
(d) the client and each server that has to store the data sends exactly one message,
(e) with high probability the system is immune against adversaries that may gain control over a limited number of servers.

Key words: security, secure data storing, onion protocol for storing data

---

[1] this research has been partially supported by KBN, grant 0 T00A 003 23

1. INTRODUCTION

Problem statement. In this paper we present a simple method for secure storing of data based on Rackoff-Simon onion protocol against traffic analysis (see [5]). Secure storing of data is a much more challenging task than encryption of this data with a secret key. Encrypted data can be destroyed even easier than unencrypted one (if we destroy only a part of this data, the rest may be worthless). Our protocol is designed for secure storing of data in a distributed environment. A solution for local data is presented in [2].

An obvious way to achieve better security is to store multiple copies of data in a pool of data servers. However, in order to limit the costs, the number of copies must be limited. In this case an adversary has to attack only a few servers actually storing this data. It only has to know, where the copies are placed.

The protocol presented in this paper solves this problem. It uses only standard symmetric and asymmetric encryption schemes. It can work in an environment where the servers and the clients communicate through a shared communication channel which provides anonymity of a sender as well as a receiver even though all messages can be read by all servers and all clients (as in an Ethernet bus or a Token Ring). The protocol guarantees that:

- the user alone chooses which servers store the data, the number of copies can be determined immediately before storing the data;
- the server storing the data has no knowledge about other servers storing the same data;
- either all honest servers chosen store the data or none of them (honest means here *the servers not overrun by an adversary*);
- the client and each server storing the data sends exactly one message (version of the protocol without ack-onions);
- with high probability the system is immune against adversaries that may gain control over a limited number of servers.

Onion protocol. In this paragraph we briefly describe Onion Routing. A more complete description and analysis of this protocol can be found in [3, 6, 7, 8, 9]. Onion protocol is based on so-called mixes [1] used to hide communication. A mix is a node which collects a number of fixed-length messages, called a batch, recodes them in a cryptographic way and sends forward in a random order.

Onion routers are designed to pass information in real time, which limits mixing and potentially weakens the protection. The network of onion routers is a clique, that is, every node may communicate directly with any other node. Connections between each pair of nodes are encrypted independently. Three logical types of virtual nodes are distinguished by the protocol:

- normal clients and servers using TCP/IP, which can work with proxies (for example: HTTP servers and web-browsers);
- onion routers -- described below;
- proxies, which manage connections initiated by clients and directed through onion routers to the servers.

All three types of virtual nodes may co-exist on the same computer.

From the logical point of view, Onion Routing has three phases called *create, data, destroy*. At the beginning (create phase) client (initiator) contacts his proxy called *onion proxy* (transparent proxy, which would not require any additional abilities from the client, could be also constructed, but the current version of onion protocol does not concern this issue) and the proxy creates connection for him in the following way:

(1) It chooses at random list of n nodes $s_0, ..., s_n$.
(2) It creates so called *onion* using the following recursive formula:

$$G_0 = E_{P(0),S}(\,\texttt{exp\_time}\,(0),\,\texttt{null},\,F_{f,0},\,K_{f,0},\,F_{b,0},K_{b,0},\,\texttt{PADDING})$$

$$G_i = E_{P(i),S}(\texttt{exp\_time}\,(i),\,s_{i-1},\,F_{f,i},\,K_{f,i},\,F_{b,i},\,K_{b,i},\,G_{i-1})$$

where $\texttt{exp\_time}(i)$ is an expiration time for this connection, s_{i-1} is a next node number (if the receiving node is the responder's proxy, it is $\texttt{null}$), (F_f, K_f) is a pair of keys applied to data moving in the forward direction and (F_b, K_b) is a pair of keys applied to data moving in the opposite direction, $P(i)$ is a public key of the node s_i. PADDING is a random bit string used for the purpose of making each onion of the same size (which makes tracking more difficult). $C = E_{X,S}(Y)$ denotes that:

1. a key $\mathcal{K}$ for symmetric algorithm S is chosen at random;
2. message Y is encrypted with symmetric algorithm S with key $\mathcal{K}$, let C_2 denote the ciphertext obtained;
3. key $\mathcal{K}$ is encrypted with asymmetric algorithm with key X, let C_1 denote the ciphertext obtained;
4. C is a concatenation of C_1 and C_2.

(3) It sends the onion G_n to the node s_n.
(4) Each node s_i decrypts the sub-onion posted, if it is incorrect the node ignores it. If the data decrypted has the format of data used to construct G_i as described in the definition of the onion, then:

- if the next node number is not $\texttt{null}$, then s_i creates a virtual connection to node s_{i-1} (and stores record for this connection), stores the keys contained in the decrypted text, expiration time, adds random bit string at the end of G_{i-1} in order to obtain a fixed size (bits at the end of G_{i-1} belong to PADDING, so if some additional bits are added at the end they do not affect any bits containing useful information, if the ciphertext is decrypted from the beginning), independent of the "layer" of the onion and sends G_{i-1} to the next node;

- if the next node number is $\texttt{null}$ (the current node is the responder proxy), it stores corresponding keys, expiration time and creates connection to the responder. This connection is not encrypted by the protocol (however, it may be encrypted itself, for example it may be an SSL connection).

When a connection is established the client can send the data to the initiator proxy, the proxy encrypts it with the keys specified in the onion, innermost first. These layers of cryptography are "peeled off" as the data travels forward through the channel, that is, each node decrypts it using its key obtained from the onion. Data from the responder is encrypted by each node, so initiator proxy has to apply decryption with keys specified in the onion, outermost first, to this stream and sends the plaintext to the initiator.

At the end of the connection *destroy* packet is sent through the connection, all nodes forward it and clear up all data relevant to this connection. All packets traveling between nodes have the same size fixed by the protocol, so an observer cannot distinguish between types *onion, data, destroy* of packets.

2. ONION PROTOCOL FOR STORING DATA

Now we describe the protocol that solves the problem stated in the previous section. We assume that a client Alice is going to store k copies of data M in a pool of file servers $S_1, ..., S_n$. Communication between the servers and the clients is through a bulletin board that hides who publishes data on it.

We assume also that the servers use public key encryption algorithm such that a ciphertext of an unknown plaintext starting with a random string does not reveal which public key was used to create it. For example, one can use RSA encryption with moduli $m_1, ... , m_n$ of the same length. However, since the ciphertexts are quite uniformly distributed over $(0,m_i)$ for each i, a ciphertext may show at once which keys could not be used, namely when the ciphertext is larger than m_j. In order to solve this problem we may apply a simple trick. We choose m so that $\max(m_1,...,m_n) < m < 2\max(m_1,...,m_n)$. When we have to create a ciphertext with the jth key of text t, we choose at random a string s and create a ciphertext c of s concatenated with t using the jth private key (so it is for the server S_j). Roughly speaking, ciphertext c is evenly distributed over the interval $[0,m_j]$. That is, probability that $c \in U$ is approximately proportional to the size of U for sufficiently large intervals $U \subseteq (0,m_j)$. Let $k=m-m_j$. We proceed as follows:

- we choose bit b at random;
- if $b=0$, then $c':=c$ else $c':=c+k$;
- if $c'<k$ or $c'>m_j$, then c' is our ciphertext and we output c' as the ciphertext produced;
- else we choose at random bit b'
    if $b'=0$, then we output c',
    otherwise we choose at random a new s and start from the beginning.

It is easy to see that the number c' is evenly distributed over interval $[0,m]$. Indeed, during one execution of the loop, if c is uniformly distributed over $(0,m_j)$, then the probability for a given $z \in (0,m)$ of outputting z is $\frac{1}{2}(m-1)$. There is a slight technicality following this construction: when a server S_i decrypts such a ciphertext c', it tries to decrypt c' and $c'-k$.

Creating an onion. First, Alice has to create an *onion* that contains all relevant information for the servers:
- Alice chooses at random a set of numbers $J=\{j(1), ..., j(k) \leq n : j(i) \neq j(l)$ for $i \neq l\}$. Alternatively, Alice may produce these numbers by a pseudo-random number generator with a seed including $H(M)$ and a secret key known only to Alice (H is a secure cryptographic hash function).

- Alice chooses at random a key K for symmetric encryption, then a random key K_0 of the same length, and finally computes $K_1 = K$ XOR K_0 (so K_0 and K_1 are shares of key K according to the 2-out-of-2 secret sharing scheme).
- Alice chooses at random strings SIG(M), $r_1, ..., r_k$, and $s_2, ..., s_k$ of a fixed length l, and sets s_1:=null (the length of s_1 is equal to l, too).
- The onion C_k is created by Alice. It has a recursive structure defined as follows. The *kernel* C_0 is a sequence of the following strings:

$C_0 := s_1, ..., s_k, K_1, \text{SIG}(M)$.

Then for $i \leq k$ the sub-onion C_i has the form

$C_i := E_{P(j(i))}(r_i, s_i, \mathscr{F}, K_0, H(C_0), C_{i-1})$

where $E_X(Y)$ denotes a ciphertext obtained from Y with a key X and an asymmetric encryption algorithm, $P(u)$ is the public key of server S_u, and $\mathscr{F}$ is a sufficiently long fixed sequence chosen by the protocol (for instance, it may contain the current date, and expiration time). $H(C_0)$ is used to check correctness of the kernel (and honesty of $S_{j(1)}$).

Sending information by Alice. The client Alice publishes on bulletin board two messages:
- the onion C_k,
- the message consisting of SIG(M) and M encrypted with the key K using a symmetric encryption algorithm.

Both messages can be published at once. However, one may also choose to postpone publication of the second message until the kernel of the onion C_k is published. This may save unnecessary transmission, if the protocol breaks down. If Alice waits for the kernel on the bulletin board, the server $S_{j(1)}$, which knows K_0 and K_1, has to publish the kernel to get the second message from Alice. We may slightly modify the protocol so that $S_{j(1)}$ will not realize that it is the first node in the onion. For this purpose it suffices to change the kernel: s_1 has to be replaced by a random string, and C_0 padded so that its length equals the length of the messages sent by other nodes.

Let us point at this place that the servers will store M and not its ciphertext. The encryption with K is used merely to hide M from communication channel that can be read at least by all servers. However, another measure can be deployed by Alice: M itself can be a ciphertext.

Processing an onion by the servers Once an onion $X = C_i$ is published on the bulletin board a server S_i performs the following steps:
- decrypts X with its private key, if the plaintext obtained has not the form

$r, s, \mathscr{F}, L, H(x), C$

where r, s are strings of length l, L is the key for symmetric algorithm, $H(x)$ is a fixed length value of hashing function, and C is a ciphertext, or forms a kernel of an onion, then S_i stops processing X. If the onion is expired (proper information about expiration time are in $\mathscr{F}$) the server also stops processing X. Most important point here is that S_i proceeds, if the plaintext obtained contains the string $\mathscr{F}$ on the proper place.
- if the ciphertext decrypted does not contain a kernel, then S_i stores s together with the key L for a later use, and publishes C on the bulletin board.
- if the decrypted ciphertext contains a kernel of an onion, say

$s_1, ..., s_k, K_1, \text{SIG}(M)$,

then S_i stores $K = K_0$ XOR K_1 and SIG(M) for a later use and puts the strings s_1, ..., s_k, K_1, SIG(M) on the bulletin board.

Storing data by servers. As soon as on the bulletin board a server S_i detects a kernel C_0 containing a string s it has saved together with K_0 while processing an onion, then S_i computes $K := K_0$ XOR K_1. Later it uses K to decrypt each encrypted data from the bulletin board: if SIG(M) appears in front of the plaintext, it saves the remaining part of the plaintext in its file system.

3. SECURITY FEATURES

Privacy of file localization. Only Alice knows where the data is stored. Each server S_i knows only its own private key, and cannot decrypt an onion encrypted with public key not related to its private key. It cannot also reconstruct an onion (add the previously removed layer) in order to find which public key was used. Indeed, it does not know random strings r_j for $j \neq i$, so cannot construct the previous layer, even if it knows the public keys that may be used to construct it. It cannot even associate the messages on the bulletin board corresponding to the same onion, since only ciphertexts are published.

"All or nothing" property. If a kernel of an onion appears on the bulletin board, all honest (see next paragraphs) servers will store it. If it does not appear, none of the servers will know the "fingerprint" SIG(M) of the message and key K used to decrypt it. In this case, after the onion expires (expiration time may be included in $\mathscr{F}$), Alice can try to choose another set of servers and try again.

Denial-of-service attacks. To avoid DoS attacks (filling chosen servers with worthless messages by another servers or clients) and preserve anonymity of the protocol, we can enclose *e-coin* (more precisely, $E_{\text{Priv}(a)}(e\text{-}coin)$, where Priv($a$) is a private key created by Alice for this transaction) in each layer (i.e. Alice can buy a card with SIG(M) and k different e-coin's in an anonymous way, similar to pre-paid cards). To avoid using the same e-coin in multiple layers, we precede each s_i in the kernel by $H(E_{\text{Priv}(a)}(e\text{-}coin))$. E-coin should require some information from the kernel. The server S_i checks if this string is in the proper place and each such a string appears only once in the whole kernel. If so, it decrypts e-coin and proceeds with storing data. Public key Priv(*a*) may be enclosed in the kernel or in the second message generated by Alice together with *M*. Of course, Alice should use these keys only in one transaction, to preserve full anonymity.

Number of messages. During each protocol solving the problem stated, Alice has to send at least one message, each server has to acknowledge that it can store the data from Alice (if not, it cannot break down the protocol in order to guarantee "all-or-nothing" property). If Alice wanted to contact directly each server (without onions and the bulletin board), she would have to send at least *k* messages, it would be more difficult to preserve anonymity and all-or-nothing property. Altogether it would require at least 2*k* messages. On the other hand, even if the onion and the data are sent separately the total number of messages in our protocol is *k*+2.

Robustness against attacks on servers. If we assume that only a few servers are overrun by an adversary, we can hope our set of servers does not contain any dishonest server. Let us assume that we have $\sqrt{n}$ dishonest servers where *n* is a total number of servers. If we choose servers at random we can assume that the probability of being dishonest is equal for all servers. Assume that Alice chooses $\lceil \log n \rceil$ of servers to store its data. Let *A* denote an event that *J*, the set of servers chosen, does not contain any dishonest server. Then:

$$\Pr(A) = \frac{\binom{n-\lfloor\sqrt{n}\rfloor}{\lceil\log(n)\rceil}}{\binom{n}{\lceil\log n\rceil}} = \prod_{i=1}^{\lceil\log n\rceil} \frac{n-\lfloor\sqrt{n}\rfloor-\lceil\log n\rceil+i}{n-\lfloor\sqrt{n}\rfloor+i} \qquad (1)$$

Thus, one can easily check that Pr(*A*) is going to 1 for *n* going to infinity. More precisely,

$$\Pr(A) \approx \prod_{i=1}^{\log n}\left(1-\frac{\log n}{n-\sqrt{n}+i}\right) \geq \left(1-\frac{2\log n}{n}\right)^{\log n} \approx 1$$

for *n* large enough.

We can see in Figure 1 that event *A* is quite probable, well above 0.5 even for moderate values of *n*. Moreover, if the adversary (or broken server) breaks down the protocol, Alice can notice it and try again. Probability of failing in *t* trials is below 2^{-t}.

The worst case occurs when the protocol does not break down, but all servers requested by Alice are dishonest and do not store the data. Let us consider a different model for the possibility of being dishonest (asymptotically equivalent). Each server (independently) is dishonest with probability *p*. Let *B* denote the probability that at least one server is honest in *J*. Then:

Pr(*B*)=1-p^k

Obviously, if *k*=log *n* and *p*=½, then Pr(*B*)= 1-1/*n*, which is asymptotically a very good result. Figures 2 and 3 present probabilities of event *B* for different, practical values of n, where $p=1/\sqrt{n}$ and $p=\frac{1}{2}$, respectively. So, even if a constant fraction of servers is dishonest, it is very unlikely that dishonest servers will prevent storing a data sent by Alice in our protocol.

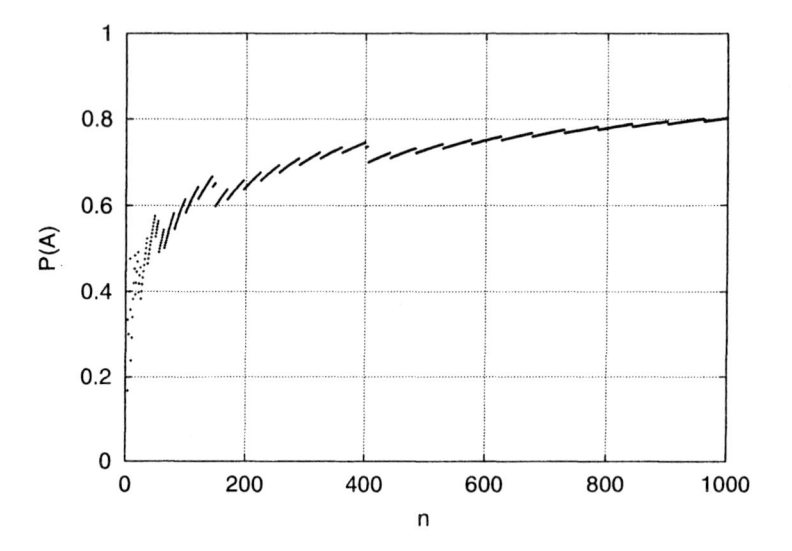

Fig. 1. Probability of event A depending on value of n.

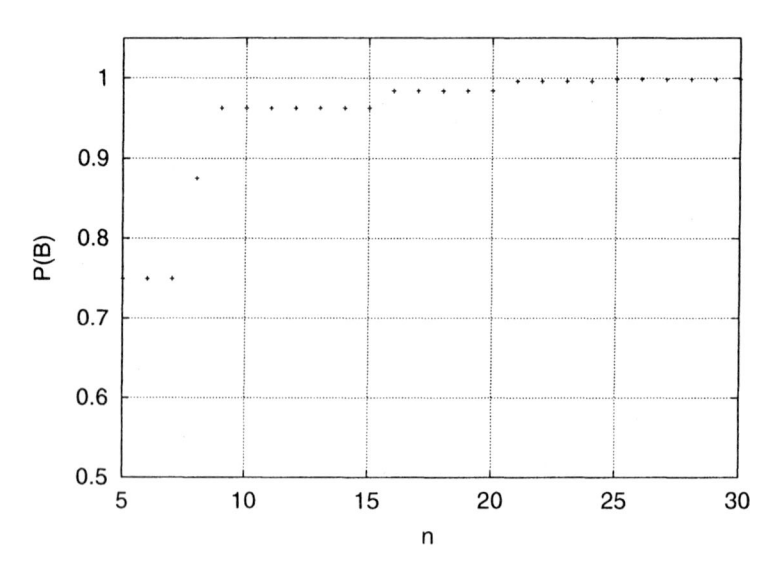

Fig. 2. Probability of event B when $p=1/\sqrt{n}$

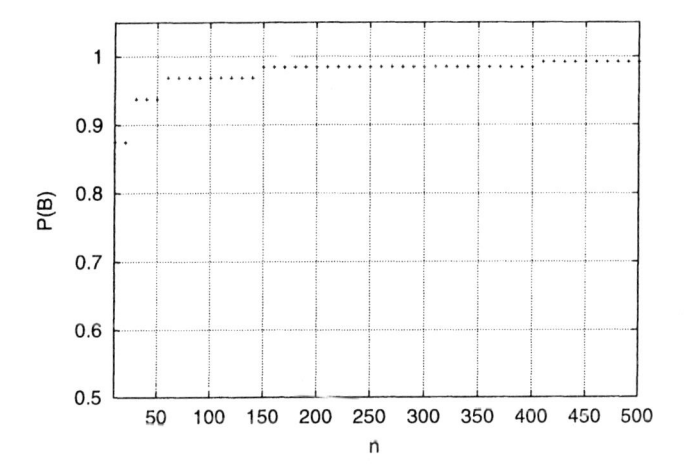

Fig. 3. Probability of event B when $p=\frac{1}{2}$

Ack-onion. If Alice uses protocol described in Section 2, she does not have any proof, suitable for a third party, that any server has responded to her request -- she could send each layer of the onion by herself. If she needs such a proof, we have to modify the protocol slightly. We can enclose electronic form in the kernel C_0 and each server will have to sign it. This extension should fulfill some conditions:
* the protocol supports anonymity of the participants involved in storing the data;
* each server cannot sign this form before downloading and decrypting the message from Alice; (of course, we still cannot say if it actually stores the data from Alice in its file system);
* the number of messages can increase at most by k.

We also assume that each message or onion sent to the bulletin board is temporarily stored by each server -- this is necessary, if communication is actually through a shared broadcast channel.

We can construct so called *ack-onion* (in fact a coupled pair of onions) in the following way: Alice chooses at random A_{k+1}, in addition to the set of indices J and for $i=k, k-1, ..., 1$ constructs sub-onions (first for $i=k$):

$A_i := E_{P(j(i))}(s_i, K_1, \text{SIG}(M), A_{i+1})$,
$F_1 := H(c_1)$.

Alice uses a pair (A_1, F_1) instead of C_0 as the kernel (compare Section 2). Server which receives the kernel signs (encrypts with its private key $\text{Priv}(j(1))$) and encrypts F_1 as follows:

$F_2 = E_{P(a)}(E_{\text{Priv}(j(1))} (x_1, F_1, H(A_1), H(M)))$

where x_1 is a random string of a fixed length. Then it sends a pair (A_2, F_2) to the bulletin board.

Each subsequent server $S_{j(i)}$ identified by s_i, decrypts A_i (it tries to decrypt all appearing messages and checks if the plaintexts obtained contain the known s_i in a proper place), chooses at random x_i, stores M in its local file system, computes $H(M)$ and $H(A_i)$, then it signs F_i in the following way:

$$F_{i+1} := E_{P(a)}(E_{Priv(j(i)}(x_i, F_i, H(A_i), H(M)))$$

and publishes the pair (A_{i+1}, F_{i+1}) on the bulletin board. As soon as Alice detects a pair (A_{k+1}, F_{i+1}) on the bulletin board she decrypts F_{k+1} and checks signatures. With this extension our protocol requires k-1 additional messages.

4. CONCLUSIONS

Protocol described in this paper provides anonymity of storing data in a pool of servers. It is designed for distributed environments and in big networks it guarantees that even if many servers are overrun by an adversary several copies of the message M are stored. This protocol also ensures the client that either all chosen servers (not overrun by an adversary) or none of them will store the message. Neither adversary nor other servers knows other servers storing particular data. So the data stored is very difficult to be destroyed. This protocol can be easily extended to provide additional functionalities (robustness against DoS attacks, proofs for third party). Total number of messages in the protocol without extensions is k+1 (or k+2 depending on the policy). However, even in the version with *ack-onion* Alice has to send message M only once.

5. REFERENCES

[1] D. Chaum: Untraceable electronic mail, return addresses, and digital pseudonyms. Communications of the ACM 24 (1985) 84—88.
[2] A. D. McDonald, M. G. Kuhn: StegoFS: A Steganographic File System for Linux. Information Hiding '99, Lecture Notes in Computer Science, vol. 1768, Springer-Verlag, Berlin Heidelberg New York (1999), 463—477.
[3] Onion Routing, www.onion-router.net.
[4] A. Pfitzman, M. Waidner: Networks without User Observability. Computers & Security 6 (1987) 158—166.
[5] C. Rackoff and D. R. Simon: Cryptographic defense against traffic analysis. ACM Symposium on Theory of Computing (STOC) '93, 672—681.
[6] P.F. Syverson, D. Goldschlag, G. Reed: Hiding Routing Information. Information Hiding '96, Lecture Notes in Computer Science, vol. 1174, Springer-Verlag, Berlin Heidelberg New York (1996), 137—150.
[7] P.F. Syverson, D. Goldschlag, M. Reed: Anonymous Connections and Onion Routing. Proc. Symposium on Security and Privacy, Oakland, California, 1997.
[8] P.F. Syverson, D. Goldschlag, M. Reed: Onion Routing for Anonymous and Private Internet Connections. Communications of the ACM 42 (1999), 39—41.
[9] P.F. Syverson, G. Tsudik, M. Reed, C. Landwehr: Towards an Analysis of Onion Routing Security. Lecture Notes in Computer Science, vol. 2009, Springer-Verlag, Berlin Heidelberg New York (2001), 96—114.

On automatic secret generation and sharing for Karin-Greene-Hellman scheme

KAMIL KULESZA, ZBIGNIEW KOTULSKI
Institute of Fundamental Technological Research, Polish Academy of Sciences
ul.Świętokrzyska 21, 00-049, Warsaw Poland, e-mail: {kkulesza, zkotulsk}@ippt.gov.pl

Abstract: The secret considered is a binary string of fixed length. In the paper we propose a method of automatic secret generation and sharing. We show how to simultaneously generate and share random secret. Such a secret remains unknown until it is reconstructed. Next, we propose a method of automatic sharing of a known secret. In this case the Dealer does not know the secret and the secret's Owner does not know the shares. We discuss how to use extended capabilities in the proposed method.

Key words: cryptography, secret sharing, data security, extended key verification protocol

1. INTRODUCTION

Everybody knows situations, where permission to trigger certain action requires approval of several selected persons. Equally important is that any other set of people cannot trigger the action.

Secret sharing allows to split a secret into different pieces, called shares, which are given to the participants, such that only certain group (authorized set of participants) can recover the secret. Secret sharing schemes (SSS) were independently invented by George Blakley [2] and Adi Shamir [11]. Many schemes have been presented since, for instance, Asmuth and Bloom [1], Brickell [5], Karin-Greene-Hellman (KGH method) [6]. In our paper we concentrate on the last method.

In KGH the secret is a vector of η numbers $S_\eta = \{s_1, s_2, ..., s_\eta\}$. Any modulus k is chosen, such that $k > \max(s_1, s_2, ..., s_\eta)$. All t participants are given shares that are η-dimensional vectors $S_\eta^{(j)}, j = 1, 2, ..., t$ with elements in Z_k. To retrieve the secret they have to add the vectors component-wise in Z_k.

For $k = 2$, KGH method works like $\oplus$ (XOR) on η-bits numbers, much in the same way like Vernam one-time pad. If t participants are needed to recover the secret, adding $t-1$ (or less) shares reveals no information about secret itself.

Once secret sharing was introduced, people started to develop extended capabilities. Some of examples are: detection of cheaters (e.g. [9],[10]), multi-secret threshold schemes (e.g., [9]), pre-positioned secret sharing schemes (e.g., [9]).

Anonymous and random secret sharing was studied by Blundo, Giorgio Gaggia, Stinson in [3], [4]. Some of ideas in automatic secret sharing and generation come from the same field.

Dealer of the secret is the entity that assigns secret shares to the participants. Usually, the Dealer has to know the secret in order to share it. This gives Dealer advantage over ordinary secret participants. There are situations, where such advantage can lead to abuse.

Automatic secret generation and sharing (ASGS) allows computing and sharing the secret "on the spot", when it is not predefined. This is typical situation, that secret helps to identify authorized set of participants upon recovery. In such an application any element from certain set (say, all l-bit vectors) can be a secret. Automatic secret generation allows random generation of the secret and elimination of the secret Owner. First feature is important even without elimination of the secret Owner. It makes the secret choice "owner independent"; hence decrease chances for the Owner related attack. For instance: users in computer systems have strong inclination to use as the passwords character strings, that have some meaning for them. The most popular choices are spouse/kids names and cars' registration numbers.

Automatic sharing of a known secret addresses problem of secret Owner not trusting the Dealer. Using such a method Owner can easily share the secret. The resulting secret shares are random. It may have added feature, that even secret Owner knows neither secret shares, nor their distribution. The later decreases chances of Owner interfering with the shared secret.

The outline of the paper is the following:

Preliminaries are given in section 2; we also state basic property of binary vectors' set. Next section brings description of methods for automatic secret generation and sharing. In section 4 outline of method for automatic sharing for the existing secret is presented. Proposed methods support extended capabilities, which apart from being interesting theoretical constructs on their own, allow greater flexibility in the applications of secret sharing schemes.

Finally, we make few remarks about procedures and algorithms presented in this paper. Short description is provided for every routine. It states the purpose of routine, describes what is being done and specifies output (when needed). Such description should be enough to comprehend the paper and get main idea behind presented methods. In selected cases (volume constrains) we give routines written in pseudocode, resembling high level programming language (say C++). Level of detail is much higher than in description part. Reading through pseudocode might be tedious, but rewarding in the sense that allows appreciate proposed routines in full extend. Pseudocode for all presented routines can be found in preliminary version of this paper [8].

2. PRELIMINARIES

In order to formally present procedures and algorithms, one needs to introduce notation. Further, we describe two devices and their functions. First comes random number generator; its output strings have good statistical properties (e.g., see [7]). Next comes the accumulator, which is a dumb, automatic device that memory cannot be accessed otherwise than by predefined functions. Its embedded capabilities are described below. In further considerations m_i denotes l-bit vector. Given set A, its cardinality (number of elements) is denoted by $|A|$.

RAND yields m_i obtained from a random number generator.
ACC denotes the value of l-bit memory register. Register's functions are:
ACC.reset sets all bits in the memory register to 0,
ACC.read yields ACC,
ACC.store(x) yields $ACC = ACC \oplus x$ (performs bitwise XOR of ACC with the input binary vector x, result is stored to ACC).

Accumulator consists of l-bit memory register together with defined above functions. It has also some storage capacity separate from memory register. Accumulator can execute functions and operations as described in procedures.

Secure communication channel. In this paper we assume that all the communication between protocol parties is done in the way that only communicating parties know plaintext. Whenever we use command like "send", we presume that no third party can know the message contents. There is extensive literature on this subject, interested reader can for instance consult [9].

Encapsulation. Entities and devices taking part in the protocol can exchange information with others only via interface. Inner state of the entity (e.g. contents of memory registers) is hidden (encapsulated) and remains unknown for external observers.

The idea of automatic secret generation and sharing is based on the following property of binary vectors.

Basic property: Let $m_i, i = 1, 2, ..., n$, such that

$$\bigoplus_{i=1}^{n} m_i = \vec{0}, \tag{1}$$

form the set M. For any partition of M into two disjoined subsets C_1, C_2 ($C_1 \cup C_2 = M$, $C_1 \cap C_2 = \emptyset$), it holds:

$$\bigoplus_{m_i \in C_1} m_i = \bigoplus_{m_i \in C_2} m_i. \blacksquare \tag{2}$$

Now we present the procedure that generates set of binary vectors M.

Procedure description: *GenerateM* creates set of n binary vectors m_i, satisfying condition (1). Procedure is carried out by the Accumulator.

Procedure 1: *GenerateM(n)*

Accumulator:
  ACC.reset;
    for $i = 1$ to $n-1$ do
      $m_i := RAND$
      ACC.store (m_i)
      save m_i
    end //for
  $m_n = ACC.read$
  save m_n
  return $M = \{m_1, m_2, \ldots, m_n\}$
end // *GenerateM*

Discussion: We claim that the generated set M satisfies condition (1). First, statistically independent random vectors $m_i, i = 1, 2, \ldots, n-1$ are generated, while $m_n = \bigoplus_{i=1}^{n-1} m_i$, so $\bigoplus_{i=1}^{n} m_i = \left(\bigoplus_{i=1}^{n-1} m_i\right) \oplus m_n = \left(\bigoplus_{i=1}^{n-1} m_i\right) \oplus \left(\bigoplus_{i=1}^{n-1} m_i\right) = \vec{0}$. ∎

3. AUTOMATIC SECRET GENERATION AND SHARING

Longman's "Dictionary of Contemporary English" describes secret as "something kept hidden or known only to a few people". Still, there are few basic questions about nature of the secret, that need to be answered:
- When does the secret existence begin?
- Can secret exist before it is created?
- Can secret existence be described by binary variable?
- Can secret exist unknown to anyone; do we need at least one secret holder?
- If secret is shared, how one can verify its validity upon combining the shares?

In our approach secret existence begins, when it is generated. However, for the secret that is generated in the form of distributed shares, moment of creation comes when shares are combined for the first time. Before that moment, secret exists only in some potential (virtual) state. Nobody knows the secret, though secret shares exist, because they have never been combined. In order to assemble it, cooperation of authorized set of participants is required.

In such a situation, there are only two ways to recover secret: by guess or by cooperation of participants from the authorized set. The first way can be feasibly controlled by the size of the secret space, while the other one is the legitimate secret recovery procedure.

In case of the KGH (see [6]) secret sharing scheme, the process of creating secret shares destroys original copy of the secret. Once shares are combined, the secret is recovered. Recovered secret has to be checked against original secret in order to validate it. Hence, there must exist primary (template) copy of the secret. This can be seen from different perspective: recovered secret allows to identify and validate authorized set of participants, so, the template copy is required for comparison. For instance, consider opening bank vault. One copy of the secret is shared between bank employees that can open vault (the authorized set of secret participants). Second copy is programmed into the opening mechanism. When the employees input their combined shares, it can check whether they recover proper secret.

We propose the mechanisms, that allow automatic secret generation, such that:
a. The generated secret attains a randomly generated value.
b. Two copies of the secret are created.
c. Both secret copies are created in a distributed form.
d. Nobody knows the secret till the shares from the authorized set are combined.
e. Distributed secret shares can be replicated without compromising the secret.
f. The secret shares resulting from replication have different values then the source shares.

3.1 Basic secret shares generation

In this section we present algorithm that creates a secret simultaneously in two distributed copies.

Let $s_i^{(1)}$ and $s_i^{(2)}$ be some secret shares in KGH secret sharing scheme, let S denote the secret shared. Now, we show how to generate two authorized set of secret shares $U^{(1)} = \{s_1^{(1)}, s_2^{(1)}, ..., s_d^{(1)}\}$ and $U^{(2)} = \{s_1^{(2)}, s_2^{(2)}, ..., s_n^{(2)}\}$, such that $\bigoplus_{i \in U^{(1)}} s_i^{(1)} = S = \bigoplus_{i \in U^{(2)}} s_i^{(2)}$. $U^{(1)}$ is authorized set of primary secret shares that is used for verification of $U^{(2)}$. $U^{(2)}$ is called authorized set of user secret shares or, for the reasons that will become clear later, authorized set of master secret shares. To generate $U^{(1)}$ and $U^{(2)}$ algorithm *SetGenerateM* is used.

Algorithm description: *SetGenerateM* creates $U^{(1)}$ and $U^{(2)}$, such that $|U^{(1)}| = d$, $|U^{(2)}| = n$. First, *GenerateM* is used to create set M, such $|M| = d + n$. Next, M is partitioned into $U^{(1)}$ and $U^{(2)}$. The Accumulator executes algorithm automatically.

Algorithm 1: *SetGenerateM(d , n)*

Accumulator:
    GenerateM($d + n$)
        for $i = 1$ to d do // preparing $U^{(1)}$
            $s_i^{(1)} := m_i$
            save $s_i^{(1)}$
        end //for
        for $i = d + 1$ to $d + n$ do // preparing $U^{(2)}$
            $j := i - d$

$$s_j^{(2)} := m_i$$

save $s_j^{(2)}$

end //for

return $U^{(1)} = \{s_1^{(1)}, s_2^{(1)}, ..., s_d^{(1)}\}$, $U^{(2)} = \{s_1^{(2)}, s_2^{(2)}, ..., s_n^{(2)}\}$

end// *SetGenerateM*

∎

So far, generation of secret sets $U^{(1)}$ and $U^{(2)}$, was described. In order to make use of the secret shares they should be distributed to secret shares participants. Shares distribution is carried out via secure communication channel. Little modification (using send instead of save) of *SetGenerateM* allows distribution of shares once they are created. Due to the volume constrains this topic will be omitted. Usually, one participant from the authorized set is assigned one secret share. Let $P_i^{(n)}$ denote secret share participant that was assigned the share $s_i^{(n)}$ from $U^{(n)}$. When $|U^{(1)}| = 1$, one is dealing with degenerate case, where $s_1^{(1)} = S$. It is noteworthy that, when $|U^{(1)}| > 1$, shares assignment to different participants $P_i^{(1)}$ allows to introduce extended capabilities in the secret sharing scheme. One of instances could be split control over secret verification procedure.

3.2 Secret shares replication

Algorithm 1 allows only two sets of secret shares to be created. Usually, only $U^{(2)}$ will be available for secret participants, while $U^{(1)}$ is reserved for shares verification. Often, it is required that there are more than one authorized sets of participants. On the other hand property used in Algorithm 1 does not allow creating more than two authorized sets. The problem is: how to share the secret further without recovering it's value?

This question can be answered by distributed replication of $U^{(2)}$ into $U^{(3)}$. Although all participants $P_i^{(2)}$ take part in the replication, they do not disclose information allowing secret recovery. Any of $P_i^{(2)}$ should obtain no information about any of $s_i^{(3)}$. Writing these properties formally:

1. $\bigoplus_{s_i^{(2)} \in U^{(2)}} s_i^{(2)} = \bigoplus_{s_i^{(3)} \in U^{(3)}} s_i^{(3)} = S$.

2. $P_i^{(2)}$ knows nothing about any of $s_i^{(3)}$.

Such approach does not compromise S and allows to maintain all previously discussed automatic secret generation and sharing features.

3.2.1 Authorized set replication (same cardinality sets)

The authorized set satisfies: $|U^{(2)}| = |U^{(3)}| = n$, $U^{(2)} = \{s_1^{(2)}, s_2^{(2)}, ..., s_n^{(2)}\}$, $U^{(3)} = \{s_1^{(3)}, s_2^{(3)}, ..., s_n^{(3)}\}$. Procedure *SetReplicate* replicates set $U^{(2)}$ into the set $U^{(3)}$.

Procedure description: *SetReplicate* takes $U^{(2)}$, M, such that $|M| = 2*|U^{(2)}|$. First, all participants $P_i^{(2)}$ are assigned corresponding vectors m_i. Each of them performs bitwise XOR on their secret shares and corresponding m_i. Operation result is sent to the Accumulator. Accumulator adds m_{i+n} to form $s_i^{(3)}$, which later is sent to $P_i^{(3)}$. As the result, simultaneous creation and distribution of $U^{(3)}$ takes place.

Procedure 2: *SetReplicate(M , $U^{(2)}$)*

  Accumulator:
  $n := |U^{(2)}|$
      for $i = 1$ to n
          send m_i to $P_i^{(2)}$
          $P_i^{(2)}$: $\omega_i^{(2)} := s_i^{(2)} \oplus m_i$ // ω is l-bit vector (local variable)
      end//for
      for $i = 1$ to n
          $P_i^{(2)}$ send $\omega_i^{(2)}$ to Accumulator
          Accumulator: $s_i^{(3)} := \omega_i^{(2)} \oplus m_{l+n}$
          send $s_i^{(3)}$ to $P_i^{(3)}$
      end// for
  end//*SetReplicate*

■

Algorithm *EqualSetReplicate* is the final result in this section.

Algorithm description: *EqualSetReplicate* takes $U^{(2)}$. It uses *SetReplicate* to create and distribute set $U^{(3)}$, such $|U^{(2)}| = |U^{(3)}| = n$.

Algorithm 2: *EqualSetReplicate($U^{(2)}$)*

  Accumulator:
  $n := |U^{(2)}|$
  $M := GenerateM(2n)$
      SetReplicate(M , $U^{(2)}$)
  end// *EqualSetReplicate*

Discussion: We claim that *EqualSetReplicate* fulfils requirements stated at the beginning of section 3:

1. $\bigoplus_{i=1}^{n} s_i^{(3)} = \bigoplus_{i=1}^{n} \left(s_i^{(2)} \oplus m_i \oplus m_{i+n} \right) = \left(\bigoplus_{i=1}^{n} s_i^{(2)} \right) \oplus \left(\bigoplus_{i=1}^{2n} m_i \right) = \bigoplus_{i=1}^{n} s_i^{(2)}$ as requested.

2. All $s_i^{(3)}$ result from XOR of some elements from $U^{(2)}$ with random m_i, m_{i+n} hence they are random numbers. ∎

3.2.2 Authorized set replication (different cardinality sets)

For $|U_2| \neq |U_3|$ there are two possibilities:

Case 1: The authorized set satisfies: $n < d$, $U^{(2)} = \{s_1^{(2)}, s_2^{(2)}, ..., s_n^{(2)}\}$, $U^{(3)} = \{s_1^{(3)}, s_2^{(3)}, ..., s_d^{(3)}\}$. The algorithm *SetReplicateToBigger* takes $U^{(2)}$. It uses SetReplicate to create and distribute set $U^{(3)}$, such $n = |U_2| < |U_3| = d$.

Algorithm 3 description: *SetReplicateToBigger* takes d and $U^{(2)}$. It generates M, such that $|M| = d$. Next, it uses *SetReplicate* to create and distribute first n elements from $U^{(3)}$. As the result participants $P_i^{(3)}$ for $i \leq n$ have their secret shares assigned. Remaining participants $P_i^{(3)}$ are assigned m_i ($i > n$) not used by *SetReplicate*. As the result $U^{(3)}$, such $n = |U_2| < |U_3| = d$ is created and distributed. ∎

Case 2: The authorized set satisfies: $n > d$, $U^{(2)} = \{s_1^{(2)}, s_2^{(2)}, ..., s_n^{(2)}\}$, $U^{(3)} = \{s_1^{(3)}, s_2^{(3)}, ..., s_d^{(3)}\}$. The algorithm *SetReplicateToSmaller* takes $U^{(2)}$. It uses SetReplicate to create and distribute set $U^{(3)}$, such $n = |U_2| > |U_3| = d$.

Algorithm 4 description: *SetReplicateToSmaller* takes d and $U^{(2)}$. It generates M, such that $|M| = n + d - 1$. Next, it uses *SetReplicate* code to create n secret shares $s_i^{(3)}$. First $d-1$ shares are sent to corresponding participants $P_i^{(3)}$. Remaining $s_i^{(3)}$ ($i \in \{d, d+1, ..., n\}$) are combined to form $s_d^{(3)}$ that is sent to $P_d^{(3)}$. As the result $U^{(3)}$, such that $n = |U_2| > |U_3| = d$ is created and distributed. ∎

3.3 Remarks

1. All three algorithms meet requirements stated at the beginning of the paper. Combing this fact with security proof for KGH secret sharing scheme [6], encapsulation and use of secure communication channels, enables us to consider them as secure. Certainly, detailed proofs of security are yet to be constructed.
2. To obtain many authorized sets of participants, multiple replication of $U^{(2)}$ takes place. In such instance $U^{(2)}$ is used as the master copy (template) for all $U^{(n)}$, $n \geq 3$. For this reason it is called authorized set of master secret shares.

3. Proposed algorithms can accommodate arbitrary access structure, when combined with cumulative array construction (e.g. see [10]).

4. AUTOMATIC SECRET SHARING

To share secret S, secret Owner has to generate set $S^{(o)} = \{s_1^{(o)}, s_2^{(o)}, \ldots, s_n^{(o)}\}$, such $\bigoplus_{i=1}^{n} s_i^{(o)} = S$.

Automatic secret sharing algorithm takes away responsibility, for proper construction of the secret shares, from the Owner. Algorithm *FastShare* provides an automatic tool to complete this task. Next, comes algorithm *SaveShares* that adds up two more capabilities:
a. Shares are prepared using secret mask provided by an external Dealer.
b. Owner knows neither distributed shares, nor their assignment to the participants. Once the shares are distributed by *SaveShares*, they have to be activated by the algorithm *ActivateShares*.

Finally, we discuss how automatic secret sharing can be used to implement secret sharing schemes with extended capabilities (e.g. see [9]).

4.1 Known secret sharing

FastShare is the tool that provides fast and automatic sharing for a known secret.
Algorithm description: *FastShare* takes secret S and n (number of secret participants). Accumulator generates random $s_i^{(o)}, i = 1,2,\ldots,n-1$. Every $s_i^{(o)}$ is added to the ACC and simultaneously saved. To obtain $s_n^{(o)}$ the secret S is added to ACC. Next, ACC value is read and saved as $s_n^{(o)}$. Algorithm returns $S^{(o)} = \{s_1^{(o)}, s_2^{(o)}, \ldots, s_n^{(o)}\}$.

Algorithm 5: *FastShare(S , n)*

Accumulator:
ACC.reset
    for $i = 1$ to $n-1$
        $s_i^{(o)} := RAND$
        ACC.store($s_i^{(o)}$)
        save $s_i^{(o)}$
    end// for
Owner: Send secret to Accumulator
Accumulator:
ACC.store(S) //adding secret to the accumulator

$s_n^{(o)} := ACC.read$

save $s_n^{(o)}$

return $S^{(o)} = \{s_1^{(o)}, s_2^{(o)}, \ldots, s_n^{(o)}\}$

end//*FastShare*

Discussion:
1. We claim that *FastShare* produces random secret shares, due to the fact that all of them originate from a random number generator. First $n-1$ shares are purely random, while the last one results from bitwise XOR of the secret and random number. More formally, $s_n^{(o)} = \bigoplus_{i=1}^{n-1} s_i^{(o)} \oplus S$. So, $s_n^{(o)}$ is random.
2. All secret shares combine to S. Just observe:

$$\bigoplus_{i=1}^{n} s_i^{(o)} = \bigoplus_{i=1}^{n-1} s_i^{(o)} \oplus s_n^{(o)} = \bigoplus_{i=1}^{n-1} s_i^{(o)} \oplus \left(\bigoplus_{i=1}^{n-1} s_i^{(o)} \oplus S\right) = S. \blacksquare$$

4.2 Confidential secret sharing

We present two algorithms. First, algorithm *SaveShares* will be described, algorithm *ActivateShares* follows. *SaveShares* shares secret S using secret sharing mask M provided by Dealer. In the method the following conditions hold:
a. Dealer does not know S;
b. Secret Owner does not know M;
c. Secret Owner does not know secret shares and their assignment to the secret participants

Algorithm 6 description: *SaveShares* requires cooperation of two parties: Dealer and Owner. First, Dealer uses *GenerateM* to create secret sharing mask M, such that $\bigoplus_{m_i \in M} m_i = \vec{0}$. He also creates set K of encryption keys k_i, such that $\bigoplus_{k_i \in M} k_i \neq \vec{0}$. M elements are encrypted using corresponding keys from K to form encrypted mask set C. $\begin{bmatrix} m_1 \\ m_2 \\ \vdots \\ m_n \end{bmatrix} \oplus \begin{bmatrix} k_1 \\ k_2 \\ \vdots \\ k_n \end{bmatrix} = \begin{bmatrix} c_1 \\ c_2 \\ \vdots \\ c_n \end{bmatrix}$ or $M \oplus K = C$.

Dealer stores K and sends C to the Owner. Owner shares original secret S using *FastShare* to obtain $S^{(o)}$. Using C and $S^{(o)}$ he obtains $S^{(p)}$, which elements are randomly distributed to the participants. $\begin{bmatrix} c_1 \\ c_2 \\ \vdots \\ c_n \end{bmatrix} \oplus \begin{bmatrix} s_1^{(o)} \\ s_2^{(o)} \\ \vdots \\ s_n^{(o)} \end{bmatrix} = \begin{bmatrix} s_1^{(p)} \\ s_2^{(p)} \\ \vdots \\ s_n^{(p)} \end{bmatrix}$ or

$C \oplus S^{(o)} = S^{(p)}$

Participants receive secret shares from $S^{(p)}$ and store them. ∎

ActivateShares is used to activate secret shares that were distributed to secret participants using *SaveShares*.

Algorithm 7 description: *ActivateShares* requires cooperation of two parties: Dealer and Owner (of the secret). Dealer contacts participant P_1. Once participant's identity is established participant obtains one key from the set K. Participant combines k_i with $s_i^{(p)}$ to obtain activated share $s_i^{(a)}$. Action is repeated for all participants.

The algorithm yields $S^{(a)} = S^{(p)} \oplus K$, where $S^{(a)} = \{s_1^{(a)} \; s_2^{(a)} \; \ldots \; s_n^{(a)}\}$. ∎

4.3 Remarks

1. Security discussion is analogous as in the section 3.3.
2. To create single authorized set of participants both algorithms have to be executed. Hence, to obtain many authorized sets of participants, multiple execution of *SaveShares* and *ActivateShares* take place.
3. Extended capabilities. Algorithms defined above can be easily adapted to enable pre-positioned secret sharing. In [9] pre-positioned secret sharing schemes are described as that: „All necessary secret information is put in place excepting a single (constant) share which must later be communicated, e.g., by broadcast, to activate the scheme." In order to implement this capability in our case it is enough to separate execution of *SaveShares* from *ActivateShares*. Scheme is initialized by *SaveShares*. When the time comes, it is activated by using *ActivateShares*. In addition, algorithm *ActivateShares* can be modified, so it will send key values only to selected secret participants. For instance, assume that only one participant is selected. To activate the scheme he obtains $\bigoplus_{k_i \in M} k_i$ as the key. Another possible modification can lead towards public initialization. In this case value of $\bigoplus_{k_i \in M} k_i$ is made public by algorithm *ActivateShares*, so secret participants make use of it to recover original secret.

5. FURTHER RESEARCH

We hope that of the paper we managed to present in comprehensible way all basic algorithms for ASGS. However, much work still needs to be done. Major research tasks are:
1. Generalization into arbitrary access structures. This seems to be relatively simple task nevertheless it requires proper formalization.
2. Adding more extended capabilities to both methods. Some of possibilities were outlined in the paper. Set of extra functions that can be embedded into secret sharing scheme is much bigger. Authors are busy working in this field.
3. Construction of security proofs.

6. AKNOWLEDGMENT

The paper was partially supported by State Committee for Scientific Research, grant no.8 T11D 020 19. The authors wish to thank our friends: Kris Gaj, Karol Górski and Konrad Kulesza for discussion and useful comments.

7. REFERENCES

[1] Asmuth C. and Bloom J. 1983. 'A modular approach to key safeguarding'. *IEEE Transactions on Information Theory* IT-29, pp. 208-211
[2] Blakley G.R. 1979. 'Safeguarding cryptographic keys'. *Proceedings AFIPS 1979 National Computer Conference*, pp. 313-317.
[3] Blundo C., Giorgio Gaggia A., Stinson D.R. 1997.'On the dealer's randomness required in secret sharing schemes'. *Designs, Codes and Cryptography* 11, pp. 107-122.
[4] Blundo C., Stinson D.R. 1997.' Anonymous secret sharing schemes'. *Discrete Applied Mathematics* 77, pp. 13-28.
[5] Brickell E.F. 1989. 'Some ideal secret sharing schemes' *Journal of Combinatorial Mathematics and Combinatorial Computing* 6, pp. 105-113.
[6] Karnin E.D., J.W. Greene, and Hellman M.E. 1983. 'On secret sharing systems'. *IEEE Transactions on Information Theory* IT-29, pp. 35-41.
[7] Kotulski Z. 2001. 'Random number generators: algorithms, testing, applications'. (Polish) *Mat. Stosow.* No. 2(43), pp. 32-66.
[8] Kulesza K., Kotulski Z. 2002. 'On automatic secret generation and sharing, Part 1,2' *Proceedings of the 9th International Conference on Advanced Computer Systems*, ACS'2002, pp. 81-96.
[9] Menezes A.J, van Oorschot P. and Vanstone S.C. 1997. '*Handbook of Applied Cryptography*'. CRC Press, Boca Raton.
[10] Pieprzyk J. 1995. '*An introduction to cryptography*'. draft from the Internet.
[11] Shamir A. 1979. 'How to share a secret'. *Communication of the ACM* 22, pp. 612-613.

The FSR-255 family of hash functions with a variable length of hash result

TADEUSZ GAJEWSKI, IZABELA JANICKA-LIPSKA, JANUSZ STOKŁOSA

Poznan University of Technology, Institute of Control and Information Engineering, pl. Sklodowskiej-Curie 5, 60-965 Poznan, Poland, e-mail: Stoklosa@sk-kari.put.poznan.pl

Abstract: In the paper a family of cryptographic hash functions with a variable length of hash result, called the FSR-255 family, is presented. The hash functions are defined by some processing structures based on seventeen 15-stage nonlinear feedback shift registers. The feedback functions can be modified by the user to customize the hash function. An algorithm for computing the hash result of length $r \leq 255$ is given. It was successfully tested against the birthday attack: no collisions have been found. The FSR-255 family hardware implementation is presented at the level of logical structure. The circuit is designed for implementing as a full custom ASIC, and is optimized to increase the processing rate. The device is capable of working on-line, and can be customized by the user.

Key words: cryptography, cryptographic hask functions, ASIC

1. INTRODUCTION

Information security is strongly related to transferring and storing of data. The expanding use of information, by sending or saving it, has stimulated a rapid development of effective tools to guarantee that data are not read, changed or damaged by those who do not have the authorization to do so. From a cryptographic point of view, it is necessary to provide services that ensure confidentiality, integrity, authentication, access control and nonrepudiation. Data integrity is understood as a security service by which the data are protected from unauthorized or accidental modification.

Hash functions are used most frequently for data integrity and authentication of data with digital signatures. Other cryptographic applications of hash functions include: construction of message authentication codes, protection of passwords in access control, key derivation processes, pseudorandom number generation, confirmation of knowledge [4, 6, 8].

A hash function is defined as a computationally efficient algorithm (or function) mapping binary strings of arbitrary length to binary strings of some fixed length, called hash results. A cryptographic hash function should additionally be one-way, and either weak collision resistant or strong collision resistant [4, 8].

In this paper we present an extension and generalization of some earlier results [1]. We define here the FSR-255 as a class of cryptographic hash functions that can be customized by the user. The FSR-255 family of cryptographic hash functions, with a variable length of hash result, is based on some processing structures defined over seventeen 15-stage nonlinear feedback shift registers [7]. We present an algorithm for the FSR-255 family of hash functions, and the results of experiments proving their resistance against collisions. Furthermore, we show a general idea of the FSR-255 hardware implementation. The device is designed for implementing as a full custom ASIC. The circuit consists of three major parts, called units, corresponding to the three basic operations of the algorithm. Our device is capable of working on-line, and can be customized by the user. We give an estimation of the processing rate for this implementation.

2. ALGORITHM

For any finite nonempty set S we denote by S^n the set of all words (sequences of elements from S) of length n. The set $\{0,1\}$ will be denoted by B, and the concatenation of words x_1 and x_2 by $x_1\|x_2$. The symbol $\oplus$ will be used to denote the exclusive-or operation (xor) defined in $B^n \times B^n$.

Let $p: \{1,2,\ldots,n\} \to \{1,2,\ldots,n\}$ be a permutation. The *bit permutation* (BP) *function* $f_p : B^n \to B^n$ associated with p is defined as follows: $f_p(x_1, x_2, \ldots, x_n) = (x_{p(1)}, x_{p(1)}, \ldots, x_{p(n)})$ for all $(x_1, x_2, \ldots, x_n)$ from B^n. The bit permutation function f_p will be denoted by BP_p, or shortly by BP if p is fixed.

We have selected, and fixed for the FSR-255 family, the following permutation $\pi: \{1,2,\ldots,255\} \to \{1,2,\ldots,255\}$ given in Table 1. In what follows the symbol BP will denote the bit permutation function f_π associated with π.

Table 1. Permutation π. The (i,j)-cell contains $\pi(i+j)$.

	0	1	2	3	4	5	6	7	8	9	10	11	12	13	14	15	16	17	18	19
0		175	10	174	209	155	182	244	193	219	26	22	107	214	236	173	14	215	44	97
20	153	28	8	185	254	204	25	164	37	195	255	231	154	158	159	29	19	243	151	6
40	90	200	4	252	206	94	118	95	42	191	218	116	180	110	65	93	17	190	117	136
60	144	87	140	88	162	40	123	115	71	52	226	132	147	53	250	248	32	80	116	64
80	225	15	166	232	86	251	160	83	187	181	101	129	130	201	33	249	176	125	109	146
100	30	41	138	76	34	27	127	85	78	3	47	106	228	213	48	61	75	178	230	57
120	72	23	111	1	100	20	247	55	212	13	227	12	81	145	62	188	39	246	133	245
140	38	135	235	2	221	241	56	5	237	170	224	233	184	202	114	203	70	124	113	239
160	103	156	196	177	148	59	122	210	220	168	242	92	36	194	51	84	186	63	99	238
180	46	102	171	18	142	149	89	137	161	112	31	119	120	50	98	253	108	134	192	217
200	79	167	43	234	143	199	163	179	69	45	198	152	9	157	121	58	77	11	189	105
220	49	150	183	223	21	91	66	165	74	216	96	141	169	229	104	54	131	7	240	126
240	82	67	68	207	222	24	35	73	197	139	128	208	60	172	205	211				

A *nonlinear processing block* (NPB) is a processing structure (shown in Fig. 1a) which consists of bit permutation function BP and seventeen 15-bit nonlinear feedback shift registers $NFSR_1,...,NFSR_{17}$ with state cycles of the maximum length.

The *NPB function* $f_{NPB} : B^{255} \to B^{255}$ is defined for all x from B^{255} by the following four-step procedure:
1. Split x into seventeen 15-bit words x_i such that $x=x_1\|x_2\|...\|x_{17}$.
2. For each $i=1, 2, ..., 17$:
    ♦ set the initial value of $NFSR_i$ to x_i,
    ♦ execute 19 elementary operations (clock cycles) of $NFSR_i$.
3. Form the word $z=z_1\|z_2\|...\|z_{17}$ where z_i denotes the state of $NFSR_i$.
4. Compute $BP(z)$.

The NPB function f_{NPB} will be denoted shortly by NPB.

A *linear permutation block* (LPB) is a processing structure (shown in Fig. 1b) which consists of:
- 256-input multiplexer MUX with i-th data input connected to i-th bit of the input word,
- 8-bit linear feedback shift register LFSR with state cycle of the maximum length,
- 255-bit shift register SR (used as a data buffer) with serial data input connected to the output of MUX.

The *LPB function* $f_{LPB} : B^{255} \to B^{255}$ is defined for all x from B^{255} by the following three-step procedure:
1. Set the initial value of LFSR to 00000001 (in the binary notation).
2. Execute 255 elementary operations (clock cycles) of LFSR and SR. At each operation, one bit selected from the input word by MUX (addressed by the state of LFSR) is loaded into SR through its serial input.
3. Take the contents of SR (the bit connected to MUX output is the leftmost bit).

The LPB function f_{LPB} will be denoted shortly by LPB.

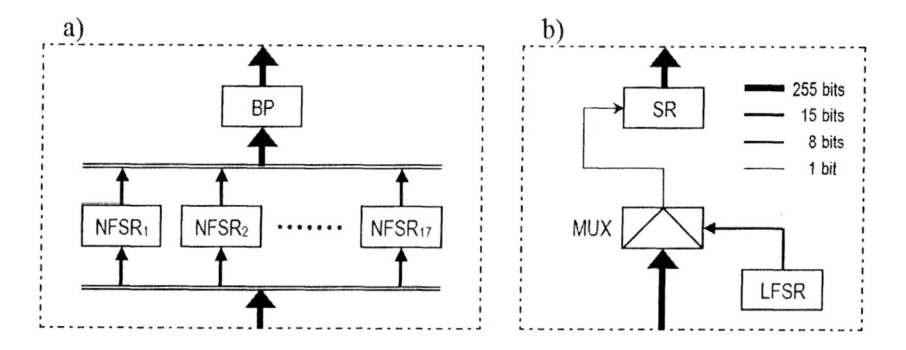

Fig. 1. Processing structures: a) Nonlinear Processing Block, b) Linear Permutation Block

The operations of NPB and LPB will be used to define a class of hash functions called the FSR-255 family. The hash functions will be defined constructively by an algorithm for computing the hash result.

Algorithm 1 (The FSR-255 family of hash functions)

Input: a message m of length n (n is an arbitrary nonnegative integer).
Output: the hash result of length $r \leq 255$.
Method:
1. *Extending the message*
   Append extra bits to the message m so that the extended message m' is of the form $m'=m\|10^k\|b$ where b is the binary representation of n mod 2^{32}, and k is the least nonnegative integer such that the length of m' is a multiple of 2040.
2. *Splitting the extended message*
   Divide m' into 255-bit words m_1', m_2',..., m_q' such that $m' = m_1'\|m_2'\|...\|m_q'$.
3. *Initial processing*
   ◆ Set the initial values: $H_0 = \alpha$ and $y_0 = \alpha$ where α=(511C, 1B59, B4D, 333, 979, 4F4, 9AC, E0F, 4FA, FC3, 1EB, 353, 1FA, 674, C50, E98, A75).
   ◆ *Notation*: a 255-bit word is presented as a sequence of seventeen 15-bit words written in hexadecimal (0–7FFF) with leftmost zeros omitted.
   ◆ Compute $H_1 = \text{NPB}(m_1 \oplus y_0) \oplus H_0$ and $y_1 = \text{RL}_4(y_0)$
   ◆ where $\text{RL}_4(x)$ denotes the "rotate to the left by 4 bits" operation.
4. *Iterative processing*
   For each $i=2, 3, \ldots, q$ compute:
   ◆ $H_i = \text{NPB}(m_i \oplus y_{i-1} \oplus H_{i-1}) \oplus H_{i-1}$
   ◆ $y_i = \alpha$ if $i \equiv 0 \pmod 8$,
      $y_i = \text{RL}_4(y_{i-1})$ otherwise.
5. *Final transformation*
   Compute $\text{LPB}(H_q)$ and take r leftmost bits as the hash result $h(m)$.

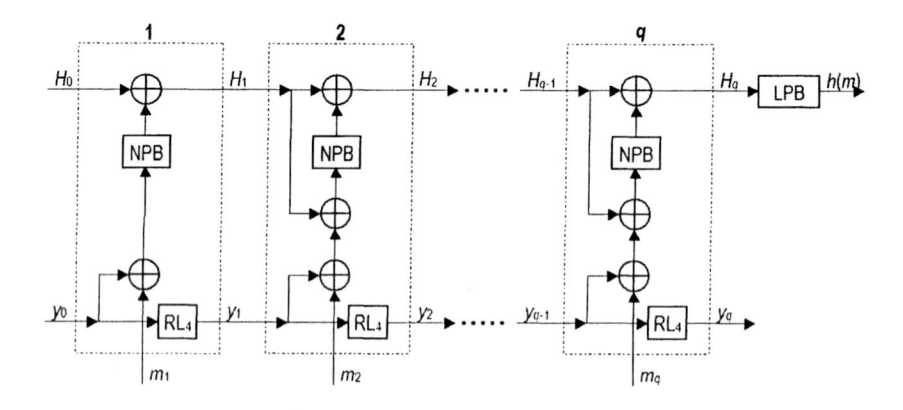

Fig. 2. Block diagram of FSR-255 computations

A block diagram of Algorithm 1 is shown in Fig. 2. Since both NPB and LPB contain feedback shift registers as variable elements, Algorithm 1 defines a class of hash functions called *the FSR-255 family of hash functions*. A single hash function from the FSR-255 family can be specified by defining all feedback shift registers in NPB and LPB. It is essential that all registers have state cycles of the maximum length. Algorithms for finding nonlinear feedback functions such that the feedback shift registers generate sequences of the maximum length are presented in [2, 9].

3. CRYPTOGRAPHIC PROPERTIES

The FSR-255 family of hash functions has been tested thoroughly to determine its cryptographic properties and verify ideas supporting the FSR-255 design. The results of experiments can be found in [2]. As an example of experiments carried out, we present here the effects of attacks to show that the FSR-255 hash functions can be used as a tool to ensure data integrity.

The tests presented here have been conducted for the following FSR-255 hash function defined by the linear feedback function $g = x_0 \oplus x_2 \oplus x_3 \oplus x_4$ and seventeen nonlinear feedback functions $f_1, f_2, \ldots, f_{17}$. The nonlinear feedback functions have been selected by an algorithm presented in [2]. All eighteen feedback functions are such that the feedback shift registers generate sequences of the maximum length. The functions $f_1, f_2, \ldots, f_{17}$, given in truth tables with 2^{15} values for each function, can be found in [3].

Because of a specific construction of the FSR-255 hash function, it is possible (for the purpose of testing) to choose a desired length r of hash result ($1 \leq r \leq 255$). In our experiments r was changed from 10 to 128. The hash results were computed for all $2^{w+1}-1$ input strings of the length from $w=0$ (the empty string) up to $w=20$ (the string 11...1 of the length 20). The results of experiments confirm the fact that the length $r=128$ of hash result seems to be sufficiently secure.

We have tested FSR-255 against the memoryless birthday attack [3,7]. The algorithm of the attack is as follows:

Algorithm 2 (The memoryless birthday attack)

Input: randomly chosen messages m_1 and m_2.
Output: the number c of collisions and the pointer p of the first collision.
Method:
1. Set to zero the collision counter ($c:=0$), the iteration counter ($i:=0$) and the pointer of the first collision ($p:=0$).
2. Compute $h(m_1)$ and $h(m_2)$.
3. If $h(m_1)=h(m_2)$ then
    ♦ if $c=0$ then $p:=i$,
    ♦ $c:=c+1$.
4. $i:=i+1$.
5. While $i<2^{r/2}$ do
    5.1. Select randomly (a,b) from the set $\{(1,2),(2,1)\}$.
    5.2. Select m_a' as a modification of m_a.
    5.3. Compute $h(m_a')$.
    5.4. If $h(m_a')= h(m_b)$ then

- if $c=0$ then $p:=i$,
- $c:=c+1$.

5.5. $i:=i+1$.

For each experiment two 250-byte messages were randomly chosen. They were padded with 5 bytes 80 00 00 07 D0 (in hexadecimal). The modification of 250-byte message *m* has been made by one of the following methods:
- select randomly *l* bytes from *m* ($1 \leq l \leq 9$) and replace them with the results of xor operation performed, respectively, on those bytes and *l* randomly chosen 1-byte words,
- select randomly one bit from *m* and replace it with its negation.

We have carried out 1000 series of experiments (each with a new pair of randomly chosen messages m_1 and m_2), and no collisions have been found.

4. HARDWARE IMPLEMENTATION

The FSR-255 family of hash functions is particularly suitable for hardware implementation. Basic operations of Algorithm 1 are defined by some processing elements composed of typical digital circuits. The structure of the algorithm is modular with mostly local exchange of data. Furthermore, many operations can be performed in parallel.

There are two distinctive features of our design: it implements a *class* of hash functions (the FSR-255 family) and is capable of working *on-line*. The variable elements of the algorithm can be modified by the user. The device is designed for implementing as a full custom ASIC (*Application Specific Integrated Circuit*).

We present here a general idea of the design at the level of logical structure, leaving out technical details. Consequently, the control circuit and input/output interface are omitted. We focus on data paths optimization for increasing the device speed (processing rate). The circuit consists of three major parts called units which correspond to the three basic operations of the algorithm. A block diagram of the FSR-255 hardware implementation is shown in Fig. 3.

4.1 Extension Unit

Extension Unit is designed to implement Step 1 and Step 2 of the algorithm. Appending extra bits to the message is necessary if the hash function is to be computed on-line with no pre-processing by supporting software. Extension Unit performs the following operations (refer to Fig. 3 and 4).
- *Initializing*. The unit is initialized for each new message. A 32-bit value *b* (representing the length of *m*) is loaded to 32-bit register R_1 and 33-bit counter C_1 while 3-bit counter C_2 is cleared.

- *Basic operation.* Each successive word m_i of the message is loaded to 255-bit input register R_1. At the same time the contents c_1 and c_2 of counters C_1 and C_2, respectively, are modified as follows: $c_1:=c_1-255$ and $c_2:=c_2+1$. Further operation depends on c_1 and c_2. All conditions are tested in combinational circuits F_1 and F_2. The output signals of F_1 and F_2 are used to control other circuits: D, IF and M_1.
- *Passing the word.* If $c_1 \geq 255$, no extra bits are appended. The word m_i is passed on to Processing Unit as it is a 255-bit (full) word of the message.
- *First appending.* If $0 \leq c_1 < 255$, register R_1 contains the last word m_p (of length c_1) of the message. The word m_p should be completed with extra bits starting with "1". The number c_1 is decoded by 8-to-256 decoder D (as "0" on the output bit No. c_1), and passed to iterative combinational circuit IF. The outputs of IF form 255-bit extended word $m_p' = m_p \| 10^k$ where $k-255-c_1$.
- *Next appending.* If $c_1 < 0$, the word 0^{255} should be appended. To carry out this operation decoder D is disabled (forcing "1" on its all 256 outputs) and circuit IF is enabled through its cascade input (forcing "0" on its all 255 outputs).
- *Last appending.* If $c_1 \leq 221$ and $c_2=0$, a 32-bit value b (representing the length of m) should be appended. This operation is performed together with either "first appending" or "next appending" operation. The condition $c_1 \leq 221$ ensures that there is enough space for the 34-bit minimum appendix of the form $10\|b$. If both conditions are true, the outputs of register R_1 (containing b) are selected by multiplexer M_1.

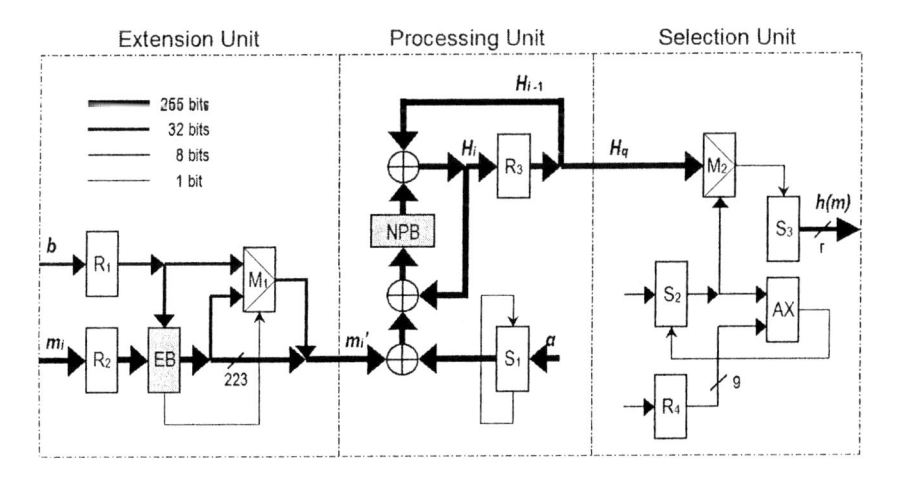

Fig. 3. Block diagram of FSR-255 hardware implementation

4.2 Processing Unit

Processing Unit is dedicated to the implementation of Step 3 and Step 4 of the algorithm. The basic structure of the unit is a result of embedding the algorithm

246

graph, and optimizing 255-bit data paths to increase the processing rate. The Nonlinear Processing Block is designed for implementing the user-defined feedback functions. The unit carries out the main processing tasks, and is largely responsible for the time needed to compute the hash result. Processing Unit performs the following operations (refer to Fig. 3 and 5).

- *Initializing*. The unit is initialized for each new message. Register R_3 should be loaded with initial value α. Because of data path structure (optimized for iterative processing) this simple operation is carried out in three steps. In the first step, register R_2 is loaded with initial value $\beta = BP^{-1}(\alpha)$ while registers R_3, S_1 and NFSR are cleared (the symbol NFSR denotes the parallel composition of $NFSR_1, \ldots, NFSR_{17}$). In the second step, NFSR is loaded with the output of $R_2 \oplus S_1 \oplus BP(NFSR)$ that is $\beta \oplus 0 \oplus BP(0) = \beta$. In the third step, register R_3 is loaded with the output of $BP(NFSR) \oplus R_3$ which results in $BP(\beta) \oplus 0 = \alpha$.

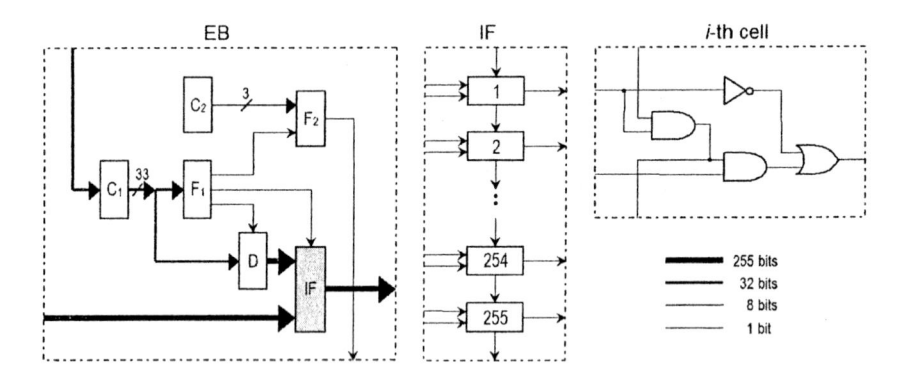

Fig. 4. Organization of the Extension Block (EB)

- *Initial processing*. This operation carries out Step 3 of the algorithm by processing the first word m_1' sent by Extension Unit. First, register NFSR is loaded with the output of $M_1 \oplus S_1 \oplus BP(NFSR)$ that is $m_1 \oplus 0 \oplus BP(\beta) = m_1 \oplus \alpha$. Then NPB operation (described below) is executed. Finally, register R_3 is loaded with $NPB(NFSR) \oplus R_3$ which results in $NPB(m_1' \oplus \alpha) \oplus \alpha = H_1$. Furthermore, register S_1 is loaded with α and operation RL_4 is executed so that S_1 holds y_1.

- *Iterative processing*. This operation implements Step 4: a central part of the algorithm. The structure of Processing Unit has been optimized to increase performance for this operation as it is executed most frequently. The result H_i of the preceding operation is available at the input of register R_3. The operation begins with two simultaneous transfers: register NFSR is loaded with $m_i \oplus y_{i-1} \oplus H_{i-1}$ and register R_3 is loaded with H_{i-1}. Then NPB operation (described below) is executed. The final result $H_i = NPB(m_i \oplus y_{i-1} \oplus H_{i-1}) \oplus H_{i-1}$ is available at the input of R_3 for the next iterative step. The NPB operation is executed in parallel with RL_4 operation over the contents of register S_1, and the result y_i is ready for the next operation.

- *NPB operation*. This operation is executed by the Nonlinear Processing Block (shown in Fig. 5). It is a central part of the two above operations: initial processing and iterative processing. The nonlinear feedback functions are implemented in seventeen memory blocks (look-up tables). It has been shown in [2] that each nonlinear feedback function $f_i(x)$ can be expressed in the form $f_i(x) = x_1 \oplus f_i(x_1=0)$ where x_1 is the most significant input variable and $i=1,2,...,17$. This fact has been used to reduce the required memory size by a half. The NPB module contains seventeen $16K \times 1$ memory blocks which can be written (programmed) by the user. The NPB operation is performed in 19 clock cycles. The minimum time τ needed for each clock cycle is limited by the memory access time which depends on the implementation technology.
- *Fetching feedback functions*. This operation is carried out to implement a new hash function (from the FSR-255 family). The truth tables of seventeen nonlinear feedback functions, defined by the user, are stored in the NPB memory blocks. The values of each function are fetched into proper memory locations in the order specified by the maximum length state cycle so that no additional circuits are required for memory addressing.

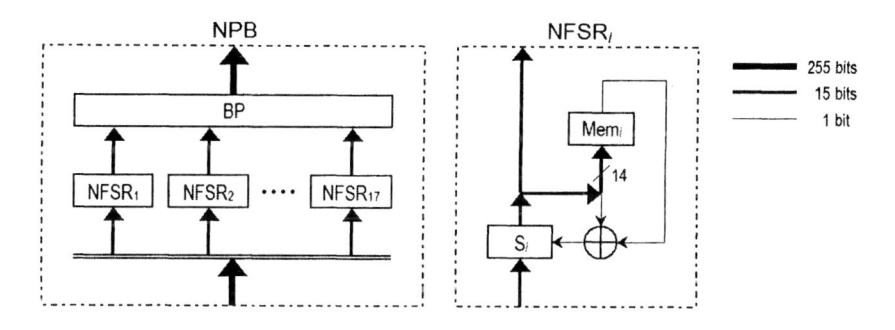

Fig. 5. Organization of the Nonlinear Processing Block (NPB)

4.3 Selection Unit

Selection Unit provides circuits for implementing Step 5 of the algorithm. The unit is designed by embedding the basic structure of Linear Processing Block (refer to Fig. 3). The user can define a linear feedback function by selecting a sequence $(a_0, a_1, ... , a_8)$ of coefficients of an affine function $a_0 \oplus a_1x_1 \oplus ... \oplus a_8x_8$. The coefficients are loaded to 9-bit register R_4. The function is realized in the circuit AX (nine 2-bit AND gates with outputs connected to 9-input XOR gate). The unit is initialized by loading register S_2 with initial value 00000001 (in the binary notation). When the input word H_q is ready for final transformation, the unit performs its operation by executing r clock cycles. The r-bit hash result is held in register S_3 (the bit connected to the output of M_2 is the most significant bit).

4.4 Processing rate

The primary reason for implementing an algorithm in hardware is to increase its speed. For a hash function it is measured by the *processing rate* defined as the quotient of the message length by the time needed to compute the hash result. It is assumed that successive 255-bit words of input message are loaded to the input register R_2 (by input/output control) with no delay, at the rate sufficient to ensure the device's continuous work. Each 255-bit word of the input message passes through Extension Unit and Processing Unit while the Selection Unit waits for its operation until the last word is processed and the result H_q is computed (refer to Fig. 3). The time required for processing each 255-bit word is restricted by the time of NPB operation performed by Processing Unit. The NPB operation is executed in 19 clock cycles. The minimum time τ needed for one clock cycle is limited by NPB memory access time, and can be specified for a given technology of ASIC implementation. For longer messages the operation time of Selection Unit can be neglected. Therefore, the processing rate v of the whole device – as the quotient of message length $255q$ by the time $19\tau q$ (in seconds) of computations – can be estimated by the expression:

$$v \approx \frac{255}{19\tau} \text{ [bits/sec]}.$$

In general, it is at least by one order higher than the processing rate of a software implementation.

5. REFERENCES

[1] Janicka-Lipska I., Stoklosa J., FSR-255 cryptographic hash function. W. Burakowski, A. Wieczorek (eds.), NATO Regional Conference on Military Communications and Information Systems 2001, Zegrze, Poland, 2001, vol. I, 277–280.
[2] Janicka-Lipska I., Nonlinear feedback functions of maximal shift registers and their application to the design of a cryptographic hash function (in Polish), Ph. D. thesis, Poznan, 2001.
[3] Janicka-Lipska I., Truth tables of some nonlinear feedback functions for 15-bit feedback shift registers with the maximum length of state cycles.
http://www.sk-kari.put.poznan.pl/janicka/functions/.
[4] Menezes A. J., van Oorschot P.C., Vanstone S. A., *Handbook of Applied Cryptography*. CRC Press, Boca Raton, FL, 1997.
[5] Pieprzyk J., Sadeghiyan B., *Design of Hash Algorithms*. LNCS 756, Springer, Berlin, 1993.
[6] Preneel B, *The state of the cryptographic hash functions*. Damgård I. (ed.), Lectures on Data Security. Modern Cryptology in Theory and Practice. LNCS 1561, Springer, Berlin, 1999, 158–182.
[7] Stoklosa J., Integrity of data: FSR-hash. Bubnicki Z. (ed.), Proceedings of the 12th International Conference on Systems Science, Wrocław, 1995, vol. III, 120–125.
[8] Stoklosa J., Bilski T., Pankowski T., Data Security in Information Systems (in Polish). Wydawnictwo Naukowe PWN, Warszawa, 2001.
[9] Yang J.-H., Dai Z.-D., *Construction of m-ary de Bruijn sequences* (*Extended abstract*). Seberry J., Zheng Y. (eds.), Advances in Cryptology – AUSCRYPT '92. LNCS 718, Springer, Berlin, 1993, 357–363.

Using Backward Strategy to the Needham-Schroeder Public Key Protocol Verification[1]

MIROSŁAW KURKOWSKI[2], WITOLD MAĆKÓW[3]

[2] *Institute of Mathematics & Computer Science, Pedagogical University of Częstochowa, al.Armii Krajowej 13/15, 42-200 Częstochowa, Poland, phone, fax (+48 34) 3612269. e-mail: m.kurkowski@wsp.czest.pl*
[3] *Faculty of Computer Science & Information Systems, Department of Programming Techniques, Technical University of Szczecin, 49, Żołnierska st., 71-210 Szczecin, Poland, phone (+48 91) 4495662, fax. +4891 4876439. e-mail: wmackow@wi.ps.pl*

Abstract: When dealing with secure distributed systems it is essential that entities (principals, persons, hosts, computers, etc.) are able to prove their identities to each other. The process of proving the identity is called entity authentication. Cryptographic protocols are very good tools to achieve this goal. These protocols are precisely defined sequences of communication and computation steps that use some mechanism such as encryption and decryption. In this paper we present applying a new fast method of verification of cryptographic authentication protocols to verification of the Needham-Schroeder Public Key Authentication Protocol. We present a verification algorithm, its implementation and some experimental results. Our method is a kind of model checking. To decrease the number of states in the space, which describe executions of authentication protocols in real net, we use a partial order reduction. For the verification of correctness property we apply a backward induction method.

Key words: cryptographic protocols, authentication protocols, verification, backward induction.

---

[1] This research was partly supported by Polish Scientific Research Committee Grant No. 7 T11C 01 521.

1. INTRODUCTION

Authentication is the process by which participants in a computer network prove their identity. Usually, each participant shares a secret and by proving possession of this secret, can establish trust in its identity. Authentication in a large, distributed system is challenging because participants communicate over a network that is vulnerable to many Intruders attacks. A passive Intruder can be on a line and obtain sensitive information. An active Intruder can obtain and modify messages and insert his own data to the net. Such an Intruder can impersonate some participant in the computer network and intercept his rights and privileges. The Needham and Schroeder Authentication Protocol (with symetric and asymetric key) given in [10] revolutionized security in distributed systems. Adaptations of this protocol (or its modifications), such as Kerberos [11] is still working. However, it was not long before a flaw was found in this protocol [1, 3, 4]. This research focuses on the development of protocols, and is accompanied by a greater and more interesting problem, the analysis of authentication protocols.

The problem of looking for methods of correctness verification of the cryptographic authentication protocols is still important. In the last decade many methods and results are introduced and published. These methods allowed to discover many kinds of attacks upon the authentication protocols [3,4,5,6,7,8,9].

In this paper we present the application of a new method of verification of cryptographic authentication protocols to verification of the Needham-Schroeder Public Key Authentication Protocol (described below by NSPK). We present a main method concept, a verification algorithm, its implementation and some experimental results.

2. ALGORITHM

In our consideration we investigate one of the kinds of attacks upon the authentication protocols. Sometimes an Intruder can impersonate some participant in the computer network and intercept his rights and privileges. In the papper [2] the mathematical model of the real computer network have been presented. This structure allows express sending between participants messages when authentication protocols are executed. This model permits defining of mentioned above kind of attack. We say that there exists an attack upon the authentication process iff, there exist(s) execution of the given protocol (or few paralel executions) where an Intruder uses other users identifier. In the paper [2] was given an algorithm to automatic check of the above property. Our method is a kind of model checking. To decrease the number of states in the space, which describe executions of authentication protocols in real net, we use a partial order reduction. For the verification of correctness property we apply a backward induction method.

Here we present a short version of verification algorithm and introduce its implementation for automatic verification of the NSPK properties. The presented below algorithm lets us know if there exists an execution of a protocol, which thanks to it mutual authentication cannot be realized. If the answer is affirmative the algorithm generates this kind of execution or a few parallel executions.

In our considerations we assume that: 1)encrypting algorithm in the protocols are correct, meaning that to decrypt a message, the possesion of the suitable cryptographic key is necessary; 2)the necessary condition of efficiency of an attack on the authentication protocol is the execution of any step, in which a cheated user is taking part.

Algorithm

Input data
1. We define the number of users of an examinated protocol.
2. We define what cryptographic keys the users may use.
3. We define individual steps of sending messages while executing a protocol.
4. To every user we map informations send in the protocol, which he should to generate during the execution of the protocol.
5. We define which participant of the protocol (initiator or receiver) should be cheated.

Main section
6. A scheme (or schemes) of the execution of an attack is generated.
7. To the set of users taking part in the execution of a protocol an Intruder is added.
8. For every user his confident information is automatically generated.
9. Every possible executions of a given protocol where all of the users (the Intruder too) play every role in the protocol are generated. (Honest users use only their own identifiers, confident data and cryptographic keys. In executions with an Intruder, he may use arbitrary identifiers and confident data.)
10. For every executions of the step of a protocol the set of Initiator step knowledge and Responder step knowledge is generated.
11. A step of the execution of a protocol, in which the Intruder uses identifier of another user is found. This step will be the base to creating a derivation tree.
12. Starting from the given step a derivation tree is constructed. One by one execution steps, in which the set of ending knowledge is subset of the set of initiator knowledge of the given step are found.
13. Some of the constructed paths turn out contradictory. The creation of a tree path is breaking in three cases, when:
    a) the added node is conflicted with rest of path (failure);
    b) there's no steps to add on and to fulfil existing conditions (failure);
    c) all passed on conditions are fulfilled (success).
14. If uncontradictory path contains not only prefixes of executions suitable steps must be added to the path.

Output data
15. The derivation tree and the attack path(s).

3. IMPLEMENTATION

Input data.

All information needed for a protocol analysis should be prepared in the form of script. Following keywords may be used in a script:

- **sides** (mandatory) –indicates the number of sides participating in a protocol;
- **secrets** (mandatory) – indicates the maximal count of secrets generated by each side;
- **steps** (mandatory) –indicates the number of steps in protocol;
- **secrets_modif** (optional) – modifies settings obtained from **secrets** for a single side;
- **pstart** (mandatory) – indicates a protocol section beginning (a section consists of a description of all protocol steps – communication direction, message format, ...);
- **pend** (mandatory) – indicates a protocol section end;
- **afrom** (mandatory) –defines an attack-from position;
- **ato** (mandatory) – defines an attack-to position;

Last two parameters (**afrom** and **ato**) are related to *position*. In this case we understand this as the side position. All sides are sorted by their first occurrence in protocol steps description – side position may be defined as a side index in this sorted array.

In protocol section we can use following symbols: **1)** *A1, A2, A3, ...* – protocol sides names (up to *A9*); **2)** *NA1_1, NA1_2, ...* – secret names for *A1* side (similarly for *A2*: *NA2_1, NA2_2*, and so on); **3)** *KA1, KA2, KA3, ...* – public keys names for sides: *A1, A2, A3, ...*; **4)** *{...} KA1* – message encrypted with *KA1* key; **5)** | - concatenation; **6)** > - direction of a transmission (for example: *A1 > A2* – "*A1* sends a message to *A2*"); **7)** : - separator between a direction indicator and a message field.

We are presenting an example of a script describing Needham-Shroeder protocol in Figure 1. We define two sides (A1, A2), each one holding one secret and one public key pair (we explicitly show in a script only public keys). Attack should start from position 1 (the Intruder will be protocol initiator) and aim at position 2.

```
sides 2
secrets 1
steps 3
afrom 1
ato 2

pstart
a1>a2:a1|a2|{na1_1|a1}ka2
a2>a1:a2|a1|{na1_1|na2_1}ka1
a1>a2:a1|a2|{na2_1}ka2
pend
```

Figure 1 Example of a protocol script (Needham-Shroeder)

CScript is the base class of our program. This class is designed to load the protocol script from a file and to prepare this script for farther analysis. It's also designed as a container for all other classes and functions dealing with protocol analysis. Communication with these classes is possible only through the CScript methods. Some of the most important of all methods and required order of their calls are shown in Figure 2.

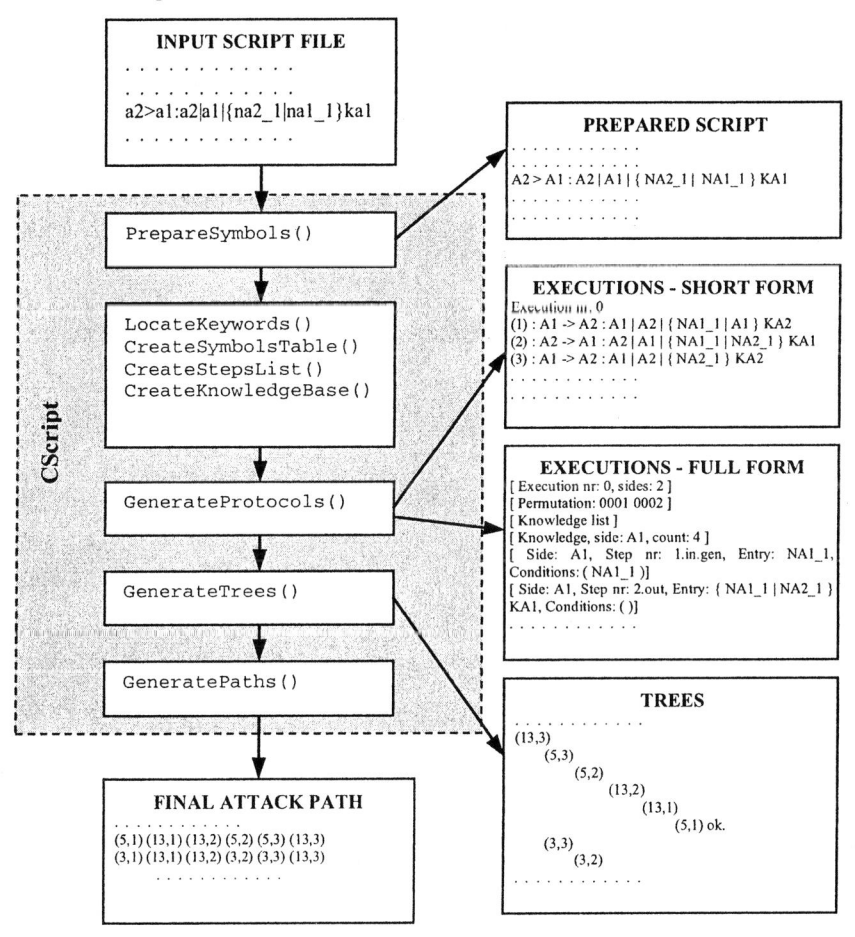

Figure 2 General scheme of the program execution

We may split protocol analysis into some independent stages. Each stage is initialised by a different method. At the end of the each stage we may preview intermediate results and then we may make next method call dependent on these results. Below we shortly present some of the most important methods:

`CScript( AnsiString aScript)` – *CScript* class constructor, parameter *aScript* holds a file name.

`PrepareSymbols()` – pre-processes script text, i.e. translating all characters to uppercase, removing leading and trailing space characters, removing comments, separating all keywords and symbols by single space character. We may preview the pre-processed script after successful execution of this method.

`LocateKeywords()` – searches pre-processed script for keywords (sides, steps, etc) and their values. The function can generate comments connected to possible script errors.

`CreateSymbolsTable()` – generates space of all possible symbols on the basis of data from *LocateKeywords* (i.e. A1, NA1_1, KA1, etc). Only symbols placed in this set may be used in the protocol. Then above function creates a list of *CSide* class objects, called *SidesList*. Each list entry describes another protocol side. The first entry (index 0) contains information about the Intruder (symbol I), next is the first honest side "A1" and so on. Information from *secrets* and eventually from *secrets_modif* says about the number of secrets for each side. This information is passed on to *CSide* object constructor (with a side name), and then used for generating all names of side secrets.

```
CSide *side = new CSide( "A1"/*side name*/, 5
/*secrets number*/)
```

`CreateStepsList()` – analyses the protocol section in a pre-processed script. This function creates the *StepList* list, consisting of objects of *CStep* class. Each list entry contains a single protocol step specification. Some individual fields are separated from each script line, which describes the protocol step (see also *CStep* description) (see Figure 3).

```
CStep *step = new CStep( stepNr, from, to, message);
```

A1 > A2 : A1 | A2 | { NA1_1 } KA2

stepNr	from	To	message
1	A1 >	A2 :	A1	A2	{ NA1_1 } KA2

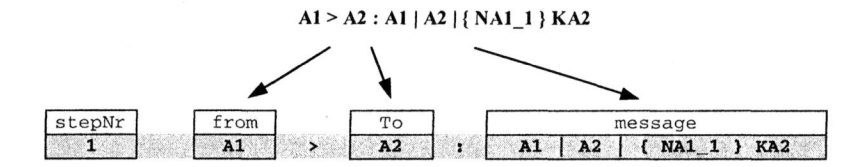

Figure 3 Basic deconstruction of single step

`CreateKnowledgeBase()` – generates "maximal" knowledge base for each protocol side, getting information separately from each protocol step. This information indicates which secrets and under which conditions are owned by side, before and after step (see also *CKnowledge* description).

`GenerateProtocols()` – prepares a set of possible permutations of sides positions. Then the function creates an object of *CProtocol* class (for original sides' positions) and it creates *Protocols* list. Each list entry is created as a copy of original

CProtocol object and then it is modified for suitable position permutation (see also *CProtocol* and *CPermut*).

`GenerateTrees()` — checks step by step all executions from *Protocols* list, taking all executions suitable for successful attack. For each of these executions a new object of *CTree* class is created. Then the above function creates the *Trees* list using *CTree* objects (see also *CTree* description).

`ExtractGoodPaths()` - checks step by step all of the trees from the *Trees* list, looking for all leaves indicated as a correct one. Then this function moves upward, from a leaf to a root, completing the path with missing executions. Each of the path are added to the *Path* list (see also *CPath* description).

Objects of a *CStep* class contain information about a particular step of protocol. The *Message* field holds the message part of step description, in the form of a tree. This tree is built with recursively-repeated objects of classes *CFields and Cfiled*. Deconstruction of an example message is shown in Figure 4.

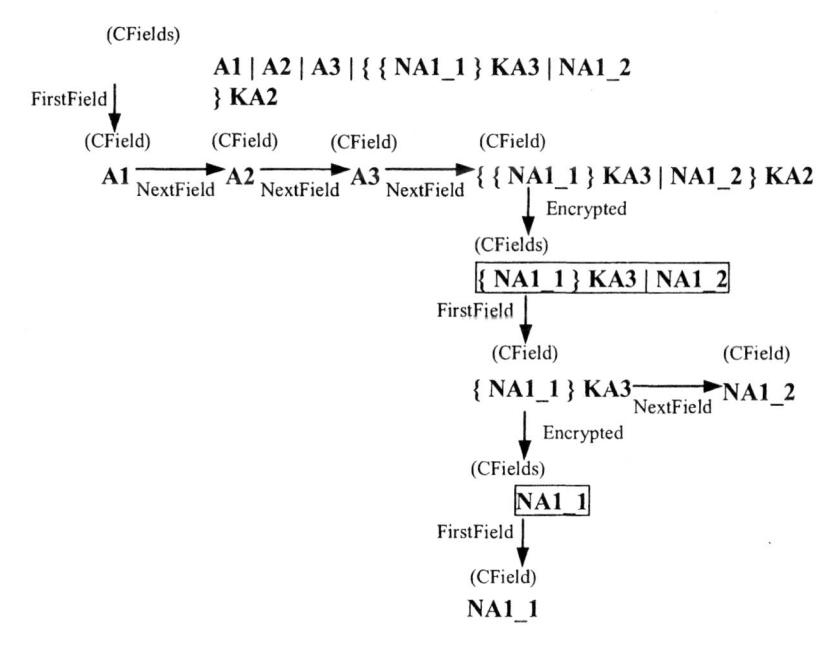

```
        (CFields)
                    A1 | A2 | A3 | { { NA1_1 } KA3 | NA1_2
FirstField ↓        } KA2
        (CField)    (CField)      (CField)       (CField)
        A1 ────→ A2 ────→ A3 ────→ { { NA1_1 } KA3 | NA1_2 } KA2
           NextField  NextField  NextField
                                              ↓ Encrypted
                                           (CFields)
                                           { NA1_1 } KA3 | NA1_2
                                    FirstField ↓
                                          (CField)              (CField)
                                          { NA1_1 } KA3 ────→ NA1_2
                                                       NextField
                                              ↓ Encrypted
                                           (CFields)
                                           NA1_1
                                    FirstField ↓
                                          (CField)
                                          NA1_1
```

Figure 4 Deconstruction of an example message: A1|A2|A3|{{NA1_1}KA3|NA1_2}KA2

Each *CStep* object also owns a *Trigger* field. In this field a set of conditions (which may be empty) is kept. These conditions should be fulfilled before the execution of this step. Triggers can also hold a list of secrets known for step initiator. *Trigger* information is stored in a form of tree (classes *CSFields* and *CSField*), similarly as *Message*. A small example of such a trigger is shown in Figure 5.

Example 1
A1>A2 : {A1|NA1_1|{NA2_1}KA3}KA2|NA1_2|A1|A2|A3

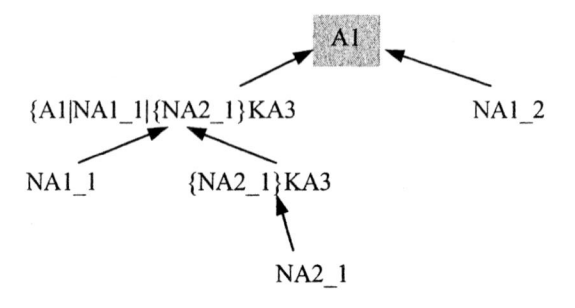

```
                        A1
                       ↗  ↖
   {A1|NA1_1|{NA2_1}KA3}   NA1_2
        ↗      ↖
    NA1_1   {NA2_1}KA3
                ↑
             NA2_1
```

Example 2
I(A1)>A2 : A1|A2|{NI | I}KA2

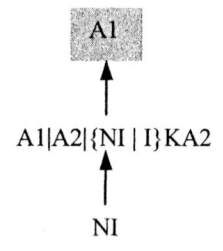

```
          A1
          ↑
    A1|A2|{NI | I}KA2
          ↑
          NI
```

Figure 5 Two examples of triggers for a specific steps

We mentioned about knowledge base in a description of *CreateKnowledgeBase* function. Each entry of this base contains an information about secrets known to a different side. Some conditions are bound to each secret We may present conditions as some kind of statements, for example: *"side knows this secret only under the condition of knowledge of a particular private key"*. Below, in a Table 1, we present simplified knowledge base for NSPK protocol script (see Figure 1). It's a knowledge base for original positions of sides (A1 is an initial side in step 1, A2 is an initial side in step 2, and so on). Some secrets may be repeated (for example NA2_1 for side A2) – all steps are treated independently. In honest execution it doesn't matter, but it makes sense in executions with the Intruder. This original knowledge base is used during the creation of triggers of newly generated protocol executions.

As we said before, all possible permutations of positions are generated. For the NSPK protocol we obtained 18 possible permutations. There're some honest executions in this set and some intruder-including executions (for example: intruder uses the identity of A1 and the secret of A2).

Side A1 (4 secrets)	Side A2 (5 secrets)
NA1_1 (1.in.gen), if A1 is honest	
	{ NA1_1	A1 } KA2 (1.out), no condition
	NA1_1 (1.out), if A2 knows private key for KA2
	NA2_1 (2.in.gen), if A2 is honest
{ NA1_1	NA2_1 } KA1 (2.out), no condition	
NA1_1 (2.out), if A1 knows private key for KA1	
NA2_1 (2.out), if A1 knows private key for KA1	
	{ NA2_1 } KA2 (3.out), no condition
	NA2_1 (3.out)

Table 1 Simplified knowledge base for Needham-Shroeder protocol (two entries: one for side A1, and second for side A2)

Between generated of the executions we choose these, which correspond to the attack definition. From each executions we took a suitable step. This step is treated as a root of a new attack tree. We pass on an execution like this to the constructor of *CTree* class, starting automatic creation of the entire tree. There's recurrent *CreatSubTree* function, taking as parameters current tree node (connected to an execution step) an additionally some extra conditions. These conditions are kept in an object of the mentioned before *CTriger* class. In this object we transfer conditions not fulfilled in the upper part of a tree (on the current path). There's a simple example passing on of conditions in Figure 6.

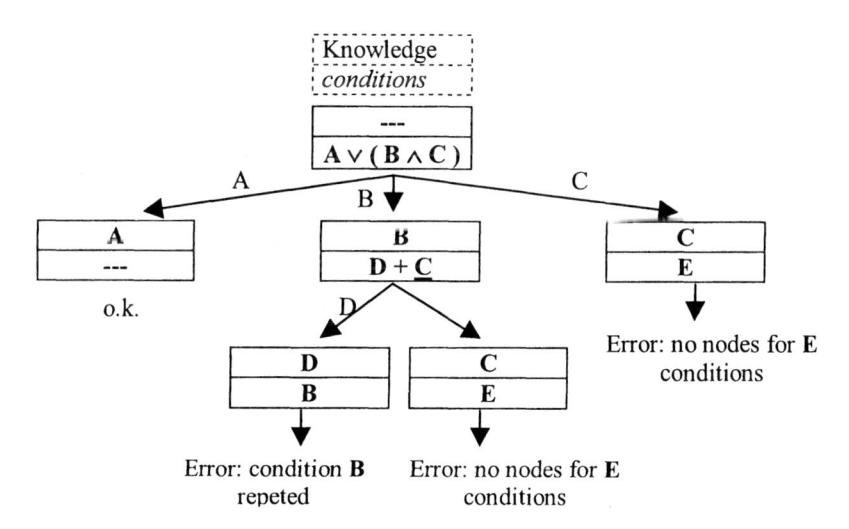

Figure 6. Example of passing on condition

According to an algorithm we should check each newly added node, looking for any conflicts. Conflicts may appear on the path leading to the root (for example the same condition appears twice or the same step will be processed twice, etc.). The creation of a tree path breaks in three cases, when:

1. the added node is conflicted with rest of path (failure);
2. there's no steps to add on and to fulfil existing conditions (failure);
3. all passed on conditions are fulfilled (success)

In case of success we add a last node to the auxiliary list called *Leaves*. Further creation of a final attack paths starts from nodes stored in this list. We should complete paths with the lacking steps of a given execution. We are looking for a conflict after each addition, similarly as during the creation of a tree.

4. EXPERIMENTAL RESULTS

Experimental results were done on the Intel Pentium 4 - 1,7 GHz, 512 MB RAM computer. For the NSPK protocol 18 possible, hipothetical executions of the protocol were found. The derivation tree which we have automatically created consists of only 22 nodes (protocol executions steps). We obtained the attack path due to the Lowe's attack given in [3, 4]. The time needed to generate possible executions, analyse, create the derivation tree and find the attack path is given in Table 2.

Also we investigated an attack from the responder position. In this case the derivation tree had all contradictory paths. The full time needed to this calculation is 33 ms.

We have examined the corrected version of the NSPK protocol given in [4] too. Our method give an answer that there is no attack upon this protocol version in the time 38 ms.

The analysis of the protocol script	1 ms.
Generating executions, conditions and knowledge sets	16 ms.
Generating derivation tree	15 ms.
Generating attack path	1 ms.
TOTAL	33 ms.

Table 2. Time of verification of NSPK Protocol

5. CONCLUSION AND FUTURE WORK

In this paper we have presented the application of a new method of verification of cryptographic authentication protocols to verification of the Needham-Schroeder Public Key Authentication Protocol. We have presented a main method concept, a verification algorithm, its implementation and experimental results. Our method is a kind of model checking with a partial order reduction of the state space. For the verification of correctness properties we have applied a backward induction method. It is possible that a verification of many cryptoprotocols which uses this method will be very fast. We will investigate that problem by the verification of some other authentication cryptographic protocols.

This paper is due to the Mirosław Kurkowski's doctoral dissertation which be submitted to The Institute of Computer Science, Polish Academy of Sciences under the supervision of Professor Marian Srebrny.

This research was partly supported by Polish Scientific Research Committee Grant No. 7 T11C 01 521.

We would like to thank Marian Srebrny for usefull discusions and Małgorzata Berezowska for help at work with the text.

6. REFERENCES

[1] **Denning D., Sacco G.**, *Timestamps in key distribution protocols*, Communications of the ACM, 24(8), pp. 533-536, August 1981.
[2] **Kurkowski M.**, *Using Backward Induction to Cryptographic Protocols Verification*, to appear in ICS PAS Report
[3] **Lowe G.**, *An attack on the Needham-Schroeder Public-Key Authentication Protocol*, Information Processing Letters, 56, (1995) pp. 131-133.
[4] **Lowe G.**, Breaking and Fixing the Needham-Schroeder Public-Key Protocol Using FDR, In Proceedings of TACAS, (1996) 147-166, Springer Verlag.
[5] **Lowe G.**, Casper: A Compiler for the Analysis of Security Protocols, Proceedings of the 1997 IEEE Computer Security Foundations Workshop X, (1997) 18-30, IEEE Computer Society Press.
[6] **Meadows C.**, *Language Generation and Verification in the NRL Protocol Analyzer*, Proceedings of the 1996 IEEE Computer Security Foundation Workshop IX, (1996) 48-61, IEEE Computer Society Press.
[7] **Meadows C.**, *The NRL Protocol Analyzer: An overview*, Journal of Logic Programming, Vol. 26, No. 2, (1996) 113-131.
[8] **Meadows C.**, *Using the NRL Protocol Analyzer to examine Protocol Suites*, Proceedings of the 1998 LICS Workshop on Formal Methods and Security Protocols, (1998) \\ http://www.cs.bell-labs.com/who/nch/fmsp/program.html
[9] **Mitchell J.C., Mitchell M., Stern U.**, *Automated Analysis of Cryptographic Protocols Using Murϕ*, Proceedings of the 1997 IEEE Symposium on Security and Privacy, (1997) 141-151, IEEE Computer Society Press.
[10] **Needham R., Schroeder M.**, *Using encryption for authentication in large networks of computers*, Communications of the ACM, 21(12):993--999, December 1978.
[11] **Steiner J., Neuman B., Schiller J.**, *Kerberos: An authentication service for open network systems*, In Usenix Conference Proceedings, pp. 191-202, Dallas, Texas, February 1988.

OF-FMEA: an approach to safety analysis of object-oriented software intensive systems

TADEUSZ CICHOCKI[1], JANUSZ GÓRSKI[2]
[1] *Bombardier Transportation (Zwus) Polska Sp. z o.o.,*
Modelarska 12, 40-142 Katowice, Poland,
e-mail: tadeusz.cichocki@pl.transport.bombardier.com
[2] *Gdańsk University of Technology,*
Narutowicza 11/12, 80-952 Gdańsk, Poland, e-mail: jango@pg.gda.pl

Abstract: The paper presents an extension to the common FMEA method in such a way that it can be applied to safety analysis of systems (hardware and software) that are developed using a recently popular object oriented approach. The method makes use of the object and collaboration models of UML. It assumes that the system components are specified formally using the CSP notation. The method supports systematic way of failure mode identification and validation. Selected failure modes are injected to the specification of "normal" behaviour and their consequences are analysed with the help of an automatic tool. The verification process provides hints for possible redesign of components. Experiences of using the method for a railway signalling case study are also reported.

Key words: Safety critical systems, FMEA, formal analysis.

1. INTRODUCTION

Failure Modes and Effects Analysis (FMEA) and its variants, like FMECA (*Failure Modes and Effects Criticality Analysis*), have been widely used in safety analyses for more than thirty years. With the increase of application domain of software intensive systems there was a natural tendency to extend the use of (originally developed for hardware systems) safety analysis methods to software based systems. SFMECA (*Software Failure Modes and Effects Criticality Analysis*) was such an extension proposed for FMEA. In this method software faults are identified based on a generic classification. Another extension of FMEA, known as SEEA (*Software Error Effect Analysis*), applicable to software was proposed in [2].

Although less standardised then FMEA they were successfully applied to many industrial cases. A good survey and a list of related bibliography can be found in [1].

FMEA is focused on safety consequences of component failures and takes a risk-based approach to failures. Identified failure modes of a component are analysed case by case. The analysis process results in an explicit and documented decisions that take into account the risk associated with a given failure mode. The decision can be just the acceptance (supported by a convincing justification) of the consequences of the failure or it can suggest necessary design changes to remove (or mitigate) the consequences or causes of the failures. Documentation is an important output of FMEA. This documentation can be then referred to by a safety case for the considered system.

In FMEA the analysis of failure mode consequences is mostly qualitative. As this approach is in most cases sufficient for hardware systems it can cause problems when applied to software. The reason is that an approximate analysis does not provide sufficient assurance then. As software is discontinuous, due to its discrete nature, a very small deviation of its data or code can cause a very big difference in its behaviour. Testing does not help much as to achieve a very high assurance the number of test cases becomes too large. A standard approach to remove this difficulty is to use formal methods. The advantage is that formal analysis explores all possible behaviours and therefore provides very high confidence in the results. Disadvantage is that formal proofs are labour consuming, error-prone (when performed by hand) and quickly face the barrier of computational complexity. The difficulties can be partially removed by choosing a proper scope of analyses (to control complexity) and applying tools (to decrease human effort and errors).

In this paper we present an approach to application of FMEA to software intensive systems. We assume that to analyse failure mode consequences formal methods are being used. This way we provide for a very high assurance of the results of the analyses. We concentrate on systems that are object-oriented. This is because we appreciate that object-orientation is becoming a leading approach while developing software based systems. We call our approach OF-FMEA (*Object-oriented Formal FMEA*). OF-FMEA follows the FMEA approach while analysing system designs. It is a specialisation of the 'classical' FMEA in two aspects: (1) it assumes that the analysed system is being developed using an object-oriented approach, and (2) the object-oriented models of the system are supplemented with their formal specifications.

We work on OF-FMEA within the context of a railway signalling application. The system is called LBC (*Line Block System*) and is presently under development. For short introduction to the LBS system and more technical details related to OF-FMEA we refer to [3, 4].

2. OVERVIEW OF OF-FMEA

The objectives of OF-FMEA are consistent with the objectives of FMEA in the sense that both approaches aim at analysing the dependence of system behaviour on possible failures of its components. OF-FMEA extends FMEA in three aspects:

- assumes that the analysed system is being developed using the object-oriented approach,
- assumes that the object-oriented models of the system are supplemented with their formal specifications,
- assumes that the analysis of failure consequences is based on the formal specifications and is supported by an automatic tool.

The choice of the object-orientation as the system design approach was motivated by the increasing popularity of this paradigm in the system developing community, especially as far as software development is concerned (compare [6]). Object models are general enough to represent systems (people, software and hardware) and can then be specialised towards representation of software components. As the consequence, system development can proceed without a major switch of the modelling approach while changing the attention from the system to software aspects. This is an important advantage during the analysis as we can pass the borders between heterogeneous components of the system (both, hierarchically and horizontally) without being forced to work with heterogeneous models.

Formal methods are an important weapon to fight problems resulting from discrete nature and high complexity of software. Informal approaches to software safety analysis can not provide a very high level of confidence in the results of the analyses. In contrary, formal approaches, if applicable, can provide a very high level of assurance. A common limitation in application of formal methods is the rapid increase of computational complexity of analytical processes. However, the recently emerging tools provide help in this respect and open the way to wider industrial application of formal methods.

In OF-FMEA we have chosen CSP (*Communication Sequential Processes*) [5] as a formal base for object-oriented models. The motivation behind this choice was that CSP is well suited to modelling co-operating components that interact by passing messages along communication lines. And it was exactly the situation we were facing during our case studies (related to railway switching). The system we were working with is composed of components with a relatively little state information. The components exchange messages with their environment through defined communication channels. A natural way of specifying such components is by describing their possible interactions with the surrounding world. This way of viewing interfaces is well suited to the way FMEA considers the system components: it concentrates on failures, i.e. on what is visible to the environment and to much extend disregards the mechanism (the component's interior) that led to the failure.

It is assumed that before we start OF-FMEA an adequate environment to support the work has been set up (see Fig.1). Part of this environment is object-oriented models of the system of interest. Of particular interest are two categories of models:

- The *object model* that presents the system in terms of its constituent objects and relationships among them; of particular interest is the *decomposition* relationship as it shows how the system decomposes into its components.
- The *object collaboration diagrams* showing how objects interact through communication channels; the channels may model the actual communication links (if the objects are already designed and implemented) or show the designers' intentions concerning the further development of the system.

```
                    ┌─────────────────────────────┐
                    │   Environment of OF-FMEA    │
                    └─────────────────────────────┘
                                 ◇
       ┌──────────────────┐    │    ┌──────────────────┐
       │ Description of OF-│───┼────│ Component failure│
       │   FMEA steps     │    │    │    checklists    │
       └──────────────────┘    │    └──────────────────┘
                               │
       ┌──────────────────┐    │    ┌──────────────────┐
       │   Object model   │    │    │ Failure mode patterns │
       │   showing the    │────┤    └──────────────────┘
       │ decomposition of │    │
       │    the system    │    │
       └──────────────────┘    │
                               │
       ┌──────────────────┐    │    ┌──────────────────┐
       │  Collaboration   │    │    │ Documentation of CSP │
       │ diagrams showing │────┤    └──────────────────┘
       │ how components   │    │
       │ interact to implement │    ┌──────────────────┐
       │ higher level objects │────│     FDR tool     │
       └──────────────────┘    │    └──────────────────┘
                               │
       ┌──────────────────────────────────────────────┐
       │ Training of project participants concerning the OF-│
       │     FMEA objectives, scope and process       │
       └──────────────────────────────────────────────┘
```

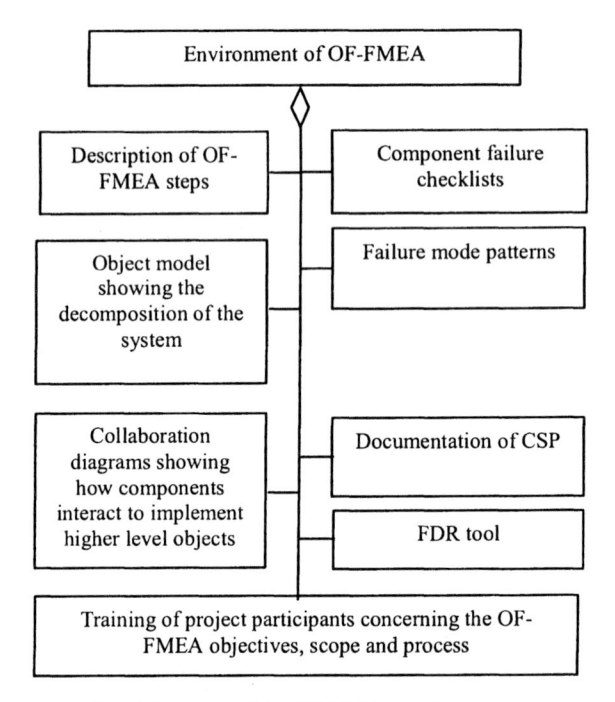

Fig. 1. Structure of the OF-FMEA environment

We assume that the models have been checked against relevant consistency and correctness criteria (e.g. by checking them against documentation standards and by passing them through an inspection process).

Failure checklists are based on experience, producer recommendations, sectoral norms and engineering judgement and support identification of component failure modes. To support modelling of the identified failure modes we provide a set of patterns. Each pattern suggests how to modify the specification of a "normal" behaviour of the component (and possibly of some co-operating components) in order to model a given failure mode. An application of a pattern to represent a given failure mode in the specification of a component is called *failure mode injection*. The specifications with injected failure modes are then verified against safety properties to check for possible failure consequences.

The OF-FMEA method comprises the following steps:
- Choosing the scope of the analysis.
- Formal modelling of the system.
- Analysis of component failures.
- Failure mode injection campaign.
- Interpretation of the results.

The steps are presented in more detail in the subsequent sections.

3. CHOOSING THE SCOPE OF THE ANALYSIS

While applying OF-FMEA we concentrate on the decomposition hierarchy of the object model. This hierarchy shows how the higher level components are built out of the lower level ones. On top of this we can see the whole system as a single component. Its required properties specify what is considered important concerning the mutual influence of the system and its environment, e.g. for a critical system we postulate that the system should be safe. The lower level decomposition shows the system components and explains how they interact. In our case study the system of interest is LBS – the *Line Block System*. It controls the traffic of trains between adjacent railway stations. The related decomposition structure is shown in Fig. 3 (see the next page). At Level 0 we have a generic railway system and its only attribute represents our (the public) concern that the system should be safe. Level 1 shows the signalling system and its relevant co-operating components. The next Level 2 shows the place of LBS within the signalling system. This is the level with respect to which we interpret the railway signalling rules derived from the railway regulations. The rules impose safety constraints on the model.

With respect to the hierarchy shown in Fig. 3 the rules can be understood as the explanation of what "safe" of Level 0 means in terms of levels 1 and 2 of our decomposition. Levels 3 down to 6 represent design decisions (explain the structure of LBS in terms of its components and their interactions).

We chose Level 2 as the reference level during our analysis that means that by "safe" we understand that the system is compliant with the railway safety regulations. And we chose Level 6 as the lowest component level (we did not consider further decomposition levels). Our goal was to analyse how possible failure modes of the components can affect the safety properties expressed with respect to Level 2.

Object models represent the structural aspects of the system design. Communication among objects is represented by collaboration diagrams that belong to the suite of models recommended by UML [6]. An example collaboration diagram is shown in Fig. 2. It explains how components of Level 4 co-operate to implement the i-th Local Control Point object.

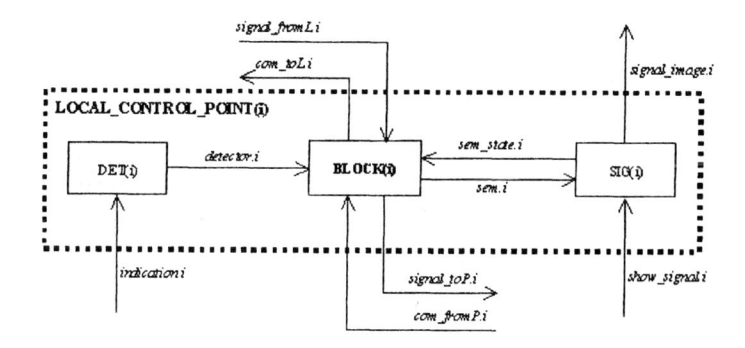

Fig. 2. Collaboration diagram of the components of the i-th Local Control Point object.

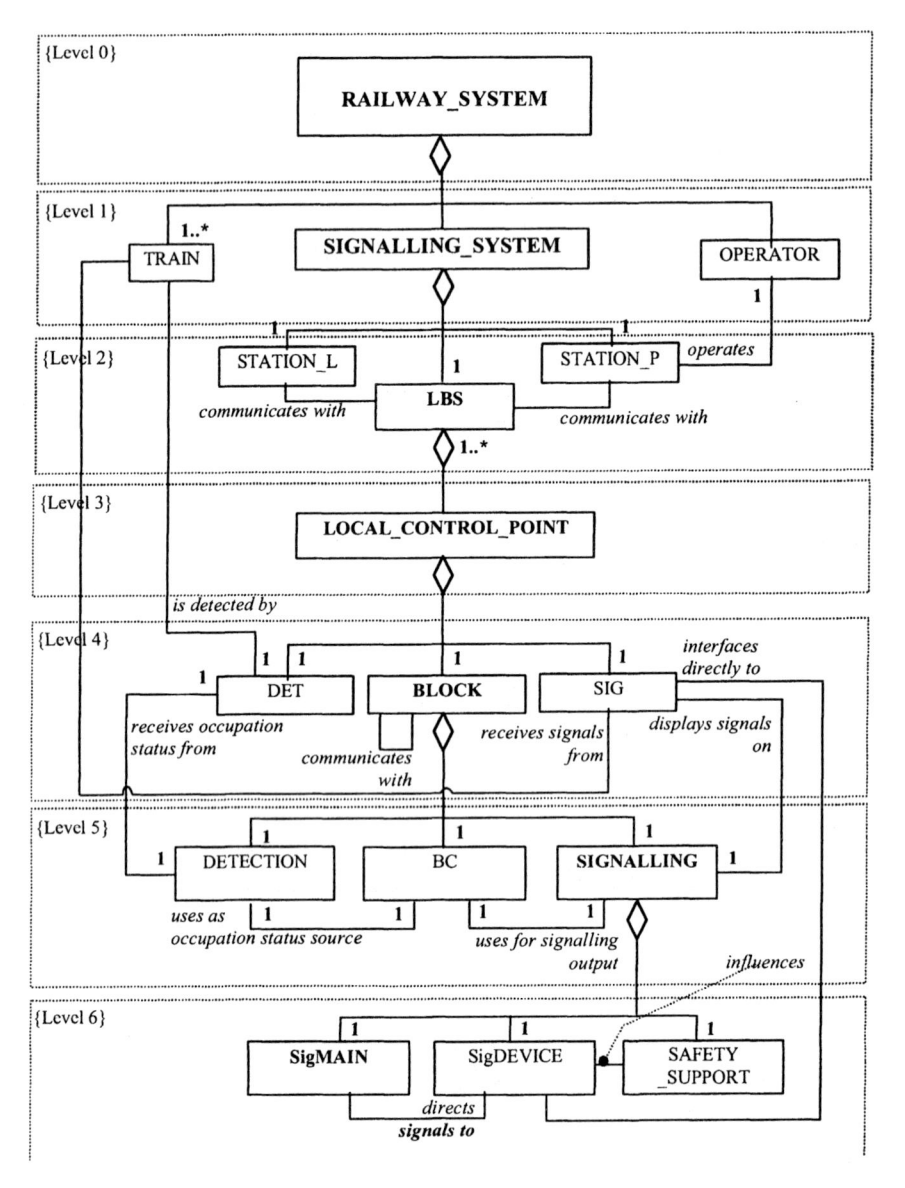

Fig. 3. Object model of a railway system. Shadowed blocks show the objects that are subjected to further decomposition. The objects of lower levels were not included in our case study.

4. FORMAL MODELLING OF THE SYSTEM

The object and collaboration diagrams are input to the OF-FMEA method. From this input we develop formal specification of component interactions. For this purpose we use CSP. Each component of the collaboration diagram becomes a CSP process with input and output channels as shown in the diagram. In addition to this we develop formal models of safety requirements of the system. The requirements are derived from the railway safety regulations. Each requirement is modelled as a CSP process and imposes some restrictions on the ordering of events in the system. The requirements refer to the events that are visible on Level 4 of our decomposition.

We can verify consistency of the formal specifications using the FDR tool [7]. During verification we compare the specification of the system (seen as composition of its components) with the specification of the safety requirements. During verification we check for each safety requirement if the following relation holds:

$$TS \subseteq TSR,$$

where TS denotes the set of event traces of the system (restricted to events visible on Level 4) and TSR denotes the set of event traces of the process modelling a safety requirement. This verification process can follow the design process (in a sense that after we design the next decomposition level we can verify it against the specification of the safety requirements).

Formal specifications that were positively verified against the safety requirements are the input to the next step, the analysis of component failures.

5. ANALYSIS OF COMPONENT FAILURES

Failures are modelled as deviations from the "normal" behaviour of a component (observed on the component's interface). The modelling is achieved by altering the specification of a component and its interaction with other components. To provide for completeness of failure modes we follow a systematic procedure of failure mode identification. The problem is to formulate hypotheses about potential failure modes of a component X and to decide which of them are included in further analyses (by accepting or rejecting the failure hypotheses). In order to control the completeness of failure hypotheses we apply the following criteria.

C1. We look at the domain associated with a given communication channel and admit that the values passed through the channel can be changed.

C2. We admit that a communication channel can pass values that are beyond the domain of values associated with the channel.

C3. We admit that after accepting an event a component can switch to a different (defined) state, i.e. there is a faulty transition to the state that is already in the specification.

C4. We admit that after accepting an event the component can switch to a different (undefined) state, i.e. there is a faulty transition to a state that was not included in the specification of 'normal' behaviours.

The above criteria form a sort of a checklist to be followed while formulating the failure hypotheses for a component. The criteria C1-C4 protect against omissions but cannot be solely used as a tool to identify valid failure hypotheses. Application of C1-C4 can force us to consider a large number of possible failure modes, disregarding their credibility. To provide for a more focused set of failure modes we apply additional criteria that provide for early rejection of incredible failure modes. Those that withstand this selection are passed to the subsequent analysis step.

During validation of the failure mode hypotheses we apply the following criteria:
- Checklists of failure modes of a considered type of component that can be found in sectoral norms and guidelines (e.g. [8], [9], [10], [11]). For instance, [10] recommends some standard failures of communication channels in railway applications.
- Experience reports provided by users of similar systems.
- Failure profiles of components (e.g. delivered by producers of components).
- Suggestions coming from the project stakeholders (e.g. designers' intentions concerning the components structure and the ways of their interaction).

The above criteria are used to accept/reject failure mode hypotheses. The result of this selection process is a list of credible failure modes that is passed to the subsequent step, the failure mode injection campaign.

6. FAILURE MODE INJECTION CAMPAIGN

The list of selected failure modes is an input to the failure mode injection campaign. The objective of this step is to analyse the consequences of each particular failure mode on the system safety properties. Each failure mode is modelled by altering the CSP specification of the system.

Let assume that a given component X co-operates with another component Y. In terms of CSP, this means that X and Y are connected through a common communication channel as shown in Fig. 4.

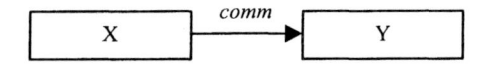

$$X \xrightarrow{comm} Y$$

Fig. 4. Component X connected with component Y by a communication channel *comm*.

As X is connected with Y, a failure of X will possibly affect the behaviour of Y. We identified and classified possible patterns of failure related to the co-operation of X and Y and called them *failure modelling patterns*.

We apply common techniques used for conditional compilation to control activation and deactivation of those parts of the specification that implement failure modes.

After injecting a failure mode into the system specification we check, using the FDR tool, for its safety consequences.

If the verification confirms that the analysed failure mode has no negative effects on system safety, the failure mode can be accepted. In the opposite case however we know that the failure mode, if actually occurs, can affect the system safety properties. In such case FDR can provide example event scenarios that lead to a contradiction of safety. Those scenarios can then be very helpful while considering possible redesign of the component objects. The results of the failure mode injection campaign are collected in the OF-FMEA table.

In Fig. 5 the scope of OF-FMEA while analysing a hypothetical component X is presented.

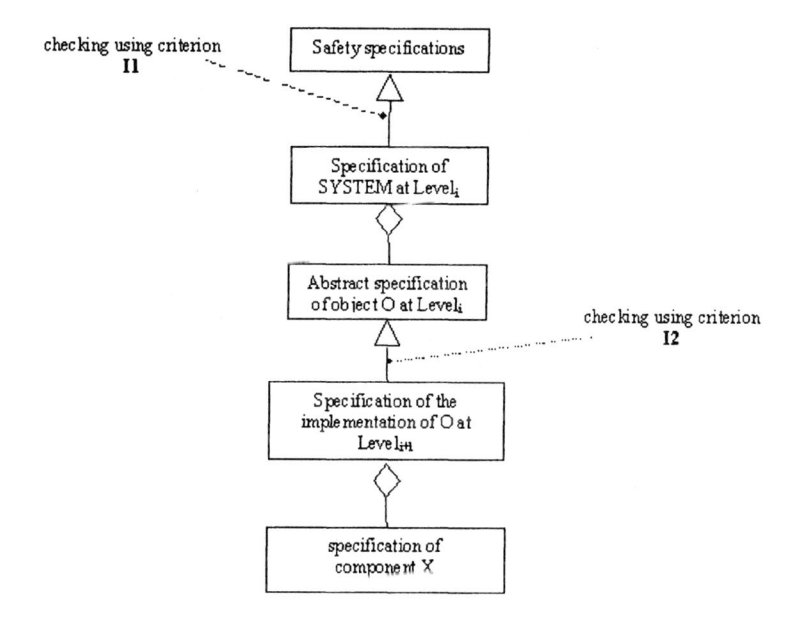

Fig. 5. The scope of OF-FMEA while analysing failures of component X.

The results of the fault injection campaign are interpreted by undertaking the following decisions: failure mode acceptance, failure mode handling or failure mode elimination.

The choice between the above interpretations depends on the judgement of the analysts/designer and is beyond the OF-FMEA method. The criteria used to support such decision include availability of the resources for redesign, availability of candidate components to replace a given one, and the assessment of the credibility of the considered failure mode.

7. CONCLUSION

In the paper we presented an overview of OF-FMEA, an approach to applying FMEA to object-oriented software intensive systems. The approach makes use of formal specifications. Building formal specifications is an additional investment and an obvious question to ask is if it is well justified. In our case study we realised that building the formal CSP specifications from the UML collaboration diagrams was very straightforward.

In our case study the components had very little internal processing and the data types were very simple. The complexity was on the side of complex patterns of interaction with the environment. This however is in many cases a typical situation in control systems and such systems are the application domain of our method.

Formal specifications were helpful in the process of identification and selection of failure modes of components. Checklists used to provide for completeness of analyses and the precise meaning of specifications were very helpful in understanding the semantics of failures.

The tool (FDR) was able to provide example scenarios showing how a given failure breaks system safety. It was very helpful while considering component re-design.

Although we basically experimented with single failure mode at a time our method of failure mode specification does not prevent analysing consequences of combined failure modes.

8. REFERENCES

[1] Lutz R. R., Woodhouse R. M.: Requirements Analysis Using Forward and Backward Search. *Annals of Software Engineering*, 3, 1997, 459-475 (JPL California Institute of Technology Technical Report, May 2, 1997).

[2] Noé-Gonzales E.: The Software Error Effect Analysis and the Synchronous Data Flow Approach to Safety Software: Method, Results, Operational Lessons. *Proc. of 13th International Conference SAFECOMP*, 1994, Los Angeles (USA), pp. 163-171.

[3] Cichocki T., Górski J.: *Failure Mode and Effect Analysis for Safety-Critical Systems with Software Components*, in: Springer Lecture Notes in Computer Science, vol. 1943, 2000, pp. 382-394

[4] Cichocki T., Górski J.: *Formal Support for Fault Modelling and Analysis*, in: Springer Lecture Notes in Computer Science, vol. 2187, 2001, pp. 190-199.

[5] Roscoe W.: *The Theory and Practice of Concurrency*, Prentice-Hall, 1998 (580 pp), ISBN 0-13-674409-5.

[6] OMG: *Unified Modelling Language Specification*, Version 1.4, September 2001 (http://www.omg.org/technology/documents/formal/uml.html).

[7] Formal Systems (Europe) Ltd.: *Failures-Divergence Refinement, FDR2 User Manual*, 24 October 1997.

[8] Mü 8004: *Answeisung zu den technischen Anforderungen für die Zulassung von Sicherungsanlagen*, Eisenbahn-Bundesamt, Münich 1999.

[9] DIN V VDE 0801/01.90: *Safety of computerized systems* (orig. Grundsätze für Rechner in Systemen mit Sicherheitsaufgaben), Beuth-Verlag, Berlin, 1994 (pp 182).

[10] EN 50159, *Railway applications – Communication, signalling and processing systems*: Part 1 and 2 - Safety related communication. 1997/1998, CENELEC, Central Secretariat, Brussels.

[11] European Rail Research Institute/UIC: *ETCS Functional Requirements Specification*, FRS, ver. 4.0, 1996, Utrecht, Netherlands (pp 176).

Providing for continuous risk management in distributed software projects

JANUSZ GÓRSKI, JAKUB MILER
Department of Applied Informatics, Technical University of Gdańsk, Gdańsk, Poland
Faculty of Computer Science & Information Systems, Technical University of Szczecin, 49, Zolnierska st., 71-210 Szczecin, Poland, e-mail: {bburchard, kniemczyk}@wi.ps.pl

Abstract: The paper presents a concept of continuous risk management in distributed software development projects. The concept is particularly relevant for critical software applications where risk management is among main project management activities. Our approach recognises that effective and open communication is the prerequisite for successful risk management. Therefore, it concentrates on providing to the project stakeholders a broad and highly available communication channel through which they can communicate risk-related information. The channel has unlimited memory – it registers all incoming information much as the "black box" device memorises all relevant data during an aircraft flight. The collected information can then be analysed from different angles to select and prioritise the most important risks or to analyse the project history in order to find out how risk perception developed during the project course. The description of a tool that embodies those concepts and reports from some validation experiments are also included.

Key words: software development, risk management, collaboration, distributed project

1. INTRODUCTION

Software projects are exposed to various risks and risk management in such projects is still inadequate as is shown by the percentage of failed, delayed or too expensive projects [2]. Risk management is listed among the key knowledge areas related to project management [6]. In relation to software project risks, a good surveys can be found in reports of Software Engineering Institute (SEI) [9] or in [2].

The importance of adequate project management is well recognised by standards and guidelines in the critical systems domain (e.g. [7]). It becomes even more important if the product or the process of its development are distributed.

Issues related to product distribution in computer-based safety related systems were addressed e.g. in [1].

The goal of any project is to deliver, in time and within the budget constraints, a product that meets stakeholders' needs and expectations. The essential factors of the project success are the quality (and in particular, safety), the time and the budget. Present software projects are often facing expanding and changing client demands and are put under schedule pressure. The systems are growing in size and become increasingly complex. To shorten the development time, the systems are built out of reused (but often not reusable) components. The personnel turnover is high and the size and diversity of project groups are growing.

Risk management means that we change our attitude towards risks. A project without risk management faces serious problems only after the risks came to the surface as a material fact (the deadline is not met, the budget is overrun, the quality is poor). Then, the only thing to do is to strive to minimize the negative impacts of those facts on the project. The reaction is always expensive and time-consuming. A project with risk management aims at early identification and recognition of risks and then actively changes the course of actions to mitigate and reduce the risk. This requires open communication, forward-looking view and team involvement in the management and the maintaining a knowledge base of typical problems. The lack of these exposes a project to a great risk of failure.

The objective of this paper is to present a concept of continuous risk management in distributed software development projects. We have recognized effective, continuous and open communication as the prerequisite for successful risk management. Therefore, we concentrate on providing to the project stakeholders a broad and highly available communication channel through which they can communicate risk-related information. The channel has unlimited memory – it registers all incoming information much as the "black box" device memorizes all relevant data during an aircraft flight. The stored information can then be analysed from different angles, e.g. to select and prioritise the most important risks or to analyse the project history in order to find out how risk perception was developing during the project course.

In the subsequent sections, we introduce the concepts related to risk communication and point out to some techniques supporting risk identification. We also present experiments performed to validate our approach and the plans for the future.

2. RISK COMMUNICATION AND RISK MEMORY

Open and unrestricted communication facilitates the key activities related to risk management. It seems, however, that the "bandwidth" of the communication channel that is necessary to support effective realization of the basic risk management activities is not even, as is shown in Fig. 1.

The most broad communication channel is necessary for thorough risk identification. The channel should be open to any project stakeholder to provide for communicating risk-related information from any relevant viewpoint. It should "absorb" information generated by using diverse identification techniques such as checklists, questionnaires, brainstorming sessions and individual observations.

Moreover, it should be constantly open to protect against the risk-related information being lost (e.g. a risk has been recognized but there was no input to pass this information to, so nothing was done and the information "disappeared").

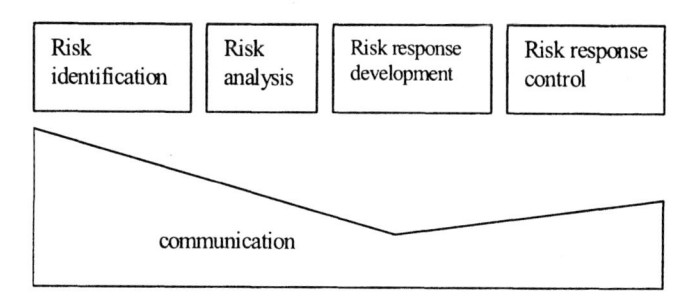

Figure 1. Communication in risk management activities

During risk analysis there is still much communication necessary as this activity is much like a consensus building process during which the parties involved communicate their views of the identified risks in order to agree on risk evaluation, priorities and possible remedying actions.

Risk response development is more related to building plans, securing resources and assigning responsibilities for handling the high priority risks. It is more on the managers' side and therefore the need for open communication is lower.

Risk response control is again the activity that heavily relays on communication, as it needs to trace the evolution of the identified risks and eventually triggers actions that are included in the risk response plans. Nevertheless, the "bandwidth" of the communication channel is not as wide as during risk identification, as here the attention is mainly focused on the already recognized risks.

From the above model, we can observe that providing a broad and highly available communication channel as early as possible is a necessary condition to successful risk identification. It strongly influences the success of all other risk management related activities. This channel should allow project stakeholders to apply diverse risk identification techniques. It should in particular allow to pass information that reflects a given person's intuitions and concerns even if this information were not obtained with the help of any defined risk identification techniques.

The conditions for successful risk identification can be summarized as follows:
- providing a constantly open communication channel,
- involvement of all relevant viewpoints,
- application of diverse identification techniques,
- effective control of the scope,
- learning from the past ("memorizing" risk related information).

As the project advances, risks can be identified either during scheduled project activities or informally, e.g. when people talk to each other at lunchtime, travel or during their leisure time. The idea of *risk black box* comes from the fact that memorizing this risk-related information should be effective and as complete as possible (much like it is done during the aircraft flight). The difference to the aircraft black box is that we want to use this information with the proactive attitude, although we do not exclude its use for retrospection (e.g. to analyse the risk history after the project success/failure).

3. RISK ASSESSMENT

Our risk assessment is based on three concepts: *reviews*, *snapshots* and *reports* that underpin the three layers of processing the risk-related information: identification, analysis and reporting. Reviews establish the framework for risk identification. Snapshots pass the identified risks for further analysis. Reports communicate the results of risk assessment. The three layers are presented in Fig. 2.

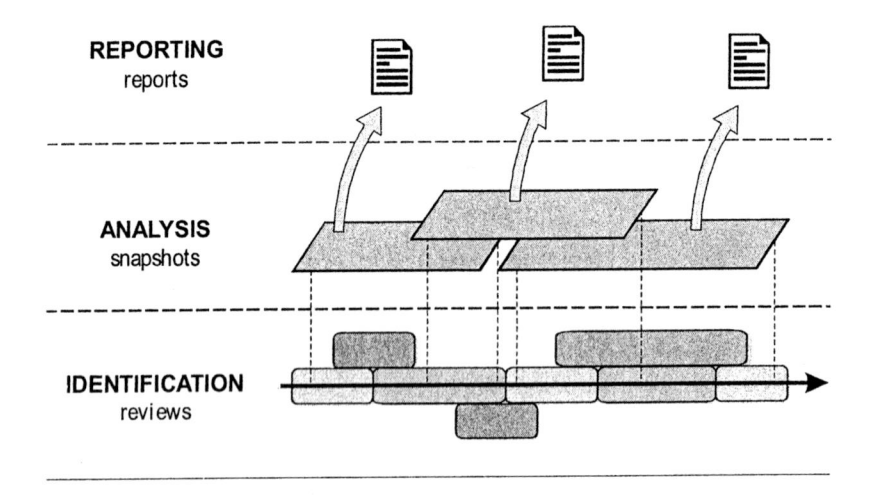

Figure 2. Three layers of risk assessment

The risk identification layer uses *reviews* to gather risk-related information from a project. Reviews differ in terms of their scope, duration, participants and identification techniques. It is possible that two reviews overlap in time, however differing in their scope and/or participants. Risk-related information collected during a review is represented as *risk indication* and identifies a particular risk, the involved project stakeholder, timestamp, the identification technique and possible comments. The idea of risk indications is presented in Fig. 3.

For any defined period we define *risk snapshot* as a summary showing, in a predefined form, all the risks identified during this period. Thus, a snapshot is a sort of the "map of identified risks" with removed redundancies. A snapshot can be constantly "open" presenting to the risk manager how the situation (in terms of risk indications) changes during an active review.

This provides a deeper insight into the risk-related information collected during the review and may be used to decide on closing the review and passing to the analysis phase. The idea of risk snapshot is illustrated in Fig.4.

Risk snapshots form the input to the risk analysis. After the analysis, a risk assessment report is being generated. The report is a sort of "risk summary" of the present view at risks. It can then be used as an input for risk mitigation related activities. It may also be taken as an input to the next risk review action. The cycle of risk identification and analysis is shown in Fig. 5.

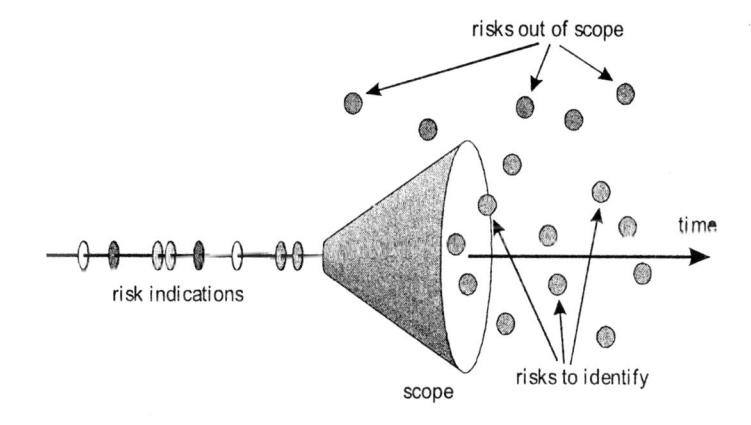

Figure 3. The idea of risk indications

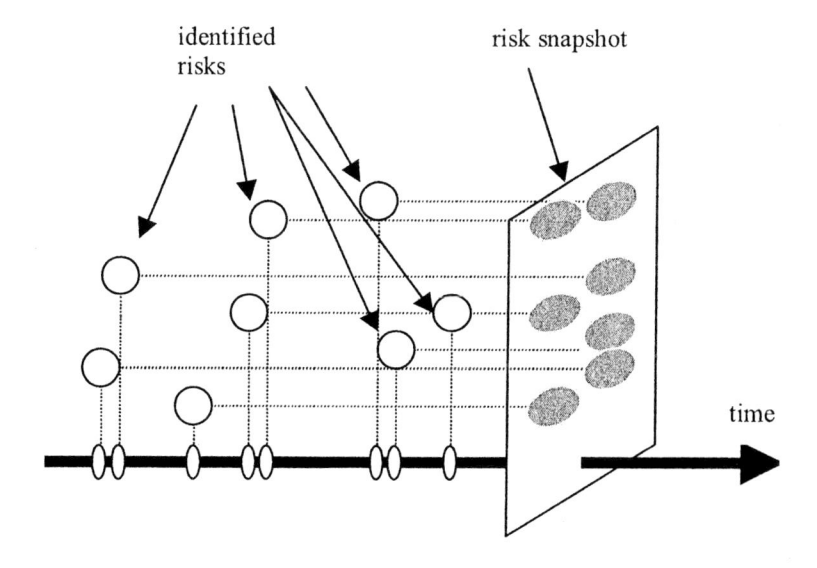

Figure 4. The idea of risk snapshot

4. THE PROCESS

Opening a channel to communicate and memorize risk related information is not enough, as it does not guarantee that anything is actually communicated and memorized. It is the manager's task to cause that the information is actually generated. We assume that there is a risk identification and analysis process *performed* by the project stakeholders and *controlled* by the risk manager (the role usually played by the project manager except large projects where it could be assigned separately). The process is structured as a sequence of *reviews*, as shown in Fig.6.

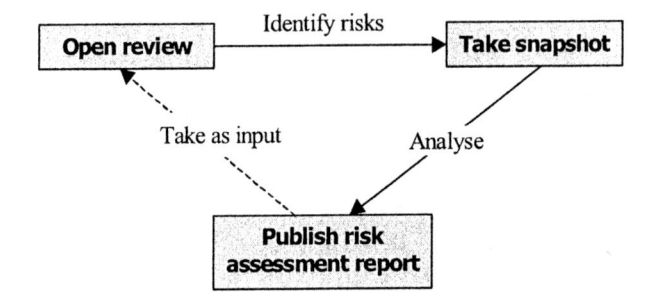

Figure 5. The risk identification and analysis cycle

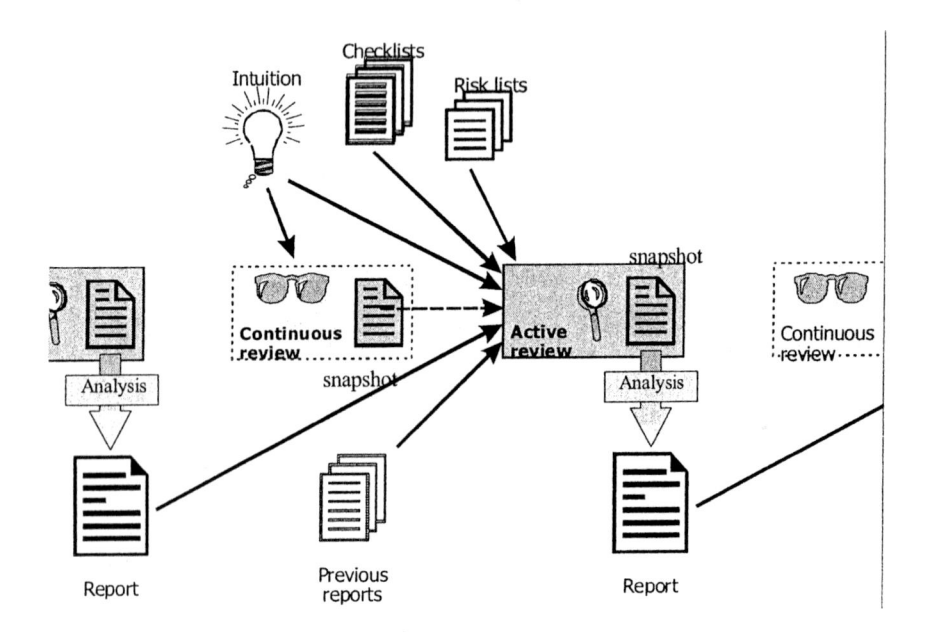

Figure 6. Review-based risk identification and analysis process

It is assumed that at any time some review is *open*. The review remains open over its *time window*. Time windows of subsequent reviews are adjacent. We distinguish between two types of reviews:
- *active review* – its starting and ending times are set by the risk manager as well as its scope and participants (the stakeholders involved in the review). The review has a defined set of inputs (reports, checklists, questionnaires, etc.) and associated risk identification techniques. As a rule, the *snapshot* from the last *continuous* review, is included as an input of the active review. The active review ends with the risk analysis session that aims at assessing and prioritising the identified risks and produces a relevant report.
- *continuous review* – it starts with the end of the previous review and ends with the start of the next review (being it active or continuous). It just keeps the communication channel open enabling the communicated risk information being memorised. Any project stakeholder can pass risk-related information disregarding the way of its generation.

Typically, a snapshot is taken at the end of each continuous review to provide input to the subsequent active review. A snapshot is also taken at the end of an active review to summarize the effects of risk identification activities (as shown in Fig.7.). The risk assessment report is generated at the end of an active review.

We assume that the process has the active and continuous reviews interleaved, their extent (in time) and scope (in terms of inputs and participants) being controlled by the risk manager. This way we achieve the following benefits:
- communication channel is constantly open,
- identification actions are being planned (as active and continuous reviews),
- all communicated risk-related information is being memorized,
- the identified risks are periodically reviewed and assessed and the frequency and scope of those assessments is under control of the risk manager,
- the results of the analyses are kept in the form of reports and are available downstream of the process (can support further identification and analysis)

5. REPRESENTATION OF RISKS

The risk management process must be supported by adequately defined data structures maintaining the risk-related information generated and used in this process. The proposed generic model is presented in Fig. 7 in a form of a class diagram using UML notation.

First, the risk itself must be defined giving the description of the undesired event that may possibly occur. The *risk definition* can be a simple statement expressed in a natural language, a formal expression in a certain notation or a scenario showing how we can get to the undesired state/event.

Risk indications point to a risk definition and declare that this particular risk is being present in the project. Many stakeholders may indicate the same risk as well as it may be reported many times by the same stakeholder (e.g. in different reviews).

To process the risk-related information we distinguish two types of risks, namely *analysed risk* and *reported risk* that inherit a related risk definition. The indicated risks are mapped to the analysed risks using the concept of the snapshot as presented earlier in the paper. An analysed risk comprises additional information like: priority, evaluation of its likelihood, severity etc. It is important to provide for backward and forward traceability between the various risk representations to provide for visibility of the analyses and retrospection. The most important analysed risks are selected for publication in the risk assessment report. A reported risk is an analysed risk extended with a risk response related information, e.g. contingency plans.

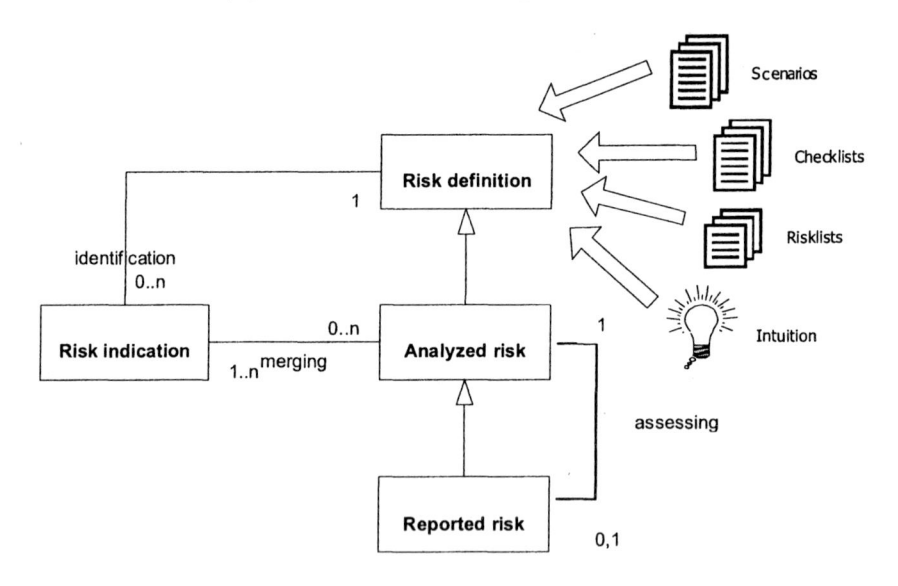

Figure 7. Representation of risks

6. TOOL SUPPORT: THE RISK GUIDE SYSTEM

To experiment with the concepts proposed above, we have elaborated and implemented a risk management tool named ()RiskGuide [5]. It is an Internet application and can be accessed simply by a web browser [10]. It makes it applicable in distributed software projects. It supports risk reviews, indications, snapshots and reports. Multiple project members can post risk indications simultaneously and those are then automatically lined up in the risk repository. The tool supports multiple projects at a time with independent risk identification and assessment processes.

Presently the system offers a knowledge base of two components: the *open knowledge base* that includes the Taxonomy-Based Questionnaire [8] and Complete List of Schedule Risks [3, 4], and the *restricted knowledge base* that includes a more advanced proprietary questionnaire and the related list of risks. This latter questionnaire comprises some 404 questions that cover the following areas of a project: project type and size; contract; upper management support; project planning; collaboration with the customer; target system and its environment; system development process; system design and implementation; configuration management; quality management; personnel management.

The following techniques to identify risks are presently supported:
- automatic generation of risk indications based on the answers to a questionnaire,
- explicit selection of a risk from the list of risks,
- supplying a new definition of a specific risk (e.g. identified by intuition and/or engineering judgement) and then referring to it
- referring to the previously identified risks

The tool supports management of checklists and lists of risks as well as provides for evolution of risk definitions (by means of versioning).

Anytime the risk manager can take a snapshot of already identified risks. As soon as the snapshot is taken, all open reviews are closed and further identification requires opening a new review. The analysis of risks is carried out in two phases: evaluation of each risk and assignment of priorities to risks. The risks can be evaluated in three dimensions: possibility, severity and timeframe. For each dimension ◯ RiskGuide offers a qualitative evaluation scale. An overall risk evaluation is calculated from individual assessments using the risk evaluation matrix. In addition, a comment can be added to the evaluation to justify it or to express its certainty. The priorities can be assigned automatically according to the evaluation or based on manager's decision. The list of risks analysed is ordered, so the most important risks are available on top of the list.

Once the analysis is completed, the resulting list of the most important risks is published in a risk assessment report. The tool also offers various options supporting risk tracking and risk history analysis and includes adequate access control mechanisms.

7. THE EXPERIMENTS

On our way towards an integrated environment for risk management we plan and carry out experiments to test our concepts. As for February 2002, two experiments are already completed and the third one was just started.

The first experiment aimed at evaluation of the ease of use of ◯ RiskGuide and assessing the effectiveness of its support in a single risk assessment cycle (according to Fig. 6). It was carried out in the academic year 2000/2001 during the Software Engineering Project Management course at our university. Risks were considered while building the detailed project plan and developing risk mitigation plans. In total, 38 groups took part in the experiment. The experiment was then evaluated using a questionnaire. The results confirmed the value of providing a common environment to focus participants' attention on risk management and provided numerous suggestions of user interface improvements.

The second experiment took place in the period October 2001 – January 2002. It aimed at the evaluation of the concepts of snapshots and reports as well as assessing the effectiveness of support in relation to schedule risks. Full recurring assessment process (as presented on Fig. 7) was being followed. Two small projects were involved in the experiment (each of 5 team members). The participants were software engineers coming from local companies. Both projects had the same goal (development of a billing system for a telecom switch) and were run during an industrial training course in software engineering. Assessment of the results was by phase and summary reports as well as by a detailed questionnaire at the end of the project, and by examination of the risk management history recorded in () Risk Guide. The experiment confirmed the help of the tool in increasing team awareness of risks and focusing at particular risk areas. The present knowledge base of () Risk Guide was highly evaluated.

The above experiments were using the open knowledge base of () Risk Guide.

The third experiment that uses the proprietary knowledge base of () Risk Guide has just started (end of February 2002). It relates to a real project of development of a GIS system to support management of a heat generation and distribution infrastructure in one of the major cities of the country. The experiment is planned for the period March – July 2002. Its goal is to assess the support offered by () Risk Guide in more quantified terms.

Several other software companies expressed their interest in incorporating the tool into their projects.

8. CONCLUSION

In the paper, we emphasised the essential role of communication in the risk management process and proposed a concept of a risk "black box" memorizing all risk-related information arising in the project. We distinguished three layers of risk assessment and explained how they interact. We also presented the structure of a process of continuous risk management taking benefit from the above ideas.

Risk management can benefit from tools that support communication and collaboration. We described an Internet tool that can be offered to a software development team disregarding the actual geographic dislocation of team members. The tool supports the previously defined process of continuous risk management.

We also described experiments that were performed and are being planned to check the validity of our approach in real projects. The already obtained results from those experiments are very encouraging.

Although the risk identification support that is presently offered by () Risk Guide is based on questionnaires and lists of risks (both, open and restricted) we do not intend to restrict the ways of risk definition and identification. We assume that a wide range of risk definition techniques can be applied from just giving a name of the risk with a possibly short textual description down to advanced techniques of presenting risk scenarios, like fault trees, event trees and others. In addition to the questionnaires we are also considering other, more advanced project risk identification techniques, e.g. applying HAZOP to project process models.

We are also considering experimenting with more advanced risk analysis methods that result in more exact assessment than just giving a list of N topmost risks, e.g. presenting risks using risk scenarios supplemented with quantitative or qualitative information on the likelihood and severity associated with a particular risk

Although our work is applicable to general software development projects we see it as particularly relevant to critical projects for which the risk of failure is high. With the widening market of safety and in particular security related applications and with the tendency of distributing projects geographically (e.g. through outsourcing) effective tool support offered to projects in the area of risk management seems to be a worthwhile attempt.

9. REFERENCES

[1] Anderson S., Górski J. (Eds.), EWICS TC7 Guidelines in Achieving Safety in Distributed Systems, Standards, ISA – The Instrumentation, Systems and Automation Society, USA, (http://www.isa.org/standards/)
[2] Jones C., Assessment and Control of Software Risks, Prentice Hall, 1994.
[3] McConnell S., Code Complete, Microsoft Press, 1993.
[4] McConnell S., Rapid Development, Microsoft Press, 1996.
[5] Miler J., Górski J., Implementing risk management in software projects, Proc. of 3rd National Software Engineering Conference, Poland, 2001.
[6] PMBOK Guide, 2000 Edition, Project Management Institute, 2000
[7] Schoitsch E. and Redmill F. (Eds.), EWICS TC7 Guidelines for the Project Management of the Development of Critical Computer Systems, Standards, ISA – The Instrumentation, Systems and Automation Society, USA, (http://www.isa.org/standards/)
[8] Sisti F. J., Joseph S., Software Risk Evaluation Method, SEI report CMU/SEI-94-TR-19, Carnegie Mellon University, Pittsburgh PA, December 1994.
[9] http://www.sei.cmu.edu/
[10] http://mkzlway.eti.pg.gda.pl/riskguide

About Some Application of Risk Analysis and Evaluation

IMED EL FRAY
Technical University of Szczecin, Faculty of Computer Science & Information Systems
ul. Zolnierska 49, 71-210 Szczecin, e-mail: imed.elfray@wi.ps.pl

Abstract: Electronic data exchange in wide-world networks have become the necessity for the companie's competition on the market. This data exchange expose the safety of the computer system on different threats, including pirates and hackers activity, viruses, information revealance and modification. In the presence of those threats every company which want to exist on the market should introduce consistent security policy and risk management mechanisms within the company to guarantee information accessibility, confidentiality and integrity. The introduction of consistent and consequent policy results in requirement of essential financial expenses and adequate methods of the risk management. The most of existing risk management methods are similar and derived from the ISO/IEC 17799 standard, ITSEC criteria and the Orange Book. This paper is focused on risk evaluation based on some model enterprise (E-Bisiness system) and in accordance with known and accepted risk management methods

Key words: risk management, risk analysis and evaluation,

1. INTRODUCTION

A security management in the case of computer systems is the process leading to obtain and maintain adequate levels of: confidence, integrity, accessibility, etc.. The rules for implementation of such a management system are given for example in ISO/IEC 17799-2 standard [1,2,4] and presented in Figure 1.

The company has to constitute its internal policy concerning the design and implementation of its security policy to increase the security level of its IT system (including procedures covering access control mechanisms and hardware and software security as well). It should also implement, adequately to its environment, an appropriate strategy of the risk management containing efficient methods for fighting against intended and accidental threats.

The methods of risk analysis are described in mentioned above ISO/IEC standard [1,2,3,4] and consist of elements shown on Figure 2.

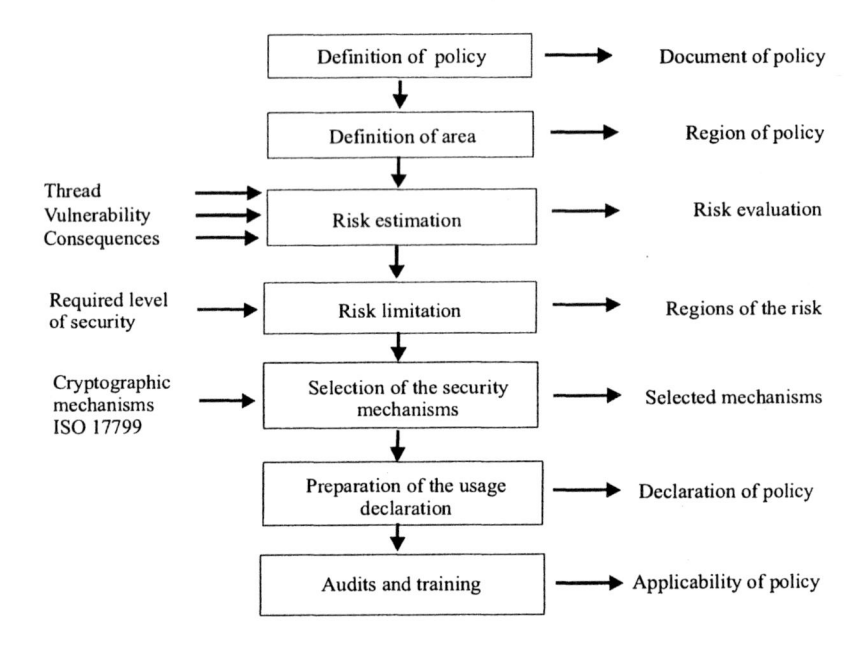

```
                          ┌─────────────────────┐
                          │ Definition of policy │ ────▶ Document of policy
                          └─────────────────────┘
                                    │
                                    ▼
                          ┌─────────────────────┐
                          │  Definition of area  │ ────▶ Region of policy
                          └─────────────────────┘
                                    │
Thread                              ▼
Vulnerability    ───▶     ┌─────────────────────┐
Consequences              │   Risk estimation    │ ────▶ Risk evaluation
                          └─────────────────────┘
                                    │
Required level                      ▼
of security      ───▶     ┌─────────────────────┐
                          │   Risk limitation    │ ────▶ Regions of the risk
                          └─────────────────────┘
Cryptographic                       │
mechanisms       ───▶               ▼
ISO 17799                 ┌─────────────────────┐
                          │ Selection of the     │ ────▶ Selected mechanisms
                          │ security mechanisms  │
                          └─────────────────────┘
                                    │
                                    ▼
                          ┌─────────────────────┐
                          │ Preparation of the   │ ────▶ Declaration of policy
                          │ usage declaration    │
                          └─────────────────────┘
                                    │
                                    ▼
                          ┌─────────────────────┐
                          │  Audits and training │ ────▶ Applicability of policy
                          └─────────────────────┘
```

Fig. 1. Security policy according to BS 17799-2 standard

The risk analysis based on four mentioned above methods (the strategy of the risk management) should be carried out in the manner suitable for the company size, activity and services, and its environment as well.

There are several methods regarding the risk management used worldwide. Those methods allow to make the analysis, the evaluation (including financial incomes) and the minimization of the risk with respect to the system, application and data sets basing on environmental properties and organizational procedures. The most popular methods in Europe are CRAMM, BSI, MARION, MELISA and MEHARI. These methods are traditional and compatible with ITSEC and Orange Book methods, and with ISO/IEC 17799 standard as well as.

2. RISK ANALYSIS BASED ON THE MEHARI METHOD

The risk analysis using MEHARI method [6, 7] is supported by knowledge about resources identification and evaluation, the risk level evaluation and vulnerability in the case of particular threats. Generally the analysis is focused on the four areas concerning security (integrity, confidence, accessibility, non-repudiation).

MEHARI method enables to make an analysis on a high level of generalization, hence it makes possible to concentrate all countermeasures in the region of a higher risk; it also deals with the specific risks on the lower levels.

Figure 3 presents the strategy of the risk analysis according to MEHARI. It consists of three main elements:
- risk scenario (the system set in the role of the potential attack target),
- risk prevention scenario (methods and tools preventing the system from and securing it against the risk),
- influence and scale of threats evaluation for the system.

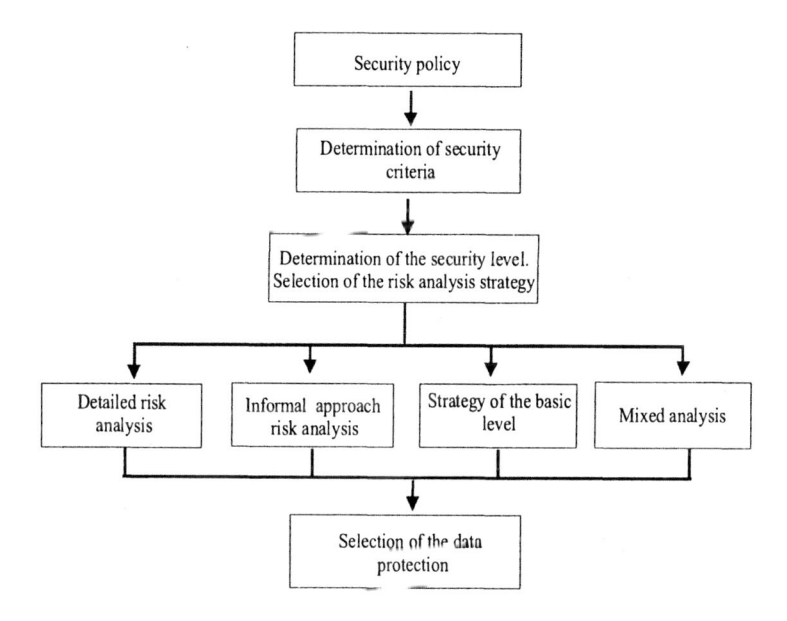

Fig 2. Strategy of the risk management

The last mentioned element (regarding threats evaluation and their influence of potential consequences on the system) is composed of the residual risk estimates which are analysed later detailly as it is demonstrated on Figure 3. An example of the analysis of the risk evaluation is presented in Table 1.

Probability of the threat	Risk				
	The seriousness of the threat			
	Disregardable	Small	Medium	Very high
Extremely high	3	4	4	4
Very high	2	3	3	4
Medium	1	1	2	2
Low	1	1	1	1

Tab. 1. Predefined risk table

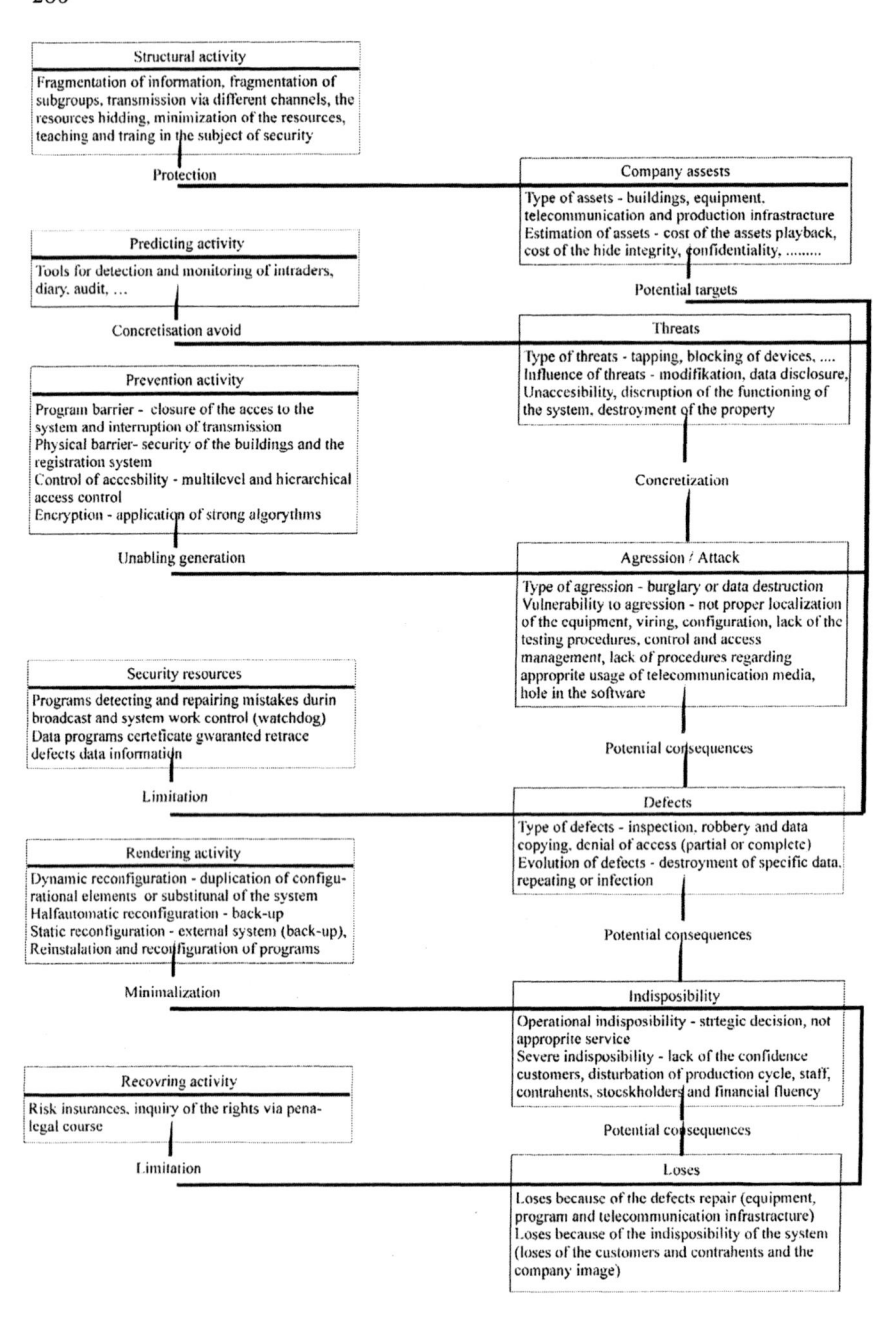

Structural activity		Company assests
Fragmentation of information, fragmentation of subgroups, transmission via different channels, the resources hidding, minimization of the resources, teaching and traing in the subject of security		Type of assets - buildings, equipment. telecommunication and production infrastructure Estimation of assets - cost of the assets playback, cost of the hide integrity, confidentiality, ...
↓ Protection		↓ Potential targets
Predicting activity		**Threats**
Tools for detection and monitoring of intruders, diary, audit, ...		Type of threats - tapping, blocking of devices, ... Influence of threats - modifikation, data disclosure, Unaccesibility, discruption of the functioning of the system, destroyment of the property
↓ Concretisation avoid		↓ Concretization
Prevention activity		**Agression / Attack**
Program barrier - closure of the acces to the system and interruption of transmission Physical barrier- security of the buildings and the registration system Control of accesbility - multilevel and hicrarchical access control Encryption - application of strong algorytluns		Type of agression - burglary or data destruction Vulnerability to agression - not proper localization of the equipment, viring, configuration, lack of the testing procedures, control and access management, lack of procedures regarding appropriate usage of telecommunication media, hole in the software
↓ Unabling generation		↓ Potential consequences
Security resources		**Defects**
Programs detecting and repairing mistakes durin broadcast and system work control (watchdog) Data programs certeficate gwaranted retrace defects data information		Type of defects - inspection, robbery and data copying, denial of access (partial or complete) Evolution of defects - destroyment of specific data, repeating or infection
↓ Limitation		↓ Potential consequences
Rendering activity		**Indisposibility**
Dynamic reconfiguration - duplication of configurational elements or substitunal of the system Halfautomatic reconfiguration - back-up Static reconfiguration - external system (back-up), Reinstalation and reconfiguration of programs		Operational indisposibility - strtegic decision, not appropritc service Severe indisposibility - lack of the confidence customers, disturbation of production cycle, staff, contrahents, stocskholders and financial fluency
↓ Minimalization		↓ Potential consequences
Recovring activity		**Loses**
Risk insurances, inquiry of the rights via pena-legal course		Loses because of the defects repair (equipment, program and telecommunication infrastructure) Loses because of the indisposibility of the system (loses of the customers and contrahents and the company image)
↓ Limitation		

fig. 3. MEHARI strategy of the risk manegement

3. RISK ANALYSIS AND EVALUATION BASED ON THE MODEL E-BUSINESS SYSTEM

The architecture of the E-Business includes the WEB server, application software and the data-base server. Every component of this architecture can be considered as a weak point and can loose its security. Some additional systems are installed (internal and external routers, firewalls, IDS systems for monitoring and intruders' detection, system switches) with the purpose of E-Business security enhancement.

Figure 4 shows an example of E-Business architecture; this one will be the subjected of the analysis [5].

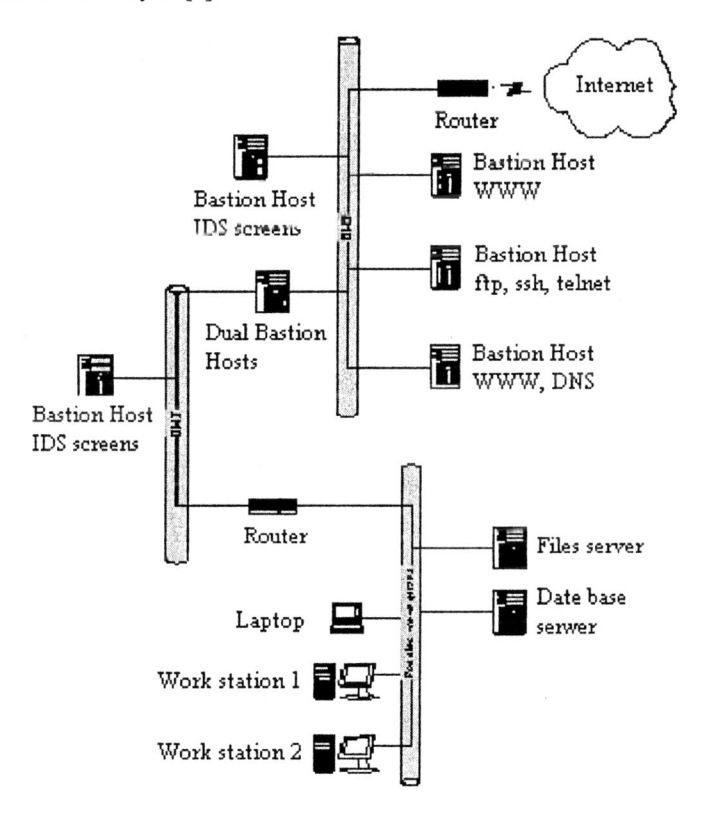

fig. 4. Example of E-Business architecture

As can be seen from the Figure 4, the whole network can be considered safe because it is based on the multi-component router network. However, during the analysis of the components from the security point of view it contains many weak points, namely bastion hosts and internal network offering an access for external and internal users (ftp, ssh, http, DSN, telnet, file server, data-base server). Taking control over the one of the hosts may lead to capture of the DMZ-head, and to breake of the security.

The risk analysis requires appropriate selection of different services. It is possible to select such services and security tools to provide the predefined risk level.

Techniques of the risk analysis are based on the following issues:
- selection of threats – selection is based on the list of threats acting on the system (accidents, natural phenomena, information disclosure, robbery, etc.)
- identification of system vulnerabilities – determination of the risk instantiation probability, expressed by the value from 0 to 1. It should be underlined there is no zero probability in computer sciences.
- determination of the threats' influence on the system – every threat has its own seriousness value in the system security context; it is different in the case of the integrity, confidence and accessibility features. The value of the seriousness is from 1 to 4.

Based on this technique, a careful selection of threats in the system has to be established. The risks resulting from the location of the network (building, technical equipment), the state of wiring and physical security are not considered in this analysis.

List of threats a in the system is presented in Table 2.

Item no	Type of threat	Sources
1	Tapping of the network	Telnet, POP3, ftp, http
2	Usage of forbidden tools – ports and addresses scanning	ICMP
3	Changes within the programs – viruses, logic bombs, modification, deletions	POP3
4	Program traps - troian horses, covered channels, trapdoors	users
5	Illegal copying and instalation of the programs	users
6	Data forgery –denial of services (overloading, unaccessibility, data destruction)	ftp, ICMP
7	Impersonation and the super user authorization taking over	ftp, telnet, WWW, http

Tab. 2. List of threats in the system

In the second step the system vulnerabilities have to be identified; the probability of instantiation of potentisal threats and the probablity of the risk should be evaluated. Evaluation of the probability of threats instantiation is carried on the basis of network topography, type of services and security policy of the company. The probability of threats instantiation is presented in Table 3.

The risk model can be constructed using detailed data concerning the probability of threats instantiation. The risk model will contain multiplied probabilities of threats instantiations according to the risk scenarios defined for the system. Appropriate scenarios and their probability are presented in Table 4.

Z	Vulnerability type	A1	A2	A3	A4	A5	A6
Z1	possibility of easy access to the E-Business server	-	-	-	0.50	-	-
	possibility of tnet transmission tapping	-	0.50	0.25	0.50	-	-
	lack of information concerning the confidentiality	-	-	-	-	-	0.25
Z2	system connected to the network and commonly accessible	0.50	0.50	-	-	-	-
		0.25	-	-	0.50	-	-
	easy access to the E-Business server and usage of hidden ports	-	-	0.50	-	-	-
	possibility of external usage of the data	-	-	-	0.25	-	-
	possibility of the access control omittance	-	-	-	-	0.75	-
	lack of the moral and ethical norms	-	-	-	-	0.75	-
	authorization of the rights not resulting from executed activities	-	-	-	-	0.50	-
	additional authorization	-	-	-	-	-	0.25
	possibility of resources usage without control	-	-	-	-	-	0.25
	lack of knowledge regarding usage of the equipment						
Z3	possibility of data and applications modification	0.25	0.50	0.25	-	-	-
	possibility of program files deletion or changes	0.25	0.50	-	-	-	-
	possibility of programs instalation (viruses and others)	0.25	0.50	0.25	-	-	-
	manipulating users, conflict situations	-	-	-	-	0.75	-
	lack of information concerning security problems	-	-	-	-	-	0.25
	lack of policy for IT usage	-	-	-	-	-	0.25
Z4	possibility of creation and modification of system commands and changes within applications	0.25	0.50	0.25	-	-	-
	possibility of instalation of illegal programs, implementation of nonvisible functions	0.25	0.75	-	-	-	-
	possibility of deletion and changes within program files	0.25	0.50	-	-	-	-
	possibility of easy access to the E-Business server	-	-	-	0.50	-	-
	possibility of taking over the access control	-	-	-	0.25	-	-
	manipulating users, conflict situations	-	-	-	-	0.75	-
	additional authorization	-	-	-	-	0.50	-
	lack of security inspection during instalation and implementation	-	-	-	-	-	0.25
Z5	possibility of the work with pirate programs	0.50	0.50	-	-	-	-
	possibility of telecopying of the programs	-	-	0.50	-	-	-
	lack of the respect for the internal policy	-	-	-	-	0.75	-
	lack of the control over operations performed by users	-	-	-	-	-	0.25
	lack of information and politic regarding author rights	-	-	-	-	-	0.25
Z6	system enables the accesss to data base	0.25	-	-	-	-	-
	possibility of influence on data transmitted via network	-	0.50	0.50	-	-	-
	possibility of easy access to the E-Business server	-	-	-	0.50	-	-
	possibility of taking over the access control	-	-	-	0.25	-	-
	manipulating users, conflict situations	-	-	-	-	0.75	-
	additional authorization	-	-	-	-	0.50	-
	lack of poliicy for IT usage	-	-	-	-	-	0.25
Z7	system connected to external netork	0.50	0.50	-	-	-	-
	interception of system functions and higher authorization acquisition	0.50	0.50	-	-	-	-
	system makes possible to obtaining unauthorized rights	-	-	0.50	-	-	-
	lack of moral, athical rules and respect for policy	-	-	-	-	-	-
	additional authorization, possibility of resources usage	-	-	-	-	0.50	-
	lack of the internal control procedures	-	-	-	-	-	0.25

A1-Software & hardware, A2-Internal network, A3-External network, A4-E-Business server, A5–Users, A6–Organization, Z–threat, 0.25 – minimal risk, 0.50 – medium risk, 0.75 – very high risk

Tab. 3. Probability of the risk instantiation

Z	Type of risk	Probability -PR
Z1	Intruder penetrated E-Business server	0.75*0.50 =0.38
	Intruder tapped transmission because of the lack of security	0.75*0.50*0.25 =0.10
	Intruder tapped transmission and penetrated E-Business server	0.75*0.50*0.50 =0.13
	Intruder tapped transmission because of the lack of security policy	0.75*0.50*0.25 =0.10
Z2	Intruder penetrated network (system network)	0.75*0.50 =0.38
	Intruder penetrated E-Business server via hidden ports	0.75*0.50*0.25 =0.10
	Intruder penetrated E-Business server despite acess control	0.75*0.50*0.25 =0.10
	Intruder caught transmission during remote usage of resources	0.75*0.50 =0.38
	Users are using systems which are not compliant with their duties	0.75*0.25 = 0.18
	Users are using different resources due to additional authorization	0.50*0.25 =0.13
	Users are using different resources despite access control	0.75*0.50*0.25 =0.10
Z3	Intruder penetrated network and modified data and system files	0.75*0.25 =0.18
	Intruder penetrated network, deleted system files, installed viruses	0.75*0.25*0.25 =0.05
	Users are penetrating system and use resources without authorization	0.75*0.50 =0.38
	Users are penetrating system because of the lack of usage regulations and policy	0.75*0.50*0.25 =0.10
	Users are modifying and deleting system files, installing viruses	0.75*0.50*0.50 =0.13
Z4	Intruder penetrated network and modified commands and deleted system files	0.75*0.25*0.25 =0.05
	Intruder penetrated E-Business server	0.75*0.50 =0.38
	Intruder penetrated E-Business server and installed nonvisible programs	0.75*0.50*0.25 =0.10
	Users are modifying data and system commands	0.75*0.25 =0.19
	Users are penetrating system and installing nonvisible programs	0.75*0.50*0.25 =0.10
	Users are installing unlegal programs due to additional authorization	0.75*0.25*0.50 =0.10
	Developers penetrated system due to nonvisible programs	0.75*0.25 =0.19
Z5	Users installed illegal programs necessary for their work	0.50*0.50 =0.25
	Users are telecopying programs	0.50*0.25 =0.13
	Users are telecopying remote resources	0.50*0.25 =0.13
	Users are telecopying unlegal programs	0.75*0.50=0.38
Z6	Intruder copied the data base contents	0.75*0.25 =0.19
	Intruder penetrated E-Business system because of the lack of appropriate protection	0.75*0.25*0.50 =0.10
	Intruder tapped unprotected transmission	0.75*0.25 =0.19
	Users are using data base resources due to authorization rights not compliant with their duties	0.25*0.50 =0.13
	Users are penetrating E-Business system despitethe access control	0.75*0.50*0.25 =0.10
	Users are using data base resources without authorization	0.75*0.25 =0.19
Z7	Intruder penetrated network and received administrator rights	0.75*0.50*0.50 =0.13
	Intruder tapped unprotected transmission and obtained authorization	0.75*0.50*0.50 =0.13
	Users penetrated system and use resources due to authorization rights which are not coplinat with their duties	0.75*0.50*0.50 =0.13
	Useres penetrated the system despite the access control	0.75*0.50*0.25 =0.10
	Users used resources because of the lack of security policy	0.50*0.25 =0.13
	Users made resources accessible for unauthorized external third parties	0.75*0.75*0.50 =0.28

Tab. 4. Probability of the risk as results of threats

The last stage of the risk analysis is determination of the threat influence on the system (Table 5).

As can be seen from Table 5, the highest value of risk seriousness and probability has to be considered during estimation of the risk. Evaluation of the risk for E-Business system (according to Table 1) in the context for integrity, confidantiality and discretionary is presented in Table 6.

Z	R	Type of the risk	I	C	D	PR
Z1	R1	Intruder penetrated E-Business server	3	4	2	0.38
		Intruder tapped transmission because of the lack of security	-	4	-	0.10
		Intruder tapped transmission and penetrated E-Business server	3	4	2	0.13
		Intruder tapped transmission because of the lack of security policy	-	2	-	0.10
			3	4	2	**0.38**
Z2	R2	Intruder penetrated network (system network)	3	4	2	0.38
		Intruder penetrated E-Business server via hidden ports	3	4	2	0.10
		Intruder penetrated E-Business server despite acess control	4	4	2	0.10
		Intruder caught transmission during remote usage of resources	3	4	-	0.38
		Users are using systems which are not compliant with their duties	2	2	-	0.18
		Users are using different resources due to additional authorization	-	1	-	0.13
		Users are using different resources despite access control	-	3	-	0.10
			4	4	2	**0.38**
Z3	R3	Intruder penetrated network and modified data and system files	4	4	2	0.18
		Intruder penetrated network, deleted system files, installed viruses	4	4	3	0.05
		Users are penetrating system and use resources without authorization	4	4	2	0.38
		Users are penetrating system because of the lack of usage regulations and policy	2	3	2	0.10
		Users are modifying and deleting system files, installing viruses	4	4	4	0.13
			4	4	4	**0.38**
Z4	R4	Intruder penetrated network and modified commands and deleted system files	4	4	3	0.05
		Intruder penetrated E-Business server	3	3	2	0.38
		Intruder penetrated E-Business server & installed nonvisible programs	3	3	2	0.10
		Users are modifying data and system commands	4	2	2	0.19
		Users are penetrating system and installing nonvisible programs	3	4	2	0.10
		Users are installing unlegal programs due to additional authorization	4	2	2	0.10
		Developers penetrated system due to nonvisible programs	3	3	2	0.19
			4	4	3	**0.38**
Z5	R5	Users installed illegal programs necessary for their work	3	-	1	0.25
		Users are telecopying programs	-	-	-	0.13
		Users are telecopying remote resources	-	2	-	0.13
		Users are telecopying unlegal programs	2	-	1	0.38
			3	2	1	**0.38**
Z6	R6	Intruder copied the data base contents	2	4	-	0.19
		Intruder penetrated E-Business system because of the lack of appropriate protection	3	4	1	0.10
		Intruder tapped unprotected transmission	-	3	-	0.19
		Users are using data base resources due to authorization rights not compliant with their duties	-	2	-	0.13
		Users are penetrating E-Business system despitethe access control	2	3	2	0.19
		Users are using data base resources without authorization	2	3	2	0.19
			3	4	2	**0.19**
Z7	R7	Intruder penetrated network and received administrator rights	4	4	4	0.13
		Intruder tapped unprotected transmission and obtained authorization	3	4	4	0.13
		Users penetrated system and use resources due to authorization rights which are not coplinat with their duties	-	2	-	0.13
		Useres penetrated the system despite the access control	3	3	2	0.10
		Users used resources because of the lack of security policy	2	3	2	0.13
		Users made resources accessible for unauthorized external third parties	-	4	-	0.28
			4	4	4	**0.28**

I – integrity, C – confidentiality, D – disposability, R – Risk, Z – threat, PR - Probability

Tab. 5. Influence of type of the risk

	Risk seriousness												
	integrity				confidentiality				discretionary			
Probability of the threat	Disregardable	Small	Medium	Very high	Disregardable	Small	Medium	Very high	Disregardable	Small	Medium	Very high
Extremely high	3	4	4	4	3	4	4	4	3	4	4	4
Very high	2	3	3	4	2	3	3	4	2	3	3	4
Medium	1	1	2	2	1	1	2	2	1	1	2	2
Low	1	1	1	1	1	1	1	1	1	1	1	1

Tab. 6 Risk evaluation in the context of system integrity, confidentiality and discretionary

Based on Table 6, estimated risk for the E-Business system is **2** (the probability of the risk is at medium level, and the influence of threats on the system is very high). Estimated risk take into account the highest risk seriousness and highest probability referenced to three issues: integrity, confidentiality and discretionarity.

It can be seen from presented results that the main attention has to be focused of the service systems, which have the highest rank from the risk and security policy inside the institution point of view. Detailed analysis of the data presented in tables 5-7 can be confirmed by additional penetration tests.

4. CONCLUSIONS

The analysis presented in this paper, concerning potential ways of attack and disadvantages of the E-Business architecture, allows to indicate directions of protection. Proposed method makes possible to indicate the sources of the errors during design of such a system. This method also allows to minimise probability of intruder success and the consequences of such attack. Detailed risk analysis is time consuming and expensive, however if properly performed is an important source of the knowledge about E-Business system.

5. REFERENCES

[1] Andrukiewicz E. "Polska Norma PrPN ISO/IEC 17799 - jak tworzyć bezpieczeństwo systemów informatycznych w przedsiębiorstwie", ENIGMA 2001, Poland
[2] BS 7799 - ISO/IEC 17799 –"Code of Practice for Information Security Management"
[3] Wołowski. "metodyka prowadzenia analizy ryzyka dla sektora bankowego i finansowego", ENIGMA 2001, Poland
[4] El Fray I, Pejaś J. „ Zasady projektowania bezpiecznych bankowych systemów informacyjnych" , II Krajowa Konferencja Naukowa E-finanse, Szczecin, 20, 21 November 2001, Poland
[5] Kostecki R: "Techniki zabezpieczeń sieci LAN ze stałym łączem do internetu", diplomma work, Szczecin 2001, Poland
[6] www.clusif.asso.fr
[7] www.scssi.gouv.fr

Linear Approximation of Arithmetic Sum Function

KRZYSZTOF CHMIEL
Poznań University of Technology
pl. Skłodowskiej-Curie 5, 60-965 Poznań, Poland, e-mail:Chmiel@sk-kari.put.poznan.pl

Abstract: In the paper the results concerning the linear approximation of n-bit arithmetic sum function are presented. In particular, the computationally effective algorithms are formulated, to compute values of the approximation tables and the distribution of values in these tables as well as the algorithm to generate the list of effective approximations, ordered decreasingly by the approximation effectiveness measure.

Key words: Cryptanalysis, linear approximation, arithmetic sum function.

1. INTRODUCTION

Linear approximation of a cipher algorithm constitutes a basic concept of linear cryptanalysis – one of the most important, general methods of cryptanalysis [3, 4, 6, 7, 8, 9, 10, 11, 12]. By a linear approximation we mean a linear equation, relating input bits to output bits of an algorithm. The equation is satisfied with some probability p for randomly chosen input and corresponding output. The magnitude of $|\Delta p| = |p - 1/2|$ represents the *effectiveness* of the approximation. Approximations with nonzero value of the effectiveness measure are said to be effective.

In the case of iterative block ciphers, the calculation of the most effective linear approximations is carried out typically in two main steps. First, as a result of composition of approximations of component functions, the effective approximations of a single iteration are calculated. One of the used component functions, for example in the algorithms Blowfish and IDEA, is the considered in the paper arithmetic sum function. Next, as a result of composition of approximations of consecutive iterations, the linear approximation of the entire algorithm is obtained.

Approximation of an algorithm, enables the identification of the key bits, for sufficiently large family of known pairs: plaintext – ciphertext. Unlike the differential cryptanalysis, which is essentially a chosen-plaintext attack [1, 2, 5, 9], the linear cryptanalysis is essentially a known-plaintext attack and moreover is applicable to an only-ciphertext attack under some circumstances [11].

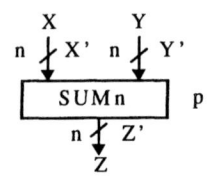

In general, the *linear approximation* of function $Y = h(X)$: $\{0,1\}^n \to \{0,1\}^m$ is defined as an arbitrary equation of the form:

$$\bigoplus_{i \in Y'} y_i = \bigoplus_{j \in X'} x_j,$$

satisfied with approximation probability $p = N(X',Y') / 2^n$, where $Y' \subseteq \{1,..,m\}$, $X' \subseteq \{1,..,n\}$ while $N(X',Y')$ denotes the number of pairs (X, Y) for which the equation holds. For simplicity the above equation is written in the following form:

$Y[Y'] = X[X']$.

The sets of indexes X', Y' are called input and output *mask* respectively and the function $N(X',Y')$ is called the *counting function* of the approximation.

The linear approximation *characteristic* is defined as a sequence $(X', Y', \Delta p)$, where X', Y' are masks or sequences of input and output masks and p is the approximation probability. Among characteristics we distinguish the *zero-characteristic* (Φ, Φ, 1/2), corresponding to the *zero linear approximation*, which probability is equal to 1 for arbitrary function h.

Composing linear approximations, it is necessary to formulate so called *approximation conditions* and to calculate the approximation probability of the composition. The approximation conditions eliminate the bits of the internal variables from the resultant equation. The probability Δp of the composition of n approximations with probabilities Δp_i, is calculated as follows:

$$\Delta p = 2^{n-1} \prod_{i=1}^{n} \Delta p_i.$$

2. APPROXIMATION TABLES

The general form $Z[Z'] = X[X'] \oplus Y[Y']$ of the linear approximation of n-bit arithmetic sum function $Z = SUMn(X, Y)$, is illustrated in figure 1.

Fig. 1. Linear approximation of function *SUMn*

Linear approximations of function *SUMn* can be described in the form of the *approximation table TASUMn*. The element *TASUMn*[X', Y', Z'] of the table, is defined as the number of triples (X, Y, Z) satisfying equation $Z[Z'] = X[X'] \oplus Y[Y']$, decreased by the half of all the triples. Thus, it can be calculated by the formula:

$$TASUMn[X', Y', Z'] = N(X', Y', Z') - 2^{2n-1}.$$

Approximation table *TASUMn* is obtained by examination, for each mask triple (X', Y', Z'), of all input triples (X, Y, Z) and contains the complete description of linear approximations of function *SUMn*. In other words, table *TASUMn* represents all the characteristics $(X', Y', Z', \Delta p)$ of function *SUMn*, where probability Δp can be calculated as follows:

$$\Delta p = TASUMn[X', Y', Z'] / 2^{2n}.$$

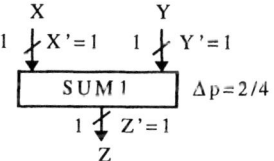

X', Y'	Z' 0	Z' 1
0, 0	2	0
0, 1	0	0
1, 0	0	0
1, 1	0	2

Fig. 2. Approximation table *TASUM1* of function *SUM1*

The approximation table of function *SUM1* is presented in figure 2. There are only two effective approximations of the function: the zero-approximation with characteristic (0, 0, 0, 1/2) and the approximation with characteristic (1, 1, 1, 1/2) called in the following, the *one-approximation*.

X', Y'	Z'=0	Z'=1	Z'=2	Z'=3
0, 0	8	0	0	0
0, 1	0	0	0	0
0, 2	0	0	0	0
0, 3	0	0	0	0
1, 0	0	0	0	0
1, 1	0	8	0	0
1, 2	0	0	0	0
1, 3	0	0	0	0
2, 0	0	0	0	0
2, 1	0	0	0	0
2, 2	0	0	4	-4
2, 3	0	0	4	4
3, 0	0	0	0	0
3, 1	0	0	0	0
3, 2	0	0	4	4
3, 3	0	0	-4	4

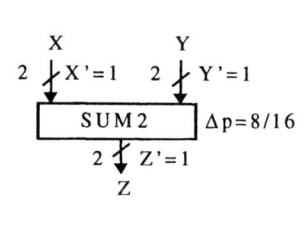

Fig. 3. Approximation table *TASUM2* of function *SUM2*

The approximation table of function *SUM2* is presented in figure 3. Besides the zero- and one-approximation with probability $\Delta p = 1/2$, there exist 8 effective approximations of the function with probability $|\Delta p| = 1/4$.

X', Y'	Z'							
	0	1	2	3	4	5	6	7
0, 0	32	0	0	0	0	0	0	0
1, 1	0	32	0	0	0	0	0	0
2, 2	0	0	16	-16	0	0	0	0
2, 3	0	0	16	16	0	0	0	0
3, 2	0	0	16	16	0	0	0	0
3, 3	0	0	-16	16	0	0	0	0
4, 4	0	0	0	0	8	-8	-16	0
4, 5	0	0	0	0	8	8	0	0
4, 6	0	0	0	0	16	0	8	-8
4, 7	0	0	0	0	0	0	8	8
5, 4	0	0	0	0	8	8	0	0
5, 5	0	0	0	0	-8	8	0	-16
5, 6	0	0	0	0	0	0	8	8
5, 7	0	0	0	0	0	16	-8	8
6, 4	0	0	0	0	16	0	8	-8
6, 5	0	0	0	0	0	0	8	8
6, 6	0	0	0	0	-8	8	16	0
6, 7	0	0	0	0	-8	-8	0	0
7, 4	0	0	0	0	0	0	8	8
7, 5	0	0	0	0	0	16	-8	8
7, 6	0	0	0	0	-8	-8	0	0
7, 7	0	0	0	0	8	-8	0	16

Fig. 4. Reduced approximation table *TASUM3* of function *SUM3*

In figure 4 is presented the reduced approximation table of function *SUM3*, obtained by omitting the zero rows from the table *TASUM3*. There are 50 effective approximations of the function: 2 approximations with probability $\Delta p = 1/2$, 16 approximations with probability $|\Delta p| = 1/4$ and 32 approximations with $|\Delta p| = 1/8$.

TA-SUMn(X', Y', Z', n)
1. BIT-XOR(X, n)
2. $w \leftarrow 0$
3. **for** $i \leftarrow 0$ **to** $n - 1$ **do** $w \leftarrow w \oplus X_i$
4. **return** w
5. N(C_0, X', Y', Z', n)
6. $w \leftarrow 0$
7. **for** $X \leftarrow 0$ **to** $2^n - 1$ **do**
8.   **for** $Y \leftarrow 0$ **to** $2^n - 1$ **do**
9. $Z \leftarrow (X + Y + C_0) \bmod 2^n$
10.   **if** BIT-XOR(X and X', n) $\oplus$ BIT-XOR(Y and Y', n) =
11.   BIT-XOR(Z and Z', n) **then** $w \leftarrow w + 1$
12. **return** w
13. **return** N(0, X', Y', Z', n) $- 2^{2n-1}$

Fig. 5. Basic algorithm, computing the values of the approximation table of *SUMn*

For clarity, in figure 5 is presented the basic algorithm computing the values of the approximation table of function *SUMn*. Auxiliary function BIT-XOR(...) computes the XOR of the n least significant bits of parameter X. Function N(...) is the counting function of the approximation, extended by parameter C_0 of input carry.

The main function TA-SUMn(...) returns the value $N(0, X', Y', Z', n) - 2^{2n-1}$. The computational complexity of the algorithm is $O(n \cdot 2^{2n})$ and therefore it can be used for small values of n.

The distribution of values in the approximation tables of functions *SUM1-6* is presented in figure 6. For each function, the upper row contains the possible values and the lower row the number of occurrences of the value. On the right side, in the form of the fraction, is given the number of effective approximations related to the number of all approximations of the function.

SUM1	0	2										(2/8)
	6	2										

SUM2	-4	0	4	8								(10/64)
	2	54	6	2								

SUM3	-16	-8	0	8	16	32						(50/512)
	4	12	462	20	12	2						

SUM4	-64	-32	-16	0	16	32	64	128				(250/4096)
	6	36	56	3846	72	60	18	2				

SUM5	-256	-128	-64	-32	0	32	64	128	256	512		(1250/32768)
	8	72	224	240	31518	272	288	120	24	2		

SUM6	-1024	-512	-256	-128	-64	0	64	128	256	512	1024	2048	(6250/262144)
	10	120	560	1200	992	255894	1056	1360	720	200	30	2	

Fig. 6. Distribution of values in the approximation tables of functions *SUM1-6*

The distributions presented, were obtained by the complete look up of the approximation tables and enable to observe many regularities with the increase of the number n of sum bits. Calculation of distribution of function *SUMn* in this way, requires 2^{3n} calls of function TA-SUMn(...) and thus, with use of the function from figure 5, requires $O(n \cdot 2^{5n})$ operations.

3. ALGORITHMS

Approximation scheme of function *SUMn* is presented in figure 7. Function *SUMn* is composed of n identical cells, containing the carry function f. The values of masks C_0' i C_n' are fixed to 0.

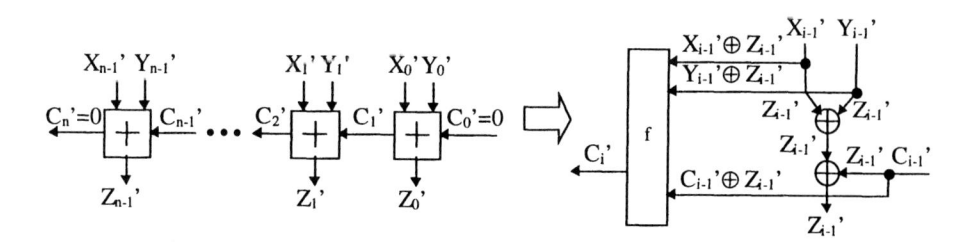

Fig. 7. Approximation scheme of function *SUMn* and of a single cell $i \geq 1$

In the approximation scheme of a single cell, for both XOR functions, input masks are equal to the output mask. Thus, the necessary and sufficient condition of effectiveness of XOR approximation is fulfilled. The XOR values of appropriate masks as input masks of function f, follow from the approximation conditions of a single cell.

The approximation table *TAC* of carry function f is shown in figure 8. Besides the zero-approximation, there exist 4 effective approximations with probability $|\Delta p| = 1/4$.

a', b', c'	d'=0	d'=1
0, 0, 0	4	0
0, 0, 1	0	2
0, 1, 0	0	2
0, 1, 1	0	0
1, 0, 0	0	2
1, 0, 1	0	0
1, 1, 0	0	0
1, 1, 1	0	-2

Fig. 8. Approximation table *TAC* of carry function f

In figure 9 a recursive algorithm, computing the values of the approximation table of function *SUMn* for masks X', Y', Z' is presented. Argument *TAC* denotes the approximation table of carry function f and argument i denotes the current cell number. Argument C', in which additionally successively computed bits of carry mask are stored, is used to input the value of output carry mask C_i' of cell i. In the first call of the function, TA-SUMn(*TAC*, X', Y', Z', n, 0), it is necessary to fulfil the condition $C_n' = 0$.

TA-SUMn(*TAC*, X', Y', Z', i, C')
1. $C_{i-1}' \leftarrow C_i' \oplus X_{i-1}' \oplus Y_{i-1}' \oplus Z_{i-1}'$
2. $w_i \leftarrow TAC[\, X_{i-1}' \oplus Z_{i-1}'\,,\, Y_{i-1}' \oplus Z_{i-1}'\,,\, C_{i-1}' \oplus Z_{i-1}'\,,\, C_i'\,]$
3. **if** $i > 1$
4.   **then return** $w_i \cdot$ TA-SUMn(*TAC*, X', Y', Z', i-1, C')
5.   **else return** $w_i \cdot 1/2$

Fig. 9. Algorithm computing the values of the approximation table of *SUMn*, first call: TA-SUMn(*TAC*, X', Y', Z', n, 0)

For this and the next presented algorithms, important are relations between the approximation probability and the values of approximation tables of individual cells and of entire function *SUMn*. Denoting by w_i the value of table *TAC* for cell i, the probability Δp of composition of n cells can be calculated as follows:

$$\Delta p = 2^{n-1} \cdot \prod_{i=1}^{n} (w_i/8) = 1/2^{2n+1} \cdot \prod_{i=1}^{n} w_i.$$

Let w denote the value of the approximation table of function $SUMn$. For w we obtain the following equation:

$$w = \Delta p \cdot 2^{2n} = 1/2 \cdot \prod_{i=1}^{n} w_i.$$

The algorithm from figure 9, calculates the above value of w. Correctness of the essential for the algorithm step 1, is based on the following argumentation. For each nonzero value of the approximation table TAC, holds:

$a' \oplus b' \oplus c' \oplus d' = 0.$

Substituting the values from the approximation scheme (fig. 7), we obtain

$(X_{i-1}' \oplus Z_{i-1}') \oplus (Y_{i-1}' \oplus Z_{i-1}') \oplus (C_{i-1}' \oplus Z_{i-1}') \oplus (C_i') = 0.$

Thus

$C_{i-1}' = C_i' \oplus X_{i-1}' \oplus Y_{i-1}' \oplus Z_{i-1}',$

is unambiguously defined for all effective approximations of function f in cell i. For not effective approximations, considering that $w_i = 0$, the calculated value of C_{i-1}' is of no significance for the final result $w = 0$. The complexity of the algorithm from figure 9 is $O(n)$ which is much better in comparison to the complexity $O(n \cdot 2^{2n})$ of the basic algorithm from figure 5.

In figure 10 a recursive algorithm, generating effective approximations of function $SUMn$ for a given carry mask C', is presented.

```
GEN-FOR-C(TAC, C', i, X', Y', Z', w)
1.    for each sequence (a', b', c', d') such that
2.        d' = C_i' and TAC[a', b', c', d'] ≠ 0
3.    do  w1 ← w · TAC[a', b', c', d']
4.        Z_{i-1}' ← c' ⊕ C_{i-1}'
5.        X_{i-1}' ← a' ⊕ Z_{i-1}'
6.        Y_{i-1}' ← b' ⊕ Z_{i-1}'
7.        if i > 1
8.          then GEN-FOR-C(TAC, C', i-1, X', Y', Z', w1)
9.          else write (X', Y', Z', w1)
10.              write (X' ⊕ 1, Y' ⊕ 1, Z' ⊕ 1, w1)
```

Fig. 10. Algorithm generating effective approximations of $SUMn$ for C', first call: GEN-FOR-C(TAC, C', n, 0, 0, 0, $1/2^{2n+1}$)

Argument w for a given cell number i, is equal to the product of values of TAC for cells from n to $i+1$, multiplied by the value of w in the first call. Therefore, through the value of $w1$, is written the probability Δp of the approximation. Each time, two effective approximations corresponding to the value 0 and 1 of the variable Z_0' are written. The complexity of the algorithm corresponds to the number of generated characteristics and is equal to $O(4^k)$, where k denotes the number of ones in the carry mask C'.

It should be mentioned, that for a given k all the generated approximations have the same probability $|\Delta p| = 1/2^{k+1}$. By generation of approximations for all C' corresponding to the consecutive values of $k = 0,1,2,...,n-1$ ($C_n' = 0$), the list of effective approximations, ordered decreasingly by the probability $|\Delta p|$ is obtained. Such a generation of the whole list requires $O(5^{n-1})$ operations in comparison to the number $O(n \cdot 2^{5n})$ of operations required for generation of not ordered list, based on the algorithm TA-SUMn(...) from figure 5.

In figure 11 an algorithm, computing the distribution of the absolute values in the approximation table of $SUMn$, is presented.

DISTRIBUTION-ABS-TA-SUMn(n)
1. write $(0, 2^{3n} - 2 \cdot 5^{n-1})$
2. **for** $k \leftarrow n-1$ **downto** 0 **do** write $(2^{2n-(k+1)}, 2 \cdot \binom{n-1}{k} \cdot 4^k)$

Fig. 11. Algorithm computing the distribution of the absolute values
in the approximation table of $SUMn$

The number of all approximations is equal to 2^{3n}. From figure 8 it follows, that for carry function f of cell i there exist 5 effective approximations: for $C_i' = 0$ the zero approximation with probability $\Delta p_i = 1/2$ and for $C_i' = 1$ four nonzero approximations with probability $|\Delta p_i| = 1/4$. For n cells, considering that $C_n' = 0$, there exist then 5^{n-1} different approximations of functions f. Because each of them, gives two approximations of function $SUMn$ corresponding to the value 0 and 1 of variable Z_0', the total number of effective approximations of function $SUMn$ is equal to $2 \cdot 5^{n-1}$. Thus, the number of zeros in the approximation table is equal to $2^{3n} - 2 \cdot 5^{n-1}$.

Variable k denotes the number of cells with nonzero approximation of block f and at the same time, the number of ones in the carry mask C'. For a given k, the approximation probability of the composition of n cells can be calculated by the formula:

$$|\Delta p| = 2^{n-1} \cdot (1/4)^k \cdot (1/2)^{n-k} = 1/2^{k+1},$$

and therefore the value of the approximation table $w = 2^{2n-(k+1)}$. The number of occurrences of this value is equal to

$$2 \cdot \binom{n-1}{k} \cdot 4^k \cdot 1^{n-k},$$

where consecutive factors denote: the number of approximations of $SUMn$ for a single approximation of functions f, the number of choices of k cells, the number of effective approximations of blocks f of the chosen k cells and the number of the zero approximations of the remaining blocks f. The complexity of the algorithm is $O(n)$

assuming that calculation of the power and of the Newton binomial require unitary operations.

In figure 12 an algorithm, computing the distribution of the negative and positive values in the approximation table of *SUMn*, is presented. In contrary to the algorithm used to calculate the distributions from figure 6 of complexity $O(n \cdot 2^{5n})$, the complexity of algorithm from figure 12 is $O(n^2)$ assuming that calculation of the power and of the Newton binomial require unitary operations.

DISTRIBUTION-TA-SUMn(n)
1. COMB3(k, $m2$)
2. $w \leftarrow 0$
3. **for** $i \leftarrow 0$ **to** k **do**
4.   **if** $i \bmod 2 = m2$ **then** $w \leftarrow w + \binom{k}{i} \cdot 1^i \cdot 3^{k-i}$
5. **return** w
6. **for** $k \leftarrow 1$ **to** $n-1$ **do** write $(-2^{2n-(k+1)}, 2 \cdot \binom{n-1}{k} \cdot \text{COMB3}(k, 1))$
7. write $(0, 2^{3n} - 2 \cdot 5^{n-1})$
8. **for** $k \leftarrow n-1$ **downto** 0 **do** write $(2^{2n-(k+1)}, 2 \cdot \binom{n-1}{k} \cdot \text{COMB3}(k, 0))$

Fig. 12. Algorithm computing the distribution of the values in the approximation table of *SUMn*

The algorithm is a detailed version of the algorithm from figure 11. From among the four nonzero effective approximations of block f of cell i with probability $|\Delta p_i| = 1/4$ one approximation has the negative value of Δp_i. For the chosen k cells, the negative value of the approximation table is obtained when the number of occurrences of this approximation is odd, and the positive value when the number is even. The number of approximations for odd ($m2 = 1$) and even ($m2 = 0$) number of occurrences, is calculated by the auxiliary function COMB3(...).

4. CONCLUSION

The presented in the paper algorithms – computing values of the approximation table, generating effective approximations and computing distribution of values in the approximation table – solve the basic problems of linear approximation of n-bit arithmetic sum function *SUMn*. The method applied, enables to solve many other problems, in particular some specific generation problems which are typical for calculation of multilevel characteristics of iterative block ciphers [8].

5. REFERENCES

[1] Biham E., Shamir A. 1993. 'Differential Cryptanalysis of the Data Encryption Standard'. *Springer-Verlag*, New York.
[2] Chmiel K. 1998. 'Principles of Differential Cryptanalysis through the Example of the *DES* Algorithm'. (In Polish). *Technical Report No. 461*. Poznań University of Technology, Chair of Control, Robotics and Computer Science, Poznań (Oct.).
[3] Chmiel K. 1999. 'Principles of Linear Cryptanalysis through the Example of the *DES* Algorithm'. (In Polish). *Technical Report No. 471*. Poznań University of Technology, Chair of Control, Robotics and Computer Science, Poznań (Oct.).
[4] Chmiel K. 2000. 'Linear Cryptanalysis of the Reduced *DES* Algorithms'. *Proceedings of the Regional Conference on Military Communication and Information Systems'2000* (Zegrze, Oct. 4-6) WIŁ, Zegrze, vol. 1, pp. 111-118.
[5] Chmiel K. 2000. 'Differential Cryptanalysis of the Reduced *DES* Algorithms'. (In Polish). *Studia z Automatyki i Informatyki,* vol. 25, pp. 127-146.
[6] Chmiel K. 2000. 'Linear Approximation of S-box Functions'. (In Polish). *Technical Report No. 471*. Poznań University of Technology, Chair of Control, Robotics and Computer Science, Poznań (Oct.).
[7] Chmiel K. 2001. 'Linear Approximation of some S-box Functions'. *Proceedings of the Regional Conference on Military Communication and Information Systems 2001* (Zegrze, Oct. 10-12) WIŁ, Zegrze, vol. 1, pp. 211-218.
[8] Chmiel K. 2001. 'Linear Approximation of Arithmetic Sum'. (In Polish). *Technical Report No. 481*. Poznań University of Technology, Chair of Control, Robotics and Computer Science, Poznań (Oct.).
[9] Górska A., Górski K., Kotulski Z., Paszkiewicz A., Szczepański J. 2001. 'New Experimental Results in Differential – Linear Cryptanalysis of Reduced Variants of DES'. *Proceedings of the 8-th International Conference on Advanced Computer Systems ACS'2001*, Mielno, vol. 1, pp. 333-346.
[10] Matsui M. 1993. 'Linear Cryptanalysis Method for DES Cipher'. *Advances in Cryptology Eurocrypt'93*.
[11] Matsui M. 1998. 'Linear Cryptanalysis Method for DES Cipher'. *Springer-Verlag*, New York.
[12] Zugaj A., Górski K., Kotulski Z., Szczepański J., Paszkiewicz A. 1999. 'Extending Linear Cryptanalysis - Theory and Experiments'. *Proceedings of the Regional Conference on Military Communication and Information Systems'99* (Zegrze, Oct. 6-8) WIŁ, Zegrze, vol. 2, pp.77-84.